What is
Political Theory
and Why do We
Need It?

W0225620

What is
Political Theory
and Why do We
Need It?

Rajeev Bhargava

OXFORD
UNIVERSITY PRESS

OXFORD
UNIVERSITY PRESS

Oxford University Press is a department of the University of Oxford.
It furthers the University's objective of excellence in research, scholarship,
and education by publishing worldwide. Oxford is a registered trademark of
Oxford University Press in the UK and in certain other countries

Published in India by
Oxford University Press
22 Workspace, 2nd Floor, 1/22 Asaf Ali Road, New Delhi 110002, India

First Edition published in 2010
21ˢᵗ impression 2024

ISBN-13: 978-0-19-808839-4
ISBN-10: 0-19-808839-6

Typeset in 10.5/12.4 Dante MT Std
by Excellent Laser Typesetters, Pitampura, Delhi 110 034
Printed in India by Manipal Technologies Limited, Manipal

In memory of
Gopi, Prakashwati, Bisheshwar, and Hardev,
and for the living link with them, Saroj and Sheila

Contents

V Philosophy of Social Science

Preface

In the preface to one of his many books, political philosopher Brian Barry reminisces that on the eve of his application for the Philosophy, Politics, and Economics course at Oxford, his school teacher recommended that he read A.J. Ayer's *Language, Truth and Logic*. Twenty years later, before I left India for the same course, a reading list arrived that included Ayer's book. I had not heard of it but was drawn to its brilliant title. However, when I rummaged through it, I could not make much sense of what was going on. Everything appeared to be in sharp contrast to what philosophy meant to me. Ayer's book was written with incredible simplicity. For me, philosophy had to be dense and difficult. It contained terms that reminded me of physics lessons at school: explicit definitions; definite descriptions; empirical, factual, and general propositions; induction; verification principle; observation statements; and so on. In comparison, the philosophical terms to which I was barely accustomed were: existence, dread, ennui, anxiety, the absurdity of life, contingency, bad faith, alienation, and so on. My personal and emotional relationship with the language of existentialism made it impossible to grasp the sense of this other, 'simple' but more mysterious one. The former was poetic, an insightful expression of experience. The latter was bland, joyless prose concerning the role of language and philosophy in knowing a world uninhabited by humans. For one, philosophy was a deeper articulation of experience lived on the edge of the world, for the other, it was pure analysis, cold-blooded dissection.

The assumption of an extremely tight connection of analytical philosophy with logical positivism came naturally to me, as did a few months later, its identical link with liberalism. It took many years to realize that neither logical positivism nor liberalism have necessary ties with at least some forms of analytical philosophy. Once its rigidity and many contingent accretions were removed, analytical philosophy became a useful tool for precise arguments and lucid propositions that need not bear the imprint of positivism or philosophical liberalism. Careful attention to the use of words, conceptual clarification, and soundness of argument is important not only for philosophers but indeed for any scholar. Despite limitations, some aspects of analytical philosophy can usefully be employed to serve the moral and social world of human communities. Its 'rational' kernel can be separated from the dispensable shell!

Readers might complain that the book has begun by flogging a dead horse—worn out exchanges between philosophers and social scientists that were dominant in the 1950s and the 1960s. However, themes emerge with varying inflection and urgency in different societies. A non-issue in one society is a livewire in another. Would the debate between modernists and traditionalists have concerned anyone in France or Germany between 1960 and 2000? Or, for that matter, the fierce public battle over secularism? Issues that have rocked India for over two centuries and which only now, at the turn of century, have begun to shatter Anglo-Saxon and European complacency. It seems more necessary and urgent to emphasize the utility of analytical tools and the significance of reasoning over values within social science circles in India than elsewhere.

The decades of the 1950s and 1960s witnessed a crisis in the identity of western political theory. The principal worry that plagued several practitioners then was whether or not systematic political reflection can aspire to scientific truth. Once this concern dissipated, there has been nitpicking among political theorists over the true nature or core value of their enterprise but the entity called political theory is more or less unquestioned. Since art, religion, philosophy, and the sciences are clearly differentiated in the West, few have thought it relevant to start a discussion of political theory by comparing or contrasting it with music or seek resemblances at some deeper or higher level! However, political theory has no such trajectory in India where philosophy and politics seem to be everything and everywhere. No identity crisis is experienced in India by political theory because it appears not to have a distinct identity in the first place. So, it might not seem odd to talk in the same breath about art and political theory, as if the two were identical.

However, while this flexibility and open-mindedness has advantages, it has deep problems too; this extreme fluidity and seamlessness also hampers the practice of political theory. In the Indian context, a tentative clarification of what political theory is and how it relates to other modes of understanding and self-understanding is crucial.

All essays in this book were born from a conviction that public justification is required for suggestions, proposals, claims, and policies. Provided a realistic and non-rationalist understanding of reasons is available, it can safely be assumed that even when unarticulated, reasons guide actions. These reasons must be accessible to anyone who cares for them now or later. Equally, those who propose or oppose a certain course of action in society must give reasons. I do not mean to suggest that in every case actors must themselves furnish them. Every society has some people who properly articulate reasons, others who communicate them, some who simply receive them, others who are persuaded by them, some who guide or rationalize their own actions in their terms, and others who are provoked enough to question and challenge them. My point is not that every actor must perform all of these but rather that this work must be collectively done in every society.

A second conviction that guides these essays is that moral and ethical perspectives are constitutive of most reasons for individual and collective actions. Human beings are inescapably evaluative, even judgemental. They may be unable to choose or compelled not to articulate their evaluations, but they cannot help make them. Many such evaluations have an ethical or moral character; they are good or bad for the well-being of oneself or good/right or bad/wrong for others. Besides, formal education is not a necessary condition for such evaluations. It may fine-tune them but as easily create a cacophony. Sound moral and ethical judgements are dependent less on classroom lessons and more on rich lived experience.

Interestingly, perspectives that guide most human beings are internally driven, laden with deeply conflicting multiple values. If so, single-value doctrines that claim a monopoly of cognitive and moral truth are dangerous, even destructive. Many of these essays take cognizance of this imminent moral complexity and insist on the need for balancing values in human lives. In many situations, the best humans can do is make life tolerable. In certain contexts, an aspiration for minimal decency may be heroic. This does mean that dreams and strivings for higher ideals must be eschewed. But, the cost of realizing them must be squarely faced. No single formula captures the shape of human lives, no recipe exists to improve their quality, replete as they are with surprises, even miracles. But small, delicately taken avalanche-avoiding steps are as astounding as great revolutions and background conditions that make either of these possible are, as Marx famously observed, 'not of our own making'.

As I reread these essays, I realized that I have, if not directly challenged, at least endeavoured to avoid received dichotomies or polarities: religious versus secular (a deeper alliance between theists and atheists is possible, partly because what really matters is the quality of life we lead—how we relate to ourselves, to others, and to our natural environment, not whether or not we believe in god); liberal versus socialist/ communitarian (left–liberal; individual and community-specific rights can and must coexist); traditional versus modern (alternative modernities); individualist versus collectivist (social formation of individuals; we aspire to be by ourselves and with others). The list can be multiplied. This stems from an ever deeper conviction that human needs are too diverse to be pigeonholed into any single ideological system. We, those who admit and those who deny, those who belong easily to many worlds and those who claim to belong only to one, not only inhabit but actually value many worlds. The most dogmatic person lives by values whose nourishment comes from many sources.

Some friends have been close collaborators for long—Sudipta Kaviraj, Bhikhu Parekh, Kumar Shahani, Alok Rai, D.L. Sheth, Tani Sandhu, Javeed Alam, Andrew and Peggotty Graham, Achin Vanaik, Anu Chenoy, Yael Tamir, and Neeladri Bhattacharya. I must thank them as also others who helped me think through some issues in this collection: Dennis Thompson, Michael Walzer, Jose Casanova, Akeel Bilgrami, Partha Chatterjee, Alfred Stepan, T.N. Madan, Nilufer Gole, Ashis Nandy, Christophe Jaffrelot, Craig Calhoun, Tariq Modood, and Pratap Mehta. Many of these essays would not have been written but for the conducive scholarly environment provided by several institutions. These include the Centre for Ethics and the Professions, Harvard University; Institute of Advanced Studies, University of Bristol; Centre for the Study of Developing Societies, Delhi; Institute of Advanced Studies, Hebrew University, Jerusalem; The British Academy; and Sciences Po, Paris. I am grateful to Vinay Jain and Sanjeev Bhargava for the cover, to Oxford University Press for their encouragement to publish these essays, and for prodding a busy administrator to get on with this other, equally important, task of getting the book out on time.

This collection owes much to one-time students who taught me more than I will ever realize—Valerian Rodrigues, K. Srinavasulu, Bishnu Mohapatra, Thangevelu, Vidhu Verma, Sanjay Prasad, Arun Patnaik, Nivedita Menon, Yogendra Yadav, Aditya Nigam, Garimella Subramanian (Subbu), Ajit Jha, Prabhat Sarangi, Shefali Choudhury, Asha Sarangi, C. Laxmanan, Anubha Kakkar, Lopamudra Tripathi, Ajay Kumar, G. Harindranath, Prathama Bannerjee, Abdul Fakhri, Mita Radhakrishnan, Y.P. Rao, Rinku Lamba, Jakob de Roover, Mohinder Singh, Prakash Sarangi, Saroj Giri, Mohammad Mohammadi, Aryama, Manas Bhattacharya, Swaha Das, V. Sriranjini, Rajesh Seth, Jaya Gupta, Aparjita Narain, Sunalini Kumar, E. Arvind, Monika Dhami, and Jaby Mathew.

It owes everything to one-time teachers who gradually became close friends and intellectual associates. The gentle, suave, and insightful, Alan Montefiore is a reservoir of empathy and can read mental states of people by a mere glance at their eyes. He gave solace to a melancholic, lonely student at Oxford and gave him the confidence that he can read and understand Kant and Wittgenstein. Christopher, the Master of Balliol, and Bridgette Hill exuded such warmth, simplicity, and humility that I forgot I was in the presence of one of the great historians of our times in the still very imperial Great Britain. The immensely intelligent, sprightly Steven Lukes made me understand the difference between a polemicist and a scholar in my very first tutorial with him. But for him, I would never have come back to Oxford to do my DPhil. Formally, Charles Taylor taught me for just one year in the mid-1970s. But, by example, writing, and conversations, he has continued to teach me since. A wonderful friend over three decades, he provides the larger grid with which to think, one that may recede to the back of my mind but never leaves me. Jerry Cohen's *Karl Marx's Theory of History* was a master class in clear thinking and sound argument. The virtues of analytical philosophy came home to me when I read and reread this wonderful book. Jerry supervised parts of my thesis when Steven left for Florence. It did not take me long to realize that defeating him in an argument was the only way to his heart. I had memorable sessions with him in his beloved room at All Souls. I was, in his own words, his 'benefactor' who brought him to India where we quickly struck a very warm friendship. His sudden passing away has deprived me of an unlikely older brother, my own JerryDa! Jerry was influenced by two Marxs, one bearded who—but not his principal ethical values—appeared gradually to have left him, the other clean-shaven who always accompanied and intermittently took hold of him. Tani and I will miss his bizarre, Groucho-like sense of fun, his outrageous jokes, and mimicry as much as his friendship and philosophy.

Publisher's Acknowledgements

The publisher acknowledges the following for permission to include articles/extracts in this volume.

Pearson Education for 'What is Political Theory?', in Rajeev Bhargava and Ashok Acharya (eds), *Political Theory: An Introduction*, New Delhi, 2008, pp. 2–17.

Pearson Education for 'Why do We Need Political Theory?', in Rajeev Bhargava and Ashok Acharya (eds), *Political Theory: An Introduction*, New Delhi, 2008, pp. 18–37.

Oxford University Press for 'Political Secularism', in John Dryzek, B. Honnig, and Anne Phillips (eds), *A Handbook of Political Theory*, Oxford, 2006, pp. 636–55.

Economic and Political Weekly for 'The Continuing Relevance of Socialism', vol. XXVII, no. 40, 3 October 1992, pp. 2161–9.

Oxford University Press for 'How Should We Respond to the Cultural Injustices of Colonialism?', in J. Miller and R. Kumar (eds), *Reparations: Inter-disciplinary Inquiries*, Oxford, 2007, pp. 215–51.

Princeton University Press for 'Restoring Decency to Barbaric Societies', in Robert I. Rotberg and Dennis Thompson (eds), *Truth v. Justice: The Morality of Truth Commissions*, Princeton, New Jersey, 2000, pp. 45–67.

The New Press for 'Ordinary Feelings, Extraordinary Events: Moral Complexity in 9/11', in Craig Calhoun, Paul Price, and Ashley Timmer (eds), *Understanding September 11*, New York, 2002, pp. 321–31.

xvi   Publisher's Acknowledgements

Tamkang Literary Review for 'Literature, Censorship, and Democracy', vol. XXVI, nos 1 and 2, Autumn and Winter 1995.

Sage Publications for 'Religious and Secular Identities', in Bhikhu Parekh and Upendra Baxi (eds), *Crisis and Change in Contemporary India*, New Delhi, 1995, pp. 317–49.

Shipra and India International Centre for 'Are there Alternative Modernities?', in N.N. Vohra (ed.), *Culture, Democracy and Development in South Asia*, New Delhi, 2000, pp. 9–26.

Routledge and Kegan Paul for 'Holism and Individualism in History and Social Science', in Edward Craig (ed.), *Encyclopedia of Philosophy*, London, 1998, pp. 482–8.

Rawat Publications for 'What Makes Something Social?', in Bijoy Barua and R.S. Mishra (eds), *Social Reality and Tradition*, New Delhi, 2006, pp. 37–55.

Sage Publications for '"Objective Significance" in Critical Social Theory', in Bhikhu Parekh and Thomas Pantham (eds), *Political Discourse*, New Delhi, 1987, pp. 97–119.

I
WHAT IS POLITICAL THEORY
AND
WHY DO WE NEED IT?

1

What is Political Theory?*

A cursory glance at the newspaper brings us face to face with dozens of political issues. The Supreme Court pronounces that there should be no reservations in private colleges, university students demonstrate against the government to demand the proper implementation of the National Rural Employment Guarantee Act (NREGA), women organizations complain bitterly about the unequal treatment of women and girls in our society, trade union leaders condemn police brutality against workers, animal right activists demand better protection for endangered species of tigers, the prime minister apologizes to the Sikh community for moral indifference and neglect by the Congress government at the time of 1984 massacre of Sikhs, the government gives up the sale of public sector units (PSUs), the Rajya Sabha passes a bill to grant Hindu women an equal right in ancestral property, the chief minister of Gujarat insists that Gujarati identity and pride is wounded by opponents of the Sardar Sarovar project.

What in your opinion makes all these issues political? Do all these issues have some one thing in common which defines them as political? Consider the examples that refer to reservations, NREGA, the massacre of Sikhs, equal rights to women in ancestral property, and the sale of PSUs. All these refer to some institution of the state: the judiciary, the government, the legislature, the office of the prime minister. They also refer to the decision-making power of these institutions. Does it follow that the term 'political' refers to any public agency with the

* Originally published as 'What is Political Theory?', in Rajeev Bhargava and Ashok Acharya (eds), *Political Theory: An Introduction*, New Delhi: Pearson Education, 2008, pp. 2–17.

power or authority to take decisions and its action? Notice, too, that all these decisions possess the potential to have an impact on almost every member of the society in question. Even when a particular decision appears to target a specific group, it relates to and has an impact on other groups. Does the term 'political' then refer to the common power to take decisions about the common life of a society?

It would be a mistake to confine this term only to this common power of state institutions. Consider once again the example of women's organizations protesting against the exclusion or unequal treatment of women. On the understanding of 'political' arrived thus far, this action of a group of women is *not* political. Why so? Because women's organizations are clearly not part of the state. But surely, on any intuitive understanding of a political act, such a protest by a women's group is political. If so, this must compel us to change or broaden our understanding of the term 'political'. This protest is political not merely because it is a collective act by a group against some continuing social practice or an earlier decision of the government but also because the very object of this protest, namely, the unequal treatment of women is part of what we understand by the term 'political'. And why is this so? Because to treat women unequally is to exercise power over them— men make women do things which, left to themselves, they may not do. This exercise of power is also part of what we mean by 'political'.

A closer look at most of the examples points to another feature of the political. The political is that domain or dimension of our collective life where we fight for our interests, make claims, including moral claims, on each other, where important and urgent issues are contested. But demands, claims, protests, and complaints cannot but generate conflict. The political, it appears, is inherently conflictual. Finally, we might look at political in a still different sense. Implicit in almost every example is a vision of a future world, one where all are equal, or where even animals are treated with some respect, or where force is replaced by deliberation, and so on. The political then is also where new worlds are imagined. Clearly, the term 'political' has no fixed or unique meaning. It has multiple, though related meanings. One objective of these introductory chapters is to enhance our understanding of the political and to draw the attention of the reader to its multiple meanings.

Our second task is to understand what we mean by the term 'theory'. Though not easy, it is important that this be done so that eventually we can put the two terms, 'political' and 'theory', together and have a better grasp over what is meant by political theory. Consider once again the examples in the first paragraph. Many of us have an opinion on most of these issues. Some of us are interested in seeking an explanation of the actions of the police, the Supreme Court, and the government. Are there any motives behind the actions of these agencies? Do their actions serve the interest of the entire community, or the narrow interests of a class, or perhaps, a tiny political elite? For instance, some might argue that the issue of Gujarat identity is used to further the interests of rich peasants. Others may claim that identity is a non-issue, that the real motive underlying every public action is class interest. The academically minded amongst us may claim that there exist structural reasons underlying these actions. For example, the slow implementation of NREGA might be due to systemic institutional biases hidden from the consciousness of power wielders.

Is doing political theory the same, then, as explaining an act, practice, event, or process? This does not appear to be so. Although explaining is part of political theory, surely, it is not the whole of it. And, this is so for two different reasons. First, because an explanatory statement does not on its own constitute a theory. If I say that I fell down because I stumbled unknowingly upon a stone, I have offered an explanation of why I fell down, but have I offered a theory of what has happened? Or, if I said that the USA has invaded Iraq in order to have easy access to oil, I would have offered some explanation of why the US state acted the way it did. But is this the same as articulating a theory of it? No. Why so? Probably because one explanation does not make a theory. Some other features are required, in conjunction with which it will become an explanatory theory. Second, all theories are not explanatory. There are other kinds of theories. For example, some theories offer justifications of actions. Take the examples of the first paragraph again. Some of us might silently condemn equal rights to women in ancestral property or justify police brutality. Others may disagree. They might denounce police action as violative of the most basic human rights or rejoice that equality now covers an important gender issue that had hitherto been neglected. These justificatory statements do not constitute theory but they may be its crucial components. Moreover, in denouncing police action, we are necessarily evaluating it negatively. All justifications presuppose evaluation. Behind these evaluative judgements are deeper issues. Why should women and men be treated as equals? What is the appropriate response of the government to mass killings? What is the connection between ensuring employment to everyone and social justice? What is the proper function of the police in a modern democratic state? Workers are beaten up apparently for disobeying the state. But why should we obey the state at all? Why should we be law-abiding citizens? Similarly, we might ask: why should tigers, who sometimes turn man-eaters, still be protected? Such questions have to do with right and wrong, good and bad; in short, with ethics and morality, with the normative. Admittedly, answers to these questions may not on their own constitute theory but what additional features are necessary for them to be deemed theoretical?

As theory, political theory must share features with theories of other phenomenon. It may even have some features in common with theories of the physical or the biological world. However, by virtue of being political theory, it must possess characteristics that are distinctive. Some of these distinctive features separate it from theories of nature but not from theories pertaining to human affairs more generally. But, its truly distinctive features must flow from its focus on the political. In what follows, therefore, we outline the more general features of any theory and in particular, elucidate features of a theory of human condition and action. In order to do so, we relate theory to and differentiate it from other forms of systematic reflections such as art, literature, and religious world views. Finally, we ask the question, 'what is political', and outline the specific features of political theory.

WHAT IS THEORY?

Humans as Concept-bearing Animals

Allow me to state a few truisms. No one denies that we are physical creatures, part of the physical universe and subject to the same laws of physics that apply to other physical objects. Nor will anyone deny that unlike purely physical objects but like other biological creatures we are sentient creatures: we breathe, we eat, we grow, and have sensory experience. However, what distinguishes us from most, though perhaps not all biological creatures is that we are concept-bearing animals. As conceptual creatures, we are born in a world that is already arranged thoughtfully in particular ways. Consider the following. A child is told to sit on a chair. From a purely physical point of view, chairs are just wood, nothing else. But it would be odd to tell the child to sit on a piece of wood. What we wish to convey to the child is that a particular piece of wood, when crafted in a particular manner serves a particular purpose, namely, that it is something on which we sit or with which we can do certain things such as eating, reading, writing, talking, and so on.

It is these purposes that we wish to convey to the child, purposes which would not exist unless conceptually formulated.

This is true not only of objects such as chairs, tables, blackboard, chalk, the classroom in the school building but also of human beings themselves. A student interacts with the person standing in front of the blackboard and talks to her not as if she is any odd person but as one who is there to perform a certain role, that of a teacher. Once again, no teaching is possible unless all of us already have a rough idea of the social role of students and teachers. The same is true of bus conductors, drivers, ticket inspectors, shopkeepers, government officials, and so on. A society cannot function without these elementary understandings and so, every child is initiated into the social world by an informal instruction in these concepts. Unlike the purely physical, chemical, or the biological world, the human world is conceptual through and through. It is already imbued with significance.[1] The German philosopher, Edmund Husserl, called it the life-world. Plants and most lower-order animals live in the world and sense it, but by virtue of living the world through concepts, humans do not merely have sensory experience. Because their experience is mediated by images, concepts, and representations, we might say that human experience is always laden with thought and significance. Humans do not merely live but have thoughtful experience in the life-world—what we might call lived experience. What to us appears as immediate experience of a red chair, a computer, a medical doctor, a painting is always already mediated by meaning and significance.

Concepts Embedded in Practices

As hinted earlier, most concepts that we use in everyday living are not formally learnt in the classroom but are acquired by participating in various practices. Since we use concepts, we may liken them to tools but this should not lead us to think that we have mental boxes in our head from which we pick them out as and when we need them. Much of our conceptual understanding is available to us as a practical skill or is directly embedded in practices. We are not even aware most of the time that we possess this skill or understanding. This may appear implausible to you at first. But really, the matter is quite simple. Several activities you do routinely are not thoughtless but are mostly absent in the stream of your consciousness. (How many times do you really

---

[1] Some of these issues are discussed in Chapter 16 of this volume.

interrupt the flow of your activity and think?) You just do them without explicitly thinking about them, just as the bus driver changes gears without first asking himself whether or not he should. You see the object in front of you as a table or a book and you understand that what you are doing is sitting at the table and reading. When we see a person entering the poll booth and approaching the ballot box, we understand that he is voting. This understanding is direct and practical, not inferred from something that first takes place in your consciousness. It is usually the same with people and social relationships. We might call this an *embedded understanding* of things, practices, people, and relationships.

Human Expressions

All humans have the ability not only to have thoughtful experience and embedded understanding but to express these thoughts and understandings in different media. A child experiences a piece of wood as a chair or a table but she may express this experience in a drawing, by representing these objects on paper. An actor, a mime artiste, or a dancer may use her body to say the same thing. A photographer may use the camera for the same purpose. There are multiple ways of expressing an experience, some word dependent and others not. Besides, we may express this experience in words to other people: 'Hey! I see a table there.' Or, I may express it to myself, privately, 'That's a table, isn't it?'. So, some of these expressions are in the outer world, in public spaces and some may occur inside, privately, as ideas in our heads. These private expressions may be called subjective reflections, a kind of mirroring of the world in our own heads.

Ad hoc and Systematic Reflections

All expressions, including subjective reflections, may occur randomly, on the spur of the moment or be arranged systematically. All of us, from time to time have spontaneous and random reflections. The chalk with which I unthinkingly and effortlessly write on the blackboard starts crumbling one day. When that happens, I may interrupt the flow of my action, examine the chalk and ask if I could not have chalk of better quality. I have an embedded understanding of what a chalk is and practical knowledge of what is to be done with it but confronted with a piece of chalk literally melting in my fingers into dust, I may think to myself, just what it is made of, whether it really is what it is meant to be. 'Is this really a piece of chalk?' Such random thoughts may occur and then disappear for no ostensible reason but they arise invariably when there is an unexpected interruption of my activities, when I am faced, for example, with a problem.

Word-dependent and Word-independent Reflections

Suppose then, that I don't let this thought disappear, I engage with it, indeed pursue it obsessively. Suppose that I now examine not merely the chalk in hand but the entire box, indeed not just one but all the boxes bought by the department of my college, and arrive at the conclusion that the entire lot is defective. I identify the manufacturer and begin to look at the quality of other lots used elsewhere. Quite obviously, I have begun a kind of sustained and systematic empirical enquiry. When I write a report on chalk produced by the manufacturer, it becomes an expression of systematic reflection on an issue selected for sharper focus. A report is systematic and word dependent. But humans have the ability to systematically reflect and express themselves in a variety of non-linguistic media. Systematic expressions and reflections on the world and on ourselves are also found in music, sculpture, painting, dance, pottery, architecture, and so on. A filmmaker or a painter may reflect on the human condition, on a social environment, on the problems of a society in transition, on the predicaments of modernity, or on the futility of war but without deploying words to convey their meaning. Have you seen the paintings in Ajanta caves? Or, Madhubani and Worli paintings? Or, a replica of the Spanish painter Pablo Picasso's Guernica? Many of you may have heard Amir Khan's rendering of Bhairavi or Kumar Gandharv's of Bhim Palasi. These too are systematic reflections. Other forms of systematic reflections use language but in interestingly different ways.

Varieties of Word-dependent Reflections

Word or language-dependent systematic expressions or reflections can also be accomplished in multiple modes, in interestingly different ways. The essay is one form. A written dialogue is another. Poetry is yet another. Newspaper articles, a mixture of short description and analysis, provide another form. A record of one's experience in a village, the ethnography of a good anthropologist is a systematic expression of collective lived experience. Folk tales, moral fables, myths and legends, epic poetry, short stories, and novels are all systematic reflections.

What has all this got to do with theory? I propose that theory too be seen as a particular form of language-dependent systematic expression different from but related to other forms of systematic reflections on the world. Like other expressions, a theory articulates, in a particular medium, a conceptual world lived practically by a specific set of human agents. Moreover, it does so in its own distinctive way. What marks a theory out from other language-dependent systematic expressions? I propose that there are six such features, four of which it necessarily shares with philosophy and two that are specific to it.

But before I outline them, I must set aside a fundamental objection: someone might say that the question I seek to answer is misplaced. We should not ask what theory is but rather teach people how to use the word 'theory'. Learning how to use 'theory' is to understand the concept of theory and this concept is acquired by learning the relevant skills. One simply has to do theory. Does this not follow from what I said earlier about the acquisition of concepts? So, the best way to teach political theory is not to provide learners with a list of its constitutive properties but to ask them to listen to someone theorizing or to read an exampler, say, Hobbes' *Leviathan*, or John Rawls' *Theory of Justice*, or Gandhi's *Hind Swaraj*. One learns to do theory by example and practice not by formal instruction stated in propositional form, precisely what the question, 'what is theory', seeks to ask. I am sympathetic to this view but not totally satisfied with it.

While the view of language as practice is extremely important, it is not exhaustive. True, we learn to pick the use of many words in practice, but as we become more self-reflective we frequently wish to acquire a general idea of the practice before entering it. This general idea helps to orient us towards that practice. Indeed, many of us might want to have a general idea of a practice, even though we may not be ourselves inclined to participate in it. I can think of many students who wish to get some idea of theory before trying a hand at it. I can also imagine people who don't wish to theorize but are interested in a clarification of what theory is. Even people who theorize might wish to articulate what they do. As long as we know that we will not learn to do political theory simply by rattling off the features mentioned next and that to properly learn to do it, we must try doing it ourselves, I see little wrong in attempting an answer to these questions. Besides, something in our intellectual context compels me to ask them the question: what is X? This is frequently raised when X is in crisis, is unfamiliar or new, the point underlying it has been forgotten, there is confusion about it or when the tradition behind it has to be retrieved or reinvented. I believe something of each of these is part of our specific intellectual context. It is in this spirit and with these minor anxieties that I seek to answer questions, such as what is theory and what is political theory?

THE DISTINCTIVENESS OF THEORY

The first feature is an almost obsessive and self-conscious concern with the internal structure of concepts, with how concepts relate to one another and come in clusters and how, in turn, they mark their own boundaries. A philosopher or a theorist—for my purpose I will often use these terms interchangeably—focuses on the meaning of words, on the different ways in which the words are used so that she can eventually answer questions such as what is justice? What is the meaning of the phrase 'social revolution' and how is it different from 'social reform' or 'social engineering'? What is the core idea of freedom, if there is one? What are the different interpretations of this core idea? Is the notion of *swaraj* linked to republican notions of liberty? What is the relationship between freedom and equality? And between freedom, equality, and justice? What distinguishes power from influence, force, violence, or persuasion? In ordinary life, we use words more or less unselfconsciously and we are not normally compelled to ask such questions. But philosophers must raise these questions and understand them in a particular way. When asked what time is, we don't expect philosophers to look at their watches and tell us the precise time of the day. Philosophers are expected to convey to us what the meaning of time is and what it is for us to live in time. Likewise, if a philosopher is asked a question about basic needs, he is not expected to supply us a list of our most urgent desires but rather to make us understand how needs are different from ordinary desires and what the distinction is between our most inescapable and significant needs and others that, at least temporarily, we may live without.

As long as our purpose is served, we don't ordinarily care whether a word is used literally, or metaphorically, or both. Poets, novelists, and essayists use words self-consciously and with extreme care, but it is not their business to elucidate why they have chosen to use this rather than some other word or to make explicit connections between different concepts. The job of a philosopher and in so far as philosophy is part of theory, the job of a theorist is to accomplish precisely this. A full-blooded sensitivity to the entire web of concepts and a commitment to its articulation is the first feature of theory.

Let me illustrate this further with an example. Suppose that someone gives a call for freedom: we should all be free! What are people to make of this call? For a start, they must understand what it means to be free. Once they have understood the meaning or rather the different meanings of freedom, they may ask why they should be free or, at least, why they should be free in this rather than in some other sense. (Sometime ago, some traditions of political theory reduced it to analysis of political concepts, but the significance of such analysis is considerably reduced if it is not included in and used to clarify larger political arguments.) To be free of or from something is to get rid of it. What you wish to get rid of must be something that you evaluate negatively. In the literature on freedom, such things that you wish to get rid of are usually called constraints. So, to be free is to be free from constraints. But what is the nature of these constraints? Surely, our ideas of freedom will depend upon our understanding of what these constraints are. Are these constraints purely physical? Take the paradigmatic example of freedom. A man is in chains. Get rid of the chains and he is free. The same is true of birds in a cage. The cage is imprisoning, restricting the flight of the bird; that which it is most prone to doing and is its nature. To set the bird free is to get rid of the cage. In the same way, prisoners are set free when they are released. Have you noticed that our notion of constraint may already have changed with this last example? For, at issue here is not merely the idea of physical but of legal constraints. A person may have been put behind bars because he has been caught stealing. He stole because he was physically free to steal and yet, he was imprisoned because it is illegal to do so. Appropriating a thing that by law belongs to another is illegal and it is because of the presence of this legal constraint that the man was put in jail. To be free then is to be free not just from physical but from legal constraints.

Is this all there is to freedom? Notice that both physical and legal constraints are external to the agent. Can a person be unfree not because of the presence of physical and legal constraints—there may be none— but by virtue of psychological barriers, obstructions that are present within his mental make-up. So, consider a slave who is set free and who is now pronounced as formally equal to his former master. Suppose that they both compete in an open exam, and while the former master always does well, the former slave simply cannot perform. Centuries of slavery have taken away from him the basic self-confidence required for a good performance. He is unable to achieve his objectives not because of physical or legal constraints but due to internal psychological ones. A conception of freedom that conceives freedom in purely physical or legal terms is unable to capture the mechanism of unfreedom which is at work here. We can similarly talk about constraints which are neither purely external nor purely internal but a bit of both—I mean social constraints. A person is physically and legally free to enter the higher education system. He has done well in his school examinations, well enough to get a place in a decent college. But higher education is costly. There are no subsidies or scholarships. The person is confident that he would do well and he has every reason to feel so. And yet, he cannot get higher education. He is severely handicapped by his relative poverty which is a major socio-economic constraint on what he wishes to do. Implicit in this is a still different conception of freedom: freedom from not merely physical, legal, and psychological but also socio-economic constraints.

Hitherto we have focused on constraints. However, our conception of freedom changes with our ideas about what we should do once freed from constraints. Some argue that it is enough that we are able to fulfil whatever we happen to currently desire. So, if I desire to smoke and no constraints exist to prevent me from doing so, then I am free. Others argue that by a focus on current unevaluated desires we misunderstand what is really at issue in discussions of freedom. Such people work with a less instrumentalist, more robust conception of reason and argue that one is free only when there is absence of constraints and a real opportunity to do what we evaluate to be good for us. In this view, if information that cigarettes are gravely injurious to health is available to us but we continue to both desire smoking and fulfil this desire then we are not really being free. We are not free because we succumb to a habit or addiction completely bypassing, ignoring, or evading what our reason says is good for us. To fall prey to one's current unevaluated desires, in this view, is to be in a state of unfreedom. Freedom is a condition of leading a life and of doing things that are evaluated to be good for us, to fulfil desires that are judged to be worth having in the first place. This view slowly leads to the idea that freedom is identical with self-realization. The detailed elaboration of different conceptions of freedom is one task of political theory. The other one is to reason why we should choose one rather than the other conception. Why, if at all, one conception is better than others.[2]

[2] The articulation of conceptions and the attempt to demonstrate via argument why one or some are better than others or what we must do in order to realize better conceptions is something I do in most chapters of this book, notably in Chapters 4 (secularism), 7 (cultural injustice), 11 (different forms of religious and secular identities), and 14 (different conceptions of the social).

This brings me to the second distinctive feature of theory or philosophy, that is, that all said and done, it is a rational enterprise, where the term rational is understood very broadly to mean that the conclusion arrived or hinted at has some discernable structure of reasons behind it. To say this is not to imply that philosophers or theorists do not rely on instincts, emotions, or flashes of insight. Nor does it mean that a philosophical or theoretical enquiry must possess a definite argumentative structure of the kind made familiar by logicians, although some philosophies and theories may have some such pattern. However, it does mean that philosophers and theorists are not satisfied with bland assertions, the flat announcement of a claim, or the presentation of a readymade proposal. When they make an assertion or proposal, they must state why they do so. In other words, they must give a reason. Indeed, they cannot be satisfied with providing one reason and stopping the process of questioning at this point. There can be a reason for a reason already supplied and a reason for the reason for the initial reason. In other words, whether stated explicitly or not, there is a chain of reasons that is discernable in a theoretical or philosophical work. Does this mean that we can reach the final reason, a reason beyond which there is no reason—the foundation of all reasons? Some philosophers appear to be obsessed with this idea of ultimate cause or justification of an event or act. But, I doubt if we humans can ever get to the bottom of all things.

Take the example of scientific theories. Suppose that it is claimed that water is a compound. This must be backed by some evidence demonstrating that it is composed of two elements, hydrogen and oxygen, and that this composition is not a mere mixture of features of both but rather a new substance with features of its own. Furthermore, this evidence must itself be supported by more general claims about the mechanism by which such a process takes place. Similarly, suppose that it is proposed that all children must be provided elementary education and suppose in answer to the question, 'why?', it is asserted that education is a fundamental right, then it must also be argued further that at least in modern times, there is a connection between education, employment, and a life of dignity, and further that a dignified life is a crucial component of human flourishing, and so on. This rational structure of theories, their internal requirement that they persistently ask for reasons makes them, albeit with some qualifications, subversive—with the potential to transform societies.

The rational component of theory also illuminates another of its important features, the third feature, namely, its aspiration to truth and objectivity. This claim must be made very cautiously but clearly. The truth that social and political theories, aspire to is not valid for all times and places. The truth of most theories is context dependent and therefore, limited to specific times and places. Only the very exceptional theories have a reach that cuts across time and space. Nor is this very achievable but limited truth in any way final. We must rid ourselves of the illusion that like god, we humans can stand outside all perspectives and attain god-like objectivity or an eternal truth of the matter. The truth that we achieve is dependent on the collective reasoning of human beings and even if all rational persons can agree at any given point of time that they have arrived at the truth of a certain matter, new information or a flaw in an argument detected much later by other reasonable beings can force us to revise our earlier truth claims. Human knowledge can neither altogether escape subjective viewpoints nor be imprisoned within the subjective biases of wealthy classes, powerful political blocs, or even intellectuals. Such views may pass off as knowledge for sometime but sooner or later, their limitations are bound to come to light. We might then arrive at some acceptable version that can rightfully be claimed as the truth of the matter; an achievement not possible without the use of reason, although reason alone cannot help us attain it.

I see no harm in repeating myself a bit. If we cannot stand outside all perspectives and if we can relate to our world only with the help of some perspective, then some interest, pre-judgement, presupposition, and prejudice will always be found in the 'foundation'. A more effective and fruitful way forward is to acknowledge and articulate them and then engage self-critically with them. Ignoring them or living in the illusion that we have transcended them will take us away from a humanly possible truth and objectivity and plunge us into further ignorance. This is the great insight of social philosophers such as Gadamer. Quite simply, we need to steer clear of the trappings of the futile search for absolute rational certainty, decisive evidence, and tightly deduced conclusions.

A fourth feature of philosophy/theory is that it is committed to unearthing the background assumptions and presuppositions of our statements, beliefs, actions, and practices. For example, the force of gravity is presupposed by all our situated action. We don't always articulate this, nor are many of us aware that this is so. Yet, without the force of gravity, embodied persons cannot exist on this earth. Similarly, when we set out to attend a class we make many assumptions which remain in the background, as part of our pre-reflective understanding. For example, the classroom is exactly where we left it on the previous day, that the teacher would arrive to take the class, that at least some other students would be present, that the teacher will give the lecture in a language that we speak or understand, and so on. All of us exist, think, and act with these assumptions and presuppositions but do not always articulate them. To take another example, in seventeenth century England, politicians had begun to think and speak of politics without appeal to religious principles. But frequently, they did not acknowledge this. It was left to Hobbes to articulate these new background assumptions and to show that it was possible to conduct politics in a purely secular manner. Thus, within reasonable limits, philosophers and theorists are committed to articulating these background assumptions and presuppositions.

Unearthing such presuppositions has cognitive value. It helps to sharpen our sense of what is really at stake. Take, for example, the debate between methodological individualists and non-individualists.[3] It is a frequently held belief that in studying any human phenomenon—understanding and explaining it—scholars and researchers must not ignore human action. Action is behaviour guided by intentions, by beliefs, desires, purposes, and so on. These intentions simply have to be in the heads of individuals. Therefore, to explain any human phenomenon, collective or individual, one must refer to entities located in individuals. Quite simply, one must be an individualist, if for nothing else, at least for methodological purposes. But, are human actions exclusively located in or owned by individuals? A theorist or philosopher must re-examine this claim by digging deeper. It might be uncontroversial that action is guided by intention, but must intentions always be in the heads of individuals? The unequivocal answer is in the affirmative if one assumes that intentions are mental entities, mental events that occur in the minds of individuals, and that the meanings of intentions, what intentions are about can be individuated by elements in the minds of each individual. These two modern assumptions, found in Descartes and Locke, are central to the individualist's claims and the articulation of these assumptions is crucial to the theorist examining them. Once this is done and assumptions examined, the individualist

---

[3] This debate is discussed at length in Chapters 13 and 14 of this volume.

claim may be endorsed or rejected. At any rate, it can be challenged. Perhaps intentions exist, also, outside the minds of individuals and their meanings are individuated by elements found largely in the external environment of actors, say, in their community. If these assumptions hold, the individualist view seems far less tenable.

The fifth feature of theory—and here philosophy and theory may begin to diverge—is this: a theory aspires to some degree of generality and abstraction. It does so because it aims to cover a wide variety of related but disparate phenomena. This does not mean that all theories must be universal in scope. But, it does mean that a theory cannot deal only with a concrete particular, something in the singular. Thus, we have a theory of motion that applies equally to planets as it does to rolling stones. Such a theory has a very high degree of generality appropriate to the object of its study. There cannot be a theory exclusively for rolling stones. Likewise, we could have a descriptive study of Indian nationalism or an empirical study of the causes of Indian nationalism. But, it is unlikely that we will have a theory of nationalism that applies to India and to India alone.

Finally, a sixth feature of theories, one that is a product of modern conditions and has emerged more particularly with the birth of modern science, has to be mentioned. Modern theories cannot be *purely* speculative and must pass through and then transcend the empirical world. They cannot bypass the empirical world altogether. This feature is related to the point mentioned earlier. The data collected by the sciences, the collective lived experience of a people captured in the work of insightful observers or participants, socially engaged thinkers, or consummate social scientists cannot be ignored by theorists. These general and interconnected reflections must take into account all these. For this very reason, a theory must be simultaneously rooted in and transcend the lived experience of a people, the collective practices of a society, and the embedded understandings and common sense of a community. There is no theory if there is mere description of lived experience and common sense, but we have theory only in name if theoretical propositions are altogether disconnected from experience, practices, and the data collected by sound empirical enquiries.

Let me sum up. A theory is a form of systematic reflection with six features: (i) conceptual sensitivity; (ii) rational structure; (iii) aspiration for a humanly achievable truth and objectivity; (iv) generality; (v) an explicit mandate to unearth assumptions and presuppositions; and (vi) strong non-speculative intent—the need not to bypass results of micro-enquiries into the particular. It is not identical to any one feature but must more or less possess all six. Thus, a theory must be distinct from ad hoc reflections, speculation, empirical enquiry into the particular, rich insights, imaginative but fictive prose, and other related narratives. It must also be distinguished from ideology, world view, and cosmology—a point that will emerge more clearly next. A rare specimen of theory may be universalist or reach the foundation, but, on the whole, the constitutive features of a theory do not include a commitment to foundationalism or universalism.

COSMOLOGIES AND COMMON SENSE

I have used the terms embedded understandings and common sense earlier. Let me remind the reader what I mean by them. I made a distinction between conceptually organized lived experience and reflection on that experience. This distinction presupposes that though conceptual, lived experience may not be present in our consciousness, we may use our concepts in practice but be unable to speak about them, quite like a skilful cook who can make delectable dishes without being able to tell us how. (Conversely, the possession of a good recipe book is not sufficient to make a good cook.) By embedded understanding, I mean this practical knowledge that remains pre-reflective and inarticulate. It is an understanding we acquire by being initiated into the practices of a society. The term common sense is broader and covers embedded understanding but also, at the very least, our spontaneous and ad hoc reflections, including reflections that are closely aligned to our practices, which might be called practical reflections. It usually also includes stories, epics, folk tales, legends, myths that have been passed on from one generation to another and with the help of which we make sense of and evaluate the entire universe. The common sense of a society can never be defined or delimited. From this, it does not follow that it is infinite or that it includes everything. But, it is in the nature of common sense that it is something loose, flexible, and fluid. Its limitations show up when certain practices do not work or are misshapen.

Virtually every society, however, has tried to give some order to common sense. Myths, fables, folk tales grow out of and get back into a society's common sense but when they are systematized, elaborated, and partially conceptualized, their reach becomes deeper and wider. Such partly systematic but non-theoretical reflections which knit together in a seamless web the physical, biological, social, mental, and spiritual worlds may be called cosmologies. Cosmologies frequently inform and become part of a society's common sense.

If this is true of the relationship between cosmologies and common sense, can it also be true of the relationship between theories and common sense? Can theories shape and inform our common sense. Though they can do so (indeed, good theories must aspire to do so), the two remain and perhaps must remain distinct entities. The common sense of a society is the collective possession of an entire people. A theory is a specialized activity or product dependent on and generated by specific skills. Does this mean that theorizing is an elite activity from which the common man will remain forever estranged? I don't think so. First, distance does not mean estrangement. Many cricket lovers in India have never played cricket. Some do play it but quite badly. Still others play well but are not exceptional. But all of them can love or admire the skills of a Sachin Tendulkar or Azharuddin. In some ways, they are distant from them but surely no one can claim that distance here necessarily means estrangement. Second, and more importantly, though the practice of theory involves skills, these, in principle, can be acquired by anyone who has some talent and a lot of opportunity and commitment. Just as cricket is not the preserve of a special class or caste of people, just so theory is not the monopoly of a particular kind of people. To think so is to be committed to a deplorable and outdated form of casteist brahminism. We must avoid both the view that theory is the monopoly of the special, naturally talented or genetically endowed group and the claim that it is available effortlessly to the masses or as my colleague, Ashis Nandy, says, that it can also grow in slums. There is wealth of lived experience in slums which is crying out to be theorized but it should not be confused with theory. To the objection that there is a sense in which everyone is a philosopher or a theorist, an appropriate response is to draw the distinction between having a philosophy/theory and doing it. Though all of us have a philosophy, we do not all *do* philosophy. Everyone may have a systematic world view, a theory of the world, a philosophy, but it does not follow that all these are the result of his or her own theorizing/philosophizing.

Lest I be misunderstood, it is important here to clarify a point. I mentioned that theory is a specialized and skill-dependent activity. It does not follow that such a skill can be learnt only within the parameters of particular, well-demarcated disciplines in academic institutions. For a start, we must jettison the thought that political theory is done or learnt only in the Departments of Political Science. Departments of

Social Science, History, Literature, and Philosophy provide equally good settings for the birth and teaching of political theory. Political theory is inherently inter-disciplinary. More importantly, the most crucial component of theorizing is imaginative thinking which can also be learnt outside university settings. Indeed, quite often the disciplinary structures of academic institutions can throttle imaginative thinking. If university institutions are so arranged that they turn skills into techniques and stifle imagination, then theory can only be generated outside them. It is true that most of us learn to do theory as part of a disciplinary practice in academic institutions. But the disciplinary framework of academic institutions cannot be made a constitutive feature of the activity of theorizing.

The emphasis on the distance between theory/philosophy and common sense as also between theory and practice should not be misunderstood or exaggerated. As I pointed out earlier, there is also a close relationship between theory and common sense and between theory and practice. As we will see in Chapter 2, the most fundamental questions asked by philosophers are the same to which answers are implicit in our practice and in common sense. A philosophy of the human world articulates what is already implicit in human practice. In this sense and unlike what many believe, philosophy is down to earth. Yet, it is also up there. It takes flight and is up there because like other systematic reflections—and this close relationship between theory and the arts is equally worth emphasizing—it frequently tries to do more than merely describe human practice. It also attempts to explain and justify it in general terms and less directly to endorse, modify, or change it.

WHAT IS 'POLITICAL'?

The term 'political' has multiple meanings. The first goes back to classical Greece and is derived from the word 'polis', which literally means 'the city' but is better, more properly understood as a place with a common world or even more simply, a community. 'Political' then pertains to whatever is done within or by the community. More specifically, it refers to *decision making* within and about the community. Decision making itself has a specific connotation. To be political, to live in the polis, as Hannah Arendt tells us, means that everything is to be decided through words and persuasion and not through force and violence.[4]

[4] Hannah Arendt, *The Human Condition*, Chicago: University of Chicago Press, 1958, p. 26.

The term 'political' then points to a specific mode of decision making—by words, not force. However, the term 'political' also refers simultaneously to what decisions are about. When we use the term 'political' in this first sense, we speak not merely about life but necessarily about the *good* life of a community. Thus, we may ask, given that we live by a certain conception of the good life, who is to be a member of the community and why; who is to rule, that is, take fundamental decisions about the community and for what reasons; and how resources are to be distributed, to whom and why. In this conception, as we can see, the empirical and the normative are completely intermeshed. Nor has the distinction emerged in this context between political and social spheres. Nothing that we now consider to be merely social, that is, falling between the public–political and the private–household is outside the political. On this classical view then, there is no distinction between social and political theory. Political theory is about how and with what justification decisions are made concerning the good life in a community.

Over a period of time and particularly with the advent of modernity, the meaning of the term 'political' appears to have changed. To understand this change lets go back to what I said earlier. In classical Greece, the term 'political' had to do with fundamental decision making about the affairs of the community. To make decisions, however, one must first have the power to do so. If the entire community is involved in decision making, then decision making presupposes the collective power of the entire community. The term 'political' then may also refer to this collective power, to the use of this power to make decisions, and political science or philosophy may be viewed as the study of this collective power. This conception is based on two assumptions. First, that there exists an undifferentiated, uncontested collective power of a single, difference- and conflict-free community. Second, that all major decisions are collectively taken by everyone within the polis. Both these assumptions are false or at least, can be strongly contested.

Few communities are undifferentiated or act in unison. Nor is there a single, enduring common good of the community. Virtually every known community comprises of individuals and groups with different and conflicting interests and values. One conception of the political seizes on this fact and makes much of it. On this view, given radical differences, various groups in any community must fight to find out who would be the decision makers. This more fundamental decision cannot be reached without conflict and struggle. The political is the arena of this fundamental conflict over which group and which conception of the good would prevail in the community. In this fundamental struggle, some groups will discover something in common with one another and deep differences with other groups. Friends and enemies are found and forged in this struggle. This is why politics frequently involves, as Carl Schmitt famously pointed out, friends and enemies.[5] In politics, no one can escape taking sides.

Second, decisions are rarely taken by everyone who inhabits the arena where they are made. As is well known, even in Greek societies, decisions were not taken by everybody. Power was not exercised by everyone. Slaves, women, and aliens were excluded from the decision-making process. One might then say that decisions about the entire community were taken by some only by excluding others from the processes within which they were made. Some people had power to make decisions about everyone only on condition that they also exercised power over some others. Of course, this can be said only with hindsight. People living at that time did not see their own condition as we now describe it. But, perhaps one reason why they did not see this is because the classical conception of the political masked another emerging conception. It did so by not properly asking: who exercises power? Who decides?

With the advent of modernity, this other meaning of 'power' became far more explicit. Indeed, the classical meaning of power as the collective capacity to decide about the community was almost completely obscured and replaced by the second meaning of power as the capacity of some people to act in a manner that thwarts the significant interest of others, that marginalizes and excludes them, so that they are left with no ability or capacity to take decisions about themselves or about the whole community. Power came simply to mean power *over* others. Correspondingly, the term 'political' refers to this power over others. Political science, then, came to mean an empirical enquiry into the exercise of this power, and political theory, the most general reflection on the processes, mechanisms, institutions, and practices by which some people are excluded by others from significant decision making. Its central question becomes: who wields power over whom and how?

This conception of political leads in two related directions. First, if politics means the exercise of power over others, their exclusion from

[5] Carl Schmitt, *The Concept of the Political*, Chicago: University of Chicago Press, 1996.

the process of decision making, then contra Arendt, it must be seen as that which shuts people up, silences them. It is a conversation stopper in order to facilitate the making of decisions which are undisputed and therefore, final, authoritative, and absolute. The political is that which ends all dialogue so that a monologue can begin. The subject of the monologue, the decision maker, is the sovereign and the political is the domain of the sovereign.

A related conception does not rule out discussion and dialogue but also places it outside the political. Discussion is intelligent but insignificant chatter largely irrelevant to the making of key decisions. Alternatively put, this view admits the existence of a space of dialogic decision making but since it is the nature of internally differentiated, multi-people arenas that they never generate any final and uncontested decision, such decisions are outside the ambit of the sovereign and therefore, the political. Commonplace or general decisions may be generated in dialogic spaces but every exception to the general belongs to the domain of the sovereign. Politics then becomes largely the space where the sovereign decides on exceptions.

Yet another related meaning emerged under conditions of modernity when major sites of decision making were relatively separated from the rest of society and were concentrated in a specific set of institutions designated by the term state (this is related to the point that a new concept of the social emerged which was distinguished from the political). If politics, considered as a comprehensive enquiry, is the study of decision-making power, then the birth of the modern state naturally implied that the major object of study of political science and political theory is the state. Indeed, the term political was itself identified with anything pertaining to the state rather than to the entire society. Political science and political theory studied how, for what reason (interests, values), and with what justification the institutions of the state—the government, the judiciary, the bureaucracy, the military, the police, etc.—arrive at their decisions (policy, programme, position). Sociology and social theory, on the other hand, studied all those structures, processes, and institutions that fell outside the state. Some people continued to believe that a study of the state was the study of how power was exercised on behalf of and in the interest of all the individuals who make up a particular society. Others, cynical of this view, saw political science and political theory as the study of how these institutions take major decisions on behalf of a small elite or the dominant class to the exclusion of the interests of the subordinate classes or subaltern people.

To summarize, the term 'political' has at least seven different meanings:

1. The collective power to produce decisions about every aspect of the good life in the community. Notice that political here refers both to power and to ethical values.
2. The conflict between irreducibly different power groups over who would be the decision makers and whose conception of the good will prevail.
3. The power of some groups to control or subordinate others in order to realize not the good of the entire community but their own narrow interests. In short, to get others to do things that might go against their own interest. Here the term 'political' is used to relate power and self-interest.
4. The power of the sovereign to silence others and to take final, undisputed decisions, especially about exceptional issues in exceptional circumstances. It also refers to power embodied in a separate institutional apparatus, that is, the state.
5. State power used to realize the common good/values.
6. State power used to exercise domination by one group over others.
7. There exists a view of the political that leans on some conceptions just mentioned and opposes others but appears to radically depart from all. In this conception, the political continues to be the domain of power but power does not emanate from the sovereign and is embodied less in state institutions and far more in disciplinary social institutions and norms (hospitals, schools, prisons, welfare departments). Power functions less to command or directly control others and more to make everyone conform. Here, the political merges once again with the social and what it does is less to generate subject-related (individual, group, sovereign) domination or realize ethical or moral values and more system-conformity, whatever the nature of the system.

But how can (1) or (5) coexist with, say, (3) or (6)? How can the entire community take decisions when a group excludes others from collective decision making? Well, in this case, we might say that a split has occurred between the empirical and the normative. The subordinate group may be excluded from decision making but may have the desire to forge a new world where everybody is involved in taking decisions about shared interests and values. (1) and (5) then become normative/ethical notions capturing something which is hitherto unrealized or realized very marginally, while (3) and (6) capture what really exists on the ground. A final meaning is related to but still different from how we have hitherto conceived (1). The reader may have noticed that so far (1) refers to the good life of the community, to values of specific communities. But, what if we begin to use the term 'political' for values common to the entire humanity in abstraction from both power and specific communities? What if it refers to values common to all living species? Here polis coincides with cosmopolis. So (1) splits into two and gives us the eighth meaning of the political. This meaning, (8), refers to values common to the entire humanity, even all living species. Recall also that the political sphere may also include the art of imagining new values and devising new worlds. Since (8) refers to possible worlds, it can be maximally abstracted from really existing lives. Thus, today, we use the term 'political' in each of the eight senses and as both an empirical and a normative concept.

Political theory then is a particular form of word-dependent systematic reflection (with each of the six features mentioned earlier) on any or all of the following:

1. The collective power to take decisions about the good life of a community (this has been the main focus of a great deal of modern political theory, both empirical and normative, that deals with the public institutions of the nation-state).

2. The fundamental conflict over who would be the decision makers and whose conception of the good will prevail (empirical theories such as the Marxist theory of class conflict and more general Schmittean theories).

3. The mechanisms by which power is exercised by one group over another (this takes place at both sub-national and supra-national levels. Much modern political theory has interrogated how ethnic groups, males, castes, classes have dominated minorities, indigenous peoples, women, outcastes, poor peasants, and workers within particular nation-states. Political theory has also dealt with colonialism, imperialism, immigration, and trans-national corporations).

4. The power of the sovereign to silence others and to take final, undisputed decisions, especially about exceptional issues in exceptional circumstances (the study of emergency powers under conditions of war and terrorism and how such power is normalized even after the threat of war and terrorism recede).

5. The use of state power (the power of different institutions including the government) to achieve the good of the community (the

empirical and normative study of modern welfare states, secular states, and constitutional democracies).

6. The use of the state by one group to exercise power over other groups.

7. On the values and principles by which a particular community and its state governs its life, in abstraction from matters of power and interest (contemporary normative political theory provides umpteen examples of this mode).

8. Power embodied in social norms and institutions to generate system-conformity (Foucault-inspired empirical theory).

9. There can be a grand political theory that reflects on the general condition of the entire humankind or values by which the entire humanity may govern its life (here, we might mention not only more abstract studies of humanism, Kantian theories of public morality and justice, theories of human rights but also the empirical and normative theories grounded in increasing importance of trans-national environmental issues such as global warming and climate change, ozone depletion, the nuclear threat, 'humanitarian' intervention, global economic disasters that lead to poverty, unemployment, and famine. All these raise new issues of global justice and responsibility).

I have given an exhaustive list neither of the constitutive features of theory nor of the political. Moreover, multiple meanings of both theory and the political are bound to generate markedly different conceptions of political theory. Given these differences, the meaning and function of political theory remains deeply contested. What political theory is and what its functions are themselves contentious, political issues.

2

Why do We Need Political Theory?*

What in general are theories meant to do? What are the functions of a theory? In the first chapter, some of these functions have already been listed. However, here we ask a different, deeper question. Do we really need political theory? One may ask how this question is different from the one mentioned in the previous line. Consider then the following: doctors of modern western, allopathic medicine undeniably perform a function in our society. However, we might ask, in the critical spirit of Gandhi's *Hind Swaraj*, if we really need doctors who practice modern western medicine? Can the function of healing and restoration of health not be performed by other practices and their practitioners? Analogously, we might ask: can the function of political theory be better performed by something else, say ideologies or cosmologies? Why do we need political theory?

I propose that this question cannot be answered unless we ask the really big questions of human existence and collective life. I suggest that many of these answers are now provisionally provided, by natural–scientific theories and the social sciences. However, this was not always the case. Most of them were once provided only by religions, cosmologies, and philosophy. Moreover, political philosophy simultaneously performed both explanatory and normative functions. In what follows, I suggest that political theory now performs four interrelated functions.

* Originally published as 'Why do We Need Political Theory?', in Rajeev Bhargava and Ashok Acharya (eds), *Political Theory: An Introduction*, New Delhi: Pearson Education, 2008, pp. 18–37. Both this and the previous chapter are re-arranged and edited transcripts of lectures delivered to students over many years. I have retained the tone and content of the lectures in the written version.

It explains at the most general level possible, it evaluates and tells us what we should do, and it speculates about our current and future condition. It also tells us who we are. In some sense, these functions are no different from the tasks performed by cosmologies and ideologies. Yet, I argue that political theory is distinct from both. I also try to claim that political theory has a special function under modern conditions. Far from being dead, it not only lives but needs to flourish.

THE BIG QUESTIONS OF HUMAN LIFE
Consider the following abstract but significant questions:
1. What is there/going on in the world? (Understanding)
2. Why are things there/going on in the world? (Explanation)
3. Will something that is currently going on continue to go on in future? (Prediction)
4. Is that which is there/going on good or bad, right or wrong? (Ethics)
5. What am I to do? What is to be done? (Normative)
6. Who am I? Who are we? (Metaphysical self-knowledge)

   Human life is virtually impossible without the availability of answers to each of these questions. One might say that one becomes a human being or at least, a certain kind of human being as answers to these questions are learnt. Humans can live in a society only if they have some understanding of what the nature of the society is. For example, it is crucial that, in a hierarchical society, a person has an understanding of his own rank as well as the social standing of others. A person who is part of the 'lower' order has a practical understanding of this status and knows that he must be deferential to someone superior to him. An insider understands what is going on when a person stands bowing his head, lowering his eyes before another man. He also understands why this is going on. He possesses an explanation for it. He knows that a person must bow before another person *because* he is inferior. Such understandings and explanations are part of common sense and crucial to the functioning of the society as *that* society. Similarly, members of such a society have some idea of what is in store for them in the future; indeed, what they can hope for. For the lower castes, practically nothing. For the upper castes, the permanence of privilege. And all this is linked further to a fairly common understanding of what is right and wrong, good and bad in that society and to a certain self-understanding. In a properly functioning hierarchical society, the person deemed inferior believes that bowing before his superiors is the right thing to do, that it would be wrong to violate this norm. Thus, the possession of answers to all these questions is vital to the working of a hierarchical society. The availability of different answers to roughly the same questions makes possible a functioning egalitarian society.

Of course, to possess a fairly comprehensive understanding of one's society does not mean that this knowledge is available *as answers* to questions. As a matter of fact, we do not first have questions for which we seek answers. We begin to have an understanding of our world, an understanding which is reformulated as a compendium of answers to these big questions when, as reflective creatures, we learn to raise these questions. But, what are the circumstances in which we learn to raise these questions? There are many reasons why this might happen. I mention three. It might happen, first, if, for whatever reason, an individual or a group is alienated from the rest of the community. It might then be asked by alienated persons: do I really belong here? Who really am I? This estrangement leads to a crisis of mutual understanding. Second, this could occur with the entry of the stranger whose opaque actions provoke curiosity and internal dissonance. Why is that man doing whatever it is that he is doing? How should we relate to him and others like him? Third, it may be caused by unpredictable changes in the natural world: disease, flood, earthquake, any natural disaster. Why do such dramatic changes occur in nature? Why do they cause suffering in this world? Why is there suffering in the world? Why are we born at all if we *must* suffer?

Now, I want to suggest that small communities develop their own local cosmologies—some general picture not reducible to context-specific practical understanding—in the face of any of the three changes mentioned earlier.[1] Unpredictable changes in nature, the coming of the stranger, the possibility of the breakup of the community, all of these lead human beings to seek refamiliarization with what has become

---

[1] In a sense, some form of generality is found in any kind of reflective understanding. As Berlin puts it, 'There is no human activity without some kind of general outlook' and 'To think is to generalize and to generalize is to compare. To think of one phenomenon or a cluster of phenomenon is to think in terms of its resemblances and differences with others.' See Isaiah Berlin, 'Does Political Theory Still Exist?', *Concepts and Categories: Philosophical Essays*, Oxford: Oxford University Press, 1980, p. 158. It is virtually impossible to think about a particular. To think is to think about particulars or the particular and the general. This is why all thinking is, in one way or another, a form of proto-theory.

unfamiliar. In order to make a fresh sense of the world and their own place within it or to lend larger, deeper significance to our somewhat shaken existence, revisions in common sense become necessary.

Cosmologies perform this function and help us tell a story about ourselves and our relations to others and to nature and make sense of existing chaos. By making sense of something that is going out of control, becoming meaningless, or discordant, they help to endow it with meaning, make it harmonious with other things, and bring it under some semblance of control. Cosmologies inform and refashion common sense. They frequently extend and even challenge the common sense of the day by raising some of these questions afresh. Is the world apprehended by our senses real? (A question remarkably similar in form to: is the chalk that is crumbling and falling through my fingers really a piece of chalk?) Does life end with the physical destruction of the body? Am I to be identified exclusively with the physical body? Several cosmologies provide a negative answer to these questions and thereby oppose our common sense. The world of senses is illusory or there is a life of the soul after death, they say. Whatever the case, cosmologies are never identical with or reducible to common sense.

THE EMERGENCE OF WESTERN MODERNITY

Several ancient cosmologies tied to relatively small communities tended to see these questions as pertaining to one unified universe. A distinction between the human and the natural world was neither drawn sharply nor seemed significant. Metaphysical self-knowledge was believed to be related to an understanding of the whole universe, including nature. As Charles Taylor points out, identities in these worlds were not self-defining but defined in relation to the rest of the universe.[2] Moreover, ethics frequently pertained not merely to human action but also to natural events. There was no distinction between science and philosophy, and certainly, no clear lines were drawn between a philosophy of the natural and the human world.

This judgement might seem over-simplistic about all cosmologies. But, it is certainly true of several European cosmologies and Aristotelian sciences and it is not too off the mark to claim that elements of such cosmologies are present in virtually every 'pre-modern' cosmology, including in several world religions. Let me stick, however, to 'pre-modern' European cosmologies. For example, before the rise of

---

[2] Charles Taylor, *Hegel*, Cambridge: Cambridge University Press, 1975, p. 6.

modern science, much of what we call the western world believed that
the universe is a meaningful whole, signifying something higher than
humans or embodying some important purpose, goal, or final cause
and that everything which exists was moving towards the fulfilment of
that cause. This was the great design or pattern in the world. Moreover,
some cosmologies believed that this design was part of the intention
of a transcendent god. To find fulfilment, human beings simply had to
relate to this pattern, one that existed in society, nature, and the whole
of the universe. This pattern could be known either by revelation, by
the grace of god or by pure reason.

EXPLAINING HUMAN AND NON-HUMAN NATURE

In the early modern era, a change began to occur in the intellectual
climate of several western societies. For many of its members, nature
no longer appeared to be meaningful. It expressed neither an idea
nor perhaps the intention of some trans-human subject. Aristotelian
physics was challenged by a new perspective. The elements of nature
were no longer believed to be purposeful. Fire does not move upwards
because this is its purpose; likewise, water does not flow downwards
to serve this purpose. It is mistaken to understand nature in terms of
final causes, as if its design was pre-ordained. Rather, for the moderns,
nature was composed of discrete things, in themselves meaningless
and independent of one another. They were not related to one another
by virtue of some overall design. If related, this relation was more
accidental. A ball moves because one hits it with one's foot, not because
it is destined to fit into some larger cosmic pattern. Its movement
in a particular direction is not pre-ordained. It is due to a variety of
contingent reasons, that is, a person happened to hit it with his foot and
the ball remains hit, keeps moving till some other force stops it. How
does one find this out? Not by relying on cosmologies that talk of deeper
significance. This interpretative move, the 'moderns' felt, must first be
jettisoned. Instead, one discovers this by 'seeing' the world unmediated
by these meanings. One observes what an entity is like, how it happens
to relate to other entities. If they happen to relate regularly, then this
observed, de facto regularity is what constitutes causation. There are
no final causes at work here. Explanation is nothing but recording this
pattern of regularity. By recording regularities, one can explain not
only why something occurred in the past but also why it is likely to
occur in the future. If you go near fire and feel warm and this happens
each time you have been there, then this is also likely to happen in

future. This fact can be predicted. Thus, these new sciences are not just telling stories about nature but, so it appeared to modern thinkers, also explaining and predicting it.

Before the birth of modern empirical sciences, the only form of rational enquiry abroad was philosophy which used the a priori method of reasoning to arrive at answers to each of the six important questions concerning both the worlds taken together. In other words, a speculative, largely non-empirical mode of enquiry was expected to answer all the questions. With the birth of modern natural science, the traditional role of philosophy was transformed. For it now transpired that reason by itself can not arrive at knowledge of the natural world. It could not, by itself, answer questions concerning the nature and activity of the physical world, nor explain or predict what goes on within it. This could be done only with some partnership with the human senses. Some thought that this had to be a partnership between unequals, with reason playing a subsidiary role. Others thought that reason and senses were joint authors of our cognitive world. What the precise nature of this partnership is remained contested but the sole authority of reason had been permanently debunked. This meant that philosophy became, in the now famous words of John Locke, 'a hand maiden of science'.

Several thinkers—for example, Hobbes—tried to apply to human behaviour what was earlier applied to movements in nature. Hobbes tried to replicate the idea of a unified universe by talking of an all-embracing materialism. To him, it appeared that what held true for the physical world was also true of the socio-historical world. Later, some philosophers drew the conclusion from this Hobbesian standpoint that a rational enquiry of the moral world or the self was impossible. As in the natural world, the task of the rational enquirer was to seek the guidance of the senses, to gather data about the social world, and to try and understand its structure, to explain and predict all the manifold events that take place within it. Theory was a more generalized form of explanation, rooted in and dependent upon data-based enquiry into the particular. Direct observation yielded a knowledge of particular things. Reason saw connections between all these different things and offered generalized explanations and predictions. These generalized explanations were theories of both the natural and the social world.

UNDERSTANDING HUMANS

However, soon a second perspective emerged in which the universe began to be segmented into at least two worlds. Though some questions were relevant to each, their form became different. Other questions could be raised only in relation to one of these worlds and not to the other. Let me explain. Modern understanding allows for a much sharper distinction between at least two worlds. There is, first, the non-human natural world, the world of physical and chemical objects, the world of plants and animals. Second, the world of humans, which is already constituted by pre-reflective and reflective understanding. To admit the existence of two worlds does not imply that they are completely disconnected from one another. But, no matter how deep the relationship between the two, there also exists some fundamental differences.

THE DIFFERENCE BETWEEN THE HUMAN AND NON-HUMAN WORLDS

One such difference is this: while the natural world, in principle, exists independently of human beings, the human world is largely constituted by and is therefore dependent on human action. The force of gravity will be there whether or not we exist. So will the movement of planets. Even if the entire human species were to perish tomorrow, rainfall, thunder, a flash of lightening will still occur. Not only are these independent of our actions, they are also independent of our thoughts. There is rainfall whether or not it is apprehended by us, whether or not we have a concept of it. This is not the case with the human world which is both action-dependent and concept-dependent. Let me explain.

Consider the act of raising one's arm. This is already different from the expression, 'the upward movement of the limb'. The latter is a purely physical description, while the former is an intentional *act*, a movement guided by or possessing an intention. To raise my arm, I must already be in possession of the concept of an arm and I must know what it means to raise something. The concept of raising something is constitutive of the physical movement of the hand going upwards. Now focus on the phrase 'raising my arm'. This in turn may mean different things in different settings, that is, in different conceptual or life-worlds. In the classroom, it means that the student wishes to raise a question or offer a comment on what she has heard. In the board meeting, it may signal the act of voting on an issue. On the cricket field, it signals a bye and so on. Outside these settings, it is simply the raising of the arm. Inside these settings, it signifies voting, raising a question, or signalling a bye. In each of these settings, therefore, the relevant concept of questioning, or voting, or signalling a bye is constitutive of the purely physical upward movement of the arm and involves an enrichment of the simple idea of raising one's arm.

All human actions, practices, and situations are *constituted* by concepts or concept analogues. To understand them is to understand these concepts. This is why an *interpretative* component is crucial to what we mean by the empirical in the human sciences.[3] Understanding the human world is to grasp the complicated structure of concepts which partly constitute it. This is not true of the understanding of the natural world. So, this is the first qualitative difference between empirical social sciences and natural sciences; indeed, the word 'empirical' itself has an entirely different connotation in the human sciences. The term 'empirical' is related to experience but the nature of our experience of natural world is different from experience in the human world. The natural world cannot be apprehended without concepts but it is not constituted by them. In this sense, the natural world exists independently of the concepts we have of it. As I said, it existed even before we had any concepts of it, before we even existed on this earth. This is not true of human or social phenomena.

What is true of human sciences in general is also true of social and political studies. The state is not just an ensemble of material things and movements. To describe it purely materially is absurd. Besides, such a purely physical understanding fails to distinguish the state from other social and political institutions. The modern state is a form of public power, relatively independent of the ruler and the ruled, embodied in an apparatus that has virtual monopoly of violence in a particular community or territory, and that functions to reproduce the conditions of existence and perpetuation of that community. This is just one way of understanding the state but notice how many different types of concepts we must already have learnt in order to grasp the concept of the state: power, ruling, the distinction between ruler and ruled, monopoly, violence, community, conditions of existence, and so on. Is this too complicated? Take then a relatively simple example: a man called John F. Kennedy has just died. Physically speaking, a living body has turned into non-living matter. But, we humans describe this event as death. The person in question was no ordinary man, however. He

---

[3] For a detailed discussion of the difference between the natural and the human sciences, see Charles Taylor, *Philosophical Papers*, Vol. 1, Cambridge: Cambridge University Press, 1985, chapters 1–4, 9, and Charles Taylor, *Philosophical Papers*, Vol. 2, Cambridge: Cambridge University Press, 1985, chapters 1–3.

was the President of the USA. To understand this fact about Kennedy is to already grasp a complex institutional setting. Moreover, we must ask: is it true that President John F. Kennedy simply died? Yes, and No. To say that he has died does not convey that he has been killed. Indeed, to say that he is killed still does not capture what has happened. For one can be killed in an accident. Would it then be right to say that he was murdered? This too is true but only up to a point. For, Kennedy was a President of the USA and his murder had a political motive. He was murdered probably by a network of rival political groups, state agencies, and the mafia. His was a political assassination. When a person says that Kennedy was assassinated, we assume that he understands the distinction between dying, being killed, murdered, or assassinated. Each of these concepts and the distinctions among them are part of and implicit in the event of Kennedy losing his life.

Thus, we arrive at the following conclusions:

1. Questions concerning explanation and prediction about the non-human natural world are answered by the natural sciences.
2. Given the difference between human and non-human nature, questions pertaining to the understanding, explanation, and prediction about the human world are answered by the human sciences (by political science, sociology, anthropology, economics, etc.), though always aided by humanities and the arts.

What then is the proper role of social and political theory? Why we do need it? Let me straightaway elucidate two functions of political theory which it shares with social theory. Indeed, the first is not a separate function but an integral feature of all social science, including political science. If all human phenomena are constituted by pre-reflective or conceptual understanding and if philosophy/theory helps us grasp this understanding and make it explicit, then given the first feature mentioned earlier of political philosophy or political theory, the latter is an integral part of empirical social science. You can neither identify what you wish to explain nor what you are to explain it by unless you have a conceptual grasp of what these are. Philosophy or at least one of its central components is not merely a handmaiden of the human sciences but one of its integral features. This is the interpretative and explanatory role of political theory.

The second function of political theory is this. Some social and political phenomena have such a large scale that no specific empirical enquiry can do justice to it. Nor can it result from a collection of all the empirical detail. Data gathering and controlled enquiry can never suffice for the understanding of large social formations and for the explanation of changes within them or changes from one type to another. So, the explanation of the rise of capitalism or the transition from feudalism to capitalism can never be understood or explained without some degree of speculation which is independent of empirical enquiry. Nor can we fully understand the nature of modernity, or the variety of human predicaments in the modern world, or the general attributes of subordination in a society that is colonized by another society merely by controlled empirical enquiry. This job is best done by social and political theory. The object of this enquiry is itself identified at a very general level and its fuller understanding or explanation cannot be properly controlled by empirical data but requires a speculative jump. Political theories must perform this second function of providing insight and understanding into the most general pattern of human practices and social change. Bhikhu Parekh calls this the contemplative role of political theory.[4]

To grasp the third function of political theory, it is important to register the second qualitative difference between the natural and the social world and therefore, between the natural and the human sciences. It makes no sense to ask moral and self-related questions about the physical world. It is no longer sensible to ask: how do we morally evaluate the force of gravity? Is there anything good or right about the laws of motion? Do chemical compounds have self-knowledge? However, such ethical and normative questions are at the heart of the human world.

Why is this so? Consider, once again, our claim concerning the action dependence of the human world. Also, consider any human action. It is true that human action can be explained and to explain it is to provide the reason for why it was done. In this respect, explaining an action is not different from explaining any natural event. But, in the case of human action we could ask another question: is the reason for action a *good* one? Now to say that it is a good reason, is to endorse the action, to justify it. An action is not merely explained, it is also justified, and as I said, this justification is always accomplished in the light of some idea of good and bad, right and wrong.

This idea of justification can be elucidated in another way. Take the example from cricket again. When a batsman faces a ball bowled outside his off stump, he also faces a number of distinct possibilities. He

---

[4] Bhikhu Parekh, 'Political Theory: Traditions in Political Philosophy', in Robert Goodin and Hans-Dieter Klingeman (eds), *A New Handbook of Political Science*, Oxford: Oxford University Press, 1996, p. 509.

can leave the ball alone or flash at it. If he decides to hit the ball, he must make a quick decision whether to drive, slice, or cut it, to hit the ball towards long off, to cover drive, or square cut. If he is audacious, he can even pull it towards midwicket. This judgement must be made on the spot, within a split second. Now suppose, the ball is a perfect outswinger, the batsman flashes at it, gets an edge, and is caught behind. He must ask himself if he had good reason to go after the ball, whether or not he made a correct judgement. Could he justify what he did to himself, to his captain, his team, the team's coach? Indeed, he is answerable to a much wider public. He is answerable because he could have acted otherwise. There is a reason why he got out. But it is not a *good* reason. His rash act can be explained but it cannot be justified.

Now, I want to draw a general conclusion from this example. To say that the human world is action dependent is to say that it is grounded in one set of reasons from among several available, and that the choice to act on one rather than another is made in the light of the person's own understanding and judgement of what is good or right for the agent in the context. This understanding can be evaluated by others. We can ask if the person's judgement of what is good is really so. Moreover, what is true of human action is also true of the state of affairs it brings about. Anything which is a result of human action is out there from among many possibilities and part of the reason why it is there is because the agent or agents in question undertook it in the light of their own understanding of what is good or right. Though any action is not always determined by the good or the right, it is undertaken against a background of qualitative distinction between good and bad, right and wrong. Human action and the world it creates must necessarily be evaluated because a normative component is an integral part of it.

The example I took involves an evaluative but not an ethical dimension. But, cricket does possess an ethical aspect too. Consider, once again, a bowler who has been hit for three consecutive fours. This assault is not merely on his bowling but, on his own reckoning, also on his sense of self-esteem and dignity. As he goes towards his bowling mark, he is angry and resentful. Indeed, he is so angry that he cannot contain himself. It occurs to him that to avenge the treatment meted out to him, he should bowl a beamer. Should he, really? He has a second to decide whether to do so or not. Should he use unfair means to remove the batsman from the crease? This is not all. A bookie has offered that if he is hit for four consecutive fours, he would earn twice the match fee paid to him by the board. Should he succumb to this temptation? He must assess these reasons in the light of some conception of the good life, some idea of right or wrong. A cricketer has this choice. So do all other human beings in their respective contexts. In short, a human being has some degree of ethical or moral autonomy.

Similar ethical considerations also arise in politics. Consider that the state is withdrawing from the public sector, say, public educational institutions. The policy of reservations is predicated upon the availability of seats or jobs in the public sector. If admission or employment opportunities get limited in this way, the policy of reservations becomes practically toothless. What should now be done for those such as dalits who have been historically disadvantaged? At least two options are available. One is to pretend helplessness and to become indifferent to the plight of the 'scheduled castes'. The other is to compel the private sector to have, for example, a proportion of seats or jobs reserved for them. Whatever policy the state adopts will be guided by some reason. The question is whether the reason guiding the policy is a good one. And, whether it is really good or not must take into account the policy makers' understanding of what is good or bad, right or wrong, and the assessment of this understanding by others. It will depend upon whether these considerations are given any weight at all, which itself is a matter of ethics. To fail to assess one's reason in the light of any ethics is itself unethical, if ethics has a bearing on these issues.

I hope to have shown that value judgements and 'should-questions' are critical in human affairs and particularly, in politics. Answers to questions such as 'who obeys whom?' or 'why do men obey?' can be provided by political scientists, empirical psychology, or sociology but none of these can answer the question, 'why should one obey the other?' While facts are not entirely irrelevant, they cannot on their own provide answers to these questions. Two conclusions follow from this. First, since facts alone cannot answer value-related and should-questions and since both are inescapable in the life of humans, value-based and normative enquiries can never be turned into empirical sciences. Second, since values and normativity constitute an irreducible dimension of the political, value-oriented, or normative political theory will continue to be a significant form of enquiry, one that is irreducible to social sciences and empirical theories.

DECLINE OF POLITICAL THEORY

This view that all human actions, including all political actions and public policies, can be evaluated in the light of ethical considerations was not accepted by some early modernists (Machiavelli, Hobbes) and resistance to it resurfaced among scientific-minded high modernists in the nineteenth and the twentieth centuries. A number of persons believe that a rational evaluation or enquiry of the moral world is impossible. The moral and political philosophy of yesteryears expressed merely the opinions, tastes, and preferences of the individual enquirer and did not deserve the status of knowledge. Our experience yields a wide variety of forms of self-understandings and moral opinions which cannot be rationally evaluated. If they come into conflict, reason cannot arbitrate between them.

Perhaps for this reason, several philosophers in the Anglo-Saxon world began to claim that political theory was in an irretrievable decline. If political theory is a rational and normative enterprise, as indeed classical political philosophy from Plato to Hegel had sought to be, then, after the 'new discovery' about the impossibility of such an enterprise and the rise of the empirical sciences, political theory was believed to have no future. Indeed, as someone put it, it was already 'dead'.

This view, associated with Positivism, is now widely believed to be deeply mistaken. Everything seen, heard, or touched by human beings is already constituted by concepts and therefore, everything in the human world has to be properly understood even as it is observed. Moreover, most of these concepts carry a normative import. The human world has to be, to some degree and extent, good or bad and human action, right or wrong. Really, there is no feature of the human world entirely free from evaluative significance.

Of course, from this, we could draw two different conclusions. If values are impervious to reason but constitute the human world, then all we can have is subjective opinion of this world. This means the impossibility of social sciences. This is a radical conclusion that the positivists did not reach because they rejected the first premise, namely, that facts and values are intertwined. Alternatively, we must abandon the assumption that values are beyond reason, and that therefore, it is possible to have objective knowledge of the human world. If values can be known and rationally assessed, then their permeation in the human world is no barrier to its understanding or rational assessment. This not only brings out the difference between the character and method of the natural and social sciences but also paves the way for a kind of systematic reflection that is exclusive to the human world, namely, normative, moral, or ethical theorizing.

So, in addition to two functions of political theory mentioned earlier, we have a third function, one that is special because it is exclusive to human phenomena: to bring out the normative import of concepts embedded in social practices and used in social sciences and to subject them to detailed critical reasoning. Indeed, for some people this has become the defining, perhaps even the sole function of political theory. Much of Anglo-Saxon political theory focuses only on the normative at fairly high level of generality. In contrast, political theory on the continent has frequently refused to separate the normative from the explanatory/interpretative and the contemplative.

Political theory on the continent has a broader scope for another reason which needs explication and brings into relief the fourth function of political theory, to tell us who we are. Recall the point made earlier that in a hierarchical society, people perform actions in accordance with their social role; what in contemporary parlance we might call their identity. A person stands bowed with folded hands or walks at a safe distance from others, given that he is from a lower caste and the other has a much higher rank in the caste hierarchy. What he does now depends on what goes on in society and who he is. More generally, almost everywhere, what one should do and who one is are related issues. When we ask the question, 'what are we to do?', there is another question that we do not always ask. The implicit form of the question is: given that this is what we are, what are we to do? Classical political philosophers almost always asked these questions together: given the essence or purpose of human beings, what should they do? In contemporary theory, these questions are separated. Thus, political philosophy remains both a practical philosophy, that is, one that has an action-guiding character and a systematic enquiry into the self, a kind of metaphysical self-knowledge.[5]

At the cost of repetition, let me once again answer the question: what is the function of political theory? Given that empirical political science is meant primarily to understand, describe, and explain how and by whom decisions are taken in a society and how some individuals groups or classes are excluded from such decision making, one task

[5] See, Alisdair MacIntyre, 'The Indispensability of Political Theory', in David Miller and Larry Siedentop (eds), *The Nature of Political Theory*, Oxford: Clarendon Press, 1983, pp. 17–34; John Plamenatz, 'The Uses of Political Theory', in A. Quinton (ed.), *Political Philosophy*, London: Oxford University Press, 1967. Also, see Charles Taylor, *Sources of the Self*, Cambridge: Cambridge University Press, 1989.

of political theory is to help empirical political science to perform this role. However, it performs three roles not undertaken by the social sciences. First, to offer a general reflection on 'the human condition', on the predicament of modern societies, on who we are, and so on. Second, a general reflection on a relatively narrow topic: the exercise of power in societies and the mechanisms by which power, that is, domination is exercised by some over others. This includes the most general reflection on state power but if power resides in the capillaries of a society, then political theory is a reflection not only on the state but on the myriad capillaries in society. Third, it is the study of how this power should be wielded, by whom and why, and in the light of which values and ideas of the good life. This is a prescriptive, normative, and broadly ethical enterprise. These three constitute the distinctive functions of political theory.

We can put the point differently by once again examining the six big questions. If the first three are answered primarily by the natural and the human sciences, the next three questions—of ethics, normativity, and of metaphysical self-knowledge—are answered by normative and contemplative political theory along with philosophy, humanities, and the arts.

TYPES OF POLITICAL THEORIES
Allow me to elaborate in somewhat greater detail these three different types of political theory.[6]

Explanatory
Suppose that we wish to understand the birth of capitalist socio-economic formations. In the social sciences, we have several different explanations. For example, Marx offered a general theory of fundamental social change.[7] On one version of this theory, humans have a fundamental interest in improving their material well-being and

---

[6] I do not have the space or the time to delve in detail into features that differentiate these forms of political theory. To take just one example, contemplative and empirical theory cannot have the same standards of validation. Contemplative theories do not aspire to be true or accurate but to illuminate reality, to help imagine new possibilities, or focus on something extremely significant but unnoticed.

[7] This account follows the masterly rendering of Marx's 'Historical Materialism' by G.A. Cohen in his *Karl Marx's Theory of History*, Oxford: Clarendon Press, 1978.

therefore, in raising their level of productivity. Thus, Marx believed that this interest explains why there is a constant improvement in the level of productive forces. However, he also believed that a thing became a productive force only in use and the use of productive forces presupposes that human beings relate to each other in particular ways. Marx calls these social relations of production. Marx proposed the thesis that a certain type of social relations of production is appropriate, roughly speaking, to a particular level of development of productive forces. For him, a particular type of social relations of production facilitates the development of productive forces. However, beyond a point, these very relations begin to hinder the further development of these forces. The level of productivity begins to fall, production forces gets into crises and yet, the human urge for better material well-being does not cease. In short, a contradiction develops between the ever-developing productive forces and the existing but outdated relations of production. This contradiction, Marx thought, is resolved not by preserving the level of the development of productive forces but rather by changing the social relations of production. The new set of social relations of production comes into existence in order to facilitate the further development of productive forces.

Marx developed this general theory to explain the rise of capitalism which he defined largely by the relation between capital and labour mediated by a free market. Such relations had to come into existence in order to increase human productivity at the time of the emergence of capitalism. Other thinkers offered different explanations. For example, Weber argued that capitalism could not have come into existence without a change in the cultural climate, in the altitudes of a specific set of people. This change of attitude was a component of and brought about by a transformation in the dominant religion of particular societies. For Weber, Protestant ethic that emphasized a certain degree of this-worldly asceticism and disciplined work facilitated both accumulation of capital and an efficient labour force, both of which were crucial for the emergence of capitalism.[8]

Normative

Suppose that in a poverty-stricken country such as India, there is a demand that the right to work and, therefore, the right to an adequate

---

[8] Max Weber, *The Protestant Ethic and the Spirit of Capitalism*, London: George Allen & Unwin, 1930.

minimum income be entrenched not just as a desirable goal but as a legal guarantee. Suppose also that there is a great deal of resistance to this idea. For example, it might be argued that while social justice is important, it should not take precedence over the decisions of elected representatives and that therefore the government of the day, backed by the parliament, may from time to time decide to have welfare schemes for the poor, and no welfare measure should be guaranteed by law. Thus, we have two broad positions on this issue, one for the right to work and the other against it. How do we break the deadlock? How do we advance further to resolve this dispute? We can settle the dispute in a number of ways. One, by a simple recourse to power. A position that is backed by greater power may override the other, irrespective of its moral strength. A pro-poor government may enact a law that entrenches the right to work as a judiciable right. Alternatively, a coalition of wealthy classes may buy up the fence sitters and block the constitutional entrenchment of this right. Both sides may arouse passion and let the matter be decided in the heat of the moment. In all such cases, a decision is made in favour of one or the other position without examining the merits of the case, without a detailed review of possible justifications in favour of either of the two positions. Normative political theory does not accept this way of proceeding on this issue. While it does not disregard the importance of emotion, rhetoric, negotiation, and even power, it begins with the assumption that rational argument, in whatever form, must play a pivotal role in decisions on such matters.

So, how would a normative political theorist proceed? A brief account may be as follows. The normative political theorist must begin with assumptions that most people can endorse. For example, few would deny that all citizens have a basic interest in living a minimally decent life. Nor would anyone deny that absence of physical suffering is part of a minimally decent existence. Thus, a modicum of material well-being is important for everyone, regardless of caste, religion, gender, inherited wealth, and so on. We all have an equal moral right to a minimally decent existence. Once these assumptions are accepted, we are left with the more contentious issues. Does minimal well-being include simply the absence of physical suffering that can be remedied by welfare schemes or does it include the guarantee of work? Here, we have to bring in two further issues. First, whether or not the democratically elected government of the day can be relied upon for initiating these schemes? Second, whether apart from the avoidance of physical sufferance, dignity is also an important component of well-being? What psychological impact does merely receiving benefits have on the poor? Is it not important that even the poor feel that they are not living on charity but have earned what they receive? Once dignity is included in the concept of well-being, which, if we think of humans not just as biological organisms but as persons, we must, we are committed to the view that, at least in modern societies, work is crucial for well-being. Therefore, a right to well-being, a right to be free from suffering must include the right to work.

To go to the second issue now: can we rely on democratically elected governments of the day to guarantee well-being? This is to be decided partly by the political history of societies and our understanding of the behaviour of people with wealth and power. My own answer is that the government of the day cannot be relied upon for such guarantees. This may be true even for governments with the best of intentions. Indeed, this assurance is even less likely in democratic societies where governments may change every four to five years, and people have to live with a government that might initiate policies that go against their interests. Democratic governments cannot be trusted with the promises they make, no matter how sincere they are. If so, such guarantees must be made an integral part of the constitution so that every democratically elected government is constrained to ensure the fulfilment of the right to work. An argument such as this neither undervalues democracy nor presents itself as the final word on the matter. It merely shows that this is one way in which we might proceed in democratic societies. In the last instance, it is meant to show how normative political theory may be done.

Consider another illustration of normative theory. Philosophers have long debated over what is meant by equality. But the crucial question is: equality of what? With respect to what should humans seek equality? In contemporary political philosophy, there have been three dominant answers. The first claims that egalitarians should focus on welfare. But this is rejected by philosophers such as John Rawls. Welfare egalitarianism suffers from a major defect because by focusing on mental reactions and states, it takes an extremely narrow view of what people get from goods.[9] Welfare is unsuitable as a measure for

---

[9] On this issue, see the illuminating discussion in G.A. Cohen, 'Equality of What? On Welfare, Goods, and Capabilities', in Martha C. Nussbaum and Amartya Sen (eds), *The Quality of Life*, New Delhi: Oxford University Press, 1993, pp. 9–29.

egalitarian evaluation because people adapt their mental attitudes and preferences to their own adverse conditions. It is morally troubling to find egalitarians endorsing a condition in which the rich and the poor are seen to be equals just because the rich derive little utility from their large resources and the poor derive the same amount (of utility) from the meager resources they possess. So, really we should be focusing not on welfare but on resources or on what Rawls calls primary goods. However, Amartya Sen provides a third alternative. For him, resources or goods are means and it is fetishistic to focus on means rather than what individuals do with them. For example, income and wealth are not desirable for their own sake but because of the substantive freedoms they may help to achieve. They are admirable general purpose means for having more freedom to lead the kind of lives we have reason to value.[10] Besides, differently made and situated individuals are bound to require different amounts of primary goods to satisfy the same needs. Why then try to bring about equality of means? Equality of primary goods would invariably lead then to a partially blind morality because it would not take into account the very real and ineradicable differences between individuals. 'What people get out of goods depends upon a variety of factors, and judging personal advantage just by the size of personal ownership of goods and services can be very misleading...It seems reasonable to move away from a focus on good as such to what goods do to human beings.'[11]

These objections suggest two alternatives to equality of resources. The first, welfare, already mentioned earlier, is rejected by Sen. Though free from fetishism, the welfarist perspective has a very narrow view of what people want from their lives. Egalitarians should be looking to equalizing not welfare or primary goods but basic capabilities and functionings. What does Sen mean by terms such as 'capability' and 'functioning', and how are these related to freedom? Recall that it is not the having of goods, nor the states of mind induced by goods that are crucial for Sen but what goods do to us and what we to with them. Goods are meaningless if they do not have an impact on us, if they do not constitute certain states in us. They can also be useless if we can do nothing with them. Thus, unless we are endowed with certain

---

[10] Amartya Sen, *Development as Freedom*, New York: Anchor Books, 1999.

[11] Amartya Sen, *Choice, Welfare and Measurement*, Oxford: Oxford University Press, 1982, pp. 29–30 (Introduction). Also, see his *Inequality Reexamined*, Cambridge: Harvard University Press, 1992.

capacities with which we can extract or receive certain valuable things from those goods, there is little point in having them.[12] A 'capability' is the capacity, power, or skill to do or to be something (examples: the capacity to be nourished, to feel pleasure and pain, to walk, to talk, to reason, to relate to others, to relate to oneself, to play the sitar, to enjoy the vastness and beauty of nature, etc.). A 'functioning' is what is achieved by virtue of a capability, the various things a person manages to do or be in leading a life (examples: the state of being nourished, housed, clothed, having companionship, being well read and well informed, participating in public life, etc.). Normative political theory is a continuing conversation or argument over what precisely we value in our social and political lives and why, how to understand the internal structure of our values, what the rival interpretations of these values are, which of these is better and why, and finally, what social and political institutions should be designed to realize these values.

In some of my work, I have explored the conceptual and normative structure of one political institution, that is, the secular state.[13] I have claimed that a secular state is one that separates religion from itself for the sake of some ends. I have also claimed that different ways of unpacking the metaphor of separation and variegated understandings of the purposes underlying separation yields different conceptions of secular state. I have argued that some states separate themselves from religion for amoral ends such as imperial expansion and others, for moral or ethical ends such as the enhancement of freedom, equality, and justice. Thus, there are amoral and moral/ethical secular states. Among the latter, there is considerable dispute over how to understand separation and what values ought to be served by it. Thus, there are different forms of moral/ethical secular states. I have also argued that one can reason about these rival conceptions and conclude which of these is best for which context and which among them is likely to have trans-contextual potential.

Contemplative

When I think of the contemplative tradition, I instinctively think of the Mahabharata as one of the greatest reflections on multiple human predicaments. But I shall not speak on it. Instead, I mention three other examples. In her famous book, *The Human Condition*, Hannah Arendt

[12] Ibid.
[13] See Chapter 3 of this volume.

begins by drawing our attention towards how in 1957, a satellite, an earth-born, man-made object stayed in skies, circled the earth, and 'dwelt and moved in the proximity of the heavenly bodies as though it had been admitted tentatively to their sublime company'.[14] She spoke of how, for many, this was the first 'step toward escape from men's imprisonment to the earth'. She also spoke of other new developments: the splitting of the atom as well as of the birth of a new language of mathematical symbols which was impossible to translate back into speech. With these introductory remarks, she proposed that in her new book she would offer a 'reconsideration of the human condition from the vantage point of our newest experiences and our most recent fears.'[15] For Arendt, political theory was not reducible to its explanatory or normative functions, although clearly these functions are part of its defining features. Political theory for her, as indeed for many others, continues to be what it was for classical thinkers: a deeply contemplative enquiry into the general condition of humankind either over a very long period or at a certain stage of their changing existence.

Gandhi's *Hind Swaraj* provides another example. It was perhaps the first major text to have emerged from the colonies that seriously challenged the cultural and civilizational premises of the colonizer.[16] It is a deeply normative text because it emanates from a profoundly felt experience of colonial injustice in all its multifarious forms—cultural, social, psychological, economic, and political. It embodies the first stirrings of Gandhi's struggle for justice, a moral concern that remained with him until his death. Moreover, this perfectly cut gem is profoundly contemplative. It dwells on the deeper malaise of modern civilization. By marginalizing religion and detaching morality from practice, modern West, for Gandhi, had turned into a disease. Its focus on bodily concerns (productivity) had drawn it into a vortex of ambition and avarice. By its obsessive concern with getting more than one's own legitimate share—what the Greeks called 'pleonexia'—manifest in its arrogant conquest of other societies, the West had already shown its ugly, profoundly uncivilized face to Gandhi. Though his view on modernity is somewhat reductive, there is little doubt that he had correctly grasped perhaps its most significant and dominant dimension. For this hideous

[14] Hannah Arendt, *The Human Condition*, Chicago: University of Chicago Press, 1958, p. 1.

[15] Ibid., p. 5.

[16] M.K. Gandhi, *Hind Swaraj*, Cambridge: Cambridge University Press, 1997.

and repulsive aspect of modernity has been revealed again and again throughout the twentieth century and is amply exhibited now, even to its most ardent admirers, by the gratuitously evil deeds of Dick Cheney and George Bush.

Here is my third example. In his recent work, *A Secular Age*, Charles Taylor begins by asking: 'what does it mean to say that we [he means those who live in the North Atlantic west] live in a secular age?'[17] By secular age, Taylor does not just mean the age of secularized polities (political secularity). He digs deeper. In most contemporary western societies, not only can you engage in politics without fully encountering god but a host of social practices have been emptied of god—a state very different from one in which there was virtually nothing anyone could do without encountering faith or religion. But, Taylor is not satisfied by merely asking: what is it to live in a world where most social practices have been evacuated of god and religion? (the secularization thesis). He digs deeper still to take us to another meaning of secularity. This is a condition in which 'faith, even for the staunchest believer, is one human possibility among others', something vastly different from a context where 'it was virtually impossible not to believe in God'.[18] And so, he asks not only what it means to live in such a world but how western societies moved from a condition where belief in god was the only option to one where it is one among many. In the best tradition of contemplative theory, he devotes some eight hundred pages to these two questions. For Taylor, exploring and specifying these background conditions and presuppositions is crucial to the understanding of western secularization and political secularity.

LITTLE THEORIES, GRAND THEORIES

I have claimed that there are three types of political theories: explanatory/interpretative, normative, and contemplative. But I do not wish to suggest that they are mutually exclusive. Perhaps it is better to see them as three dimensions of any political theory. All theories invariably contain each of these. But, most of them implicitly emphasize one or the other, that is, either the explanatory (example, Weber's theory on the rise of capitalism or Marx's historical materialism), or the normative (example, liberalism), or the contemplative (example,

---

[17] Charles Taylor, *A Secular Age*, Cambridge: Harvard University Press, 2007, pp. 1–3.

[18] Ibid., p. 3.

Hannah Arendt's *The Human Condition*). These might be called 'Little' theories. On the other hand, some explicitly possess all three. Let these as well as deeply contemplative theories be called 'Grand' theories (example, there are traditions of Marxism that claim to have each of the three features). Grand theories need to be distinguished from ideologies, world views, and cosmologies that possess *one* of the six features mentioned earlier, namely, generality. In addition, they may possess one or two other features, but rarely all. For example, they may attempt conceptual clarity or possess a rational structure but simply ignore the requirement to unearth hidden presuppositions. Besides, unlike theory, their commitment to even these is half-hearted. They may start off with conceptual elaboration or the construction of an argument but stop midway—arbitrarily and abruptly. Almost always, they bypass controlled enquiry into the particular and therefore, are largely speculative.

Theory and Ideology

The relationship of normative political theory and, by implication, of Grand theories to modern ideology is particularly complex. Both try to persuade—in a crude sense—if we believe that we are roughly equal, we all try to convert one another to our own viewpoint. But there are important differences. While political theory tries to give the fullest possible reason for why a certain standpoint must be adopted, or why an act must be performed on the basis of one set of principles rather than another, ideology lacks a commitment to spell out all reasons. Reason is short-circuited and principles frequently reduced to formulae. This is true not only of nationalism and fascism but also of liberalism and Marxism when they function as ideologies.

The case of liberal and Marxist ideologies shows that an ideology need not be entirely disconnected from reason. It may have a strategic connection. But, it is in the nature of strategic connection that it is snapped if it no longer serves a specified end. As explained earlier, theory has an intrinsic commitment to reason, truth, and objectivity that an ideology does not. When liberalism and Marxism function as ideologies, they have merely a strategic connection with reason. This is not so when they function as political theories. It is possible then for Marxist or liberal political theory to come into conflict with Marxist or liberal ideology.

If all that I have just said is true, then political philosophy is even more different from another mode of persuasion and conversion, that is, propaganda. For, in propaganda, conversion is sought by opaque, manipulative methods. Advertising is a good example because here anything goes. Not only is transparency abandoned and reason short-circuited but everything hinges on pure rhetoric. Lies are permitted, so are half-truths. The bad points of a product are never mentioned and the good ones are exaggerated.

Before I end this section, one misunderstanding must be dispelled. Grand theories do share with ideologies and cosmologies another feature—they all perform one function—all of them attempt to formulate a common understanding of the world as well as provide a common normative orientation. When they do both, they provide a common self-definition, an identity. In the performance of this function, Grand theories, ideologies, and cosmologies may, on the one hand, compete with, rival, and substitute one another and on the other hand, be mutually complementary. Thus, I am not suggesting that ideologies should be replaced by political theory. This can never happen. Ideologies have a crucial function in modern societies. Unlike theories, they directly inform practice. They provide us with practical self-understanding and a map with which to guide practical political action. Though they may misconstrue agents and practices, they also embody a great deal of practical knowledge. Thus, they must not be seen as non-scientific, false consciousness. The rigid distinction between science and ideology is the hallmark of scientistic, positivist thinking that wrongly or simplistically applies models appropriate to the natural sciences to human phenomenon.

Indeed, one might say that theory and ideology are linked to different motivations. For theory, it is important to get things right. For ideology, the most important value is to enable practice. Very often, theories are retrospective achievements. For good or bad, ideologies are part of the action. They get woven into practices. When conditions of theory formation are absent, ideologies are all that we have.

Finally, I must not be viewed as saying that we must always be rational and that there should be no place in the public sphere for emotion, rhetoric, or even condensed statements or formulae. I fully acknowledge that there is a rhetorical and emotional ingredient in all theory. However, it is one thing to admit this and quite another to gratuitously use rhetoric as the only means of asserting and communicating one's interests and claims. In short, my view is that none of these should have such an overwhelming place in society that political theory is seen or made to be entirely redundant.

POLITICAL THEORY AND MODERN SOCIETIES

I have proposed that there is something distinctive about political theory and implied that something socially valuable is lost without it. In other words, I have suggested that we all need political theory. This might seem an odd claim. After all, many societies have lived without political philosophy or theory. At least political philosophy has not existed as a separate entity in most societies. At best, we might say with hindsight that it lies hidden within cosmologies. My claim would be more defensible if it was made in favour of cosmologies for it is hard to imagine any society that is not accompanied by a cosmology.

One might then ask: why cannot cosmologies suffice for the functions I have claimed for social and political theory? This brings us to the question of the difference between cosmologies and theories. And to why, in modern societies, cosmologies probably do not suffice, I have three reasons to offer in support of theories. First, cosmologies are local and too tightly tied to contexts. Under modern conditions, however, we live in several contexts at once. Moreover, these contexts are not insulated from one another. They interact, intersect, and inter-communicate. In these circumstances, anything with a purely local significance will not do. We need inter-contextual thinking. We need something which does not merely pretend to be sufficiently general but is really so. Since theories possess this inter-contextual generality, they are better likely to serve us in these conditions. Besides, we live in times and in places where people with remarkably different cultural backgrounds and cosmologies have been thrown together. This has happened not merely with globalization but much earlier with the formation of nation-states. Despite their claims of cultural homogeneity, nation-states have had to deal with diverse local traditions and deep cultural heterogeneity. Nation-states bring together strangers. Recall my point that cosmologies are required to refamiliarize what was once familiar and is currently not. Now, this condition of almost permanent unfamiliarity with everything around us, including other human beings with whom we interact, is pervasive in modern societies where frequently, the very distinction between insiders and outsiders collapses.

Second, the situation in our times is one of a near permanent crisis of mutual understanding and common agreement. Nation-states are built around a rough consensus on some issues, a mixture of indifference and forgetting on the part of its members, a fair amount of illegitimate force, and huge areas of difference and disagreement. Such large societies can hardly be stable. But, they are unlikely to survive without a good deal of open communication among its diverse people. Conceptual clarity enables better communication. Through argument, differences which are the norm in our societies can be managed if not resolved. We need to give reasons to one another for and against why some policy is to be initiated.[19] We need to be more critically self-aware of why we are doing what we do. Although I do not wish to make exaggerated claims on behalf of reason, I believe the loose rational structure embedded in theories offers some hope towards a possible resolution of some of the most chronic misunderstandings and deep-rooted conflicts that plague us and reasonable disagreement over profound differences amongst humans.

Third, modern societies no longer have one locus of authority. In the past, community-based cosmologies frequently gave answers in a manner that gave the impression that they were emanating from a single authoritative source. Some theories which imitate these cosmologies give the same impression. But the truth is that such a source does not exist anymore. We have multiple sources of authority and to communicate amongst them, we need a space where reasons are offered, examined, questioned, challenged, endorsed, rebutted, or mediated. A theory provides such a space which local cosmologies may be unable to provide. Apart from these, there is a wholly separate reason: questions answered by normative political theory need to be even more urgently addressed. There are no easy answers to the questions: how are we to live?; What am I?; and What are we to do? These questions have acquired urgency because old certainties are gone, everything is up for grabs and therefore, everything needs to be justified. Nothing today can be taken for granted. Secularism, democracy, and equality cannot simply be assumed. Their ethical importance will always be questioned. Their value has to be justified not only to those who oppose but also to those who defend them. Besides, these concepts do not come in one unique form. Therefore, we have to justify which conception of secularism, or democracy, or equality is worth having in our context. Normative political theory is meant to do just that.

[19] Indeed, Isaiah Berlin frequently implies that the presence of profound differences or what he calls 'pluralism' is one of the conditions of political philosophy. He says, 'unless political philosophy is confined to the analysis of concepts or expressions, it can be pursued consistently only in a pluralist, or potentially pluralist society.' See Berlin, *Concepts and Categories*, 1978, p. 150.

To sum up, both the task of general understanding and prescribing are crucial in modern societies. A theory of both how power is really exercised and how it *should* be used is crucial for two reasons. First, because modernity disperses communities and yet, connects societies in such an intensified manner that understanding and explanations of specific groups and societies will never yield a relevant, comprehensive understanding of any issue. Disparate but related phenomena must be brought together under a general rubric to give us a satisfactory knowledge of them. Second, a host of situations exist in which traditional knowledge systems and older cosmologies are unable to tell us what we—people with diverse backgrounds and interests—need to do in common and in the light of which values. Modern political theory appears to have the potential to do so, as long as it performs this task with modesty and with the help of social science, humanities, and the arts.

HISTORY OF POLITICAL THOUGHT AND POLITICAL THEORY

I need to address one final issue before bringing this discussion to a close. I have written of political theory as if its history is irrelevant. If I have given that impression, it is because of paucity of time and space. Let me address it very briefly.[20] Consider a social practice. Suppose that it is being challenged by a group but you are not among those who oppose it. You wish to defend the practice and therefore ask the legitimate question: what is the good embedded in the practice. In fact, you may be more neutral and may wish to examine and evaluate the practice so that it may be critiqued or endorsed. But before you begin to do so, you must identify it. You need to articulate both what it is and the underlying point behind it. This, however, is not as easy as it seems. Sometimes that with which you are excessively familiar, that which appears to you to be obviously valuable is among the least understood. It is not properly understood because it has receded into the background, almost merged with it. It is so much taken for granted that one does not even notice that it exists. After all, this is precisely what is meant by taking something for granted. This excessive

---

[20] For a detailed discussion of these discussions, see Charles Taylor, 'Philosophy and Its History', in Richard Rorty, J.B. Schneewind, and Quentin Skinner (eds), *Philosophy in History*, Cambridge: Cambridge University Press, 1984, pp. 17–30.

familiarity has then become an obstruction to its proper understanding and to an understanding of its underlying values. If we are to better understand it, a change of stance towards it becomes mandatory. To begin to notice it, we need to make it unfamiliar, to defamiliarize it. Some strategy of radical estrangement is required to counter an already existing familiarity. We need to introduce a part-existential and part-reflective disquiet about the practice. Only then will we begin to better recognize it. Among the strategies of estrangement and refamiliarization is to place the practice along with other similar yet related practices. Locating a practice among others may be accomplished either by the use of one's imagination or by cross-cultural comparison. When this is done, one gains the awareness that it is one among several practices, one of the several ways in which the objective or value underlying the practice is accomplished. One realizes that what had appeared natural, what one had taken for granted is one of the many possible ways of doing roughly the same thing and that it is not a natural, permanent phenomenon but a social construction carved out of one set of choices.

Now this defamiliarization can be accomplished not just by travelling in space, that is, by moving from one cultural location to another existing at the same time but also by moving back in time. In short, by asking the question: what were the analogues of this practice in the past that achieved, if not the same, other similar values, values that belong roughly to the same family. Or else, we can go back not to the very distant past where we would find entirely different practices for comparison but to that moment of transition when this very practice began to first take shape, when it was born. Indeed, to go back to its moment of origin is useful for another reason. It is useful because when the practice was born, there may have been something startlingly new about it. Therefore, it must have been noticed by everyone. This is precisely the time when it was least taken for granted, when those in favour of it were keen to offer a fully explicit defence on its behalf and those opposed to it were equally keen to rebut it. At that period, and in that context, it is likely that a very rich set of arguments surrounded the practice, one that by now are forgotten. By going back in time, we retrieve those arguments that, one must remember, are once again desperately needed, now that it has become contentious. Rather than put all our labour into a de novo articulation of the conceptual and normative structure of the practice, understanding the history of the practice is a more economical way of achieving the same result. We rearticulate what is currently in a hopeless condition of inarticulacy.

This remembering is also a process of recovery of the richness of that practice. This is why a proper political argument about rights must take us back to the writings of, say, John Locke; a proper understanding of nationalism must compel us to return to Herder; and why to property debate about western modernity and colonialism, we cannot set aside Gandhi's *Hind Swaraj*. For a full disclosure of all the complex reasons for and against a practice, for the values that inspired it, and the murk in which it was entangled, we need to uncover the origins of that practice and to fully grasp these origins, we need to do the history of political philosophy.

3

Is There an Indian Political Theory?*

When the Anglo-Saxon world wrestled with the question: 'does political theory still exist?' or 'is political theory dead?', India might well have asked if political theory had even been born in this part of the world. Why? Because the way the identity of political theory has been constructed and the manner in which its features are distinguished from other related practices and modes of expression is itself culturally and historically structured. Once we realize that political reflections have not been structured in the sub-continent in the manner in which this has been done in the West, it is not difficult or preposterous to support the claim that a critical tradition of political theory does not exist in India or at least that political theory in India is underdeveloped.[1] That valuable political and moral treatises have been written over centuries in India is true, but these hardly add up to what is now understood as political theory.

Allow me to clarify this point by taking the example of the Indian constitution. A political theory perspective is absent in any study of the constitution. What is meant by this? First, that existing work has insufficiently elaborated the conceptual structure, and little interest is shown in the possible constitutional meanings or analysis of terms such as 'rights', 'citizenship', 'minority', or 'democracy'. Furthermore, there

* A version of this polemically charged paper entitled 'Notes on Derivative Theorizing in India' was presented at a workshop organized by the Architectural Forum at Mohile Parekh Centre, Mumbai in early 2002.

[1] This claim is made, for example, by Bhikhu Parekh in 'The Poverty of Indian Political Theory', unpublished paper that is part of the *Hull Papers in Indian Politics* (edited by Noel O'Sullivan), undated, p. 1.

is no attempt to construct a vision of society and polity conditional upon an interpretation of key concepts of the Indian constitution. A second weakness, then, is that existing work shows an inadequate grasp of the *structure of ideals* embedded in the constitution. I do not suggest that the finest work on the constitution is silent about the values it upholds. Nonetheless, it fails to properly articulate or provide critical interpretation. For example, Granville Austin uses Isaiah Berlin's distinction between negative and positive liberty and points out that the Indian constitution is guided equally by both.[2] But his discussion of normative values ends here. My claim is that we need to move deeper in this direction. My third, final point is that in order to refine, raise to a higher theoretical plane, and *justify* underlying values, the Indian constitution must be read in conjunction with the constituent assembly debates. Philosophical treatment of values is woefully incomplete if a detailed justification is not provided. When framers of the constitution chose to guide Indian society and polity by a particular rather than other set of values, they must have done so with a set of reasons, many of which are not made properly explicit. Howsoever sketchy and incomplete the argument, it is difficult to imagine that it was absent. Political theorists must articulate and refine these arguments so that an informed and meaningful debate may ensue on the character and value of the Indian constitution. Fourth, political theorists need to identify the larger background conditions that made it possible, first, for the elites and later, gradually, for others to imagine their society as constitution-bound.

This absence does not afflict only the study of Indian constitution. Nearly all concepts in Indian social and political discourse are under-analysed; precious few arguments have been systematically thought through and little attempt has been made to re-imagine the intellectual world of major thinker–activists in India. Those who call themselves political theorists rarely practice conceptual history, a history of ideas, or of social and political thought. Curiously, when it comes to thought and ideas, historians hardly fare better. Few historians write a non-reductive history of concepts. The impact of colonial modernity generated multiple streams of thought undertaken by diverse thinkers. While remarkable studies are available of movements that generated these ideas and some excellent biographies of thinker–activists who

---

[2] See Granville Austin, *The Indian Constitution: Cornerstone of a Nation*, New Delhi: Oxford University Press, 1999, p. 51.

participated in them, few historians have taken seriously the power and depth of the world inaugurated by their ideas. We have no real picture of the world opened up by them. Gandhi and Bankim Chatterjee are perhaps the only exceptions. Even Nehru's world remains opaque, unavailable for critical scrutiny. It has not helped matters that the work of social reformers and anti-colonialists has not been translated from one regional language to another or to English and Hindi. The history of Indian political thought must rate as one of the poorest disciplines in social science, humanities, and philosophy.

The absence of political theory defeats not only projects of dialogue between contemporary western and Indian political theory but also fatally undermines the emergence of political theory with any trans-national potential. Contemporary political theory reflects this. Even a cursory glance shows that even when some of its content has universal reach, its form remains parochial. Political philosophy as it exists today takes little inspiration from non-western societies. It hardly refers to their problems or takes much notice of how cross-cultural issues inflect or imbibe internal colouration at different places. Examples discussed in political philosophy almost never relate directly or immediately to specific contexts of these societies. For all talk of pluralism and multiculturalism in western political theory, a mention of how these issues arise or are tackled in places such as India is barely mentioned. Worse, political philosophers still show little curiosity about the experience of non-western societies.

Take the philosophical debate on Affirmative Action. The Indian experience of this important issue is older than that of most countries, preceding by several decades the USA experience of it, but the best articles written on this subject fail to take the Indian experiment into account. The story of other issues is not any different. Must not we conclude that western political theory remains Eurocentric or even Anglo-Saxon? To remove this bias and to come to grips with deep diversity that is an integral part of the daily life of India, political theorists across the world must consider taking an intensive course on Indian society and politics. Debates around group rights, self-determination, differentiated citizenship, gender equality, secularism, and constitutionalism will surely be considerably enriched by the Indian experience. A search for trans-cultural ideals is impossible without such cross-references.

I do not mean to rest responsibility in toto for this state of affairs with western political theorists. As already mentioned, Indian thinkers have contributed in no small measure to this state of affairs. Indians remain insulated from the experience of other Asian and African countries. How many of us care to comparatively explore conceptions of religion–state relationships in, say, Indonesia and Senegal?[3] Worse, we have unthinkingly pursued an agenda shaped entirely by the concerns of a few western countries—mainly Britain, the USA, France, and Germany. Exclusive attention bestowed on a small number of western countries is a matter of concern and self-reflection. Indeed, blindness to other European countries is shocking. Consider the Belgium experience on the issue of language. India and Belgium can certainly learn a thing or two from one another about deep cultural differences that emanate from linguistic diversity. But, can we think of a single book that discusses the comparative experience of linguistic diversity in India and Belgium? Has political theory been even faintly affected by the mutual experience of these two countries? Or take Switzerland. How many of us are aware of the interface and overlap of religion and language in Switzerland and their impact on Swiss politics. Quite clearly, the West towards which we remain almost permanently oriented comprises a handful of hegemonic countries.

So, we here have a conundrum. Existing, mainly western political theory is excessively ethnocentric but there appears to be nothing at hand to replace it. Whatever political theory exists in the rest of the world, including India, is largely *derivative*. Now to say of something that it is derivative means that its real source lies somewhere other than where it is currently located, made, or used. To be sure, derivative entities need not always be imports; in a sense, they could even be made by recipients who are among its current users. Yet, these users do not make them under background conditions that facilitate their generation. The conceptual structure of these entities is usually out of sync with the new contexts in which they are made. This dislocation may be minor or major, be easily corrected or align with new background conditions with great difficulty or indeed not at all. The original producers and users of entities have a shrewd idea of what purpose they serve. The borrowers and imitators may use it in ways and for purposes for which they were not designed. Many derivative entities not only thwart the autonomy but also distort or obscure the real interests of their new users.

---

[3] This comparison is illuminatingly crafted by Alfred Stepan, 'The Multiple Secularisms of Modern Democracies', in Craig Calhoun and Mark Juergensmeyer (eds), *Rethinking Secularism* (forthcoming).

Why is theory—in the sense specified in Chapter 1—derivative, more or less in the negative sense specified earlier, of western models? I tentatively put forward a hastily put together set of reasons that might explain why social and political theory in India is derivative of western models. First, as already mentioned, a well-developed tradition of social and political theorizing has never been available to us as a steady cultural resource. I have often been tempted to classify modes of expression and cognition in India as falling within four broad categories. First, those for which one can legitimately claim a long, well developed, and, more or less, continuing tradition, real or invented. Surely, classical and folk music, epic poetry, theories of grammar, logic, and metaphysics belong to this category. Second, those that belong to a tradition that once existed but has now broken so that their practices are invented either in ferocious opposition to older, fossilized forms or appear to many to be radically deracinated. Here, some forms of poetry, painting, architecture, and theatre come to mind. Third, those for which a tradition could not have existed in the past but does now and is thriving, that is, for example, cinema, film music, and novels. Fourth, practices where a tradition neither existed in the past nor has been invented; probably, autobiographical writing. Where to locate social and political theory—in the second or the fourth category? It is a difficult choice but I am tempted to put it in the latter.

Second, unlike cinema, why have we not built a new tradition of social and political theorizing? Here several reasons can be cited. The site where traditions of social and political theorizing develop are almost wholly occupied by vibrant, deeply entrenched cosmologies that continue to orient people to define their world and to normatively view it in ways that inhibit critical theorizing (cosmologies are speculative, non-rational, thrive on ambiguity and polysemy, and are disinclined to examine their own presuppositions or assumptions). In their identity-constituting function, existing cosmologies and Grand theories compete for the same space. Extant cosmologies restrict the development of Grand social and political theories. This in turn impacts the growth even of little theories.

A third possible reason why theorizing in India cannot but help being derivative is the lack of self-confidence and self-esteem, crucial to the development of a new tradition of social theory built on equal terms with the West and appropriate to our conditions. Ashis Nandy has argued that colonialism should not only be viewed in economic and political terms but also as a socio-psychological phenomenon.[4] If so, the termination of political, even economic colonialism need not entail the end of socio-psychological colonialism. Indeed, it can be argued that a new, second phase of colonialism began in India with the departure of colonial rulers, when the newly liberated educated class released all self-imposed inhibitions and began to openly, uncritically use cognitive categories generated in and by the West. Nandy argues that colonialism depends on the presence of a shared cultural code that encourages cultural co-option by a well entrenched mechanism that psychoanalysts called identification with the aggressor. The whole-hearted embrace of western conceptual systems exemplifies this psychological process.

Is this process entirely psychological? Not entirely, if by 'psychological' is meant non-institutional. Properly speaking, it is a psychological process transmitted by a set of institutions. Which ones? Here, my hypothesis is that this new phase of colonization begins with the academization of Indian intellectual life. The modern Indian university has borrowed an entire gamut of practices and discourses, including a near-total reliance on academic practices and books and journals that are transmitters of a new inescapable form of colonial power. The space where autonomous social and political theory develops is inhabited not only by traditional cosmologies but also by purely western political theories that come through a whole network of academic practices sustained by the university system. By reading great political theorists, we could access the world created by and in their texts. This is easy for English-speaking subjects. But we could not distinguish this textual world from the real world of ordinary men and women. We succumbed again and again to the fallacy of misplaced concreteness. We first mistook the ideal world of western political theory as lived reality of the West and then began to imagine this 'real world' as our own habitat or one where we shall live. You don't have to fly out of India to become a non-resident Indian!

Next, I submit that one reason for why better ground work for social and political theory was prepared in pre-independent rather than in post-independent India is because of the lack of academization and professionalization of Indian intellectual life during that period. It is frequently argued that as intellectual life is professionalized, it becomes self-referential. The connection with the world outside is broken.

[4] Ashis Nandy, *The Intimate Enemy: Loss and Recovery of Self under Colonialism*, New Delhi: Oxford University Press, 1983.

Intellectual debates are ignited within the academia during conversation among academics rather than fired by real political controversies or struggles. All that matters for academics is peer recognition and upward mobility within the academia. I am not unsympathetic to this view but in the Indian context, remain unimpressed. Professionalization also brings focus, rigour, and depth within a narrowly defined field. While it disconnects academics from the world outside, it connects them to fellows engaged in the single-minded pursuit of shared ends within traditions of inquiry. The western academia might overdo it, but some degree of professionalization is not such a bad thing where hitherto only amateurs are running the show. In India, academization has not gone hand-in-hand with a reasonable degree of professionalization.

This leads us to the fifth reason that the under-professionalization of certain fields of inquiry, particularly in the social sciences, brings with it another danger to which many of us in India have succumbed. There has been an over-ideologization of the academia and of the wider public sphere. Now, as mentioned in Chapter 2, ideology is necessary in the modern world. Clifford Geertz has rightly pointed out that ideology is an ordered system of cultural symbols organizing and integrating social and psychological processes into a meaningful pattern, enabling purposive action.[5] In a variety of interesting ways, ideologies combine facts and values, clarity and ambiguity, the rational and the non-rational, the particular and the general, the discursive and the non-discursive. This frees them from the confines of the academy and connects them to the world beyond. However, ideologies need not necessarily be opposed to critical rational theorizing and controlled enquiry into the particular. Therefore, by over-ideologization, I mean the following: opposition to rational critical thinking about one's preferred ideology; dogmatic, unreasonable attitudes that prohibit engagement with what the other says; wilful, manipulative use of words to enhance the cognitive prestige of one's own point of view; general reluctance to acknowledge counter evidence to one's own ideological claims; rhetoric and emotion are a running thread in all discourses. However, over-ideologization makes every statement dissimulatively rhetorical.

The under-professionalization of the academia has turned direct engagement with the political world into a disadvantage. Rather than provide it with complexity and insight, engagement with the political

---

[5] See Clifford Geertz, *The Interpretation of Cultures*, New York: Basic Books, 1973, pp. 216–18.

world over-ideologizes the thinking of academics. They forget that academics have their own mode of being political. Moreover, over-ideologization provokes among some academics extreme reactions—either self-indulgent, disengaged macro-speculation or an indiscriminate, overactive stance to totter everything that to them appears fixed. This is negative dialectic at its worst.

Finally, the pursuit of calculated, tactical thinking for short-term gains prevents impartial reflection crucial to the development of theory. Ironically, the democratic process itself, which has induced a healthy and irreversible wave of equalization, provides the impetus for calculated thinking to achieve short-term advantages; a whole new set of freshly empowered people with incipient, steady vitality have entered local and national public spheres from which they were hitherto debarred. These groups have not mindlessly wandered into these institutions but have brought along home-grown cultural norms. At any rate, they have joined these institutions with their own understanding of pre-existing norms. As a result, cultural norms and opinions on these norms have multiplied. Thus, the presence of countless norms and opinions, together with the fact that, in Andy Warhol's famous phrase, in today's world each of us snatch for ourselves 20 minutes of fame, has contributed to the growth of another feature of contemporary India, namely, a profound uncertainty about the very norms and principles we affirm with such pride. Confidence with which these are defended is matched by the lurking anxiety and doubt they cannot help but generate.

An interesting psycho-cultural fact about humans is that when faced with innumerable principles, none of which appear to be certain, they grasp at prejudice and various material interests. Amid everything evanescent, material interest and prejudice provide rock support. Principles come and go but material interest and prejudice endure! But, talk of principles cannot be entirely discarded—and can never be dispelled—and therefore, people try to disguise interest or prejudice as principles. A persistent tendency ensues to believe that, because it is the best, my opinions, tastes, values, and lifestyle are the best and provide the yardstick for all. This inexorably leads to complete distrust and cynicism about even the possibility of general standards of excellence and the absence of commonly agreed standards of judgement. In such contexts, rational enquiry suffers. A process of fragmentation, inevitable and concomitant with large numbers is set in motion, frequently accompanied by the absence of any network to connect these isolated and insulated groups of people. This network is important because new, original traditions develop not as gifts of world's historic individuals but by virtue of sustained public discussion and debate. This depends, in turn, on small interconnected and intercommunicating public spaces. However, in India, older public spaces are over-ideologized and new public arenas are governed entirely by market values.

The principles of the public sphere are markedly different from those that govern the market. In the market, a person may choose between courses of action that differ only in the way that affect him. In a public space, however, an individual is asked to express preferences over states that also differ in the way in which they affect *other* people. The market corrupts the public space by privatizing it. There is a fundamental sense in which a libertarian market obstructs the growth of liberal public space.[6] This is amply illustrated in the last two decades by the woeful distortion of our intellectual life by the electronic and print media. The wider presence of such liberal spaces is crucial for the growth of social and political theory.

To sum up:

1. Since a tradition of social and political theorizing is not available as a standing cultural resource, and because of factors induced by the second phase of colonization, a persistent tendency exists to depend entirely on the resources of western theory. People are mostly unable to see the culture-specific features of this theory, no doubt in part because its cultural location is almost always obscured by its universalistic language.

2. Academic institutions are even most strongly shaped by western categories. Hence, they are possibly new carriers of an older system of domination.

3. The identity-constituting function is better served for most people by old, somewhat revamped cosmologies, rather than by Grand theories. If it is true that Grand theories can help propel people into generating Little theories, then the marginalization of or indifference to Grand theories results in the sterility of Little theories.

4. Over-ideologization undermines critical–rational enquiry and therefore, fosters a distrust for theory.

5. Theories depend on a commitment to some broadly defined standards of impartiality that enable people to reach a consensus on what it is most reasonable to believe. A link exists between impartial

[6] On this point, see Jon Elster, 'The Market and the Forum: Three Varieties of Political Theory', in Robert Goodin and Philip Pettit (eds), *Contemporary Political Philosophy*, Oxford: Blackwell, 1997, pp. 128–42.

standards and a wide consensus across divergent interests of individuals and groups. Pervasive individual or communal egoism curtails impartiality and undermines development of theories.

6. A glut of ad hoc reflections, mostly ego-focused, solution-centred approaches in response to immediate problems has flooded the public world and large segments of the academic world. Sustained and systematic reflection is rare.

7. In the absence of sustained micro-enquiries that are crucial for theory building, whatever little systematic thinking that exists tends to be highly speculative, pretty much along lines of existing cosmologies.

How then can we circumvent this condition? Can political theorizing in India escape being derivative? Fortunately, some change is already underway. I say on the basis of personal experience of teaching political theory in India for three decades. I could divide this period into two phases. In the first phase, say between 1979–89, political theorists were obsessed with reading western texts and thinking about them. We were commentators, at best rather poor analysts of texts that came to us from the North and which make up the cannon of western political philosophy. During this period, I frequently heard questions from some students and complaints from many colleagues: these concerned 'applicability' or relevance of political theory. I found the refrain tiresome and frankly, very irritating. It was particularly frustrating to detect a change in attitude among better students who glowed with enthusiasm in class, took optional courses in political theory but began to show signs of indifference or impatience as they moved closer MPhil. Many never failed to mention how much they enjoyed political theory classes but shied away from 'doing' political theory. An unbridgeable gap opened up and two camps were formed—one for and the other against political theory. With hindsight, I feel that this division occurred from a collective inability to understand the complex, multifarious nature, and function of political theory. Neither camp really properly distinguished the two questions: (i) what is the relevance of political theory?; and (ii) what is the relevance of the kind of political theory that occupied many of us? General scepticism about political theory must be kept separate from the most specific scepticism directed against particular kinds of political theorizing. The pro-political theory camp failed to realize that in defending the more worthwhile, relevant forms of political theory, they ended up ratifying considerably less significant variants. Similarly, the anti-political theory camp sweepingly attacked largely indefensible versions but their indispensable cousins too. What was the point of endlessly explicating what this or that western thinker said or meant? No doubt this must be an integral component of studying and teaching political theory, but is this all there is to this important human practice? Even if we were interested only in normative issues, why did we not attempt a sustained defence of democracy, affirmative action, or the autonomy of institutions? Why did we fail to discern and properly distinguish an honourable religious sensibility from an ignoble, communal assertion? Why were socialists unable to distinguish different forms of equality and reflect on which inequalities may be justified?

The climate began to change by the early 1990s. Several political theorists began to reach for the kind of political theory necessary and relevant to our context. A new world of political theory opened out. The mid-1980s had already witnessed the birth of context-sensitive empirical political theory—Partha Chatterjee's work on nationalism; Sudipta Kaviraj's work on Indian state and democracy; Ashis Nandy's work on post-colonialism; D.L. Sheth's articles on caste and language; and Upendra Baxi's on law come readily to mind. The turn of the century saw the continuation of this tradition in the work of scholars such as Achin Vanaik, Nivedita Menon, and Aditya Nigam. Yogendra Yadav's articles on democracy can also be subsumed under empirical theory. The 1990s also witnessed the emergence of normative political theory. A number of political theorists, for example, Gurpreet Mahajan, Valerian Rodrigues, Thomas Pantham, Sarah Joseph, Gopal Guru, Peter deSouza, and Ashok Acharya began to explicitly write on normative issues that were India focused.[7] Their work began to relate issues of caste, religion, and culture in India to rights and democracy. Interestingly, some scholars—Pratap Bhanu Mehta, Javeed Alam, Niraja Jayal, and Neera Chandhoke—straddled both empirical and normative theory.

How do we judge political theory in this phase? How original or derivative was it? I speak for myself in the hope that many political theorists find something representative in what I have to say. Take the example of multiculturalism.[8] When multicultural discourse was first examined in India, several scholars claimed that it would not sit well

[7] I follow Bhikhu Parekh here and refer only to those Indian political theorists who reside or who wrote their work when resident in India. See Parekh, 'The Poverty of Indian Political Theory', in O'Sullivan (ed.), *Hull Papers in Indian Politics*, p. 1. I admit this list is somewhat Delhi-centric.

[8] This is discussed in greater detail in Chapter 5 of this volume.

with the criss-cross, amorphous pluralism of traditional India.[9] They shared the consensus that multiculturalism originated in Canada, later spreading to Australia, America, and Britain. Though I did not entirely disagree with this view, I saw this matter slightly differently. For a start, I am not committed to the strong programme of sociology of knowledge for which concepts and theories are rigidly located with an immovable allegiance to specific interests. For me, many concepts and theories possess a degree of flexibility and mobility that makes for multiple applications in contexts different from where they emerged. Critics of multiculturalism who saw it as an alien framework over-contextualized it hugely.

Second, I turned this critique on its head to make a stronger counter-claim. I contended that certain issues and themes of multiculturalism originate in the practices of modern India with greater salience and depth than anywhere else in the world. Multiculturalism as a practice is an Indian original.[10] At an international level where multiculturalism signals a demand for authenticity, a way of being that is uniquely one's own, a long sub-continental tradition exists of a widely shared but distinctive civilization (this must not be confused with cultural nationalism). At the second level, we have a multicultural nationalism that bitterly fought and disavowed a narrowly conceived Hindu and Muslim nationalism. Finally, at the third level, that is, within the nation-state, practices emanating from constitutionally recognized, group-specific cultural and religious rights exist.

If multiculturalist practices were formulated and long discussed in India, why were they not theorized? Why did we derive theories from the Canadian experience? Though theories emerge from practice, neither the presence of a particular set of practices nor ad hoc reflections on them generates theory. We need to rely on traditions of theorization and sustain practices of learning from them. And while these traditions and institutional apparatus to learn about them exist in the West, such traditions are non-existent or broken in India. Unless these are retrieved or invented in India, no original *theories* can be generated.

This is a difficult, rather pessimistic conclusion. What must be done in the interlude? Most theories originating in the West are bound to

[9] See Shail Mayaram, 'Recognizing Whom? Multiculturalism, Muslim Minority Identity and the Mers', in Rajeev Bhargava, Amiya Kumar Bagchi, and R. Sudarshan (eds), *Multiculturalism, Liberalism and Democracy*, New Delhi: Oxford University Press, 1999, pp. 380–99.

[10] See Chapter 5 of this volume.

initially have a strong flavour of their origin. However, rejection of the strong programme of sociology of knowledge helps to see that concepts and theories can be decontextualized, relocated, and then invested with different meaning and intonation. This complex practice of decontextualization and recontextualization must be pursued. To understand *how* to decontextualize, we need to rely on available theoretical traditions. To know *what* precisely to recontextualize, we must have a strong practical grasp of our own social practices.

This explains why multicultural practices need not always be accompanied by multicultural theories, and also why *our* multicultural theories, at least for now, will be produced by Indians at best jointly with, say, Taylor or Kymlicka. So, we will have an Indian political theory in some weak sense, that is, largely western theories with a distinctively Indian flavour. When we are engaged in political practices, reflect on issues that grow from them, and creatively use traditions of theorizing no matter where they are born, then something like an Indian political theory is bound to emerge. The difference between this political theory and political theory in other parts of the world, particularly in Europe and in the USA, may be tiny. But since the devil is in the detail, these little variations are bound to make a big difference to the character of Indian political theory.

Though a good step in the right direction, I do not think it goes far enough. I don't mean to suggest that we should strive for theories born out of and reflecting the 'genius' of Indians, something uniquely Indian. This is far from what I have in mind. However, something in the air these days gives me the confidence to propose that we can have Indian political theory in a stronger sense. My reason for this self-belief stems from certain world historical developments that include clear signs that the period of second colonization might be coming to an end. With great clarity, Gandhi's prophetic *Hind Swaraj* anticipated many features of the current conjuncture in which the world is witness to the dramatic, almost irreversible breakdown of the hegemony of modern western civilization.

Ideas and practices associated with the modern West have been critiqued for long, viewed with suspicion, and rejected, rightly or wrongly, in the past. But never before has the impact of this critique been profound enough to launch a transformation in the social and political imaginary of large numbers of people in the world. A new historical dynamics has been set in motion in recent times that has fundamentally altered the relationship between former centres and their peripheries.

In short, the pluralization of the centre has begun. The persistent challenge of others, and the folly of its own actions, has nearly brought the end of western hegemony. We suddenly live, as Smuel Eisenstadt tells us, in a world of shifting hegemonies. The modern West is merely one among many, just another culture with a few strengths and several weaknesses, as much in need of cure as others. It has fallen off the pedestal. True, the West still has riches as well as a capacity to use brute force but it can hardly claim to be more civilized than others. A space has emerged for real cultural and civilizational equality between a much weakened hegemon and a previously hegemonized world.

For political theorists, this is a unique opportunity to seize the moment, to think of their mode of inquiry afresh. Hitherto, attention was focused on how concepts developed in the West were used in India, the meaning and inflection they acquired. The more urgent question now concerns the internal structure of concepts evolved in India and what happened to them with the advent of colonial modernity. This requires closer collaboration of political theorists with Indian social anthropologists, sociologists, and historians and with scholars of Sanskrit, Persian, and regional languages, including Hindi.

In the rest of this chapter, I outline what such an attempt would look like. I take my first example from early Indian history. There is much talk of tolerance or toleration in Indian civilization. At its best, what did it add up to? Toleration implies that the one who tolerates refrains from interfering in the morally unacceptable or repugnant beliefs and practices of those who are tolerated even though he has the power to do so. Is this what was practised in, say, Ashoka's times? Evidence from Ashokan edicts gives a different picture. Many of these edicts acknowledge the presence of different religions as natural. All religions are seen to be worthy recipients of respect and support. Non-Buddhist faiths are seen not as errors but as a 'constructive part of reality in a morally productive society'.[11] The *praja* is advised to 'avoid extolling one's own faith and disparaging the faith of others improperly or, when the occasion is appropriate, immoderately'.[12] It follows that a proper,

---

[11] K. Scheible, 'Towards a Buddhist Policy of Tolerance: The Case of King Ashoka', in J. Neusner and B. Chilton (eds), *Religious Tolerance in World Religions*, Pennsylvania: Templeton Foundation Press, 2008, p. 321. Also, see Romila Thapar, 'Asoka and Buddhism as Reflected in the Asokan Edicts', in Romila Thapar (ed.), *Cultural Pasts*, New Delhi: Oxford University Press, 2000, p. 432.

[12] Scheible, 'Towards a Buddhist Policy of Tolerance', in Neusner and Chilton (eds), *Religious Tolerance in World Religions*, p. 323.

moderate critique of other faiths is justified. It is assumed that one who conducts such a critique does so from the standpoint of his own faith and that therefore finds his own faith at least marginally superior to others. Ashoka himself must have believed so about Buddha's teachings. So, according to Ashokan edicts, all religions are expected to share a space within which they can respect and dialogue with one another. Yet, acknowledging and respecting other religions is not the same thing as according them *equal* respect. Respect is compatible with hierarchy, which is why the use of the term 'toleration' in the context of Ashokan edicts is partly appropriate. Ashoka's edicts appear to articulate something more than toleration but somewhat less than equal respect for all religions. Clearly, we are on to a concept that does not easily fit neat categories of western political theory.

Ever since Dumont posited the essentialist idea that Indian society must be viewed as an organic whole embodying a hierarchy-ridden caste system, and partly because this was an idealization of nineteenth century social reality in India, it has been difficult for academics to conceive that a form of equality has been available as a conceptual resource in our traditions. It was. The Mahabharata, generally known to endorse the caste system, contains verses that enjoin the brahmin, Kaushika, to learn about *dharma* from a lower caste person who trades in flesh. Implicit in this is the idea of some form of *dharmic* equality. But Buddhism's challenge to Vedic brahminism, arguably, made it one of the earliest originators of the idea of social equality.[13] It made Buddhism a catalyst in opening a conceptual space which would be widely used by low caste *shudras* and outcastes in later periods.

Various movements between the seventh and the thirteenth centuries, grouped together under the generic name of '*bhakti*', contained egalitarian elements. One particular bhakti movement, the Vir Shaivite movement led by the Karnataka saint, Basavanna,[14] and popularized by the *vachana* writers in the twelfth century, was the most radical. Although a brahmin, Basavanna revolted against brahamanical or-

---

[13] For a discussion of Buddhist notion of human equality, see G. Obeyesekere, *Imagining Karma*, Berkeley: University of California Press, 2002, pp. 182–5. Also, see Romila Thapar, 'Is Secularism Alien to Indian Civilization?', in T.N. Srinivasan (ed.), *The Future of Secularism*, New Delhi: Oxford University Press, 2007, pp. 83–108.

[14] Ekantada Ramayya and the Aradhyas shaped the creed before Basavanna—the Prime Minister of King Bijjala of the Kalachuri Kingdom of Kalyana in present-day Bidar, Karnataka—took over.

thodoxy, ritualism, and discrimination on the basis of caste, creed, or gender. His movement accorded a special place to women and became the predominant factor in overturning brahamanical superiority and, to some extent, patriarchal values. The female with her powers of creation and nurturing became more important than the male, and lower castes devoid of the trappings of wealth and power were considered nearer to the god than brahmins.[15] Worshiping Shiva, the movement rejected Vedic authority over the rite of cremation, favouring burial instead. It propagated widow remarriage, condemned child and arranged marriages, and did not class women as polluted during menstruation[16] Indeed, women saints, dedicated at an early age to god, subverted many male-oriented norms. They defied their parents and escaped marriage in one of several ways: by single-minded love, turning into a courtesan, getting transformed into an unmarriageable old woman or into a male. Like several Buddhist and Jain women in the past, they also had the freedom to explicitly renounce marriage.[17] While the initial radicalism and the anti-Sanskritization of the Vir Shaivite movement did not last beyond the twelfth century and inherent socio-economic inequality (between very poor Madigas and Holeyas and very rich Okkaligas), retrenched caste hierarchies, patriarchy, and gender inequality,[18] three things stand out in the early phases of this movement: first, a defence of social equality and a rejection of caste and gender hierarchies; second, an emphasis on

[15] V. Ramaswamy, *Divinity and Deviance: Women in Virasaivism*, New Delhi: Oxford University Press, 1996, p. 147.

[16] K. Jones, *Socio-religious Reform Movements in British India*, Cambridge: Cambridge University Press, 1994, p. 11.

[17] Vinay Dharwadker, *The Collected Essays of A.K. Ramanujan*, New Delhi: Oxford University Press, 1999, pp. 271–8. On women's freedom to become renouncers, see Thapar, 'Is Secularism Alien to Indian Civilization?', in Srinivasan (ed.), *The Future of Secularism*. This quality of the empowerment of women via sainthood is also found in north India. For example, Mirabai (1498–1550) gave voice to the subordinated classes (in particular, the weaving communities in the sixteenth century) of Saurashtra and Rajasthan (western India) against feudal privilege and caste norms; stood for a cultural resistance to socially imposed marital relationships; and gave refuge to those bereft of caste. See P. Mukta, *Upholding a Common Life: The Community of Mirabai*, New Delhi: Oxford University Press, 1994; and K. Sangari, 'Mirabai and the Spiritual Economy of Bhakti', *Economic and Political Weekly*, vol. xxv, no. 27, 7–14 July 1990, pp. 1464–75, 1537–52.

[18] Ramaswamy, *Divinity and Deviance*, p. 192.

individual choice and responsibility in religious matters, including liberation unmediated by social authority or institution, thus developing the conceptual repertoire for socio-religious freedom for individuals; and finally, this freedom not only challenged established authority but also provided platform for radical dissent.

I have indicated the availability of conceptual spaces where forms of religious tolerance, social equality, and individual freedom developed in the early history of India. In the Sultanate and the Mughal periods, my focus is on notions of Sharia, state, and justice. It has been argued by others that exigencies of politics prevented Afghan and Turk rulers from imposing Sharia on entire populations of their kingdom. They followed the Quranic injunction that in matters of faith there should be no compulsion and that Muslims should coexist peacefully with non-Muslims. Not that a policy of political expediency had widespread legitimacy with the ruling elite and clergy. Rulers succumbed frequently to pressure from religious orthodoxy. For instance, Ziauddin Barani (1285–1357) opposed carriers of a false creed, who did not suppress infidels, and promoted *din* and Sharia. Since the primary function of the king was to protect Islam and Muslims, any act intended to promote the interest of Muslims is praiseworthy, however injurious to others. For Barani, royal action taken in the cause of Islam cannot be despotic. Conversely, a decision that ignores, overlooks, or offends Sunni Islam is nothing but tyrannical. The Muslim ruler had to be just but justice is established only when the king follows the commands of religion.[19]

Similarly, for Ali Hamdani (fourteenth century), the subjects of the rulers must be divided into Muslims and *kafirs*. Both enjoy divine compassion but must be treated differently by Muslim rulers. Muslim rulers were enjoined to protect the life and property of kafirs only if they did not build public places of worship. Even their private religious buildings were to remain open to Muslim travellers. No public demonstration of their rituals and customs were acceptable. The *jizya*, a special tax imposed on non-Muslims, was a heavy financial burden and a badge of inferiority, which stimulated conversions to Islam. Hindus were to be constantly reminded of their inferior status in an Islamic state.

However, this is not the whole picture. It overlooks the manner in which Sharia was reinterpreted and how justice rather than religious

---

[19] See M. Alam, *The Languages of Political Islam in India c. 1200–1800*, Delhi: Permanent Black, 2004, for a discussion of the Sultanate and Mughal period.

law was made an important value under-girding the state. First, in a context where the religious views of rulers failed to coincide with the religion of the subject, dissenters within Sunni Islam continued to invoke the Sharia but altered its meaning to legitimize an ideal city as one that is composed of diverse religious and social practices and an ideal ruler to be one who ensured not the well-being of Muslims alone but of the entire people consisting of diverse religious groups. For these dissenters, Sharia was not to be interpreted in narrow juridical but in broader philosophical terms.[20] It became a more flexible concept of practical political philosophy rather than a rigid concept of law. In the narrow juridical interpretation, found in the works of Barani and Sirhindi (sixteenth century), the rule of the Sharia meant not only the total dominance by Muslims but, if not the elimination of infidelity, at the very least the humiliation of infidels. To those who interpreted Sharia more philosophically, for example, Abul Fazl, the Sharia came to be synonymous with the *Namus* (divine law). Its most important task was to ensure a balance of conflicting interests, promote harmony between groups and to ensure non-interference in personal belief.

Second, dissenters within Sunni Islam developed a conception of a state based on justice which, if not entirely independent of Sharia, was at least not incompatible with it. This view is present in the Nasirian tradition, in *Akhlaq-i-Nasiri*. Akhlaq texts focus on man, his living, and the temporal world. Though a man's perfection cannot be achieved without adulation of divinity, it is equally impossible to attain it without peaceful social organization and cooperation. Social cooperation, in turn, depends on justice. If justice, that is, *adl* disappears, each man will merely pursue his own particular, self-related desires. This negates social cooperation. To facilitate it, a balancing agency is required. The Sharia serves this purpose but it cannot do so without being administered by a just king whose principal duty is to control people through affection and favours. Cooperation can be achieved: (i) through mutual love (*mohabbat*). However, in the absence of natural love, it can be achieved only (ii) by an artifice, that is, justice. If love among the people was present, *insaaf* (justice) would be redundant (the word 'insaaf' comes from *nasf* which means taking the half, reaching towards the middle. The *munsif*, dispenser of justice, divides the disputed object into two equal parts that can be shared). Social cooperation is achieved through

[20] Ibid.

this sharing, through justice administered in accordance with law, protected and promoted by a king whose principal instrument of control is affection, favours, and justice rather than diktat.

In the Akhlaq literature, justice in an ideal state is social harmony and balance of the conflicting claims of diverse interest/religious groups. Divergence from adl causes clashes and destruction. In a treatise of the seventeenth century compiled in the Deccan, it is argued that the objective of the Sultanate is to fulfil worldly human needs. Since human beings follow diverse religions, conflict might ensue. The role of the perfect god-sent person, Namus, or Sharia is to avoid such conditions of conflict.[21]

Justice further requires that no one should get either less or more than he deserves as a member of his class. Both excess and shortfall dislocate the nature of the union and social relations of companionship. This emphasis on the desirability of justice is argued from the point of view of a secular ethic. Justice is for all and is against discrimination of anyone on irrelevant grounds. A primary advice to a king is to a consider his subjects as 'sons and friends', irrespective of their faith. So, justice serves a real public interest. A non-Muslim but just ruler will serve society better than an unjust Muslim sultan.[22] The ancient Sassanid kings remained in power for 5,000 years even though they were fire worshippers and infidels. Akhlaq and Mutazilite theories of justice had a lot in common except that the former was dependent on the will of god and the latter, on human reason. In the Sunni tradition, the former prevailed but aspects of the second whose ethics were close to that of the first also crept into the tradition.

Akbar went even further.[23] Since the sultan was the de facto caliph in India, every Muslim ruler was dependent on the religious guidance of ulema. The Sadar-us-Sadur was the chief theologian of the state—responsible for the interpretation and application of the Shariat. In 1579, Akbar reduced the powers of this official. He also claimed that as a just ruler, he was not bound by any particular interpretation of Sharia and if there was any disagreement on a point of law, he had full authority to give a legally binding interpretation. This was a standpoint with palpably secular overtones.

[21] This introduced a degree of ambiguity in Sharia, a point mentioned earlier.

[22] Alam, *The Languages of Political Islam in India*, p. 59.

[23] See R. Aquil, *Sufism, Culture, and Politics*, New Delhi: Oxford University Press, 2007, p. 232.

He also abolished the tax on Hindu pilgrimage centres and jizya (tax on Hindus). Scholars have legitimately argued that 'these were steps dictated principally by the exigencies of state...rather than...religious tolerance...', [24] but this is true primarily of the early part of his rule. Over a period of time, he unfolded his philosophy of *Sulh-I-Kul*— 'absolute/universal peace'—by composite socio-religious tolerance.[25] He launched *Din-i-Ilahi*—independent of orthodox Islam or Hinduism and questioning both with a neutral terminology for both intra and inter controversies—heavily influenced by pantheism: 'God creates visible differences whereas the Reality is the same'.[26] He forbade forcible conversions to Islam, removed restrictions on the building of temples, and appointed Hindus in high places. He organized religious discourses open not only to Muslims but to Hindus, Jains, Parsis, and Christians. The Mahabharata and the Upanishad were translated into Persian. Various Hindu festivals were celebrated in Akbar's court. Following Hindu yogis, Akbar abstained from eating meat and had the centre of his head shaved. He named his own household servants *chelas* (disciples of yogis were known as chelas). He appointed a brahman to translate *Khirad Afza* and showed interest in the worship of fire and the sun. He had always permitted his Hindu wives to worship their idols within the palace and now showed some interest in the idea of reincarnation. He venerated Virgin Mary and gave permission to construct churches.

All this was in sharp contrast to the rest of the world where religious bigotry and intolerance were virtues. The 'Age of Akbar' coincided with the period of bloody religious wars in France and other European countries, of which the St Bartholomew's massacre (1572) was an episode. Closer home, the Ottoman emperor claimed that the enforcement of Sharia was an important part of state policy. Developed by Akbar, this tradition of equal or near-equal respect and impartiality towards all

---

[24] See I.A. Khan, 'The Nobility under Akbar and the Development of His Religious Policy, 1560–80', in Richard M. Eaton (ed.), *India's Islamic Traditions, 711–1750*, New Delhi: Oxford University Press, 2005 (reprint), chapter 5.

[25] S.A.A. Rizvi, 'Dimensions of Sulh-i-Jul (Universal Peace) in Akbar's Reign and the Sufi Theory of Perfect Man', in I.A. Khan (ed.), *Akbar and His Age*, New Delhi: ICHR, 1999, pp. 3–21; I. Habib, 'The Mughal Empire', in J.S. Grewal (ed.), *State and Society in Medieval India*, New Delhi: Oxford University Press, 2005, p. 79.

[26] For a recent analysis of this point, see M. Athar Ali, *Mughal India*, New Delhi: Oxford University Press, 1996.

religions was continued by the British. It is not far-fetched to conclude that while the Europeans learnt the idea of toleration of other sects from their own experience, the conceptual space for the idea of impartiality towards all faiths was created in the sub-continent and learnt by Europe, if at all, from colonial encounters and the legacy they inherited from the polities of their colonial subjects.

Much of the present discussion can be seen not merely as explication of concepts in separate periods of Indian history but as contributing to an anti-anachronistic, non-teleological account of the development of modern secularism in India. This account can be viewed as providing a preliminary sketch of how multiple traditions of popular Hinduism, Buddhism, Jainism, Sufism, and court Islam opened up conceptual spaces that enabled later generations to forge a distinctive conception of India's secular ideals. Ideas of minimal material well-being and decent, this-worldly social relations were developed by Buddhism. The persistent account of the denial of religious freedom is paralleled by an even more powerful account of religious toleration and religious freedom throughout Indian history. Likewise, the idea of human equality is available in some form in Buddhism, bhakti and Sufi movements, popular Islam, and occasionally, in Akbar's eclectic religiosity. Elements of resources for principled distance between state and religion can be found in deep religious diversity that goes back at least to fifth century BCE, and reinforced by developments in the Sultanate and the Mughal periods.[27]

However, these sketchy accounts are ridden with internal problems, of which I mention a few. For a start, there is the danger of being overly triumphilist.[28] Have I laid more emphasis on conditions conducive to the development of secular ideals rather than on those that undermine them? Second, chronological accounts carry with them the danger of teleological bias and an indefensible progressivism. Third, any such account closely resembles the modernist vocabulary implicit in the social reform movements of the nineteenth and the twentieth centuries. If so, I am guilty of anachronism. The claims made on behalf of the

[27] For an account of principled distance, see Chapter 4 of this volume.

[28] For example, see E. Vanina, 'Meeting of the Oceans', in her *Ideas and Society in India 16th–18th Centuries*, New Delhi: Oxford University Press, 2004 (second reprint; first published 1996), p. 82; and S. Chandra, 'Historical Background to the Rise of the Bhakti Movement in Northern India', in his *Historiography, Religion and State in Medieval India*, New Delhi: Har-Anand Publications Pvt. Ltd., 2004 (third reprint; first published 1996), pp. 110–31.

Vir Shaivite movement beg the following questions. Why did the Vir Shaivite propagate widow remarriage? Why did they attack arranged marriage? Why, unlike the orthodoxy, did they believe their women to be clean during menstruation? Unless we have answers to these questions, do we really know the differences between how lives were lived in the eleventh and the twelfth centuries and how they are lived today? Even if we were to make the not altogether implausible claim that something interesting was stirring in parts of southern India in the twelfth century—which was what we call modern and well before the advent of western modernity—we still do not get a sense of the background conditions and the social, cultural, and political imaginary of that period. We do not have a sense of how past actors understood or articulated their actions and intentions. There is too much anachronism and too little sensitivity to the radical differences between the world then and the world now.

Another difficulty concerns the meaning of crucial terms and their translation. When something is translated as equality, what exactly are we to make of that? How do we understand the claim that religious reformers such as Kabir sought to end the caste system? How do we understand notions of individual choice and responsibility? In short, we have to confront the following issue: we need to oppose ridiculous ideas such as notions of individuality, freedom, and equality were invented in the modern West and existed nowhere else. But equally, we must guard against ethnocentrism and anachronism. We must not be tempted to read modern western notions of freedom, equality, or the individual into India's past. Yet, a new language and vocabulary needs to be retrieved, our buried treasure has to be excavated so that we can reconsider not only the non-western past and present but also rewrite the story of the western past and present.

The greatest difficulty of any such account is that the fundamental categories with which it operates, its framework, has developed within western Christendom and modernity. This is true of terms like 'secular', 'state', and the idea of church–state separation partially implicit in 'political secularism'. A deeper, conceptually sensitive historical reading of sources might throw up altogether different concepts, new categorical frameworks that fundamentally question terms with which I have operated here. This just shows that to evolve a form of political theory that is suitable for us and that opens up western political theory as it exists today is a significant but arduous task. But here, the underdevelopment of political theory might be an advantage because, unlike the heavily over-professionalized discipline of western political theory, political theory in India can take real political struggles and contests as its point of departure. Indeed, the little political theory that exists already does this. The rich debate on secularism in India was incited less by professional disagreements within the discipline and more by the looming threat in the last decade the twentieth century of religious majoritarianism. Yet, without quickly cultivating a suspicion of currently dominant theories,[29] generating richer micro-enquiries that are far more focused and, most importantly, turning to traditions of reflection available to us in pre-independent India and earlier, a political theory that speaks to our urgent or enduring problems is unlikely to develop.

[29] My remarks should not give rise to a misunderstanding. I am *not* suggesting that henceforth we should ignore mainstream western political theory. Such a move would be suicidal for Indian political theorists. At any rate, it is not a meaningful option before us.

II
NORMATIVE FRAMEWORKS

4

Political Secularism*

Secularism is a beleaguered doctrine everywhere. For a start, the predicted decline of religion or its privatization failed to occur not only in non-western but also in western societies.[1] Second, political secularism, the doctrine of the separation of state and religion felt a seismic tremor with the establishment of the first modern theocracy in Iran by Khomeini. Soon, other religious voices began be heard and then, to aggressively occupy the public domain. In Egypt, people were exhorted to free themselves of the last vestiges of a colonial past and to establish a Muslim state. In 1989, an Islamic state was established in Sudan. In 1991, the Islamic Salvation Front won the election in Algeria. Islamic movements emerged in Tunisia, Ethiopia, Nigeria, Chad, Senegal, Turkey, and Afghanistan.[2] The states of Pakistan and Bangladesh increasingly acquired theocratic and Islamicist overtones.[3]

* Originally published as 'Political Secularism', in John Dryzek, B. Honnig, and Anne Phillips (eds), *A Handbook of Political Theory*, Oxford: Oxford University Press, 2006, pp. 636–55.

[1] Jose Casanova, *Public Religions in the Modern World*, Chicago: University of Chicago Press, 1994.

[2] Gilles Kepel, *The Revenge of God: The Resurgence of Islam, Christianity, and Judaism in the Modern World*, Pennsylvania: Pennsylvania State University Press, 1994; and David Westerlund, *Questioning the Secular State: The Worldwide Resurgence of Religion in Politics*, New York: St. Martin's Press, 1996.

[3] I. Ahmed, *The Concept of an Islamic State: An Analysis of the Ideological Controversy in Pakistan*, London: Frances Pinter, 1987; and Amena Mohsin, 'National Security and the Minorities: The Bangladesh Case', in D.L. Sheth and Gurpreet Mahajan (eds), *Minority Identities and the Nation-State*, New Delhi: Oxford University Press, 1999, pp. 312–32.

Movements that challenged the seemingly undisputed reign of secularism were not restricted to Muslim societies. Singhalese Buddhist nationalism in Sri Lanka, Hindu nationalists in India, religious ultra-orthodoxy in Israel, and Sikh nationalists who demanded a separate state, partly on the ground that Sikhism does not recognize the separation of religion and state, all signalled a deep challenge to secularism.[4]

Strong anti-Muslim and anti-Catholic movements of Protestants decrying secularism emerged in Kenya, Guatemala, and Philippines. Religiously grounded political movements arose in Poland and Protestant fundamentalism became a force in American politics. In Western Europe too, where religion is a personal response to divinity still largely private, rather than an organized system of practices, change has come from both migrant workers of former colonies and from intensified globalization. This has thrown together a privatized Christianity with Islam, Sikhism, and pre-Christian, South Asian religions that do not draw a boundary between the private and the public in the same way. These strange bedfellows have created such a deep religious diversity, the like of which has never before been known in the modern West.[5] As the public spaces of western societies is claimed by these other religions, the weak but distinct public monopoly of single religions is beginning to be challenged by the very norms that govern these societies. This is evident in Germany and Britain but was most dramatically highlighted by the headscarf issue in France.[6] The suppressed religious past of these societies is now foregrounded and questions the claim concerning the robust secular character of their states.

The secular state is questioned not only by politicians, civil society groups, and clerics. Secularism is contested even by academics. Indian academics were among the first to voice their opposition to secularism.[7]

---

[4] Mark Juergensmeyer, *New Cold War? Religious Nationalism Confronts the Secular State*, California: University of California Press, 1994.

[5] Bryan S. Turner, 'Cosmopolitan Virtue: On Religion in a Global Age', *European Journal of Social Theory*, vol. 4, no. 2, 2001, p. 134.

[6] C.R. Barker, 'Church and State: Lessons from Germany?', *Political Quarterly*, vol. 75, no. 2, 2004, pp. 168–76, Oxford: Blackwell Publishing; Jane Freedman, 'Secularism as a Barrier to Integration? The French Dilemma', *International Migration*, vol. 42, no. 3, 2004, pp. 5–27.

[7] Partha Chatterjee, 'Secularism and Tolerance', in Rajeev Bhargava (ed.), *Secularism and Its Critics*, New Delhi: Oxford University Press, 1998, pp. 345–79; T.N. Madan, 'Secularism in Its Place', in Bhargava (ed.), *Secularism and Its Critics*, pp. 297–320; and Ashis Nandy, 'The Politics of Secularism and the Recovery of Religious Toleration', in Bhargava (ed.), *Secularism and Its Critics*, pp. 321–44.

According to them, the external threat to secularism in India is a symptom of a deeper internal crisis—the conceptual and normative structure of secularism is itself terribly flawed. For them, secularism is linked to a flawed modernization, has a mistaken view of rationality and its importance in human life, makes an impractical demand that religion be extruded from public life, has an insufficient appreciation of the importance of communities in the life of religious people, and has a wholly exaggerated sense of the positive character of the modern state.

By the 1990s, this criticism of secularism was worldwide and included several western scholars. Hitherto, critics of secular states in the western academia only wished to fine-tune them, to make them a littler more sensitive to religion. Without challenging the fundamental framework of liberal democracy, critical academic writing in the West focused narrowly on two issues: first, whether citizens in liberal democracies can *justify* political decisions by relying exclusively on religious reasons; and second, whether they can *make* such decisions by relying solely on religious reasons rather than on secular considerations. Critics of western secularism argued either that (i) while the justifications may be public and secular, actual decision making may be grounded solely on a religious rationale[8] or that (ii) not only political decisions but their justification too, could in certain contexts, rely solely on a religious rationale.[9]

Critiques of western secularism have since become far more trenchant. Several western scholars claim that by enjoining believers to leave behind religious convictions when they step into public life, secularism shows hostility to believers, inhibits diversity, and homogenizes the public domain. Others claim that while it may be suited to Protestantism and religions that are weakly protestantized, it excludes or is actively inimical to other religions. Thus, secularism is a parochial doctrine with universalistic pretensions.[10] Still others claim that secularism denies dependence on a visceral register that it publicly

[8] Kent Greenawalt, *Religious Convictions and Political Choice*, New York and Oxford: Oxford University Press, 1988.

[9] Michael J. Perry, *Love and Power: The Role of Religion and Morality in American Politics*, New York and Oxford: Oxford University Press, 1991.

[10] Talal Asad, *Formations of the Secular: Christianity, Islam, Modernity*, California: Stanford University Press, 2003; William E. Connolly, *Why I Am Not a Secularist*, Minneapolis: University of Minnesota Press, 1999, pp. 23–5; John Keane, 'Secularism?', *Political Quarterly*, vol. 71, no. S1, Oxford: Blackwell Publishing, 2000, pp. 5–19.

denounces as irrational, that it purports to fight religious hegemony but attempts to establish itself as the sole, authoritative basis of adjudication in public life.[11] Others argue that secularism has failed to accommodate community-specific rights and therefore, is unable to protect religious minorities from discrimination and exclusion and that its peace-talk is mere sham because deep down it is a conflict-generating ideology that threatens pluralist democracies.

However, critical writing on secularism is deeply ambiguous between two claims. First, that the deep crisis of secular states signifies that we must look for alternatives to them and second, that we look not for an alternative to secular states but rather for their alternative conceptions, and by implication, for alternative conceptions of secularism. It is important, then, to begin this enquiry by asking what distinguishes secular states from their competitors and—this remains largely unclear—what precise alternatives critics have in mind when they seek to replace them. More importantly, we must ask what the merits and demerits of secular and non-secular states are. This is a sensible question, given that any sound, ethically sensitive practical reasoning must be comparative in nature, and must tell what ethical gains or losses might ensue if we are to transit from a secular state to some other kind of state that presumably grants more importance to religion. If secular states are indeed more worthy, we must also ask if this is true of all forms of secular states or only some? And, if only some, which of these? In what follows, I deal with these questions by elaborating what, in my view, is the proper conceptual and normative structure of secularism. This I hope will not only distinguish secular from non-secular states but also help individuate different types of secular states. I do this not because I have an interest in classification per say, but rather, because of the need to identify a version of secularism that meets the most important religious objections mentioned earlier and because of my belief that an indifference to this objection and the consequent smugness that ensues from this neglect bolsters otherwise indefensible anti-secular states. Finally, I explore if a search for alternative conceptions of secularism leads us towards conceptual resources that cut through the division between a modern West and a traditional East. For example, I ask if the Indian version of secularism is a genuinely modern alternative to its western counterpart, one from which everyone, including the West, may benefit in the future.

---

[11] Connolly, *Why I Am Not a Secularist*, pp. 38–9.

THE CONCEPTUAL STRUCTURE OF SECULARISM

Theocracy and States with Established Religions

To identify the conceptual structure of secularism, it is best to begin by contrasting it with doctrines to which it is both related and opposed. Such anti-secular doctrines favour not separation but a union or alliance between church/religion and state. A state that has union with a particular religious order is a theocratic state, governed by divine laws directly administered by a priestly order claiming divine commission.[12] The Islamic Republic of Iran, as Khomeini aspired to run it, is an obvious example. A theocratic state must be distinguished from a state that establishes religion. Here, religion is granted official, legal recognition by the state and while both benefit from a formal alliance with one another, the sacerdotal order does not govern a state where religion is established.

Because they do not identify or unify church and state but install only an alliance between them, states with an established church are in some ways disconnected from it. In these political orders, there is a sufficient degree of institutional differentiation between the two social entities. Distinct functions are performed in each by different personnel. Yet, there is a more significant sense in which the state and the church are connected to one another: they share a common end largely defined by religion. By virtue of a more primary connection of ends, the two benefit from a special relationship with one another. There is finally another level of connection between church and state at the level of policy and law. Such policies and laws flow from and are justified in terms of the union or alliance that exists between the state and the church. The institutional *disconnection* of church and state—at the level of roles, functions, and powers—goes hand-in-hand with the first- and third-level *connection* of ends and policies. So, this is what differentiates a state with established church-based religion from a theocracy: the second-order disconnection of church and state.

Just as a theocracy is not always distinguished from the establishment of religion, just so a distinction is not always drawn between the establishment of religion and the establishment of the church of a religion. Clearly not all religions have churches. Yet, a state may grant formal and legal recognition to a church-free religion. A majority of

---

[12] *New Catholic Encyclopedia*, Vol. 14, Washington: Catholic University of America, 1967, p. 13.

Hindu nationalists in India may wish to establish Hinduism as state religion but they have no church to establish. Early Protestants may have wanted to disestablish the Roman Catholic Church without wishing the state to derecognize Christianity as the favoured religion. Alternatively, they tried to maintain the establishment of their preferred religion by the establishment of not one but two or even more churches. The establishment of a single religion is consistent therefore with the disestablishment or non-establishment of church, with the establishment of a single church, or with the establishment of multiple churches. Finally, it is possible that there is establishment of multiple religions, with or without church. Possibly, Ashoka's reign in India came closest to it. In the second half of his reign, it was quite certainly an ideal to which the Mughal Emperor Akbar aspired and sometimes realized.

We can see then that there are five types of regimes in which a close relationship exists between state and religion. First, a theocracy, where no institutional separation exists between church and state and the sacerdotal order is also the direct political ruler. Second, states with the establishment of single religion. These are of three types: (i) without the establishment of a church, (ii) with the establishment of a single church, and (iii) with the establishment of multiple churches. Third, states with the establishment of multiple religions.

So, when anti-separationists imagine the replacement of a secular state with some other type of state, which of these do they have in mind? Undoubtedly, some religious activists fervently desire the installation of theocracy or a state that establishes its own religion or church. However, most anti-separationist academics neither endorse this position nor explicitly reject it. (Of course, there are exceptions. For example, Tariq Modood has suggested that Britain might consider having multiple establishment of religions.) They attack separation but wish to distance themselves with a wholly religion-centred polity. It is not hard to understand why. A cursory evaluation of these states shows that these are all deeply troublesome. Take first historical instances of states that establish a single church—the unreformed established Protestant Churches of England, Scotland, and Germany, and the Catholic Churches in Italy and Spain. In such cases, not only was there inequality among religions (Christians and Jews) but also among churches of the same religion.[13] When members of other

---

[13] Leonard W. Levy, *The Establishment Clause: Religion and the First Amendment*, Chapel Hill: University of North Carolina Press, 1994, p. 5.

church or religious groups possessed strength or number, then such a multi-religious or multi-denominational society was invariably wrecked by inter-religious or inter-denominational wars. If they did not, then religious minorities were not even tolerated and faced persistent religious persecution (for example, Jews in several European countries, Muslims in Spain).

States with substantive establishments have not changed colour with time. Wherever one religion is not only formally but substantively established, the persecution of minorities and internal dissenters continues till today. One has to cite the example only of Saudi Arabia to prove this point.[14] It is important to dwell on this because in so many recent critiques of secularism, a more accommodative stance towards religion is recommended with an alarming neglect of some very elementary facts about what such an alliance might entail. Consider the situation in Pakistan, where the virtual establishment of the dominant Sunni sect has proved to be disastrous to minorities, including the Muslim minorities. For example, under Article 260 of the constitution, Ahmedis have been deemed as a non-Muslim minority and forbidden from using Islamic nomenclature in their religious and social lives.[15] Ahmedis have been tried and convicted under the law for calling themselves Muslims or using the word 'mosque' to designate their place of worship. I have taken Pakistan only as an illustration. Surely, after the pogrom in Gujarat, there is no doubt how disastrous the establishment of a Hindu *Rashtra* in India would be for Muslim minorities. Or, consider the democratic state of Israel. Can any one claim that religious minorities in this Jewish state enjoy the same rights as Jews themselves?

States with substantive establishment of multiple churches or religions, such as the states of New York in the middle of the seventeenth century or in the Vijayanagar Kingdom of India in the fourteenth century, are better in some ways than states with singular establishment. For example, such states are likely to be relatively peaceful. Members of different denominations are likely to tolerate one another. There may be general equality among all churches or religions. For example, schools run by religious institutions may be financially aided on a

[14] Malise Ruthven, *A Fury for God: The Islamist Attack on America*, London: Granta Books, 2002, pp. 172–81.

[15] Rajeev Bhargava, 'Inclusion and Exclusion in South Asia: The Role of Religion', Background Paper for HDR, UNDP, 2004, p. 30; and Iftikhar H. Malik, *Religious Minorities in Pakistan*, UK: Minorities Rights Group International, 2002, p. 10.

non-discriminatory basis.[16] The state may grant each denomination considerable autonomy in its own affairs. But, states with establishment of multiple churches have their limitations. For a start, they may continue to persecute members of other religions and atheists. Second, they are indifferent to the liberty of individuals within each denomination or religious group. Closed and oppressive communities can thrive in such contexts. Third, they may not have legal provisions that allow an individual to exit his religious community and embrace another religion or to remain unattached to any religion whatsoever. Fourth, such states give recognition to particular religious identities but fail to recognize what may be called non-particularized identities, that is, identities that simultaneously refer to several particular identities or transcend all of them. Fifth, such states are unconcerned with the *non-religious* liberties of individuals or groups. Finally, such states are entirely indifferent to citizenship rights.

Secular States

So, are secular states better, from an ethical point of view, than theocracies and states with establishment? It would be hasty to answer this question in the affirmative. From a moral point of view, at least some secular states are deeply troublesome. To further understand this issue and individuate different forms of secular states, allow me to distinguish three levels of disconnection to correspond with the already identified three levels of connection. A state may be disconnected from religion at the level of ends (first level), at the level of institutions (second level), and the level of law and public policy (third level). A secular state is distinguished from theocracies and states with established states by a primary, first-level disconnection. A secular state has free standing ends, substantially, if not always completely, disconnected from the ends of religion or conceivable without a connection with them. States with established religions have something in common with secular states—institutional disconnection. But secular states go further in the direction of disconnection; they break away completely, refusing to establish religions or if already established, formally disestablishing them by withdrawing privileges that established churches had earlier taken for granted. In a secular state, no official status is given to religion. No religious community in such a state can say that the state belongs exclusively to it. No one is compelled to pay tax for religious purposes

---

[16] Levy, *The Establishment Clause*, p. 12.

or to receive religious instruction. No automatic grants to religious institutions are available.

Theoretically, two things follow from the abovementioned. First, a non-theocratic state is not automatically secular because it is entirely consistent for a state neither to be inspired by divine laws nor run by a priestly order, but instead have a formal alliance with one religion. Second, because it is also a feature of states with established churches, the mere institutional separation of the two is not and cannot be the distinguishing mark of secular states. Political secularism cannot be identified with church–state separation.

VARIETIES OF SECULAR STATES

A state may be disconnected from religion even at the level of law and public policy. This third-level disconnection can take diverse forms and may serve different ends. This generates different forms of secular states. To begin with, this disconnection may be entirely opportunistic and serve the self-aggrandizing purposes of the state and its political class, for example, those states that wish to maximize power and wealth. Despite moral pretensions, such states have no commitment to values such as peace, liberty, or equality. I shall call them self-aggrandizing, amoral secular states. Usually, they are imperial and autocratic. A good example of such a predominantly secular state, despite the not infrequent allegation of its biased, Christian character, is the British colonial state in India that, motivated almost exclusively by power, wealth, and social order, had a policy of tolerance and neutrality towards different religious communities. This is not surprising, given that empires are interested in the labour or tribute of their subjects, not in their religion.

Distinct from these amoral states are value-based secular states, that is, states guided by values such as peace, liberty, or/and equality.[17] For example, secular states defend the rights of individuals to not only criticize the religion into which they are born but, at the very extreme, to reject it and further, given ideal conditions of deliberation, to freely embrace another religion or even remain without one. Likewise, they make active citizenship rights such as the right to vote or stand for

[17] On the importance of inter-denominational peace, see Michael W. McConnell, 'Taking Religious Freedom Seriously', in Terry Eastland (ed.), *Religious Liberty in the Supreme Court*, Cambridge and Michigan: Eerdmans Publishing Company, 1993, pp. 483–96. On the relationship between secular states and values such as liberty and equality, see Donald Smith, *India as a Secular State*, Princeton: Princeton University Press, 1963.

public office available without discrimination to everyone, regardless of religion.

This third-level disconnection may be made not only for different ends but take different forms. Disconnection may first be identified with strict exclusion. Secularism here becomes a doctrine of political taboo and generally prohibits contact between state and religion. This exclusion itself may take two forms. The first, called one-sided exclusion, is typified by the French and the Turkish model. Such states exclude religion from their domain but intervene in religion to control or regulate them and sometimes, to even destroy them. They are anti-religious and may justify this disconnection on epistemological grounds, for example, that religion is false consciousness, or obscurantist, or superstitious. Or, they may do so in the name of a single value such as equality, because of the belief that important values can be realized only by controlling or eliminating religion. Their aversion to religious freedom makes them illiberal.

The second form, exemplified by the American model, conceives disconnection as mutual exclusion. Such a view proposes that religious and political institutions live as strangers to each other, at best with benign or respectful indifference. When a state is disconnected from religion at all three levels in this particular way, then we may say that a 'wall of separation' has been erected between the two. On the wall of separation conception of secularism, religion must be outside the purview of the state, and in this sense, must be privatized. Such liberal–democratic states are not anti-religious but give religion a particular form and protect religious liberty, liberty more generally, and equality of citizenship.

Liberal–democratic secular states usually enjoin their citizens to support only those coercive laws for which there is public justification. Why so? Because if others are expected to follow a law in terms that they do not understand and for reasons they cannot endorse, then the principle of equal respect is violated.[18] If other reasonable and conscientious citizens have good reason to reject a particular rationale in support

---

[18] Robert Audi, 'The Place of Religious Argument in a Free and Democratic Society', *San Diego Law Review*, vol. 30, Fall 1993, p. 701; Charles Larmore, *The Morals of Modernity*, Cambridge: Cambridge University Press, 1996, p. 137; Stephen Macedo, *Liberal Virtues: Citizenship, Virtue and Community in Liberal Constitutionalism*, Oxford: Clarendon Press, 1990, p. 249; John Rawls, *A Theory of Justice*, Cambridge: Belknap Press, 1971, pp. 337–8; Lawrence Solum, 'Faith and Justice', *DePaul Law Review*, vol. 39, 1990, p. 1095; Paul Weithman, 'Religion and

of a coercive law, then this rationale does not count as public justification. Because a religious rationale is a paradigmatic case of a reason that other citizens have good reasons to reject, it does not count as public justification and because it does not count as public justification, a law grounded solely on a religious rationale must never be enacted. In short, purely religious convictions or commitments have no role to play in democratic and pluralist polities.

Critics who wish to rehabilitate religion in political life usually contrast states more hospitable to religions with self-aggrandizing amoral or mindlessly anti-religious secular states. This is an unfair comparison. An attempt is made here to antecedently shift judgement in favour of religiously friendly states by deliberately pitting them against the worst forms of secular states. This comparison may serve a point: there is not much to choose between theocracies or states with established church on the one hand and amoral or absolutist secular states on the other. Both fare miserably on any index of freedom or equality. But surely, when evaluating the relative merits of religious and secular states, it is this liberal–democratic model which must be kept in mind and not the routinely debunked, severely anti-religious or self-aggrandizing secular states. Little is to be gained from damning secularism by citing the atrocities of Hitler and Stalin or crimes committed by 'secularists' such as Saddam Hussain or Ali Hyder.[19] Nor is any point served by deriding secularists for failing to realize that Sharon does not need to invoke passages of the Torah to kill and terrorize the Palestinians. Secularism, a value-based doctrine, is as committed to denouncing these secular states as it is to berating religious states that violate principles of liberty and equality. Not all secular states abide by the principles of secularism! In short, the word 'secular' is mostly used in a descriptive sense, while 'secularism' is an evaluative term with moral and ethical connotations.

Likewise, it is astonishing to read the claim that 'in modern democratic politics, there is not much reason to fear a religious majority more than a secular majority'.[20] Charles Taylor's arguments about the

---

the Liberalism of Reasoned Respect', in Weithman (ed.), *Religion and Contemporary Liberalism*, Notre Dame: University of Notre Dame Press, 1997, p. 6.

[19] Asad, *Formations of the Secular*, p. 10.

[20] Peter van der Veer, *Imperial Encounters: Religion and Modernity in India and Britain*, Delhi and Princeton: Permanent Black and Princeton University Press, 2001, p. 20.

exclusionary tendencies in modern democratic states with religious or ethnic majorities point clearly towards the inherent possibilities in these states towards de facto singular establishment and the wide range of exclusions and injustices that make them what they are.[21] To say, at this point, that religious majorities are no worse than secular majorities because different religious communities have lived in the past without coming into violent conflict is both ambiguous and misses the point. It is ambiguous because it is hard to understand what a secular majority means. If by this is meant a group of hard-nosed secular absolutists who are deeply anti-religious, then the statement is true. But if by this is meant, a majority that wishes not to politicize religion in all kinds of unprincipled ways, then this statement is deeply wrong. The statement misses the point because peace between communities is entirely compatible with all kinds of exclusions from the domain of freedom and equality. A fearful minority is willing to buy peace at any cost—something that Indians painfully learnt again after the Mumbai riots in 1992–3.

Critiques of Liberal–Democratic Secularism

The more important and serious question then is whether this model, call it the idealized version of the American model or liberal–democratic secularism (also, perhaps the dominant western model), has serious problems that are emphasized by highlighting the persistent problems it faces in practice or when it is contrasted with other non-western variants. The criticisms of this model are many. First, the requirement that religious reasons be excluded from liberal–democratic politics is offensive to religious persons who, like others, wish to support their favoured political commitments on the basis of their conscience.[22] If people believe that their politics must be consistent with their morality, then, why should they be discouraged or stigmatized for doing so? Besides, it is mistaken to assume that only religious people bring passion and sectarianism into politics or, as Richard Rorty believes, that only religion is a conversation stopper.[23] By asking a religious person to exer-

---

[21] Charles Taylor, 'Democratic Exclusion', in Rajeev Bhargava, Amiya Kumar Bagchi, and R. Sudarshan (eds), *Multiculturalism, Liberalism and Democracy*, New Delhi: Oxford University Press, 1999, pp. 138–63.

[22] Michael J. Sandel, 'Freedom of Conscience or Freedom of Choice', in Eastland (ed.), *Religious Liberty in the Supreme Court*, pp. 483–96.

[23] Quoted in Christopher J. Eberle, *Religious Conviction in Liberal Politics*, Cambridge: Cambridge University Press, 2002, p. 393, n65.

cise restraint and exclude religious reasons in their justification for a coercive law, liberal secularism forces her to act against her conscience, and in doing so, it fails not only to respect the moral agency of that person but also violates its own principle of equal respect. Indeed, the demand that restraint be exercised is counterproductive because exclusion from the larger public sphere forces the religious to form their own narrow public where resentment and prejudice will flourish.[24] This would lead not only to the freezing of identities but to the building of unbreachable walls between the religious and non-religious citizens. Therefore, 'engagement with religious people is typically better than shunning them'.[25]

Second, this secularism does not understand the believer's life as it is lived from the inside. It misses out on perhaps the most significant feature of most religions that they encourage their members to choose to live a disciplined, restricted, rule-bound, and desire-abnegating life. A religious life is not just a life of personal and whimsical attachment to a personal god but one in which one submits to his commands and lives obediently by them. This may be a nightmare for a standard liberal but gets the constitutive features of most religions rather better than liberal secularism does. Third, by interpreting separation as exclusion, it betrays its own sectarianism; it can live comfortably with liberal, protestantized, individualized, and privatized religions but has no resources to cope with religions that mandate greater public or political presence, or have a strong communal orientation. This group-insensitivity of secularism makes it virtually impossible for it to accommodate community-specific rights and therefore, to protect the rights of religious minorities. In short, while this secularism copes with intra-religious domination, it does not possess resources to deal with inter-religious domination.

Fourth, western secularism is largely a product of protestant ethic and shaped by it. Therefore, its universal pretensions are perhaps its greatest drawback. Moreover, it presupposes a Christian civilization that is easily forgotten because over time, it has silently slid into the background. Christianity allows this self-limitation and much of the world innocently mistakes this rather cunning self-denial for its disappearance.[26] But if this is so, this 'inherently dogmatic' secularism cannot

---

[24] Jeff Spinner-Halev, *Surviving Diversity: Religion and Democratic Citizenship*, Baltimore: Johns Hopkins University Press, 2000, pp. 150–6.

[25] Ibid., p. 155.

[26] Connolly, *Why I Am Not a Secularist*, p. 24.

coexist innocently with other religions.[27] Given the enormous power of the state, it must try to shape and transform them—a clear instance of illegitimate influence, if not outright violence. Thus, with all its claims of leaving religions alone, of granting religions liberty, this secularism is hostile to non-liberal, non-protestant believers.[28] Overall, it would not be wrong to say that western secularisms force upon us a choice between active hostility or benign indifference. Fifth, liberal secularism relies excessively on a rationalist conception of reason that imposes unfair limits on the manner in which issues are to be brought in the public domain. Some issues are constitutively emotive; others become emotive because they are articulated by people who are not always trained to be rational in the way liberals mandate.[29] In short, the model of moral reasoning typical of secularism is context-insensitive, theoreticist, absolutist (non-comparative), enjoining us to think in terms of this or that, and too heavily reliant on monolithic ideas or values considered to be true, or superior, or wholly non-negotiable.

These are powerful critiques with some of which I agree. But, I also have serious disagreement with the conclusion that they rebut secularism altogether. I agree that in our imagination of social and public life, greater space must be given to non-liberal religions; such ways of life have moral integrity that liberal secularism frequently fails to realize. Yet, in our effort to accommodate such religions, we cannot ignore that these very religions also continue to be a source of severe oppression and exclusion. States that align with these religions frequently condone these morally objectionable practices. In Pakistan, the religiously sanctioned law of evidence, *Qanoon-e-Shahadat*, holds on par the evidence of two women or two non-Muslims with that of a single male Muslim, thereby establishing the intrinsic superiority of Muslim men over women and minorities and contravening the fundamental principle of equality.[30] In Hinduism, religiously sanctioned customs related to purity and pollution, for example, the bar on the entry of menstruating women in several temples in India, continues to exclude women from the affairs of their own religion and perpetuate an institutionalized system of subordination of women. This violation

[27] Keane, 'Secularism?', p. 14; Madan, 'Secularism in Its Place', in Bhargava (ed.), *Secularism and Its Critics*, p. 298.

[28] Philip Hamburger, *Separation of Church and State*, Cambridge: Harvard University Press, 2002, pp. 193–251.

[29] Connolly, *Why I Am Not a Secularist*, p. 27.

[30] Malik, *Religious Minorities in Pakistan*, p. 18.

of the religious rights of women severely compromises the secular character of the Indian state.

What does all this show? It demonstrates three things. First, that we must be sensitive simultaneously to the moral integrity of liberal and non-liberal religious ways of living as well as to religion-based oppression and exclusions. Second, states that are strongly aligned to religions may be sensitive to the moral integrity of non-liberal religions but not always to their oppressions. Third, that a policy of non-interference (mutual exclusion), typical of liberal secularism, is self-defeating. In short, a conception of secularism needs to be worked out that, without ignoring liberal values, goes beyond them, and does justice to both dimensions referred to earlier. Do we have a version of secularism that escapes some of these critiques and imaginatively opens up new possibilities of expanding our horizon. I believe such a model was developed in the sub-continent. It is neither wholly Christian nor western. It meets the secularist objection to non-secular states and the religious objection to some forms of secular states.

INDIAN SECULARISM

Seven features of Indian secularism make it distinctive.[31] First, its multi-value character. Indian secularism more explicitly registers its ties with values forgotten by western conceptions—for example, peace between communities—and interprets liberty and equality both individualistically and non-individualistically. It has a place not only for rights of individuals to profess their religious beliefs but the right of religious communities to establish and maintain educational institutions crucial for the survival and sustenance of their religious traditions. Second, because it was born in a deeply multi-religious society, it is concerned as much with inter-religious domination as it is with intra-religious domination. Although community-specific political rights (special representation rights for religious minorities such as Muslims) were withheld for contextual reasons, the conceptual space for it is present within the model. Third, it is committed to the idea of principled distance, poles apart from one-sided exclusion, mutual exclusion, and strict neutrality or equidistance. Fourth, it admits a distinction between depublicization and depoliticization as well between different kinds of depoliticization. Because it is not hostile to the public presence of religion, it does not aim to depublicize it. It accepts the importance of

[31] Also see Bhargava (ed.), *Secularism and Its Critics*.

one form of depoliticization of religion, namely, the first- and second-level disconnection of state from religion but the third-level depoliticization of religion is accepted on purely contextual grounds.

Fifth, it is marked by a unique combination of active hostility to some aspects of religion (a ban on unsociability and a commitment to make religiously grounded personal laws more gender-just), with active respect for its other dimensions (religious groups are officially recognized, state-aid is available non-preferentially to educational institutions run by religious communities, no blanket exclusion of religion as mandated by western liberalism). This is a direct consequence of its commitment to multiple values and principled distance. The Indian model accepts the view that critique is consistent with respect, that one does have to choose between hostility and respectful indifference. In this sense, it inherits the tradition of the great Indian religious reformers who tried to change their religions precisely because they meant so much to them. Sixth, it is committed to a different model of moral reasoning that is highly contextual and opens up the possibility of different societies working out their own secularisms. In short, it opens out the possibility of multiple secularisms. Seventh, it breaks out of the rigid interpretative grid that divides our social world into the western modern and traditional, indigenous non-western. Indian secularism is modern but departs significantly from mainstream conceptions of western secularism.[32]

Principled Distance

Let me further elucidate two of its features: the idea of principled distance and its contextual character. As seen earlier, for mainstream western secularisms, separation means mutual or one-sided exclusion. The idea of principled distance unpacks the metaphor of separation differently. It accepts a disconnection between state and religion at the level of ends and institutions but does not make a fetish of it at the third level of policy and law (this distinguishes it from all other models of secularism, moral and amoral that disconnect state and religion at this third level). How else can it be in a society where religion frames some of its deepest interests? Recall that political secularism is an ethic whose concerns relating to religion are similar to theories that oppose unjust restrictions on freedom, morally indefensible inequalities,

---

[32] On this point, also see Marc Galanter, 'Secularism, East and West', in Bhargava (ed.), *Secularism and Its Critics*, pp. 234–67.

inter-communal domination, and exploitation. Yet, a secularism based on principled distance is not committed to the mainstream enlightenment idea of religion. It accepts that humans have an interest in relating to something beyond themselves, including god, and that this manifests itself as individual belief and feeling as well as social practice in the public domain. It also accepts that religion is a cumulative tradition[33] as well as a source of people's identities. But it insists that even if turned out that god exists and that one religion is true and others false, then this does not give the 'true' doctrine or religion the right to force it down the throats of others who do not believe it. Nor does it give a ground for discrimination in the equal distribution of liberties and other valuable resources.

Similarly, a secularism based on principle distance accepts that religion may not have special public significance antecedently written into and defining the very character of the state or the nation, but it does not follow from this that it has no public significance at all. Sometimes, on some versions of it, the wall of separation thesis assumes precisely that. As long as religion is publicly significant, a democratic state simply has to take it into account. Indeed, institutions of religion may influence individuals as long as they do so through the same process, by access to the same resources as anyone, and without undue advantage or unduly exploiting the fears and vulnerabilities that frequently accompany people in their experience of the religious.

But, what precisely is principled distance? The policy of principled distance entails a flexible approach on the question of inclusion/exclusion of religion and the engagement/disengagement of the state, which at the third level of law and policy depends on the context, nature, or current state of relevant religions. This engagement must be governed by principles undergirding a secular state, that is, principles that flow from a commitment to the values mentioned earlier. This means that religion may intervene in the affairs of the state if such intervention promotes freedom, equality, or any other value integral to secularism. For example, citizens may support a coercive law of the state grounded purely in a religious rationale, if this law is compatible with freedom or equality. Equally, the state may engage with religion or disengage from it, engage positively or negatively, but it does so depending entirely on whether or not these values are promoted or undermined.

---

[33] Wilfred Cantwell Smith, *The Meaning and End of Religion*, Minneapolis: First Fortress Press, 1991, pp. 154–69.

Principled distance is different from strict neutrality, it is the stance for which the state may help or hinder all religions to an equal degree and in the same manner, that if it intervenes in one religion, it must also do so in others. Rather, it rests upon a distinction explicitly drawn by the American philosopher, Ronald Dworkin, between equal treatment and treating everyone as an equal.[34] The principle of equal treatment, in the relevant political sense, requires that the state treat all its citizens equally in the relevant respect, for example, in the distribution of resources or opportunity. On the other hand, the principle of treating people as equals entails that every person or group is treated with equal concern and respect. This second principle may sometimes require equal treatment, say, equal distribution of resources but it may also occasionally dictate unequal treatment. Treating people or groups as equals is entirely consistent with differential treatment.

What kind of treatment do I have in mind? First, religious groups have sought exemptions from practices in which states intervene by promulgating a law to be applied neutrally to the rest of society. This demand for non-interference is made on the ground either that the law requires them to do things not permitted by their religion or prevents them from doing acts mandated by it. For example, Sikhs demand exemptions from mandatory helmet laws and from police dress codes to accommodate religiously required turbans. Elsewhere, Jews seek exemptions from Air force regulations to accommodate their yarmulkes. Muslims women and girls demand that the state not interfere in their religiously required *chador*. Principled distance allows then that a practice that is banned or regulated in one culture may be permitted in the minority culture because of the distinctive status and meaning it has for its members. For many republican or liberal theories this is a problem because of their simple, some what absolutist morality that gives overwhelming importance to one value, particularly to equal treatment or equal liberty.

Religious groups may demand that the state refrain from interference in their practices but they may equally demand that the state interfere in such a way as to give them special assistance so that these groups are also able to secure what other groups are able to routinely get by virtue of their social dominance in the political community. It may grant authority to religious officials to perform legally binding

---

[34] Ronald Dworkin, 'Liberalism', in Stuart Hampshire (ed.), *Public and Private Morality*, Cambridge: Cambridge University Press, 1978, p. 125.

marriages, to have their own rules or methods of obtaining a divorce, its rules about relations between ex-husband and ex-wife, its way of defining a will or its laws about post-mortem allocation of property, arbitration of civil disputes, and even its method of establishment of property rights.

However, principled distance does not merely allow special exemptions or dispensations. Considering the historical and social condition of all relevant religions, it may require state intervention in some religions more than in others. For example, if the aim of the state is to advance social equality, then this may require that the state interferes negatively in caste-ridden Hinduism more than, say, Islam or Christianity. However, if a diversity-driven religious liberty is the value to be advanced by the state, then it may have to intervene in Christianity and Islam more than in Hinduism. If this is so, the state can neither strictly exclude considerations emanating from religion nor keep strict neutrality with respect to religion. It cannot antecedently decide that it will always refrain from interfering in religions or that it will interfere in each equally. Indeed, it may not relate to every religion in society in exactly the same way, or intervene in each religion to the same degree or in the same manner. All it must ensure is that the relationship between the state and religions is guided by non-sectarian motives consistent with some values and principles.

Contextual Secularism

A context-sensitive secularism, one based on the idea of principled distance, is what I call contextual secularism. Contextual secularism is contextual not only because it captures the idea that the precise form and content of secularism will vary from one context to another and from place to place, but also that it embodies a certain model of contextual moral reasoning. This it does because of its character as a multi-value doctrine. To accept that secularism is a multi-value doctrine is to acknowledge that its constitutive values may come into conflict with one another. Some degree of internal discord and therefore, a fair amount of instability is an integral part of contextual secularism. For this reason, it forever requires fresh interpretations, contextual judgements, and attempts at reconciliation and compromise. No general a priori rule of resolving these conflicts exist; no easy lexical order, no pre-existing hierarchy among values or laws that enables us to decide that, no matter what the context, a particular value must override everything else. For example, the conflict between individual rights and group rights cannot always be adjudicated by a recourse to some general and abstract principle. Rather it can only be settled case by case and may require a fine balancing of competing claims. The eventual outcome may not be wholly satisfactory to either but still be reasonably satisfactory to both. Multi-value doctrines such as secularism encourage accommodation—not the giving up of one value for the sake of another but rather their reconciliation and possible harmonization, that is, to make each work without changing the basic content of apparently incompatible concepts and values.

This endeavour to make concepts, viewpoints, and values work simultaneously does not amount to a morally objectionable compromise. This is so because nothing of importance is being given up for the sake of a less significant thing, one without value or even with negative value. Rather, what is pursued is a mutually agreed middle way that combines elements from two or more equally valuable entities. The roots of such attempts at reconciliation and accommodation lie in a lack of dogmatism, in a willingness to experiment, to think at different levels and in separate spheres, and in a readiness to take decisions on a provisional basis. It captures a way of thinking characterized by the following dictum: 'why look at things in terms of this or that, why not try to have both this and that'.[35] In this way of thinking, it is recognized that though we may currently be unable to secure the best of both values and therefore, be forced to settle for a watered-down version of each, we must continue to have an abiding commitment to search for a transcendence of this second best condition. Two things follow from the abovementioned. First, that the practice of secularism requires a different model of moral reasoning than the one that straightjackets our moral understanding in the form of well-delineated, explicitly stated rules.[36] Second, that secularism is an ethically sensitive negotiated settlement between diverse groups and divergent values.

IS SECULARISM A CHRISTIAN AND WESTERN DOCTRINE?
What then of the claim that secularism is a Christian, western doctrine and therefore, is unable to adapt itself easily to the cultural conditions of, say, India, infused as they are by religions that grew in the soil of the sub-continent. This necessary link between secularism and Christianity

[35] Granville Austin, *The Indian Constitution: Cornerstone of a Nation*, New Delhi: Oxford University Press, 1972, p. 318.

[36] Charles Taylor, 'Justice after Virtue', in John Horton and Susan Mendus (eds), *After MacIntyre*, Oxford: Polity Press, 1994, pp. 16–43.

is exaggerated, if not entirely mistaken. It is true that the institutional separation of church and state is an internal feature of Christianity and an integral part of western secularisms. But, as we have seen, this church–state disconnection is a necessary but not a sufficient condition for the development of secularism, even in societies with church-based religions. It is clearly not a necessary condition for the development of all forms of secularisms. Moreover, as I have argued, the mutual exclusion of religion and the state is not the defining feature of secularism. The idea of separation can be interpreted differently. Nor are religious integrity, peace, and toleration (interpreted broadly to mean 'live and let live') uniquely Christian values. Most non-Christian civilizations have given significant space to each. Therefore, none of them are exclusively Christian. It follows that, even though we find in Christian writings some of the clearest and most systematic articulation of this doctrine, the western conception of secularism is not exclusively Christian.

All right, one might say, secularism is not just a Christian doctrine, but is it not western? The answer to this question is both yes and no. Up to a point, it is certainly a western idea. More specifically, as a clearly articulated doctrine, it has distinct western origins. Although elements that constitute secularism assume different cultural forms and are found in several civilizations, one cannot deny that the idea of the secular first achieved self-consciousness and was properly theorized in the West. One might then say that the middle history of secularism is almost entirely dominated by western societies. However, the same cannot be said of its later history. Nationalism and democracy arrived in much of the West after the settlement of religious conflicts, in societies that had been more or less religiously homogenized (with the exception of the Jews, of course, who continued to face persistent persecution). The absence of deep religious diversity and conflict meant that issues of citizenship could be addressed almost entirely disregarding religious context; the important issue of community-specific rights to religious groups could be wholly ignored. This had a decisive bearing on the western conception of secularism. However, for non-western societies such as India, the case is different. Both national and democratic agendas in countries such as India had to face issues raised by deep religious difference and diversity. In India, nationalism had to choose between the religious and the secular. Similarly, the distribution of active citizenship rights could not be conceived or accomplished by ignoring religion. It could be done either by actively disregarding religion (as in all political rights) or by developing a complex attitude to it, as in the case of cultural rights, where it had to balance claims of individual autonomy with those of community obligations, and claims of the necessity of keeping religion 'private' with their inescapable, often valuable presence in the public. By doing so, Indian secularism never completely annulled particular religious identities.

In addressing these complex issues, the idea of the political secularism was taken further than had been evolved in the West. The later history of secularism is more non-western than western. Mainstream theories or ideologies in modern, western societies take little notice of features constitutive of the Indian model or have forgotten them. Hence, they are struggling to deal with the post-colonial religious diversity of their societies. To discover its own rich and complex structure, the dominant model of western secularism can either look backward, to its own past or else look sideways, at Indian secularism that mirrors not only the past of secularism but, in a way, also its future. It certainly needs to closely examine and properly theorize its own evolving practices in response to problems of religious diversity. Doing so will certainly benefit the secularisms of many western societies. For example, French secularism needs to look beyond its own conceptions of laicite in order to take into account its own multicultural and multi-religious reality. It cannot continue to take refuge in claims of exceptionalism. A good hard look at Indian secularism could also change the self-understanding of other western secularisms.

5

The Multicultural Framework*

A number of interrelated themes are put together by the term 'multi-culturalism': the need to have a stable identity, the contribution of cultural communities to the fulfilment of this need and the link between identity and recognition, the importance of cultural belonging, and the desire to maintain difference. The modest objective of this essay is to formulate an analytical framework with which to understand these themes of multiculturalism. Some preliminary remarks are in order, however. For a start, a distinction needs to be made between the fact and the value of multiculturalism. As a fact, multiculturalism simply registers the presence of many cultures. Its abstract enumerative character, its indefinite quality, and surface, decontextualized form makes it amenable to different interpretations, open to different ideological incarnations, with applicability across space and time. Hence, the possibility of an Indian multiculturalism. As value, multiculturalism morally endorses the presence of many cultures, even perhaps celebrates them. Put simply, multiculturalism as fact and value challenges the fact and value of a single-culture society.

Current interest in multiculturalism can hardly be understood without the acknowledgement of a shift in background theoretical conditions, a large intellectual move away from the mainstream tradition of enlightenment political philosophy. For much of the twentieth century,

* A version of this paper was first presented as part of introductory remarks at a conference on multiculturalism held in Kasauli in March 1995. It was subsequently published as 'Introducing Multiculturalism', in Rajeev Bhargava, Amiya Kumar Bagchi, and R. Sudarshan (eds), *Multiculturalism, Liberalism and Democracy*, New Delhi: Oxford University Press, 1999, pp. 1–57.

Anglo-Saxon political theory not only emphasized a particular set of ethical values but also interpreted them in a specific way. It concerned itself with freedom understood as a condition without constraints on meaningful choices and—what is widely believed to be a necessary condition of free life—with equality or justice in the distribution of material resources. These values were then given a pronounced individualist inflection: the primary unit of analysis in theories of distributive justice is the individual conceived in abstraction from the communities to which he belongs; the point underlying equality of material resources is to improve the well-being of people, where well-being too is understood from an individualist point of view. Finally, the unit of decision making is believed to be the individual, not the group.

This appears to have changed over the last two decades. First, communitarian writing emphasized the need to have a stable identity and explicitly registered the relevance of cultural communities to the formation of identities. Second, that a culture-relative self-esteem matters to people as much as the fulfilment of material needs was belatedly recognized. Equally significant was the recognition that the sense of identity and self-worth of persons derives from cultures that they not only know well but can and may call their own. Therefore, not culture in general, rather a *particular* culture matters to people. This foregrounds issues of cultural belonging as well as the interest people have in ensuring the survival of particular cultures, even when other cultures may suffice. Third, philosophers such as Charles Taylor, drawing upon the work of Hegel, pointed out that identity and self-worth are dialogic notions, and rich empirical work in sociology demonstrated that well-delineated identities as well as well-demarcated cultural communities to which these identities are linked, are formed through dialogic interaction and struggle. A further implication of such work is this: if cultural particularity is pervasive and valuable, and if the number of political communities can never be the same as the number of cultural communities, then it is neither feasible nor desirable to have uni-cultural polities. In short, it is imperative to design multicultural polities. In what follows, I try to amplify some of these points.

IDENTITY AND COMMUNITY

Identity is an overused term in both ordinary discourse and social science. But, what the term refers to is of fundamental importance to human beings, particularly under conditions of modernity. Discourses on identity try to answer the question: who am I? We can approach this question from many vantage points. One way of answering it is this: I am what I understand myself to be. This self-understanding, in turn, is conceptually dependent on the beliefs and desires with which I identity, that I call my own. My identity, the understanding I have of myself, is crucially dependent on the content of my beliefs and desires.

But surely, all my beliefs and desires are not identity constituting. I believe that if it is raining, there must be clouds in the sky. This tells me something about myself, namely, that I have the capacity for logical reasoning but, by itself, it would be odd to claim that it is this capacity which lends me my identity. To uphold this claim, I must further establish that of the many capacities that I have, for instance, the capacity to breathe, drink water, eat food, sleep, play football, swim, and so on, it is the capacity for logical reasoning that I really and enduringly value. I would die if I lost my capacity to breathe or drink water and I might be unhappy if I forgot how to play football but I would be hugely diminished in my own eyes and would be virtually lost in the world if I lost the capacity to reason. If I strongly value logical reasoning and the exercise of this capacity gave meaning to my life, I would lose what anchored me to the world.

The point I am making has already been most illuminatingly formulated by Charles Taylor, who argues that a person cannot have an identity in the absence of qualitative distinctions between the worth of different desires and beliefs because only such distinctions furnish the criterion of relevance constitutive of identity.[1] I call these identity-constituting beliefs and desires. Since such beliefs and desires are formed within an enduring framework, not to possess such a framework is to fail to have an identity. What is relevant to a person's identity is what he values strongly. The identity of a person is defined not by any odd set of beliefs but only those held firmly, with good reason, and by values that cannot be reduced to mere desires, are judged by him or her to be more important than unevaluated desires. Only those beliefs and desires that a person strongly values, and finds worthy, are crucial to his or her identity.

A framework provides a person with a springboard from which to aspire to do or be something. This aspiration to be moved by something regarded as valuable is central to the notion of commitment. To strive for some value, no matter how unattainable, is to be deeply engaged

---

[1] See Charles Taylor, *Sources of the Self*, Cambridge: Cambridge University Press, 1989.

with it, to have entrusted oneself to it. It is to constantly judge our desires and to hope to guide our actions by standards set by these values. It is to want our lives to be directed by them. Hence, the tie between commitment and identity. Indeed, the identity of a person is defined by the commitments and identifications which provide the frame within which he or she tries to determine, from case to case, what is good or valuable, what ought to be done, what he or she endorses or opposes. In other words, it is the horizon within which a person is capable of taking a stand.[2] No wonder that the identity of most of human beings is defined in terms of religion or the ethical framework of one's culture or intellectual perspective.

Two points are worth noting. First, to identify with strongly held and valued beliefs and desires is to identify with something which is ineluctably social, necessarily shared with others. A human individual recognizes his identity in socially defined terms. Indeed, since these desires and beliefs emerge through interaction with others, it might be legitimate to assert that the identity of a person is largely a matter of social construction. This is true as much for a manufactured identity as for an identity engendered by the more gentle, almost invisible process of social interaction.

Second, beliefs and desires have two modes of existence; they exist as mental representations of which individuals are conscious but also directly in action.[3] Much of our knowledge of such wants, and of beliefs about how to fulfil them, is neither theoretical nor stored in a propositional form. Indeed, it is frequently not even represented in our consciousness. All we possess is a practical sense of these beliefs and desires and this sense is enough to guide our behaviour. Furthermore, some beliefs and desires are embedded not exclusively in the behaviour of one individual but rather in an interlocking behavioural system of several individuals at once. When this happens, we obtain what can be called a social practice.[4] A social practice consists of actions of several individuals whose individuating descriptions are social and precisely because they do not exist as internal mental states, are never immediately available to agents. Many of our identity-constituting beliefs and desires exist directly embedded in such social practices and therefore, are irreducibly collective. I propose to define 'community' as a network of

[2] Ibid., p. 27.
[3] On this, see Rajeev Bhargava, *Individualism in Social Science*, Oxford: Clarendon Press, 1992, p. 209.
[4] Ibid., pp. 205–12.

such practices in which identity-constituting beliefs and purposes are embedded. It follows that the identity of a person is directly embedded in particular communities and its knowledge is not fully present in the person's consciousness. The link between the identity of a person and his or her community lies deep and is not entirely explicit. I suspect this explains why issues of identity sometimes appear not to matter at all, and at other times, nothing matters more than them; the very existence of a person hinges on such issues.

IRREDUCIBLY DIFFERENT COLLECTIVE GOALS

Several implications emerge from the brief discussion of identity, culture, and community. One implication is the importance of irreducibly collective goals. The objective of a more equitable distribution of some collective goods such as security, prosperity, and justice can be met by policies grounded in individualist political theory. However, claims to the equal right for the expression of cultural particularity, or to national independence, or even to equal treatment in the international arena cannot be easily accommodated by them.[5] From different perspectives, both Will Kymlicka and Charles Taylor make this point. Kymlicka argues that minority rights cannot be subsumed under the category of human rights. 'The theory of rights present in modern constitutionalism is individualistically construed in that the rights protect the vulnerable integrity of legal subjects who are in every case individuals.'[6] Their 'only focus remains the individual legal person.' Taylor takes the example from the Canadian province of Quebec.[7] To safeguard its form of life from threat by Anglo-Saxon majority culture, the Francophone group has regulations forbidding the French-speaking population and immigrants to send their children to English language schools. This, for Taylor, shows how the promotion of the collective goal conflicts with the theory of individual rights. Taylor then provides an alternative that, under certain conditions, permits the restriction of rights solely in order to maintain the integrity of endangered forms

[5] For an illuminating discussion of some of these issues, see Jurgen Habermas, 'Struggles for Recognition in the Democratic Constitutional State', in Amy Gutmann (ed.), *Multiculturalism*, New Jersey: Princeton University Press, 1994, pp. 107–48.

[6] See Will Kymlicka, *Liberalism, Community and Culture*, Oxford: Clarendon, 1989.

[7] Charles Taylor, 'The Politics of Recognition', in Gutmann (ed.), *Multiculturalism*, pp. 25–74.

of cultural life. It is because of its inability to take such matters into account that liberal individualism simply evades issues of culture and community.

Another implication of the important point about the social construction of identity is also effectively drawn by Charles Taylor in a characteristically Hegelian manner.[8] He argues that identities are formed in a continuing dialogue and struggle with significant others. People know who they really are only through contact with and by confirmation and endorsement by others. Self-knowledge is mediated by others and therefore, involves not just cognition but *recognition*. To have an identity, to stabilize a sense of who one is, requires that significant others also properly see what we see in ourselves. This dialogical model of the formation and continual reinforcement of identity holds true for the wider social universe as well as for the narrower public sphere within it. It is in this second domain that a more clearly defined politics of recognition is found. People want their identities and significant attributes of their community to be not merely socially acknowledged but publicly endorsed and respected. Such recognition in the public arena may take various forms. For example, groups may be accorded special rights to express their cultural particularity, be given a voice in the political process by special representation rights, may procure special subsidies from the state, or, if concentrated within a particular territory, may even earn self-government rights and therefore, considerable political autonomy.

Keeping this in mind, multiculturalism embodies the politics of collective goals as well as a politics of difference. This is sometimes believed to necessitate the politicization of group identities and the abandonment or at least a modification of the ideal of equal treatment under common laws. Every law of the land need not be followed by all cultural groups. The demand for a strictly uniform set of laws may unfairly impose great burdens on some groups. It may, for example, be unfair to expect Sikhs to abandon their turbans in order to meet the requirements of a uniform dress code, say, in the army. Fair treatment entails that a slightly different dress code be acceptable if their religion so requires. Once again, it hasn't exactly helped western political theory to have operated with an idealized model of the polis in which fellow citizens share a common descent, language, and culture.[9] This

[8] Ibid., pp. 32–3.

[9] Will Kymlicka, *Multicultural Citizenship*, Oxford: Clarendon Press, 1995, p. 2.

has only resulted in silence on minority rights, cultural differences and recognition.

FORMS OF MULTICULTURALISM

It is important to understand the current context within which such demands for political recognition are made. To emphasize this context, it helps to situate this issue in what I call the broader dialectic of multiculturalism. The first moment in this dialectic is the moment of *particularized hierarchy*, characterized by a dominant community to which other communities are subordinate. Here, we have two or more communities in a hierarchical relation, a dominant community to which other communities are subordinate. Differences between cultural communities are maintained but only within this relation of subordination. In short, the only way in which difference is sustained is by treating communities unequally. The second moment may be called the moment of *universalistic equality*. The only way to sustain equality here is to deny the significance of cultural difference. People are equal because their membership in a cultural community is deemed inconsequential. Rather, what matters is their status as individuals and their membership in an abstracted political community. The third moment may be called the moment of *particularized equality*. Here people are different but equal. Membership in a particular cultural group is important but so is the relationship of equality among different cultural communities.

With the context unravelled, it is easy to situate current demands for political recognition as belonging clearly to the moment of particularized equality rather than particularized hierarchy. This means that recognition must be made available to everyone within society. No community and therefore, no member of it can be subordinate to other communities or its members. Recent demands for a multicultural society constitute a plea for *egalitarian multiculturalism*. Second, neither class nor level of achievement is the basis of recognition but rather one's overall way of life, a culture. Any politics that requires the exclusion of cultural identity as a condition for membership or recognition is ruled out. A demand to renounce cultural identity as a condition for free and equal citizenship is no longer viable.

Within egalitarian multiculturalism, it is useful to distinguish between liberal and authoritarian forms of it. Liberal multiculturalism is liberal because equal recognition of cultural groups must be compatible with requirements of basic individual liberties and perhaps, with even individual autonomy. Authoritarian multiculturalism affirms equal recognition of all cultural groups, including the ones that violate freedom of individuals. A good example of authoritarian multiculturalism comes from many successor states of old empires. On examining the history of empires, it is found that different cultural groups were brought together by imperial powers and divided for more effective political domination.[10] Each group was granted considerable autonomy in exchange for their acceptance of imperial hegemony. Such was the case in the Ottoman empire that developed the millet system. Groups within the system were given equal legal standing, every individual was required to identify himself with one of these and submit to its laws pertaining to marriage, divorce, inheritance, and so on. Roughly the same is true of the British empire in India where Hindus, Muslims, Parsis, and Christians were given equal legal status and every individual gradually felt compelled to identify with one of these communities and to comply with their separate laws. Mahmood Mamdani provides us with another example of authoritarian multiculturalism by showing how the construction of illiberal cultural communities was part of the system of Apartheid in South Africa.[11]

LEVELS OF MULTICULTURALISM

In the preceding sections, I claimed that multiculturalism brings together a set of issues that relate to the need for community, a sense of belonging to it, the importance of a secure sense of identity, of status and recognition, of particularity, and the need to recognize and maintain difference with others. The concerns of this framework—the

[10] On this, see M. Walzer, 'Education, Democratic Citizenship and Multiculturalism', in Yael Tamir (ed.), *Democratic Education in a Multicultural State*, Oxford: Blackwell, 1995, pp. 23–31.

[11] See Mahmood Mamdani, 'Civil Society and Community: Reflections on the African Experience', in Bhargava, Bagchi, and Sudarshan (eds), *Multiculturalism, Liberalism and Democracy*, pp. 348–63. Mamdani makes the extremely relevant point that prolonged colonial rule has set up an opposition between liberal individualism and some version of republicanism on the one hand and an authoritarian, illiberal multiculturalism on the other, neither of which yields social justice. The modernist language of rights has come to be associated with dominant groups and the language of communitarianism with internal authoritarianism that valourizes customary force. Thus, there is a breach between rights and community on the one hand and social justice on the other. Mamdani argues, therefore, for the sublimation of both modernist rights discourse and communitarian perspectives.

framework of identity and cultural particularity—smell different from issues raised within another framework that dominated mainstream political theory since the Second World War, that is, the framework of material welfare and a cultural universalism that underscored the importance of individual choice in one's profession, relationships, lifestyle, and basic moral convictions, the compulsion of a more equitable distribution of material resources and the need to belong to a wider social and political universe where neither one's class or status nor cultural inheritance was a source of advantage or disadvantage. Proponents of these broad frameworks (let me call them the multiculturalist (M) framework and the abstract universalist (AU) framework, respectively) are suspicious of one another and frequently vie for the same space.

My own view is that the two frameworks are not irretrievably opposed. Both are concerned with questions of power and hegemony as well as with questions of dignity. Whereas one concentrates on direct political domination and economic exploitation, the other focuses on the more subtle ways in which disabilities and inadequacies, loss of self-esteem and self-confidence develop within individuals and groups. In real life situations, both are frequently intertwined. Consider a system in which non-market private power has been abolished. Even in such societies, the initial conditions of inequality of wealth and access to education can permanently deny large groups of people their right to dignity as human beings, and the right to their own culture as a sign of that dignity.[12] It remains true, however, that the two frameworks cannot easily be reconciled by a subsumption of one by the other. Issues grouped under multiculturalism cannot be incorporated without remainder into the domain of social justice as conceived by the first framework. The two can be reconciled but only after they have evolved in a direction away from how they are currently conceived and formulated.

For the moment, I wish to emphasize that both frameworks operate at three distinct levels. There is first the international level, either

---

[12] Thus, the USA had to enact the Homestead Act in order to see that land belonged to cultivating farmers rather than rentier landlords, and make primary education compulsory in order to ensure that people had a certain minimum command over information regarding their rights in a republic. Even then, the USA has not been able to accord equality of opportunity to the Afro-Americans who are discriminated on the basis of non-market stigmata, stigmata which are ineradicably associated with the accident of birth. I am grateful to Professor Amiya Kumar Bagchi for drawing my attention to this point.

outside national boundaries or across them. Questions of economic justice, political domination, and sovereignty can arise within the global order, between nation-states. Territories that have turned into colonies of an empire are denuded of wealth and resources and the collective sovereignty of distinct peoples is severely curtailed. This results in forms of injustice and severe deprivation of material well-being. Likewise, dominant cultures generate stereotypes of the dominated which they get their victims to accept and that results in the loss of confidence and pervasive self-images of inferiority. People then lose respect for their own cultures and hasten the progress of homogenization induced by dominant cultures. At this level, multiculturalism challenges cultural imperialism and the cultural hegemony of the West.

The second level operates at the site of the nation-state and is concerned vitally with its basic structure. At this level, the AU-framework allows for questions such as: what is the class character of the nation-state? The M-framework enables us to ask: how relevant is religion, language, or culture to the imagination of the nation and to the determination of the criterion of citizenship? The principal issue here is whether the nation is legitimated by the ideology of an exclusionary ethno-nationalism or else by an inclusive nationalism. At this level, multiculturalism is the view which directly challenges ethno-nationalism by conceiving the nation-state as formed out of, and giving ample space to, diverse cultural groups. Perhaps it also challenges weaker versions of ethno-nationalism that enjoin the state to uphold the culture of the majority, by making its language the language of public affairs, celebrating its holidays, and teaching only the history of the majority. Multiculturalism opposes states whose only objective is the survival and well-being of the dominant cultural group.

Finally, there remains a third level operating at sites within the nation-state. At this level, the AU-framework addresses inter-class issues. Within M-framework, we ask, for example, how are minority groups to be treated? Must they be given special privilege and immunity and on what grounds? Should they be given special representation rights in the political arena? Should state subsidy be given for small but embattled cultures and if yes, what is the best justification for it? Strong multiculturalism gives an affirmative answer to these questions. Weak multiculturalism reflects the institutional history of immigrant societies. Here, all groups, including the first that displaces or subordinates the indigenous population, have an immigrant status. Over time the state is forced into a kind of neutrality, which is first expressed in religious toleration and secularism and then in a slow disengagement from the national history and cultural style of the first immigrants. Such disengagement is no doubt partial and incomplete but, in principle, each immigrant culture must sustain itself without mandatory support from the state which celebrates its own history and teaches values of toleration, neutrality, and mutual respect but not the particular values of any one group.[13]

A CHALLENGE TO MULTICULTURALISM

The delineated approach postulates a rather straightforward link between issues of identity and the domain of particular cultures. It also assumes that the identity of a person corresponds to a particular culture and that such cultures are wholes with easily discernible boundaries. Differences in identity therefore correspond to differences in clearly identifiable and mutually distinct cultures. It further assumes that cultural communities are homogeneous and cultural identities distinct and extremely well demarcated. Each of these assumptions can be questioned. For example, it is doubtful if we can speak of cultures as neatly separated, internally coherent wholes. Cultures, in fact, may be more like clusters of heterogeneous elements with varying origins.[14] A similar point is made by Shail Mayaram, who argues that existing models of multiculturalism are not only insensitive to internal differentiation within groups but also to the fluid, criss-crossing and overlapping nature of identities, at least in many non-western societies.[15] Western models of multiculturalism are anti-syncretic, she claims, because they are unable to grasp the simultaneity of or mobility within different

[13] On the discussion of this issue, see M. Walzer, 'Education, Democratic Citizenship and Multiculturalism', in Tamir (ed.), *Democratic Education in a Multicultural State*, p. 24.

[14] It does not follow that cultural differences do not exist but they are more like 'differences within climatic regions or ecosystems than like the frontiers drawn with a pen between nation-states.' See Steven Lukes, 'Moral Diversity and Relativism', in Yael Tamir (ed.), *Multiculturalism and Education*, Oxford and Cambridge: Wiley Blackwell, 1995, pp. 15–22. Nonetheless, such perceptions are fairly widespread and sustained in different degrees, at different times and places, by imperialist powers, nationalist movements, populist leaders, and social anthropologists.

[15] See Shail Mayaram, 'Recognizing Whom?: Multiculturalism, Muslim Minority Identity and the Mers', in Bhargava, Bagchi, and Sudarshan (eds), *Multiculturalism, Liberalism and Democracy*, pp. 380–99.

identities, the fact that people can be simultaneously X and Y or move easily from X to Y.

If this is true, then it must surely alter our understanding of multicultural polities. However, suppose that this assumption is dropped or at least modified to mean only that people act frequently on the belief that cultures are separate wholes and that their identity and self-esteem is linked to the culture so conceived, then it might be said that multiculturalism registers this fact about a generally held belief among a very significant number of people. Similarly, the first assumption that social identity is linked in an uncomplicated way with affiliation to a particular culture is questioned, in the American context, by Anthony Appiah; a significant intervention given that the term multiculturalism is very much a North American original.[16] Appiah notes that in the USA, cultural diversity has disappeared over the years. Much greater cultural homogeneity exists there than people generally like to believe. Most Americans share a common language, enjoy the same sport, and watch the same films and television programmes. Indeed, Judaism and Islam too are extraordinarily Americanized. Much of American Islam is as comfortable as Protestantism is with the separation between church and the state. So, if America is not culturally diverse and if, in the last instance, multiculturalism is about cultural diversity, then multiculturalism is irrelevant to the USA. If anything, the term tries to capture an altogether different phenomenon, namely, the presence in the USA of diverse social identities. A large number of people in America, Appiah tells us, insist that they are profoundly shaped by groups to which they belong, that their social identity and membership to these groups is central to who they are. They also demand that these social identities be acknowledged publicly as their authentic identities. It follows that America is marked by the presence of a variety of social identities without an accompanying cultural diversity. Each distinct identity is not necessarily co-related with a distinct culture. A uniform culture generates different identities and anxiety about maintaining such a difference.

If this is so, Appiah concludes, an appeal to cultural difference obscures rather than illuminates the situation of offence and disrespect shown, say, to the blacks because it is not black culture that the racist disdains but blacks. 'Culture is not the problem, and it is not the solution'.

[16] Anthony Appiah, 'The Multicultural Misunderstanding', *The New York Review of Books*, vol. XLIV, no. 15, 9 October 1997, pp. 30–5.

Appiah therefore pleads that 'we should conduct our discussion of education and citizenship, toleration and social peace, without the talk of culture.'[17]

Have the multiculturalists then been barking up the wrong tree? I believe all that Appiah's argument shows is that a politics of cultural difference presupposes a significant degree of cultural homogenization and assimilation but not that the recognition of cultures is 'not part of the solution to the problem'. For a start, Appiah selectively draws evidence of cultural sameness in order to downgrade the possible significance of the fact and value of cultural difference. But, even if his factual claims are entirely true, they leave unanswered the question of how and why the belief in cultural difference is so easily accepted among people who apparently are culturally very similar. Appiah is correct in rejecting the view that sees cultural difference as primordial or essential but not in jettisoning the idea that some difference, no matter what its origin, matters to a significant number of people. It is, of course, true that cultural difference is not natural and transparent but is variously constructed. No doubt it is important to recognize that cultural difference is recovered and invented halfway up a path of cultural interaction among unequals but it doesn't follow that the politics of cultural difference rests on total hoax, that difference is entirely invented, and that the real issues lie elsewhere. The plain fact is that at one level, French and English-speaking Canadians are culturally different and *this* is not altered by showing that *objectively speaking* there exists a larger quantum of cultural sameness. Appiah is right that respect for people's food and music does not guarantee that they be treated with equal dignity. They can still be looked down upon on the ground that in countless relevant respects that matter hugely in society, they are less able or inferior. Such an attitude towards blacks may well exist among, say, the middle class white professionals and even among intellectuals. However, Appiah underestimates the reach of the belief that, despite evidence of cultural sameness and even appreciation of some aspects of the culture of blacks, for example, a respect for their sport and music, current disabilities of blacks are linked in the minds of people to inferior cultural backgrounds. In such an environment, proper education in cultural matters is crucial.

Appiah suggests an additional argument against multiculturalism in which fierce inter-group conflict appears not to be due to cultural

[17] Ibid.

difference. Plenty of social friction exists in America among people who, by objective standards, are culturally quite similar. The various peoples of Bosnia—Serb, Croat, or Muslim—are fairly homogeneous in critical terms as are Hutus and Tutsis in Rwanda. There is something to chew on in Appiah's claim. The saliency of cultural difference can be created by manufacturing cultural conflict. Indeed, cultural difference is brewed by cultural conflict.

It is, of course, true that motivations for the creation of cultural difference have diverse origins. Culture alone cannot generate unbridgeable social distance or prolonged hostility between groups. But, whatever its origin and motivation and, compared to cultural sameness, no matter how small objectively speaking it is, cultural difference is significant in the minds of the relevant agents whose motivations may differ vastly from its direct beneficiaries. It is true that when looked from the outside, Serbs and Croats look strikingly similar; they speak roughly the same language and have shared the same village life for centuries. Urbanization and industrialization have further slimmed down even their religious differences. However, we will do well to remember Freud's perceptive comment that the smaller the real difference between two peoples, the larger it looms in their imagination. This 'narcissism of minor difference' implies that it is precisely when external markers point towards the absence of any major differences that people act as if they are deeply divided.[18] The objective fact of a common past should no doubt result in harmonious coexistence and subjective states of fraternity and mutual respect. What is frequently produced instead is a painful narrative of how two peoples have been at the throat of each other ever since the clock began to tick. Thus, history and collective memory frequently stand irretrievably opposed to each other.

Careful sociological examination shows that cultural homogenization tends to implode, to collapse into a black hole before it comes to fruition; just when complete cultural sameness comes to be reasonably expected, tiny, seemingly insignificant differences are first foregrounded and then consolidated as a conglomerate of major cultural divisions. By a curious dialectic, what comes to be widely accepted and legitimized, that is, cultural differentiation and division is the result of a process of cultural homogenization. The conclusion to be drawn is this: Appiah

---

[18] See M. Ignatieff, *Blood and Belonging*, New York: Farrar, Straus and Giroux, 1993, pp. 21–8.

correctly points to the absence of significant cultural difference in the initial stages of this process—that no primordial cultural differences exist—but he mistakenly concludes that it is not present at the end. The difference created *on the way* is real and cultural, a point brought out clearly by Alok Rai who claims that language was not a conventional, usual site of communal differentiation in northern India.[19] Only from 1880 through to 1930, 'a tragic wedge was inserted into the common language of north India and a great lingua franca was mutilated into two half languages, modern Hindi that belong to Hindus and Urdu that belong to the Muslims'.[20] Rai does not say that a period of supreme harmony existed prior to this differentiation. Rather, he claims 'to finesse something between subverted harmony and primordial difference'.[21] My own view is that once such differentiation and division is created, there is a foreclosing of any reversal. No simple way of undoing it is available anymore—henceforth, culture will remain both a problem and must be at least a part of the solution. Perhaps a failure to recognize this resulted in the demand for Pakistan. A failure to shift focus away from the relative absence of cultural difference at the very beginning of anti-colonial struggle and register its robust presence at the end of it led the leaders of the Indian National Congress (INC) into insisting, Appiah-like, that 'culture is not the problem and it is not the solution'. Perhaps it is the denial, not the affirmation of multiculturalism that results in prolonged, bitter, inter-group conflicts and mutual separation.

PROBLEMS OF MULTICULTURALISM

I have claimed earlier that multiculturalism comes in different guises. It is egalitarian but it can also be hierarchical, is liberal but also authoritarian. So, an advocacy of multiculturalism is not exactly free of problems. Some of these are easily explicated. First, it tends to essentialize and harden identities that generate radical exclusions of people. Second, by its encouragement of cultural particularity, it appears to deepen divisions and undermine the common foundation necessary for a viable society. Third, multiculturalism supports aggregative community power over individual freedom, and by according equal right to oppressive cultures, it corrodes values of liberal democracy.

---

[19] Alok Rai, 'Making a Difference: Hindi, 1880–1930', in Bhargava, Bagchi, and Sudarshan (eds), *Multiculturalism, Liberalism and Democracy*, pp. 248–64.

[20] Ibid., p. 249.

[21] Ibid., p. 250.

The first problem of the hardening of identities, the closure of communities, and the exclusion generated by them invariably draws attention to the notorious issue of communal exclusion. Communalism in India usually brings to mind the spectre of the exclusion of cultural communities defined predominantly by religious markers. But other forms of exclusions exist, for instance, of smaller regions and lower castes. M.S.S. Pandian has discussed this by taking up the question of citizenship and has claimed that the model of citizenship implicit in the official discourse of Indian nationalism appears to embody freedom and equality but in fact and spirit, remains upper caste, male, and Hindu—imposed almost always from above, nearly never negotiated from below.[22]

The problem of oppressive communities is addressed, among others, by Javeed Alam and Shail Mayaram in the case of India.[23] Alam contrasts modern communities in the West with pre-modern communities in India. Communities in the West, he claims, leave private space for individuals as well as a place for their autonomy. Communities in India, on the other hand, act as collective personalities, allowing no autonomy or private space for individuals and forcing into silence any dissent from a community's way of thinking and acting. Indeed, Alam argues such communities do not even allow individuals, particularly women, the right to exit.

Mayaram takes a different track on this issue, arguing that the formation of oppressive communities is a result precisely of western models of multiculturalism that first unleash a process of homogenization and then constitute communities operating with rigid distinctions and binary oppositions. These models, she claims, are also unable to see how individuals and groups can choose ambiguity and double speak. She substantiates her claims by rich data from her fieldwork on the Mer community in Rajasthan, which offers 'multiple choices with respect to sectarian affiliations as also the possibility of switching affiliation'.

[22] M.S.S. Pandian, '"Nation" from Its Margins: Notes on E.V. Ramaswamy's "Impossible" Nation', in Bhargava, Bagchi, and Sudarshan (eds), Multiculturalism, Liberalism and Democracy, pp. 286–307.

[23] See Javeed Alam, 'Public Sphere and Democratic Governance in Contemporary India', in Bhargava, Bagchi, and Sudarshan (eds), Multiculturalism, Liberalism and Democracy, pp. 323–47; and Shail Mayaram, 'Recognizing Whom?' in Bhargava, Bagchi, and Sudarshan (eds), Multiculturalism, Liberalism and Democracy, pp. 380–99.

How can egalitarian multiculturalism be prevented from becoming hierarchical? How must it be prevented from turning authoritarian? How may its liberal content be retained? How can a multicultural society formulate its laws that recognize cultures but prohibit the moral devaluation of individuals and restriction of their autonomy? How can it do so when multiculturalism also requires that proper respect be accorded to those social practices that combine traditional wisdom with oppression of individuals? Can we reconcile the conflict between future generations and the autonomy of individuals living now? It is true that individuals need larger narratives within which to fit their own life plans, with the help of which to tell their life stories. It is equally true that such narratives are provided by collective identities.[24] Given this, do individuals still have the option of choosing which features are part of the collective dimension of their identities? In other words, is there a scope for looser scripts? These are some of the dilemmas that must be faced by a defensible theory of multiculturalism.

Many of these dilemmas have already been noted within political theory, especially in the debate between liberals and communitarians. Attempts have also been made to develop fresh perspectives that resolve them. Let me go over some of that ground and link some issues of that debate with the points raised earlier.[25] To begin with, liberals and communitarians are divided over the core values of a comprehensive public morality. Liberals appear to hold on to freedom and equality as central values. Reasonable communitarians do not deny their importance but believe that individuals cannot pursue their good independent of cultural traditions and social roles. So, one difference is this: liberals value the ability of individuals to take a critical distance from social and cultural practices and if need be, to change them by generating forces within civil society, outside the arena of the state and without the help of state power. Critical distance enables individuals to see possible oppression within cultural practices when it exists and to ensure that existing social practices are not used to licence any abuse, injustice, and cruelty that may be present within the culture of a

---

[24] This way of framing this issue is found in K. Anthony Appiah, 'Identity, Authenticity, Survival', in Gutmann (ed.), *Multiculturalism*, pp. 149–63.

[25] A number of good discussions of these issues exist, including Charles Taylor, 'Cross-purposes: The Liberal–Communitarian Debate', in N. Rosenblum (ed.), *Liberalism and the Moral Life*, Cambridge: Harvard University Press, 1989, pp. 159–82. For a good overview, see J. Hampton, *Political Philosophy*, New Delhi: Oxford University Press, 1998, chapter 5.

community. Communitarians, on the other hand, believe that critical distance is at best one value among several others and cultural belonging matters even when it undermines critical reasoning. When taken to extremes this leads communitarianism, at least so the liberal fears, to turn a blind eye to oppressive cultural practices, and to ignore injustice, even cruelty within cultures. There is an obvious tension here between liberalism and communitarianism so conceived, a conflict between autonomy and cultural belonging, one of the many contentious issues subsumed under the individual versus group debate.

The general implication of what I have said has a bearing on a difference between liberals and communitarians over the nature of the state and the role it is expected to play. For the communitarian, the ideal state must use its power and authority to encourage the continuation and health of cultural traditions and roles through which each person must find her good life. On the whole, the liberal believes in keeping the state out of the pursuit of the good life by an individual. Liberals generally distrust state power, are more optimistic about the potential within voluntary associations in civil society to realize freedom and to maintain self-limiting devices to check exploitation and domination. This may have to do with differences over how they conceive the state. Although this is not always the case, the residual Weberianism in liberals can't but help view the state as an organized monopoly of power and violence, fundamentally authoritarian and therefore, always in need of being checked *from the outside*. Communitarians hold the view that the state is a political community and therefore, do not hesitate to bring about self-limiting mechanisms *inside* the state. They hope to bring controls within the state by the democratic organization of the political community. For political communitarians, reins on the authoritarian content of state power are necessary and can be effected by the presence of people within state structures, which enable them to bring virtually everything into the political process. This differentiates them from the liberal who keeps certain issues altogether out of the political agenda because they are too personal or contentious.

DEMOCRATIC MULTICULTURALISM

Notice immediately the two distinct senses in which the term community is used in the preceding paragraph. For democratically-minded political communitarians, the central issue is the need to shed the traditional liberal fear of the political domain and to bring into it everything, the most personal, even the most contentious. For cultural communitarians, the crucial issue hinges on the constitutive link between identity and particular cultural communities. A cultural communitarian is not necessarily a political communitarian. Likewise, political communitarianism can exist without a commitment to cultural communitarianism, for instance, in Rousseau's republicanism. By itself, multiculturalism has close affinities with cultural communitarianism. This is why it may enlist behind authoritarian, anti-democratic political structures. The distinctiveness of *democratic multiculturalism* is that it combines cultural and political communitarianism. Democratic multiculturalism recognizes the importance of cultural identity, the need to maintain cultural difference, *and* is committed to bring these differences into the political domain. Since these differences frequently turn into conflicts, it is also committed to their resolution through dialogue, discussion, and negotiation.

Allow me to briefly recapitulate the perspective just discussed. Multiculturalism emphasizes the importance of particular cultural communities and by implication, the need for cultural difference. Both republicanism and liberal individualism are equally blind to the importance of multiculturalism and altogether evade multicultural issues. Authoritarian multiculturalism negates individual liberty and autonomy, is obsessed solely with identity and belonging. Liberal multiculturalism recognizes the value of both but denies the entry of issues of identity or belonging into the political domain and therefore, in the last instance, antecedently tilts in favour of individual autonomy. Democratic multiculturalism is fully prepared to tackle the tension between identity and belonging on the one hand and requirements of individual autonomy on the other, and to bring into the political domain both sets of issues.

Why is democratic, rather than liberal, multiculturalism a better perspective? By denying the importance of practices and cultural traditions, the liberal individualist is unable to even notice the systemic bias and domination of these practices. Liberal multiculturalism is able to at least see these oppressions. But by making large areas of public life immune from political intervention, it simply allows inbuilt oppression and subordination to persist and by insulating the political domain from different identities, it ends up 'freezing difference'. The plain truth is that oppressive cultural practices flourish due to the indifference of the state. Unless the state uses non-punitive measures that its considerable authority makes possible, and encourages a variety of non-governmental organizations (NGOs) to move in a certain direction, subordination and oppression are likely to continue. The success and failure of Indian secularism provides ample evidence in favour of the need for democratic multiculturalism. The removal of oppression and subordination has been a function of a successful and effective democratic state. The state has had to democratically intervene in religious and cultural practices to get rid of oppressive practices. Such practices have continued, congealed, and become worse whenever the state has refrained from intervention or acted without democratic legitimacy.

Does democratic multiculturalism work in all contexts? Can conflicts always be resolved through discussion and dialogue? Is democratic multiculturalism insufficiently attentive to the depth and extent of conflicts? Is the liberal multiculturalist fear of the political domain simply an effect of its acute sensitivity to deep conflicts hidden within cultural difference? Of course, one should not be blind to differences but should we not be wary of exacerbating the morally repugnant forms that cultural conflict assumes? Suppose that the complete set of political strategies is divided broadly into two categories: the politics of involvement and the politics of detachment. The first entails an engagement with disagreement and brings every issue out into the open. The second kind compels an abstraction from the public domain, imposes restraint, and asks us to keep some issues to ourselves rather than force them into glare of the public eye. Is democratic multiculturalism a politics of involvement and is it wise to implement it no matter what the context? Perhaps the politicization of culture and collective identity is justified, but are there any limits to this? Can an issue be unwittingly over-politicized? Isn't this dangerous? I believe it is.

Elementary sociological investigation draws attention to another painful fact, that is, that involvement requires self-confidence which flows from sustained participation and the habits of winning. Those excluded from participation and those who lose persistently tend to detach themselves from politics. In this context, an assertive politics of involvement cuts both ways. It brings hitherto marginalized groups within the domain of politics. Conversely, it may help those already in politics to take complete control and exclude some groups altogether. To prevent such domination, a better strategy may well be to support mutual detachment. Occasionally, the best available strategy to contain hegemonizing forces is to get everybody to support *a politics of reciprocal detachment*. In short, a space must be found within democratic multiculturalism for liberal politics because it at least ensures that no one loses out completely—a wise choice in certain contexts—and therefore, it remains a reliable fall-back strategy. Let me reformulate this point by deploying some terms I introduced in the third section, namely, 'Forms of Multiculturalism'. When the first moment of particularized hierarchy is safely buried in the past, we can confidently move from the second moment in the dialectic to the third, final moment of particularized equality, that is, to democratic multiculturalism. If on the other hand, one step in the direction of the third really takes us two steps back to the first moment, then we must simply hold on to the moment of universalistic equality that constitutes liberal multiculturalism. Under certain conditions, the eminently liberal fear of over-politicization is justified. Since I believe that subordination is never a thing of the past but always an ever present danger in societies everywhere, even within egalitarian social structures, I cannot help but conclude that a version of liberal multiculturalism must have a permanent place in larger democratic politics.

MULTICULTURALISM AND BITTER CONFLICTS

So far in the discussion on multiculturalism, an underlying assumption has been that cultural conflicts are fairly controlled, and occur within the parameters of civic peace. But, societies may also undergo civil war or be on the verge of it. Under such volatile conditions, what if cultural communities are over-politicized? What if we are dealing with problems not of inferiority, internal oppression, or conflicts within acceptable moral limits, the usual kind that liberals take into account, but with acute, intractable, insurmountable difficulties of a multicultural society where bitter relations between groups have soured and turned rancid? Consider, for example, post-partition societies, where members cannot cope with new boundaries and borders. Michael Ignatieff reports a conversation with an East German, inhabitant originally of Upper Silesia, a German province of what is now Poland. When asked if he ever wanted to visit Upper Silesia, he said, 'not as a tourist, never. Only with a German flag.'[26] Such resentment was not exactly uncommon among Punjabi refugees in India. Consider the bitter legacy of Apartheid in South Africa or the emotional environment of hatred and revenge that exists in Palestine or Bosnia. What strategy can be devised to cope with societies with a bitter aftertaste of bitter horrific conflicts?

It is a brute, frequently neglected fact that splenetic memories of the past fester in the mind. David Hume wrote perceptively about animosities bequeathed from one generation to another.

[26] Ignatieff, *Blood and Belonging*, p. 83.

Nothing is more usual than to see parties, which have begun upon a real difference, continue even after the difference is lost. When men are once enlisted on opposite sides, they contract an affection to the persons with whom they are united, and an animosity against their antagonists; and these passions they often transmit to their posterity.[27]

Only the very dogmatic or blind analyst will fail to see that people are often divided by the mere fact that at some time in the past one group ruled over the other. It is the memory of domination, not difference by itself, which turns conflict into a downward spiral of political violence. Some societies have the luxury of ignoring the past or looking at only its pleasant dimension. Others must deal head on with it and face its ghosts, phantoms, and demons.

How do we deal with collective memory in deeply divided multicultural societies? In Chapter 7, I discuss this issue in detail. Suffice it to say here that remembering the past is always a tricky issue. For a start, it may reinforce asymmetries of power. The fear of physical suffering in the future feeds on the remembrance of past acts of violence or repression. The remembrance of the beating I received for crossing the line with my superiors prevents me from resisting them. Such remembrance encourages passivity and obedience in victims, which feed the interests of the powerful. But such remembrances cuts both ways. If memory of suffering is kept alive, reprisal may occur at future, opportune moments. Therefore, among former perpetrators, a motivated forgetfulness of their own wrongdoings, accompanied with the hope that former victims will quickly forget past suffering is not uncommon when asymmetries of power dissolve. In this context, calls to let bygones be bygones work unabashedly in favour of the perpetrators. Forgetting is not a fair compromise and should be unacceptable to victims. The demand on the victim to forget past injustice is, in reality, an injunction to forgive and not to publicly recall past injustice.

It is doubtful if forgetting is a good strategy for repairing wounds or achieving reconciliation. Usually, when a person is wronged, the message communicated by the aggressor is that in his theme of things, the victim counts for nothing. Since self-respect and self-esteem hinge upon critical opinion of the other, messages sent by the wrongdoer significantly lower self-esteem in the wronged. The insult and degradation inflicted is, in fact, a deeper moral injury. This loss of self-esteem is not addressed by demands to forget past injuries. Indeed, it inflicts further

---

[27] David Hume, *Political Writings*, Cambridge: Hackett Publishing Company, 1994, p. 160.

damage. Asking victims to forget past evils is to treat them as if no great wrong to them has been done, as if they have nothing to feel resentful about. This only diminishes them further. Indeed, forgetting eventually facilitates evil. Only proper remembering restores dignity and self-respect to the victim.

Besides, proper remembrance is necessary to fulfil the collective needs of a badly damaged society. A pervasive social condition bolstered by an argument from Hobbes challenges the pro-remembrance view. It is an ugly, uncomfortable fact that societies remember their heroic deeds but suppress memories of collective injustice. Recall Ernest Renan's remark that nations are constituted by a great deal of forgetting. In a perceptive essay, Sheldon Wolin wonders if a society can ever afford to vividly remember events in which members feel tainted by a 'kind of corporate complicity in an act of injustice done in their name'.[28] Can France remember the Saint Bartholomew massacre; America, its civil war; and India, its partition? Can these be remembered by being represented in civic rituals? One philosopher who endorsed collective forgetting was Thomas Hobbes who argued that the suppression of memories of past wrongs is a precondition of building a new society. Societies must be dehistoricized.

Is dehistoricization possible? I think not. Besides, it is to live in a fool's paradise to imagine that as grievances recede into the past and are half-forgotten, they will somehow cease to be real. As Ignatieff put it, 'Collective myth has no need of personal memory or experience to retain its force.'[29] Turks and Afghans, who also happen to be Muslims, invaded India early in the second millennium but for many Hindus, even destitute Muslims continue to be invaders who killed, destroyed, and converted. The conquest of Quebec by the English happened more than two centuries ago but the project of Quebec nationalists 'involves a reconquest of the conquest'. A simple strategy of forgetting has simply not worked.

Nonetheless, former victims in fragmented societies eventually need to get on with their lives rather than be consumed by their suffering. Perhaps victims need to forget just about as much as they need to remember. People who carry deep resentment and grievances against one another are hardly likely to build a society together. Therefore,

[28] Sheldon Wolin, 'Injustice and Collective Memory', *The Presence of the Past: Essays on the State and the Constitution*, Baltimore and London: Johns Hopkins University Press, 1989, pp. 32–46.

[29] Ignatieff, *Blood and Belonging*, p. 153.

an injunction to forget is not *entirely* unreasonable. Rather, my key point is that though forgetting at an appropriate time is necessary, a complete erasure is neither sufficient nor desirable for healing or for the construction of a minimally decent society.

Reflection on some of these uncomfortable issues shows the inadequacy of the philosophical treatment of multiculturalism. The deficiency is due to several sources. Perhaps liberal philosophy screens out the full range of experiential motivation. For instance, it wrongly supposes that grievances cease to be real just because they are in the past.[30] Quite possibly, it is too rationalist and does not give emotion its due. Could it be that a proper multicultural philosophy develops only by accepting that violence is neither feared nor hated by everyone? Could it even be true that 'liberals have not understood the force of male resentment that has accumulated through centuries of pacification of politics'?[31] Perhaps there is need to understand how ethnic revolts tap this male resentment. Alternatively, the very framing of issues may be flawed. To pin the blame for conflict on rival cultures, conceptually and ethically segregated from one another, may miss the real nature of conflict in which togetherness, sameness, and a variety of emotions which these produce play a much greater role than is allowed by rationalist traditions within liberalism.[32] Is it not true that the dialectic between ethnic and civic nationalism is determined 'as much by ethnic group as by those who wish away problems of unity or who suppose that patriotism is for fools'?[33] The hold of face-to-face interactions on nationalist imaginations, in particular the clutch of the family, may be a real factor in deep conflicts.

Communitarian advocates of cultural belonging will benefit from recognizing the relationship between violence and an intense sense of belonging. If belonging sanctions self-sacrifice, it also legitimizes killing the other. Proponents of a politics of recognition may not fully see that even when self-affirmation is unavoidable, it takes positive as well as negative forms. People justify all manner of wrong deeds in the name of self-affirmation. Only a proper appreciation of these facts gives an adequate explanation of why people who have lived peacefully with each other for long suddenly turn hostile and also, why large, abstract ideologies manage to enthuse ordinary people. Several scholars rightly

---

[30] Ibid., p. 246.
[31] Ibid.
[32] Ibid., p. 244.
[33] Ibid., p. 102.

point out that ordinary people are not fundamentalist but perhaps, like most of us, they insufficiently recognize just how enmeshed the lives of ordinary people are in little holocausts hidden within each small community. We may never hit upon a stable solution to these problems without grasping all of this.

It is in this spirit that I interpret Stanley Fish's critique of philosophical multiculturalism: that it is superficial and unable to appreciate cultural difference where it ought to matter most.[34] Some forms of multiculturalism respect other cultures up to a point, stopping short just where some value lying deep at the centre of the other culture produces an action that violates norms of 'civilized decency'. Fish aptly calls this boutique multiculturalism, that opposes the death sentence on Rushdie, is hostile to Afro-centrist curriculum, detests animal sacrifice or use of a control substance, and cannot grant legitimacy to polygamy.[35] In short, boutique multiculturalism fails at the very point where any kind of multiculturalism must succeed, namely, in arenas of deep difference over values; it cannot take seriously the core values of the cultures it ostensibly tolerates. It rejects the idea of deep difference because the core identity of humans is constituted for it by elements shared by all. Fish distinguishes boutique multiculturalism from what he calls strong multiculturalism, the view by which at least a part of our identity is shaped by differing particular cultures. For strong multiculturalism, at some level, a deep irreconcilable difference exists. But, in the last instance, even strong multiculturalism bows to some supra-cultural universal and so, like boutique multiculturalism, it misinterprets at least some conflicts between particular cultures as a clash between the particular and the universal. By elevating one particular culture wrongly on a universalist pedestal, it creates new asymmetries of power or suppresses the distinctiveness of separate cultures. The lesson to be drawn, according to Fish, is to refuse to see multiculturalism as a philosophical problem or conceptual puzzle but rather to see it as a demographic fact that generates crises diffused only by what Taylor calls inspired adhoccery. Philosophically, reconciliation may never be possible but a way can be devised of accommodating particular differences within a community without coming to blows with each other. Each situation provides an opportunity for improvization rather than annotation for the application of principles. A solution for it is bound to be temporary, anyhow.

[34] S. Fish, 'Boutique Multiculturalism, or Why Liberals are Incapable of Thinking about Hate Speech', *Critical Inquiry*, vol. 23, no. 2, 1997, pp. 378–95.
[35] Ibid., pp. 378–9.

I do not share Fish's scepticism about the possibility of trans-cultural universals. So I guess for me strong multiculturalism goes roughly along the right path. Without dismissing the possibility of universals, strong multiculturalism allows for deep difference as also for fierce conflicts. It fractures the complacency of liberal individualism, of a simple-minded republicanism, and of boutique multiculturalism. It shatters the myth that conflicts are always generated, to borrow a term from philosophy of science, under conditions of closure. I concede, however, that in more open situations, where conflicts spin out of hand and human behaviour is anything but predictable or systematic, only Stanley Fish's recommendations are likely to work. A modus vivendi is the only way out for societies where divisions go very, very deep or where relations are particularly raw.

Two other things are more or less certain. First, no strategy can work in the absence of an effective state. Conditions of peaceful co-existence are not reproduced automatically but require a fairly strong state. Second, a solution is hardly likely to work unless a modicum of democratic politics exists. A minimally democratic state may not be good enough but what it may manage to prevent is much worse.

MULTICULTURALISM, AN ALIEN FRAMEWORK?

I have referred already to the objection that multiculturalism does not sit well with the criss-cross, amorphous pluralism of traditional India. I now tackle a related objection, which has two versions. What makes them versions of the same objection is that for both multiculturalism carries a heavy ideological baggage derived from its links with the context of its origin. The first links it to a new phase of global capitalism, the other relates to the specific experience of Canada and the USA. It is alleged that such a framework, with its strong ties with the experience of highly 'developed' nations or with international capitalism, could or should not have much value or relevance in the Indian context. I understand multiculturalism differently, seeing it more as a framework that brings together a number of distinct themes such as identity, recognition, cultural belonging, etc., which all respond to common human needs but are understood and dealt with variously in different societies. These issues, I claim, emerge at several levels—across nations, at the site where nations are formed, and within the nation-state, in the wider social and the narrower political domains. For me, its abstract, indefinite decontextualized character enables it to have several ideological incarnations as well applicability across time and space.

The issue that divides such critics of multiculturalism and myself is about how to understand and evaluate the nature of concepts and theories. For critics who believe in the strong programme of sociology of knowledge, concepts and theories have a rigid location and an immovable allegiance to specific interests. For me, concepts and theories, at least some of them, possess a degree of flexibility and mobility that makes it possible for them to have multiple applications in contexts different from where they first emerged. This is why we can legitimately talk of an Indian multiculturalism, even though theories of multiculturalism are imports from Canada and the USA. So, in my view, critics of multiculturalism who allege it to be an alien framework hugely over-contextualize it.

Indeed, I would like to turn this critique on its head and make a stronger counter-claim. I contend that some issues and themes of multiculturalism originate in the practices of modern India with greater salience, depth, and togetherness than anywhere else in the world. If so, multiculturalism is not an American or Canadian but an Indian original. Let me explain. Recall the three levels at which multiculturalism emerges. First, an international level, where it connotes a struggle against western hegemony. Second, the site where nations are formed, where it fights ethno-nationalism. Third, within the nation-state, where it acknowledges group rights. Now, whereas Canadian and the American multiculturalism are situated only at the third level and have been recognized to be so situated only in the last two decades, Indian multiculturalism exists at all three levels and originates even earlier. At the international level, where multiculturalism signals a demand for authenticity, a way of being that is uniquely one's own, there exists a long Indian tradition of cultural nationalism. At the second level, despite all its internal problems, Indian nationalism has fought narrowly conceived Hindu and Muslim nationalism. Finally, at the third level, that is, within the nation-state, group-specific rights were recognized in India explicitly in the constitution. Such rights include the right to cultural particularity enshrined in Articles 29 and 30 as well as self-government rights, found, for example, in Article 370, that embody what Taylor fruitfully calls asymmetrical federalism. So, India has been multicultural at each of these three levels, and moves to become multicultural began over a century ago. Many issues currently under discussion elsewhere in the world had engaged the constituent assembly and were resolved with the framing of the constitution, which was adopted in 1950.

A question that remains unanswered relates to the need for the strong reliance on theorists like Taylor and Kymlicka. When these issues have long been discussed and formulated in India, why rely on these theories? Why are not there Indian theorists of multiculturalism? True, an occasional reliance on other cultural traditions is not troubling, but we appear to make a habit of it. Why does it happen all the time? Why are issues first theorized elsewhere and only later gain academic salience in India? This complex question needs a long and patient answer but I must gesture towards answering it. My brief answer is this. Theories emerge from practice, but the presence of a particular set of practices and even ad hoc reflections on them is not enough to generate a theory. In addition, a tradition of such theorizing is required as also the practice of learning from these traditions. Do such traditions and pedagogic practices have a substantial presence in India? The answer has to be in the negative. India has a modern multi-cultural practice, and reflection on such practice, but no tradition of theorizing on it. Such a tradition and a whole institutional apparatus to learn from it exists in the West. Unless such an apparatus also exists in India, no original *theories* will be generated here.

This is a difficult and a rather pessimistic conclusion to accept. What must be done in the interlude? My answer is quite simple. Most theories that originate in the West are bound to initially have a strong flavour of their origin. It is a mistake not to grasp this and to delude yourself into believing that they have immediate application anywhere and at anytime. No theory or concept has an immediate universal application. However, it is in the nature of concepts and theories that they can be decontextualized and when this is done, they can be relocated and invested with different meaning and intonation. This complex practice of decontextualization and recontextualization must be pursued. A condition of such pursuit is that we be well versed in the tradition of political theorizing and equally well immersed in the practices of our own society and culture. To know how to decontextualize, we must have a strong link with available theoretical traditions. To know what precisely to recontextualize, we must have a strong practical grasp of our own social practices.

I hope this explains why multicultural practices need not always be accompanied by multicultural theories and also, why *our* multicultural theories, at least for now, will be produced by us jointly with, say, Taylor and Kymlicka.

6

The Continuing
Relevance of Socialism*

In this chapter, I re-examine some aspects of the socialist ideal in the
light of events in the recent past in Eastern Europe and in what was
called the Soviet Union. Such reappraisal is understandably difficult for
many committed socialists and they may legitimately demand that a
person doing so must prove his credentials to do so or not attempt it
at all. This is easy to do for one who is currently, or has in the past, engaged in the far more tangible political project of realizing socialism in
our society. Since I cannot claim to have done this, I must straightaway
admit that I do so with very scant moral weight behind me. All I can say
in my favour is that for more than twenty years, I have had sustained
intellectual curiosity in socialist and in particular Marxist ideas and
that for over a decade now, I have sympathetically taught the difficult,
exhilarating, and often seductive ideas of Marx to a large numbers of
post-graduates.

Allow me to also make an honest confession. I belong to that quaint
group of reluctant socialists—sometimes called fellow travellers—who
have dreamt ever so often of embracing a full-fledged socialist identity
but have lacked the courage to do so. This is partly because of the spirit
of the times in which I grew up, partly to do with my class background
and profession, but, it has something also to do with a couple of things
that are no longer imprudent to mention. First, socialism has appeared

* This was delivered as a lecture organized by Veer Bharat Talwar on behalf
of a group associated with CPI(ML) in New Delhi, sometime in 1991. It was
subsequently published as 'The Continuing Relevance of Socialism', *Economic
and Political Weekly*, vol. XXVII, no. 40, 3 October 1992, pp. 2161–9.

to me to be anchored to ideals that soar so high that I have found them difficult to practice. Second, the ordinariness of my life has always found its high moral tone difficult to swallow, and paradoxically, its political realism, even when it has seemed legitimate, has offended even *my* diffuse moral sensibility. Third, I have often felt uneasy with the simplicity of vision of many of its practitioners. These three things are linked to each other. Lofty ideals frequently simplify the world and a simplified world encourages those who live in it to swing from intemperate moralism to dubious consequentialism.

I believe ordinary people in Soviet Union, reluctant socialists like myself but crushed so often by the massive weight of lofty ideals that I for one have never experienced, could just not take it anymore. It seems to me that this is the simple explanation of why the system crumbled so rapidly. That indeed is the dominant social meaning of the shattering events of 1991. Allow me to elaborate this point.

Let us squarely face hard facts. We have just witnessed the passing away of a socialist system, perhaps the only really existing socialist system. Not the end, to be sure, of socialist practices or as I would argue, of the socialist ideal, but the disappearance of that ensemble of dominant practices and institutions that makes any society socialist. There is no getting away from the fact that howsoever deviant it may have been, the system that existed there was a variant of socialism. I differ from those who argue that the events of Eastern Europe and the Soviet Union entail not the transformation of a system but a move sideways—a shift from bureaucratic state capitalism to multinational capitalism. It is also beyond doubt that this change has come from below. Whatever the eventual outcome of these changes, no one can deny that they are a result of popular movements. The ultimate irony of the events of 1989 and 1991 is that a socialist system has been overthrown by popular consent, if not exactly popular participation and revolt.

What explains this bizarre volte-face? The secondary reason is plain: people who were meant in theory to run the state had been excluded for long from decision making. Quite simply, if real socialism was to survive, democracy had to be restored. Stalinist political structures should never have come into existence in the first place and ought to have been dismantled long ago. The failure to do so in good time has resulted in this convulsion. There is little doubt that for a section of the population, particularly the intelligentsia, these events embody a victory for democracy, a triumph against Stalinism. But the more significant, primary reason is this: I believe that, over the years, people in these societies finally got to see that the only residence of their very high ideals lay in a state that owned all the means of production, and this unwanted concentration of economic and political power is precisely what denied them ordinary freedoms, a better material life, and a modicum of differentiation without which human life is unbearably dull. Liberty, prosperity, distinction—these were the key demands of the people. 'Socialist men and women' fought against socialism because for them it had begun quite literally to mean the denial of material comfort (an endless programme of austerity), the negation of political liberty (a blueprint for inescapable repression), and an absence of diversity (a strict regime of boring uniformity).

On top of this was the ever-visible relation of inequality and hierarchy, between those in power—the party officials—and those ordinary people, forever out in the cold. For the people, the following equivalences had become rock-solid: socialism = state ownership of means of production = unequal relations = denial of liberty = restraint on wants = uniformity. It all came in a suffocating package. Destroying one meant negating everything else that went along with it. People fought against socialism because they did not know any way of disentangling all these from one another. Because individual freedom and emancipated desire was perceived to be unsocialist, even anti-socialist, and because they could not but help want individual freedom and a better material life, people believed themselves to be rejecting the very ideals of socialism. Although these issues (the relation of socialism to liberalism, democracy, ordinary life, and the much larger question that has to do with the socialist idea of perfection) have surfaced from time to time, they never erupted as provocatively as during the dramatic events of 1989. This made some questions inescapable. Is to seek freedoms traditionally associated with liberalism and aspire to fulfil wants that were first realized without guilt under capitalism tantamount to going against the grain of socialism? Are material prosperity and individual freedom possible only within the framework of capitalism? Or, are we led to this conclusion because of a mistaken or inadequate formulation of the socialist ideal? Do these changes in 'socialist world' have significant implications for the socialist vision? What anyway is it?

WHAT IS THE SOCIALIST VISION?
I propose to answer this question by going deep down to the most basic elements of the socialist vision. But, why one may ask, should we need to do this. Is this not a purely defensive reflex forced by the collapse of

Soviet communism? Is this a desperate attempt to piece together the scattered splinters of a hopelessly fractured vision, a last ditch effort to build afresh an ideal that has outlived itself and now lies prostrate? It goes without saying that we have been compelled to think on these issues as a direct consequence of what has happened in the recent past. However, this does not mean that we are left with no option but to piece together an ideal that has been smashed to smithereens. A fallen ideal need not be irretrievably broken. But still, one might ask, why indulge in the pointless reiteration of mere truisms? How will it help to state the simple and the obvious?

We are all familiar with the idea that when the context that sustains the normal working of arguments vanishes, they lose almost all their force and become a clump of disconnected propositions. Likewise, a set of statements acquires its sense from a context, the disappearance of which renders it entirely meaningless. Words push to the fore their sheer physicality, becoming mere sounds or marks and, from a human point of view, hollow, vapid, and ineffective. In such situations, language suddenly finds itself in the midst of a dead ritual, and once it is fully woven into it, starts to convey almost nothing. It is precisely when this happens that it is time to look for another, simpler vocabulary to communicate one's thoughts; to recharge, not to replace the one we already have. The simpler language reilluminates the more complicated one in order to restore the force it once possessed. Taken out of this context, the simple vocabulary is a set of mere truisms but in the proper context, it opens up precisely that field within which our complicated theories acquire the ability to give us finer insights. I think we need to return to this simple language, to that plain vision without which talk of structural exploitation and systematic oppression, of state power and ideology, of class hegemony and class struggle makes very little sense. Let me repeat: I am not making the more radical proposal of jettisoning the theoretical language of socialism. Rather my plea is that one way to reinvigorate it is to enlighten it with the help of simpler principles. Far from dumping it, this is more like oiling the ideological machinery of socialism.

1. To begin, socialism is an ethical vision, in the widest possible sense of ethics, in that it proposes a view of how we should live. It specifies a conception of the ultimate human good by which we can judge individual desires or private ideas of the human good. In short, by providing us with a model of the good life it shows us exactly what it is that makes life worth living. To put it differently, socialism

embodies a teleological vision, a set of worthwhile objectives that form the locus of primary significance for human beings. Bereft of such a framework, human life is without direction. It is precisely because socialism is such a framework that it gives individuals an ethical orientation.

2. A second distinctive feature of socialism is that it offers this vision on the basis of the best available knowledge of socio-historical existence of human beings. It is a vision that connects the future and the past by an analysis of the present, accomplished with the best available skills by which elements of the human conditions can be grasped. It is an ethics that springs not from the heart alone, that flows not just from pure and good intentions but from human reason that is connected with but not reducible to feelings, desire, or instinct. In short, it is grounded in that impure and limited form of human reason often found in social science.

3. Third, it is committed to what can be called the principle of this-worldliness. Socialists believe in the existence only of one world; this one. They believe that the only world there is exists here and now, and any other world beyond this one lies only in the thought and imagination of human beings. At any rate, if indeed there is another world beyond here and now, then human beings, living or dead, have no meaningful or relevant relation to it. Now, this principle entails a number of things but the one I would like to single out for attention is this: whatever evil exists in this world inheres in it by virtue of something in this very world. I shall return to this point shortly.

4. Fourth, socialists are committed to the principle of humanism, to the view that whatever meaning exists in our world is due to the conscious or perhaps unconscious actions of human agents, that human beings make themselves, and that to whatever extent it is possible, they control their destiny, they are masters of their own fate. Moreover, whatever evil there is in the world, must, therefore, be due to the past and present acts of human agents. Therefore, salvation, any possible elimination of evil from this world, is possible by human action alone.

5. Fifth, socialists are committed to what can be called the principle of interdependence. Now this is the distinctive and individuating socialist principle. It has three different components, each of which needs spelling out. The first can be specified by recalling the problem of theodicy, namely, the problem of accounting for and overcoming evil in this world and also by reinvoking Rousseau's solution to it.

For Rousseau, the source of all evil inheres in society and can be overcome only by an act of the whole society, the entire people. Rousseau places collective or interdependent human action at the centre of the solution to the problem of theodicy. The burden of responsibility for evil in this world has shifted from god, nature, or the individual to collectivities. Marx sharpened this idea by adding that though the entire society is responsible for the existence of evil, some groups must share a greater burden of blame. Evil in this world is an outcome of the special circumstances from which some groups derive more benefit than others. The systematic elimination of evil is not possible without resistance from such groups and therefore, without struggle between groups.

The more general idea of collective or interdependent action needs to be supplemented by the notion of collective struggle. Furthermore, this emphasis on collective human action has three other equally important aspects. First, socialism cannot be made by a few for the sake of all; it must be made by all for all. All of us or almost all of us must be implicated in realizing the good life. People must know why they are involved in the making of the good society, what society it is that they are making, and only then make it for themselves. To say this is to claim that socialists are committed to the principle of autonomy. The good life cannot be imposed from above, given to the people by the few. Socialism cannot result from the acts of few individuals who alone know the secrets of history and society. Second, if and when the good life is realized, it must be shared equally by all. The fruits of good life must be available not to a few but to all. In short, the good life must be made by and be available to all. The term 'all' is meant to cover the entire human-kind. This universalism is constitutive of the socialist vision. Finally, interdependence is not of mere instrumental value. We get together not only to seek ends that cannot be individually realized but more importantly, because we value interdependence. For socialists, real human relations amongst people matter more than anything else.

To sum up, socialism is the view that the good life can be achieved here and now by collective and 'rational' human action not for a few but for all.

WHAT THE SOCIALIST VISION IS NOT
Admittedly, this is vague and general but even so, there are certain kinds of social, political, and economic life that this elementary vision rules

out. First, note that being a substantive doctrine, it is against nihilism as well as against those varieties of liberalism which are suspicious of substantive conceptions. Second, it impugns all those ideologies that attempt other-worldly solutions to this-worldly problems. It opposes, for example, those religions that espouse the idea of a radically transcendent world or a transcendent god. Third, it directly undermines most forms of individualisms, since these either have no conception of collective human action or are deeply suspicious of it. Moreover, they have no space for the view that shared human relations is of intrinsic worth. Fourth, it opposes any view that dismisses autonomy or self-determination as illusory or self-negating. Finally, it is virulently against any concentration of economic and political power, against monopolies, dictatorship, and authoritarianism. Egalitarian and democratic elements are built into the very idea of socialism.

I mentioned at the very outset that much writing on socialism hints at a conception of the good life but nowhere states what it is. Elements of an answer to this question are implicit in what has been just said. In any case, when many ways of conceiving a good socialist life exist, no single, undisputed answer can be provided. Each of us, when we are ready to judge and discriminate, can prepare a list of socialist values and rank them on the ethical scale: the good life is free, democratic; values individual creativity, gives a distinct identity to individuals; is one in which people manage their own lives both in the work place and outside it (in the public sphere) where no relevant distinction exists between work and leisure; in which constitutive links exist between the self and others; and where human beings have reconciled themselves with nature. Formulated in this general manner, I doubt very much if any socialist is likely to dispute this list. I shall not discuss it any further. My main interest here is to make one central claim that I shall proceed to state both dramatically and provocatively. For me, a socialist society that embodies the good life is not a perfect society. The struggle for a socialist society is not a struggle for the creation of a perfect human being. This claim needs clarification. Indeed, at least three separate points contained in this claim need further amplification.

IMPERFECTIONS OF THE SOCIALIST VISION
At the heart of many versions of socialism lies a view of perfection that smacks of religious utopias. Once upon a time, before they turned socialists, well-meaning rebels believed in god. This god was perfect in every conceivable sense: He knew everything, anticipated everything,

controlled everything, and accomplished anything he wished. Then they became atheists and loudly declared the death of god. However, what they discarded was not the sense of the word 'god' but its reference. The term 'god' no longer applied to an invisible, intangible entity existing beyond here and now. It referred to a being in this world. The idea was the same as before, only it was now attached to man. In short, these people apotheosized man. At long last, god had descended on earth. Human beings, who until recently were woefully limited and lived in a state of fear and ignorance, were from now on seen as possessing infinite capacities. They could know everything, predict everything, control everything, plan anything, and realize it to the T. Alas, human beings are human beings and humanism is, well, just humanism. To pronounce the death of god is not just to mark the disappearance of an entity beyond here and now but to register the complete vacuity of the very concept of god. And this means, at the very least, accepting that there lies at the heart of the human condition a radical fallibility that is futile to try to totally overcome.

Humanism is not just a slightly modified variant of theism. It rejects theism as well as what can only be called a super-humanism. To say that men and women are humans is to say that they are limited creatures, and part of what this means is that no matter what they do, however high they soar, whatever the degree of their transcendence, they will always make mistakes. Not just that, the best human beings make mistakes, the most rational person acts irrationally, the most honest person can be occasionally dishonest, and the most unambitious person can be lured by the temptation of power. In a way, the term 'evil' is merely the religious expression of this wholly secular character of humans: their potential for radical fallibility. In particular, it is the name for a fallibility that has multiplied dangerously in the absence of any institutional checks.

Let me throw another lasso on this idea. What I am saying is this: if power must corrupt some people, and if people, at least sometimes, act irrationally and if moral vacuity and radical irrationality are together known to generate horrific outcomes, then we must set up mechanisms that appear to restrict individual autonomy but, in fact, guarantee precisely those conditions of minimal rationality and freedom that make human life possible. It is not enough to have good intentions; there must be institutions to prevent us from performing those acts that we shall later live to regret. In any good society, therefore, there must be mechanisms by which mistakes can be detected before they bring irreparable damage. Not only must mistakes be identified and made public but both their sinful character and the despairing sense of shame and guilt associated with them must be expunged. People must know in advance that their mistakes can be made public and at the same time rest assured that they will not be hanged for having committed them. This requires not only a humane set of laws but also an open arena that allows unsuppressed public debate. An imperfect human society cannot survive without them.

There is a second sense in which my good socialist society is imperfect. At the centre of many socialist theories lies the ideal of a creative human being. The good person produces. She is active, a creator. There is much that is admirable in this ideal. But the brute fact is that people are not forever and always engaged in creative work. Most certainly, all human actions cannot be judged by standards that apply to creative work, by principles of self-actualization. Indeed, ways of being human exist which do not even require that men and women be active. Quite simply, human beings enjoy being passive, and as long as they are not reduced only to this state of passivity, there is nothing at all to denigrate here. My socialist society will not downgrade all forms of passivity. This point can be made slightly differently. Socialists, particularly Marxists, have had a fascinating overall view of human condition, a wonderfully rich theory and ethics of human existence, but the human situations that they best handle are all heroic. Marxism has a marked preference for heroic existence. Marxist ethics displays a profound sense of danger and of how to cope with it. It values daring, risk, sacrifice. It has a narrative that glorifies extraordinary effort and struggle. Marxists have a theory of how to live from one crisis to another but not, alas, a theory of normal existence, of ordinary life. Given their idealization of self-actualization through creative work, this is not surprising. The Marxist–socialist model of the human is the revolutionary, one who restructures entire societies; the political person, one who refashions polities; the artist, one who creates imaginary worlds; and the intellectual, one who recasts ideas. In the Indian context, the Marxist–socialist is also the ascetic and the renouncer, one who radically moulds desires. All these are models of heroic people, not of ordinary mortals: for them, ordinary life is worthless.

Socialists are generally contemptuous of time spent ordinarily, in domesticity, in the fulfilment of simple desires, and in passive enjoyment. They eschew ordinary joys. To be sure, no socialist can ever escape ordinary life, he may even enjoy it but not without guilt in having indulged in what is morally vacuous or avoidable drudgery. After all, ordinary life, that is, life spent in the pursuit of routine work, child rearing, and private enjoyment is precisely the life of the bourgeois. True, there is a sense in which it is a cultural constant but only modern bourgeois existence has lent it the moral legitimacy it earlier lacked. It no longer consists of necessary chores to be executed and set aside. From now on, it forms the very substance of a good, fulfilling life. Ardent socialists completely reject this life. Indeed, they see no value in it at all. I am afraid that in doing so they are running away not only from an inescapable part of their own selves but discarding one of the major achievements of modernity. They forget that for socialism, ordinary people matter as much as the skilled and the talented, that not only those who naturally and contingently possess socially valued features but any one, even the least privileged person, deserves to be treated with equal dignity and respect. Ordinary people can count as much as others only when ordinary life is no longer devalued. Ordinary life must matter to socialists more than it has and this means that we must re-evaluate our notions of individual desire, passive enjoyment, and privacy. However, from the ethical perspective of permanent self-creation, this is a big come down, a disappointingly imperfect ideal.

Yet another way in which my socialist society is imperfect can be illustrated by once again invoking the principle of this-worldliness. Recall that this principle states that there is only one world, that which exists here and now. But there are two interpretations of this principle, one stronger than the other. The weaker principle denies the existence of another world beyond this one but posits another world which is forever in a state of becoming. The other world is always just arriving but, I am afraid, never quite arrives. Socialists who believe in this principle permanently live for the future. They sacrifice an imperfect present for the sake of a perfect future. Indeed, this is believed to be an essential virtue of a socialist. A perfect socialist is one who is always ready to sacrifice his own imperfect present for the sake of a perfect world of future for others. The emphasis here is on *always*. Such socialists follow a weak principle of this-worldliness. Although they deny the existence of another world, they persist with the idea of an unrealizable world.

But there is a stronger principle of this-worldliness that they could follow. For this principle, each person has only one life to be lived in the only world that can possibly exist. Since she has only one life, there is no virtue in forever sacrificing the present for the sake of an imaginary future. A part of the present of living persons counts as much as the future of those who will live later. The strong principle of this-worldliness entails that there are limits to what even socialists can sacrifice. Socialists need not sacrifice all of the only life they have for the sake of a better life of future generations. It is unnecessary to impose on ourselves such absolute and harsh ideals that we can never hope to realize. Besides, the emotional quality of human life is such that when people fall below any ideal to which they have long been attached, they willingly slide so low as to actually end up negating it altogether. High ideals are always accompanied by emotions that carry with them their own opposites. Absolute ideals are never diluted gradually. Because they demand total commitment, the swing away from them is sharp and extreme, often resulting in complete rejection or outrageous degeneration. Now, I am not for a moment suggesting that all that counts in a this-worldly perspective is what the individual desires here and now. That is espoused by hedonism and socialism is not hedonism. All I am claiming is that the present, including the current desires of individuals, must have some importance in the scheme of those who take seriously the idea of this-worldliness. The socialist ideal must not be satisfied by a weak principle of this-worldliness. However, from the standpoint of strongly perfectionist doctrines, any move away from this principle involves abandoning the very idea of good life.

I have pleaded that socialists discard the godly idea of perfection. Someone may point to a paradox here. She might agree that the idea of perfection is unrealizable, illusory, even incoherent but then assert that without it, people will not be moved to act at all. No significant change occurs on this view unless people possess the very highest ideals. There is a ring of truth here but it pertains exclusively to one set of people, precisely those who have such notions of perfection. Only people with such conceptions of perfect human beings remain passive unless they are guided by ideals of perfection. There is a harmless little tautology here with disastrous consequences for the real world. Surely, men and women must learn to act for the good despite uncertainty of outcome and the fallibility of their ideals. In other words, they must learn to have modest hopes. Militancy is not incompatible with a degree of modesty and humility. Steadfastness of commitment should not be confused with passion for lofty ideals.

Two other things deserve a swift mention. First, socialists must realize that a theory of social change cannot be reduced to a theory of abolition. To change something is not always to annihilate it: the total

replacement of a thing by something else. Along with a theory of abolition, socialists require a theory of *aufhebung*, that is, a theory of subla-
tion, where things that are changed are both cancelled and preserved.
Such a theory of change makes much better sense of transformations in
ideas, in culture and tradition. Second, socialists have relied too heavily
on a fairly straightforward model of intentional action that has little
validity when applied to visions. A vision cannot be the direct object of
intentional action. It must first be translated into a set of tangible goals.
In short, it must temporarily cease to be a vision. After all, a vision is no
longer a vision if it is reduced to realizable, feasible goals.

This point can also be put differently. Every movement for social
change has an ultimate set of objectives, say emancipation. It must
also possess, distinct from its short-range tactical programme, a set of
medium-range goals. A socialist must strive to intentionally achieve
these medium-range objectives and hope that her vision will be realized
as a by-product. In short, she must work with a far more complex
notion of collective intentionality than has been hitherto supposed in
socialist practice. Nietzsche once said that man does not strive after
happiness, only the Englishman does. We might say likewise that a
socialist never tries for the direct realization of her long-term vision.
Only the capitalist does; which is precisely why, on closer scrutiny, he
does not quite have it!

Thus far, I have spoken on the dangers of lofty ideals and on the
need for concern with ordinary life. Allow me to now come to the
relationship of the socialist vision to both liberalism and democracy.

LIBERALISM, DEMOCRACY, AND THE SOCIALIST VISION
I take liberalism to be a social and political doctrine, concerned primarily to defend the values of individual privacy, of rights and justice, and
to be a doctrine about what the state may and may not legitimately
do in relation to individuals. Now there are certain presuppositions of
liberalism that we will do well to remember. There are some contexts
in which liberalism not only makes a lot of sense but is indispensable. Liberalism presupposes that no matter what the extent of their
socialization, individuals are not only different but separate from each
other. Given this fact, there exist distinct limits to their ability to come
together. Compared to the disparate character of their basic interests,
their common interests are negligible. In other words, liberalism has a
some what pessimistic view of the sociability of individuals. For liberals, the socialization of an individual does not really produce a social

person. This is not particularly disturbing for them because they value self-reliance and autonomy, and individuals with these attributes not only dislike interference from others but want to remain largely alone. They value privacy both as a condition of meaningful choice and as a context in which to lead a worthwhile life.

Liberals also believe that the disconnectedness of individuals entails a separation of their interests, that their interests clash, collide. Some basic interests of individuals conflict with each other. Liberals take the separateness of individuals and the conflictual character of their interests to be insurmountable, and the attempt to do so to be fraught with danger, to be foolhardy, if not exactly undesirable. If separateness and conflict is an inescapable and permanent condition of humankind, then an individual must have rights to protect her against all possible violation of her private space. Liberalism provides the hope not that a state can be achieved where all individuals can be collectively happy, in complete harmony with each other, as one people without any conflict, but rather the assurance that even in conditions of conflicting interest among individuals, a reasonable good life is possible for each individual. This good life is dependent, on the liberal view, upon institutions of justice and the provision of rights. Consider the language of rights. Suppose a person says that he has a right to be left alone. Now, if others habitually leave him alone, then he will never demand from them that he be left alone. He would not have to advance any such claim for the simple reason that he gets what he wants without effort, quite naturally. Nor, if indeed it was impossible for human beings to be ever left alone, would talk of rights make sense. For creatures without wings, it is absurd to demand a right to fly. The whole language of rights makes sense, therefore, only with respect to those things which a person can possibly do or have but about which he has fears that he may not be allowed to. This is just the context of separateness and conflict that I earlier mentioned. Liberalism thrives and is a critical requirement within such a context.

What is true for relations amongst individuals also holds true for relations between the individual and the state. Wherever the state has interests separate from and opposed to individuals, rights against the state have indispensable value. In a community where people wholly identify with the state or where the state does not exist at all, individuals do not need rights; indeed, they can well dispense with the entire liberal discourse. For, what is true of the language of rights holds equally for the institution of justice. Justice as a virtue is redundant in situations of shared interest and harmony. Rights and justice presuppose the presence of conflict but also that the conflict will not turn into war, that long-term peaceful coexistence is possible. This discourse encourages the belief that although they cannot be resolved, the sharper edges of conflict can be rendered blunt enough to allow for peaceable living among individuals.

How does a Marxist–socialist relate to this liberal discourse? Here, four possibilities exist. First, he may point to the very presuppositions of liberal discourse and accept that liberal discourse does not apply in conditions of war, but then claim that any condition prior to the establishment of a socialist society is a state of war in which liberalism is irrelevant. Second, he may argue for a conditional acceptance of liberalism, that liberal principles are to be followed if, and only if, those against socialism also comply with them. He accepts the validity of liberalism in normal times but has no hesitation in abandoning it in revolutionary situations. The second position differs from the first in that it allows for both peaceful and war-like conditions and therefore, accepts the restricted validity of liberalism. Third, it might be argued that whatever one's attitude to liberalism in pre-socialist society, it will be wholly redundant in a socialist society. It is superfluous because conditions of separateness and conflict are absent from every sphere in a socialist society. Finally, one may believe that some spheres of life will continue to exist, even in a socialist society, wherein separateness and conflict can neither be eradicated nor it be desirable to do so. If so, then even in the best of socialist societies, liberalism will have some restricted validity.

Marxists have generally held the first and the third position: they find liberalism irrelevant, redundant, or both. They dismiss it because they see all pre-socialist conditions to be states of total war in which liberalism cannot even begin to have any use and socialist conditions to have realized perfect harmony and peace—a utopia in which liberalism will have ceased to apply. Either way, they cannot see any use for liberalism. I do not know how many of us have this lurking suspicion that this is a far too simple view, both of pre-socialist and socialist societies. I for one cannot see pre-socialist societies in terms of the Hobbesian framework of war of all against all, where no rules apply. I say this in full awareness that for a greater part of the population of most such societies, this is how things appear to be and quite legitimately so.

But, I am not sure whether these people will not be better served by a struggle to bring them under the aegis of some liberal order rather than by a battle against it. The initial fight for a better order is a struggle for the extension of rights and justice to all and not towards their immediate abandonment. As a matter of fact, I do not believe that a socialist society will resolve all possible conflicts among humans. To be sure, in an ideal socialist society, some common identities will have been constructed but some spheres will invariably exist where identities of individuals remain distinct and potentially conflicting. In the case of these other spheres, one can only hope that rights and justice do not remain the preserve of a minority. In my ideal socialist society, there will be some spheres where all individuals will be fully and adequately covered by liberal principles. Liberal principles will, therefore, be necessary even in a socialist order. This is why a fight for liberalism is also a struggle on behalf of socialism.

It is well known that liberalism and democracy encompass two distinct set of political values. Liberalism is concerned with the private sphere of individuals, with their rights. On the other hand, democracy is primarily about political participation. Liberalism can be indifferent to political participation. A liberal society may even be undemocratic. A society where each individual is implicated exclusively and exhaustively in his or her private sphere, with a computerized programme to manage possible contact or conflict amongst them is compatible with liberalism. Likewise, a reasonably benevolent monarchy is consistent with liberalism. The co-presence of liberalism and democracy in modern capitalist societies is contingent. Not for nothing is liberal–democracy a portmanteau term.

In fact, liberalism is inconsistent with some forms of democracy. For example, liberalism and direct democracy are more or less incompatible with each other. Direct democracy requires the continuous, active participation of individuals in public affairs. Active citizenship is an abiding duty, a binding obligation on every individual. In such democracies, the public sphere far outstrips the private sphere in political value. Because individual freedom in the private domain is the cardinal value of liberalism, democracy, in liberal society, has to find another incarnation. People who value privacy but are not wholly indifferent to the public sphere must place their representatives in it. The only form of democracy compatible with liberalism, therefore, is representative democracy. Relief from public participation is crucial for a liberal society and representation alone makes this possible. Representation articulates liberalism with democracy.

Marxists are generally scornful of the half-hearted democratic order of the liberals. They are sharply critical of representative democracy and find inextricable, embryonic links between capitalism and representative democracy. Therefore, radical democrats amongst them glorify direct democracy and find representative democracy redundant under conditions of socialism. In a perfect socialist society, either no government is necessary or all persons will be so deeply involved in public affairs that representation will be downgraded.

Marxists also employ in their discourse the distinction between substantive and formal democracy. Substantive democracy is a condition of effective rather than mere formal rule by the people. The effective rule of the people is possible only under conditions of social and economic equality, in the absence of economic exploitation and social domination. Formal democracy, on the other hand, is restricted to the political sphere and is indifferent to what happens outside it. Since, as a matter of fact, what happens outside the political order is crucial to the fate of what happens inside it, formal democracy, for Marxists, is hollow. So, Marxists have generally associated formal democracy with capitalism and substantive democracy with socialism. Since capitalism and socialism are antithetical social formations, formal democracy is seen to be radically opposed to substantive democracy.

Before I offer my own brief assessment of these issues, one final distinction needs to be drawn between democracy and mobocracy. By 'mobocracy', I mean the rule of a large collection of people, even the entire people, that has suddenly, temporarily, and rather promiscuously come together for a loosely defined, more or less passing purpose. In a mobocracy, decisions are taken outside the frame of democratic norms by the majority, in the absence of rules, without procedures, with no concern for the rights of dissenting individuals. I mention this because what distinguishes democracy from other forms of government is not public participation per say but public participation within prescribed norms, within a framework of laws found generally in a constitution, and with procedures over which there is broad agreement—each of which is associated with formal rather than substantive democracy.

I started by saying that liberalism is indifferent to democracy. But now I have said that a democracy is not entirely indifferent to liberalism. In other words, while a liberal society can well do without public participation and therefore, without democracy, a democracy, if it is not to lapse into mobocracy, cannot entirely do away with some aspects of liberalism. Democracy has a healthy respect for some liberal values, even though liberalism has not always cared for democratic norms.

Our picture of democracy is now sufficiently complex to make matters difficult for one who wishes a simple, readymade answer to the question: what is a good socialist stand on democracy? I believe it is self-evident that a socialist society requires a public space within which decisions are taken. It follows that a socialist society requires a democratic form of government. I believe that the fullest possible public participation requires that exploitation and domination cease to exist everywhere, and that repression and inequality disappear from society. Surely, socialism is integrally tied to substantive democracy. The pivotal question then is whether a socialist society can turn its back on formal and representative democracy. I can think of at least one reason why this may not be possible. The feature that gives democracy its formal character is the same as that which distinguishes it from a mobocracy. As I said earlier, as crucial for a socialist society as public participation is, the form in which it takes place is equally important. This is so because unless we attend to the proper form of public participation, political domination that is irreducible to socio-economic exploitation emerges ineluctably in processes of decision making. Decisions must concern not only which but how things are done. Besides, socialists have not properly recognized that autonomy matters to people. Democracy is important precisely because we all want to be involved in the precise manner in which we achieve what we wish to accomplish. The form of public participation, the very fulcrum of formal democracy, is the all-important lever against the production of irreducible forms of political inequalities. Since socialism necessitates the end of all inequalities, it cannot be indifferent to formal democracy. Nor can it afford to dispense with it. Indeed, it is not too far-fetched to say that while the connection of capitalism with formal democracy is contingent, socialism is constitutively tied to it. Socialism is meant to be a system in which people have control over on their lives. Since the transformation of a mob into a people is brought about by constituents of formal democracy, socialism is linked to formal democracy. Furthermore, the integral ties of liberalism with formal democracy imply that socialism cannot really do away with some aspects of liberalism.

What about representative democracy? The socialist attitude to it is determined by its view on privacy. I believe that people will value privacy in any modern society, socialist or capitalist. People want both the persistent opportunity to participate in public affairs and the freedom not to participate in it, thus allowing their representatives, in faith and trust, to act on their behalf. Modernity creates the possibility for individuals to shift their involvements from the public to the private and back. A retreat into their private enclaves must be possible for individuals, should they feel the need to do so. Every society must create a space of opportunities such that all may participate sometime in some or the other public domain, but no one is under an obligation to do so all the time. I believe all of this implies the indispensability of representation. What is wrong with capitalist democracies then is not that they have representation but that they have nothing but representation and that the ground of trust and faith, so very essential to any meaningful representation, is eaten away in such systems by the all-pervasive instrumentality of human relations. In short, socialist societies must have room for representation. Socialism simply cannot be against all kinds of representative democracy.

* * *

I hope to have argued that elements of liberalism and democracy and a concern for ordinary life are a crucial part of the socialist vision. I believe I have done enough to provoke the thought that the real objective before a socialist is not to defeat formal and representative democracy but to save them from rampant capitalism. Allow me to come down from socialist ideals to the more earthy reality of a world without socialism. I said at the outset that the socialist system has all but disappeared. The people of Eastern Europe and the Soviet Union demanded liberty, democracy, and better material life. They believed that all this was not possible within the framework of socialism. They may even have believed that such goods fell right out of the framework of socialist ideals. Therefore, they appear to have turned to capitalism. Is this a correct move?

I think that these people had a right to make those demands. I also believe that they correctly grasped that, within the then existing socialist system, these demands were impossible to meet. But they have mistakenly hoped that capitalism provides the only framework within which these demands can be met. They are even more mistaken in having concluded that these are anti-socialist demands, that they are not constitutive of the socialist vision. I have already shown why these legitimate demands must be integral to socialist ideals. I now come to why capitalism is unlikely to meet these demands, why, tragically, the problems of the people of Soviet Union and Eastern Europe may not get solved all that easily. Herein also lie lessons for all of us in 'Third World' countries.

Socialists are familiar with the argument that most reforms within capitalism were introduced under pressure from working-class movements, that without socialist practices, the 'human' face of capitalism would never have surfaced. But it may need more emphasizing that these socialist practices had credibility and substance only due to the large and fearful presence of a really existing socialist system. It was only after the socialist idea, doubtless with many distortions, had been realized somewhere that substantial reforms within capitalism got going. Stalinism may have been bad for the socialist world but, ironically, ordinary people in western capitalist countries (indeed, everywhere in the world) benefited enormously from its very real presence. Anything that made capitalism tolerable for working people in the West was made possible less out of deference to the democratic demands of the people and more out of the fear that a real alternative to an unstable and flagging capitalist system existed already and could come into existence anywhere, anytime. A point even more easily forgotten and frequently stressed by Eric Hobsbawm is that were it not for socialism, formal democracy would have long disappeared from the world. But for a 'socialist' Soviet Union, the western world would 'consist of a set of variations on authoritarian and fascist regimes rather than set of variations on liberal ones'.

The implication is obvious. The collapse of the socialist world has once again brought back dangers not only of authoritarianism but of a retreat from the contingent humanity of capitalism. Furthermore, the ethical vision of liberalism has always been rather weak. It is weaker still with the setback suffered by socialism. It is always helpful to remember that liberalism and Marxist–socialism are children of a single rational–enlightenment outlook that is under persistent threat from ethical visions of the far right. Without the support of the ethical vision provided by the left, liberalism can easily be swept aside by racism, exclusivist nationalism, and religious fundamentalism. Therefore, in the absence of socialism, we may find ourselves not with a capitalist–liberal order but with a capitalist–nationalist, capitalist–racist, or a capitalist–fundamentalist one. Remember the principal demands of the people of Soviet Union and Eastern Europe—prosperity, liberty, democracy. Tragically, what they might get instead is more suffering, more repression, and an even more degrading uniformity.

I believe all I have said underlines not only the necessity of socialist reforms but also how important it was for them to have succeeded. The failure of reforms within socialist societies is a terrible setback—greater than we can imagine—precisely because of the continuing relevance of the socialist vision. It is because the support for something that is crucially necessary has tragically disappeared that socialists, even reluctant socialists, must both grieve and urgently put their act together to resume unfinished business.

III
IN THE FACE OF INJUSTICE

7

How Should We Respond to the
Cultural Injustices of Colonialism?*

Colonialism has been a recurrent feature of human history. Everywhere in the past, lands have been conquered and new settlements have emerged brutally. Marauders, who came to new lands to plunder wealth, stayed on after killing the original inhabitants and stealing their goods. All brutal invasions were unjust, even when they were not recognized to be so, but in most such cases of past injustices, circumstances have changed so drastically as to supersede them. The possible historic injustice inflicted on the people of parts of north India by the Mughal conquest in the early sixteenth century has certainly been superseded, first, because of the common suffering inflicted on both Muslims and Hindus by British colonialism and second, by the birth of political democracy in India. These past injustices of conquest and ancient colonialisms that have long ceased are not my concern in this chapter.[1]

* This paper was presented at a Conference on Reparations at Queen's University, Canada, 6–8 February 2004. It was subsequently published as 'How Should We Respond to the Cultural Injustices of Colonialism?', in J. Miller and R. Kumar (eds), *Reparations: Inter-disciplinary Inquiries*, Oxford: Oxford University Press, 2007, pp. 215–51.

[1] I am concerned with modern colonialism in this chapter but not with its most recent instances. It is arguable that the American invasion of Iraq and, more broadly, the emergence of new forces of globalization led by the USA and its allies—trans-national companies, financial and media institutions—betray the beginnings, if not the return, of a colonial empire. Whether or not this is the case, such instances of a possible, newly emerging imperial system are

Rather, I attend in this chapter, first, to injustices that started in the somewhat distant past, mostly in the early modern era, but are still continuing. Many examples of such continuing injustices exist. The plight of the blacks or the Indians in America and the suffering and marginalization of the native inhabitants of Australia and New Zealand are all a result of colonization. Arguably, the dalits in India have suffered injustice as a result of a long process of internal colonialism that persists to this day. Among continuing injustices, I deal more specifically on the injustices of modern European colonialism whose impact was felt by almost all non-western peoples. Although this chapter has a larger theoretical concern, my focus is still narrower and I concentrate largely, though not wholly, on the Indian experience of colonialism.

Modern colonialism went beyond physical violence, forcible occupation of lands, or extraction of tribute and wealth. It forcibly established a relationship between the lands of the colonizers and the colonized, and inaugurated a flow of human and natural resources that continually fed the economy of the colonizers and impoverished the colonized. As the early protagonists of the movement of Indian independence from British rule argued, there was a ceaseless drain of wealth from the colony to the metropolis. This economic injustice was accompanied by political injustice. The maintenance of economic asymmetries between the colony and the metropolis required that the latter kept a near absolute political control of the former. Neither economic nor political control could have been sustained without the pervasive belief in the cultural superiority of the colonizers. In order to establish this superiority, it was important to conquer not only the land and goods of the colonized but also their culture and mind. Colonization, therefore, involved not just economic and political injustice but also *cultural* injustice.[2] The primary focus of this chapter is the *continuing* cultural injustice of modern

---

also not the concern of this chapter. For a good overview of colonialism and post-colonialism, see Ania Loomba, *Colonialism/Postcolonialism*, New York: Routledge, 1998.

[2] Kok-Chor Tan discusses all the three forms of injustices and argues that rectification of these injustices can be framed both in terms of arguments from global egalitarian justice and in terms of reparation. My focus is narrower, on cultural injustice and my own framing of the issue of rectification avoids an appeal to global egalitarian justice and relies on a broad idea of reparation. See Kok-Chor Tan, 'Colonialism, Reparations and Global Justice', in Miller and Kumar (eds), *Reparations*, pp. 280–306.

colonialism. This injustice has neither ceased nor is present with the same force and vividity as in the past. Though somewhat faded, it has not evaporated completely, however. How do we respond to these injustices? What is the requirement of justice when the culture and the mind of a people are severely damaged by another people?

We can respond to colonial and other forms of injustices in different ways. For killing, rape, torture, and abduction, legal prosecution and punishment is appropriate, even when it is not always possible. Contemporary societies have sought to prosecute perpetrators of atrocity and sometimes, even those who benefited from the repression of communities. Less aggressive forms of retributive punishment can also be tried. For example, Czechoslovakia removed those civil servants from public office who were implicated in the old regime. However, retribution is not the only response to grave injustice. If goods are stolen and lands occupied, then justice minimally requires not only that the offender be punished but that they be restored to the original owners. Similarly, if the reins of a community have been wrongly usurped by members of another community, then justice, at the very least, requires that the members of the wronged community begin to rule themselves again. And, if retribution and restoration are either not possible or morally unsustainable, then justice requires some form of compensation to the victims. This is as true of individuals as for groups. Many societies have attempted alternative reparative responses. In Canada, First Nation groups were recompensed with land grants. In India, jobs in the government and seats in educational institutions are reserved for dalits to compensate for gross economic injustice in the past.

Other forms of reparations have also been attempted. After the overthrow of repressive communist regimes, East Germany allowed public access to secret police files. In Chile and Argentina, commissions of enquiry were set up to recover the bitter truth of mass disappearance. The South African Truth and Reconciliation Commission too combined different reparative strategies that included a search for truth and socio-psychological healing. In a sense, these are all restorative strategies to give back dignity and self-respect to those from whom they were snatched. Indeed, affirmative action programmes in India were introduced for dalits to compensate for systematic exclusion from the political sphere. Implicit in these policies, however, was an acknowledgement that a wrong against them had been committed by the rest of the community for which it was now prepared to offer an apology.

Which of these responses is appropriate, if at all, for cultural injustice?[3] Can perpetrators be punished for inflicting cultural injustice? Does justice require the restoration of cultures and the healing of injured minds? Is this even possible? If not, what other reparations are in order? I undertake three tasks in this chapter: first, to specify what I mean by cultural injustice and to identify the different forms of cultural injustice in colonialism. Second, I delineate three diverse perspectives on cultural injustices of colonialism. I offer a brief evaluation of each and specify which of these is more suited to India and related countries and why. Third, I try to explore a response to this injustice, one which goes beyond silence and denial but rules out retaliatory violence against or forcible exclusion of cultures of former colonizers. I argue that though both victims and perpetrators must work out their own separate and distinctive responses, the rectification of cultural injustice also requires a common response from both.

CULTURAL INJUSTICE

What is cultural injustice? I take it that all of us are equally entitled to make choices about how to live our lives and that it is wrong, indeed unjust, to interfere with these choices. To make these choices, we must first be able to make sense of and evaluate the situations within which they are made. This activity of interpreting and evaluating situations and choices is partly group dependent because it depends on collectively generated and sustained systems of meanings and significances. The group in question involves not just all contemporary members but their predecessors and successors as well. Thus, the generation and sustenance of this system of meanings, interpretations, and significances is historical. Culture, then, is a historically generated, collectively sustained system of meanings and significance by reference to which a group understands and regulates its individual and collective life.[4]

[3] This is not an issue that has been much addressed. Hitherto, focus has remained on socio-economic and political injustice in both national and international contexts. More recently, attention has shifted to the exploration of responses to mass atrocities and to cultural injustice within the nation-state. But there is a form of global cultural injustice which has been around for centuries. Much has been written on the injustice of cultural colonialism but not enough attempt has been made to construct a proper moral response to it.

[4] Bhikhu Parekh, *Rethinking Multiculturalism: Cultural Diversity and Political Theory*, London: Macmillan Press Ltd, 2000, chapter 5; Also see, Steven Lukes, 'Moral Diversity and Relativism', in Yael Tamir (ed.), *Democratic Education in a Multicultural State*, Oxford and Cambridge: Wiley Blackwell, 1995, pp. 15–22.

Being a system of meanings, culture is reflected in our conceptual framework, and in our language. Since culture is also a system of evaluation concerning our own life and the lives of others, our action and that of others, an inextricable link exists between culture and ethics. Since religion and ethics are frequently tied to one another and culture is the overarching structure of all meanings, culture is also tied to religion. Thus, culture is embodied in the collective memories and future visions of a group, in the group's myths, rituals, rules, norms, and customs. Since all of these—conceptual framework, language, collective memory, future visions, rules, norms and customs, myths and rituals, morality and religion—provide a sense of who we are and our self-worth, culture is inextricably linked to individual and collective identity.[5] Given its importance, every group must have access to its own systems of meanings, interpretations, and values, to its tradition and heritage, to its cultures. If members of a group are denied access to their own culture, then they suffer cultural injustice. This happens when they are born into the practices of a society that prevent them from having a knowledge of the historical and cultural traditions of their own ethnic or cultural group. Thomas calls this natal alienation.[6] If natal alienation occurs because of the forcible destruction of their culture, then there is grave cultural injustice.

Anything that is generated and sustained over time cannot remain static. Since cultures are historical, they must change over time. However, wherever humanly possible, members of a cultural community must be able to change their culture by their own light, by their own self-understandings, in terms of a set of reasons with which they identify and which they have more or less worked out themselves. When the culture of a group changes behind their backs, by acts of another group of people in terms that it does not understand, then the group loses cultural autonomy, which is another form of cultural injustice.

A culture is sustained when there is an uninterrupted transfer of cultural goods and resources from one generation to another. Just as individuals care about their children and grandchildren and are predisposed to accept a collective obligation to save and pass on resources

---

[5] Joseph Raz, 'Multiculturalism: A Liberal Perspective in Ethics in the Public Domain', in *Ethics in the Public Domain: Essays in the Morality of Law and Politics*, Oxford: Clarendon Press, 1994, pp. 155–76.

[6] Quoted in James P. Sterba, 'Understanding Evil: American Slavery, the Holocaust, and the Conquest of the American Indians', *Ethics*, vol. 106, no. 2, January 1996, pp. 424–48.

to their descendants, just so members of a cultural community care about future generations and are predisposed to accept a collective obligation to transfer cultural resources to their descendants.[7] To be sure, this transfer cannot be entirely free of interruption but nor must the interruption last too long or go too deep. If that were to happen, the fundamental ways in which a group frames its experience and thinks about, individuates, and understands the world—what I call the *basic cultural forms of a group*—can undergo a fundamental change. Even if this were to happen, it would not constitute a cultural injustice where this occurs on its own or by the group's own mistaken actions. Cultural injustice occurs when the basic cultural forms of a group are altered by the arbitrary or deliberate actions of another powerful or dominant group. An individual may appear to live her life autonomously if she acts on reasons (beliefs, desires) that she chooses or endorses but the group to which she belongs may not be autonomous if the framework within which it conceives, understands, and interprets these reasons is not collectively chosen or endorsed. A forcible alteration in the basic cultural form affects cultural autonomy in this deeper sense.

Finally, cultures are sustained by groups whose individual members possess the capacity to do so. If this capacity to sustain cultures is damaged by the deliberate or arbitrary actions of members of another cultural group, then here too there has been cultural injustice.[8] Indeed, this loss of capacity has grave consequences. If part of the culture of a people is lost or damaged but their collective capacity to repair or reinvent it is intact, then the wrong of a cultural injustice can be undone

[7] Members are not always aware of these concerns, nor do they necessarily acknowledge them, but such concerns are presupposed by a number of things they do. It is also institutionalized in the educational system sustained by teachers and educators and is part of what parents expect from the teachers of their children.

[8] Similarly, if colonial settlers and missionaries undermine the ability of indigenous people to govern themselves according to their own law, then there is grave political injustice. This precisely appears to have happened in Australia with the Aboriginal nations. On this, see Janna Thompson, *Taking Responsibility for the Past: Reparation and Historical Justice*, Cambridge: Polity Press, 2002, p. 73. Similarly, the Canadian state had launched a systematic cultural assault on Aboriginal communities of Canada by promulgating the Indian act that banned their cherished customs. The entire act presupposed the cultural backwardness and the incapacity for self-rule of these people. On this, see Alan Cairns, 'Coming to Terms with the Past', in John Torpey (ed.), *Politics and the Past*, Oxford: Rowman & Littlefield Publishers, 2003, p. 78.

relatively easily. However, if the collective capacity of a group is itself lost or badly damaged, then the harm is particularly grave. I shall call this a grave psycho-cultural injustice.

THREE PERSPECTIVES ON CULTURAL INJUSTICE

The Extreme Negative Perspective: Fanon, Cesaire, Memmi

Allow me to now examine the first view on the cultural injustice of colonialism: grave cultural injustice and frequently, grave psycho-cultural injustice is an integral feature of the system of domination that has come to be associated with modern colonialism. Without detracting from the truth or importance of this claim, I shall call this the extreme negative perspective on cultural colonialism.

The African writers, Aime Cesaire, Frantz Fanon, and Albert Memmi, passionately argued that the main consequence of colonialism was not the mere exploitation but the objectification and dehumanization of the colonized subject. Fanon declared that colonialism had so crushingly annihilated the self of the black African that after this experience, 'the black man is not a man'.[9] But what does it mean to lose one's self? Is this even a coherent idea? It is possible to make sense of what Fanon is trying to get at. At the very least, it means that as a result of colonization, the black man has lost a complete sense of self-respect. But Fanon draws our attention to something even more fundamental. A person whose self has been annihilated is one who is almost entirely what the other makes of her and one whose attributes could not have been constituted by her own conception and agency for the simple reason that she has no conception or agency of her own. Such a person cannot function as a human agent because she has lost the most crucial and fundamental relation a person can have with herself. She is devoid of basic self-confidence.[10] Those who have undergone extreme experiences of physical violation such as rape and torture are known to have been deprived of the ability to access their needs as their own and to express them without fear or anxiety. It follows that if they lose their self-confidence, the colonized must have been subjected to severe repression. They are subjected to coercion of the body, to physical violence, and severe restriction of physical movement. They are also subjected to coercion

[9] Frantz Fanon, 'Black Skin, White Masks', in Loomba, *Colonialism/Postcolonialism*, p. 8.

[10] See Axel Honneth, *The Struggle for Recognition: The Moral Grammar of Social Conflicts*, Cambridge, Massachusetts: MIT Press, 1996, p. 118.

of the will by punishment or by the threat of it. Moreover, this coercive, interfering action by the colonizer is done with impunity and at will. Because he can hardly ever be penalized, the colonizer interferes with impunity. He interferes at will because he never waits for an independent legitimating circumstance or motive. Only the power of his own capricious will restricts his own behaviour.[11] This arbitrary but persistent and coercive interference ultimately breaks the spirit of the colonized, resulting in the loss of basic self-confidence. This confirms the central point of Fanon's claim that '... de-humanisation enters the psyche and subjectivity of the colonized people'.

A person without basic self-confidence lacks the fundamental capacity to contribute to the sustenance and growth of his culture. Such a person is condemned to lose his memory, for memory is not purely a mental phenomenon. It rests upon its institutions. However, once the institutions of the colonized are demolished or petrified, he also loses a proper memory of the past.[12] From then on, 'the memory assigned to him is not that of his own people. The history he has taught is not his own. Everything seems to have taken place out of his country. Everything exists only with reference what he is not'.[13] Such a person who has been forced to turn away from his own culture and tradition suffers from natal alienation. The colonized is natally alienated because he is born into the practices of a society that prevent him from participating in or having a secure knowledge of the historical and cultural traditions of his own ethnic or cultural group. A colonized group that suffers natal alienation, and whose members have no common memory or basic self-confidence and show signs of self-hatred and pathetic mimicry of the colonizers, are victims of grave psycho-cultural injustice at the hands of the colonized.

A person who suffers from natal alienation and has lost basic self-confidence develops grave moral defects, the principal deficiency being a permanent propensity to be servile. Given the relationship between culture and identity, it is not surprising that the attributes of natal alienation and servility are frequently found in the same people. Thomas Hill's fictional Uncle Tom almost wholly echoes what Fanon

---

[11] See Philip Pettit, 'Freedom as Antipower', *Ethics*, vol. 106, no. 3, April 1996, pp. 576–604.

[12] Albert Memmi, *The Colonizer and the Colonized*, Boston: Beacon Press, 1965, p. 103.

[13] Ibid., p. 105.

and others have in mind.[14] Uncle Tom steps aside for white man, does not complain when less qualified whites take over his job, displays the symbols of deference to whites, always with a bowed stance and a ready 'sir' and 'ma'am'. He accepts without question the idea that as a black he is owed less than whites, his desires are worth nothing, and those of the white man are worth their weight in gold. In short, he believes in the intrinsic superiority of the white man and because this belief affects his character and action, he betrays complete absence of any self-respect or self-worth.

To escape their colonized condition, victims of grave psycho-cultural injustice make an earnest attempt to resemble the colonizer to the point of 'disappearing in him'.[15] Hoping that the colonizer would make them one of his own, they endeavour to forget the past; change collective habits; and adopt western language, culture, and customs. His desperate need for approval and acceptance from the colonizer goes hand-in-hand with his rejection of his true self. As he adopts the colonizer's values, he also embraces his own condemnation. 'In order to free himself, he agrees to destroy himself.'[16] His love for the colonizer is 'subtended by a complex of feelings ranging from shame to self-hate'.[17] When Negro women try desperately to uncurl their hair, which keeps curling back, or torture their skin to make it a little lighter, or when bourgeois women prefer a mediocre jewel from Europe to the purest jewel of their tradition, they succumb to the most superficial Europeanization. Superficiality is the achievement of the colonized and mimicry the process by which it is accomplished.

The 'Contact Zone' Perspective: Denial of Cultural Injustice

The most direct opposition to this extreme negative perspective on cultural colonialism comes from those who argue that while colonialism involved economic and political injustice, it generally refrained from interfering in the cultures of the exploited people.[18] Colonial empires, they argue, are known to have given the colonized a great degree of

[14] See Thomas E. Hill Jr, *Autonomy and Self-respect*, Cambridge: Cambridge University Press, 1991, p. 19.

[15] Memmi, *The Colonizer and the Colonized*, p. 120.

[16] Ibid., p. 121.

[17] Ibid.

[18] Ernest Gellner, *Encounters with Nationalism*, Oxford: Blackwell Publishers, 1994, pp. 62, 78. Gellner says, 'Rulers of dynastic states and empires were not

cultural autonomy. Over time, cultural interchange and diversity was an inevitable by-product of colonial empires and a synthesis of what has come to be called hybridity was a natural outcome of this encounter. If so, it might even be denied that cultural injustice was a feature of colonialism.

There is some evidence to support this view, particularly if it is used selectively. Undoubtedly, despite ideological pronouncements of cultural difference, colonialism brought together different groups of people in intimate contact with one another. Disparate cultures met each other in a 'contact zone' where they grappled with the other's way of looking at the world.[19] Borrowing and lending were commonplace in these social spaces and therefore, the distinction between the culture of the colonizer and of the colonized began to blur. For example, there is ample evidence to show that in the early part of the East India Company's foray into India, colonial settlers willingly embraced large chunks of Indian culture in order to feel at home. They lived like Indians at home and in the office, wore Indian dress, and observed Indian customs and religious practices. A number of them married Indian women. 'White Moghals' are clearly a case of crossover. Such crossovers came from the opposite direction when, as a by-product of colonial rule or as a result of colonial policies, Indian immigrants reached the metropolis and non-Indian colonies of the empire. Over a period of time, a degree of synthesis simply had to come about no matter who imitated whom in the initial stages of colonial encounter. If so, far from freezing identities, colonialism destabilized and made them fluid.

Second, colonial belief systems could hardly have formed without negotiation with and incorporation of indigenous ideas. Frequently, the colonizer depended on the native for access to vital information without which colonial rule would collapse. Much evidence exists to show that without local knowledges it would have been impossible for the colonizer to build dams, bridges, irrigation systems, or to collect revenue. Land management would have been impossible without traditional knowledge governing the relationship with peasants, landlords, and the state.[20] Moreover, even as western ideas were brought to colonized

---

concerned with whether their boundaries transgressed the so-to-speak ethnographic limits or even whether they reach them. They were interested in the tribute and labour potential of their subjects, not in their culture.'

[19] Mary Pratt, quoted in Loomba, *Colonialism/Postcolonialism*, p. 70.

[20] Ranajit Guha, *Dominance without Hegemony: History and Power in Colonial India*, New Delhi: Oxford University Press, 1998, pp. 158–64.

lands, their successful realization would not have been possible had local experts not grafted them onto their traditional analogues. For example, the idiom of order could not have functioned without the Indian idiom of *Danda* (an ensemble of power, authority, and punishment, emphasizing force and fear as the fundamental principles of politics). Likewise, the civilizing mission of the British required the idiom of improvement which depended for its realization on the Indian idiom of dharma, understood broadly as 'virtue, the moral duty'.[21] Similarly, travellers and conquerors were frequently dependent on the services of translators and relied on them for understanding almost everything about the natives. These translations into a suitable vernacular vocabulary were never pure or perfect; some synthesis was therefore inevitable. In such situations of dynamic cultural interaction and ambivalence, is it not hard to sustain the claim of cultural injustice?

Claims of cultural injustice can be disputed in other ways too. First, it can easily be argued that directly in the midst of economic exploitation and political despotism, there was one arena where the colonized continued to exercise near absolute sovereignty. For example, in India, elites began to resist cultural colonization by dividing the world into a material, outside sphere constituted of the economy, state-craft, science, and ideology, and a spiritual, inner-domain of culture which included religion, customs, and the family.[22] The colonized elites asserted their claim over their mother tongue and set up instruments for their dissemination. They conceded the supremacy of the West in the material world, but claimed the spiritual–cultural world for themselves and made it the essential feature of nationality, one that must be protected and defended. The state may have been given over to the colonizers but culture and the private sphere remained in the hands of the colonized. So, the colonized exercised the right to their own culture and were permitted to do so by the colonial state. If that be the case, then, so the argument might go, no matter how unjust colonial rule was from the economic and political viewpoint, surely there was no cultural injustice inflicted by it.

Second, colonialism anyway was not an unambiguous, unmitigated disaster for the colonized. It was a civilizing force. Had not the raj introjected liberal western values and helped thereby to foster social reform, combat superstition, and raise the level of indigenous culture?

[21] Ibid., pp. 24–39.
[22] Partha Chatterjee, *The Nation and Its Fragments*, New Delhi: Oxford University Press, 1998.

In particular, colonial culture was a modern culture that directly challenged the filth in indigenous traditions. Elites and people from the lower strata both benefited from modernity. Thus, westernization was adopted for purely instrumental reasons. In the late eighteenth century, reacting to the excesses of their own traditions, young men in Calcutta

openly defied the cannons of Hinduism. Many deliberately offended public opinion by their youthful exuberance, often parading in an inebriated state, blatantly challenging orthodox Brahmins by flinging beef-bones into their houses and walking the streets shouting 'we have eaten Musalman bread'.[23]

In short, hyper-westernization became a form of protest against the filth in one's own traditions, something started by Ram Mohan Roy and continued to this day by dalits (the statue of Ambedkar in a blue suit, with spectacles and polished shoes, constitution in hand is an apt reminder). Quite possibly, changes in society necessitated certain functions to be performed and, in the absence of functional analogues within existing cultural systems, this role could be fulfilled only by elements within western modernity. This explains the painless, rather smooth acceptance in India of modern educational and legal systems. As early as 1841, 'it was noticed that the Chamars, despised untouchables of northern India were not afraid to bring suits against their more powerful and privileged landlords'.[24] If the colonial modern culture served the interests of the colonized, how can the claim of cultural injustice be upheld?

Not only did the colonized benefit from colonial culture but arguably, the colonizers were harmed by it. This goes against folk wisdom for which the only sufferers of colonialism are the subject communities. However, as the Indian writer, Ashis Nandy points out, 'what Cesaire calls the decivilization of the colonizers is not an impotent fantasy but rather an empirical reality.'[25] For Nandy, colonialism is a cultural code shared by both the rulers and the ruled, the main function of which is to alter the cultural priorities on *both* sides and bring to the centre of the colonized culture, sub-cultures previously dormant, and remove from the centre of the colonizing culture that which might have been salient earlier. For example, parts of British culture which were least tender

[23] Charles Heimsath, quoted in Yogendra Singh, *Modernization of Indian Tradition*, Delhi: Rawat Publications, 1988, p. 89.

[24] O' Malley, quoted in Singh, *Modernization of Indian Tradition*, p. 100.

[25] Ashis Nandy, *The Intimate Enemy: Loss and Recovery of Self under Colonialism*, New Delhi: Oxford University Press, 1983, pp. 30–1.

and humane became prominent. The 'softer, feminine side' of human nature was made irrelevant to the public sphere and in the name of the values of competition, achievement, control, and productivity, new forms of institutionalized violence and ruthless social Darwinism was sanctified. Nandy claims that the 'tragedy of colonialism was also the tragedy of the younger sons, women, and all the etceteras and and-so-forths of Britain'. He goes on to argue that the ideology of colonialism produced an 'undeveloped heart' and encouraged the colonizers to falsely impute to themselves magical feelings of omnipotence and permanence. A culture that harmed the victor as much as the victim surely obliterates the distinction between the two and this makes it difficult to hold on to one's claim of the cultural injustice of the colonialism.

Lastly, it might be argued that even if there was cultural injustice in the colonial encounter, it was possibly due to larger social forces that, even without direct political rule, would have negatively affected cultures. If so, cultural injustice was incidental, not necessarily attributable to colonialism. On this view, colonization was only one form assumed by an expanding capitalism and a liberal democratic ethos that usually accompanies it. An emphasis on equality, individual freedom, and the resulting conception of justice would sooner rather than later have challenged the collective, hierarchical mode of thinking that characterizes non-western traditional cultures. That it did so with the help of brutal colonial politics is no doubt unfortunate but modern culture would have come to traditional societies even without colonialism. More to the point, regardless of the consequence of political conquest, the colonizers were as much in the grip of this culture as the colonized and therefore, nobody can really be held morally responsible for the results. Given the ambivalent character of the colonial encounter, the most reasonable conclusion then can only be that colonialism generated, at best, minor cultural injustices, for which some regret can be expressed but nothing more.

How seriously do we take the claim that denies cultural injustices of colonialism? For a start, the importance of crossovers and hybridity must not be exaggerated. The number of colonized who crossed over was very small. Those who crossed over tended, at least in the initial but long period, to virtually surrender to colonial culture. More importantly, the much larger number of colonized peoples had no contact with their colonial rulers. Though their lives were surrounded and deeply affected by the empire, the vast majority of Indians never saw the English administrator. They were excluded from colonial modernity and its benefits, partly by the nature of its cultural form to which they were insufficiently attuned but also deliberately by those very natives who had crossed over. Second, the assertion that Indian elites affirmed their originality in the private, cultural sphere is overstated. It fails to grasp the crucial point that the urgently felt need to be formally educated in one's own native language was itself a symptom of western, colonial influence. Under conditions of modernity, access to a shared literate high culture had become the most important possession of a person.[26] Because it gave him employment, wealth, social status, and citizenship, he had a head start if this culture was shaped by his mother tongue. A sense of importance of one's mother tongue prefigured the realization that it could bring great economic and political benefits. There was nothing particularly original in this, for it replicated the trajectory of European nationalism. Third, the proud deployment of one's mother tongue did little to prevent a deeper split between the public and the private. The Indian intelligentsia became increasing concerned with social reform in public life and continued to nurture oppressive and hierarchical values within the four walls of their homes. Thus, they managed, at the very best, to stitch together a patchwork of the colonial modern and the traditional 'feudal' and lived in this world with an unacknowledged schizophrenia.[27]

Fourth, claims concerning the civilizing force of colonial rule under-state the failure of colonial liberalism to overcome the resistance of oppressive customs and hierarchical belief systems and the many compromises imposed by these on attempts at social reform. It fails to recognize the pressing need felt by those unaffected by western influence to effect transformation in their social practices. It also underestimates the real motivation behind the introduction of modern ideas and the distorted form they assumed. This motivation had less to do with social reform or revolution and more with the maintenance of colonial rule. Much of the justification to maintain this rule came from European values and institutions. However, colonial rule also necessitated that values and institutions prevalent in colonized societies were not entirely displaced. This meant that modern values were introduced partially

---

[26] See Gellner, *Encounters with Nationalism*, p. 62.

[27] On the cultural phenomenon of patchwork, see Rajeev Bhargava, 'Are there Alternative Modernities?', in N.N. Vohra (ed.), *Culture, Democracy and Development in South Asia*, New Delhi: Shipra and India International Centre, 2000, pp. 9–26. Reproduced in Chapter 12 of this volume.

and half-heartedly. Colonial rule both introduced and held back the flow of new ideas and institutions. Many of them therefore took a mediocre, stunted form. As Guha puts it, 'ideas which were political dynamite in Europe had their critical charged doused and defused by colonialism.'[28] This might be overstating the case but not entirely wrong for at least some ideas with emancipatory intent.

But can anyone seriously contest that the colonized benefited from colonialism? Would not denying that they did be plainly wrong? However, it is hard to tell if the same benefits and many more would not have accrued without the mediation of colonialism. The historical geographer, J.M. Blaut, has argued that prior to 1492, 'the progress toward modernization and capitalism which was taking place in parts of Europe was also taking place in parts of Asia and Africa.'[29] European colonialism, in his view, probably thwarted these developments in other parts of the world and the wealth obtained from non-Europe was a necessary and important basis for the continued development of European modernity and capitalism.[30] Therefore, the view that Europe brought progress to the rest of the world is, quite simply, the colonizer's version of what happened. It is a Eurocentric picture that offers 'the colonizer's model of the world'. In any case, benefits of modernity to the colonized and its harm to the colonizer miss the point of the critic because the crux of the matter here is cultural autonomy, not gains and losses. After all, the liberty of persons and groups has frequently been impeded on the ground that such interference is for their own good, and in their own real interests. When American-Indian children were taken from their parents, sent to boarding school, and educated in white ways, the goal was not to harm but to benefit them, 'to kill the backward Indian and to save the man'. No consent was obtained from their parents. No matter how beneficial modernity is to the colonized, the real issue is whether or not he and other members of his group are authors of the conceptual and cultural frame that gives their life meaning and significance. Colonial cultural modernity can be seen, at best, as a case of cultural paternalism.

The truth is that it is hard to ignore the historical fact that the meeting of disparate cultures took place in highly asymmetrical relations of domination and subordination, and though the ambivalence of colonial

---

[28] Guha, *Dominance without Hegemony*, p. 169.

[29] J.M. Blaut, *The Colonizer's Model of the World*, New York: The Guilford Press, 1993, p. 152.

[30] Ibid., p. 10.

relations may not have been a product of pure imperial duplicity, nor can it be construed as an outgrowth of an innocent encounter between equals. Not that all those who draw attention to these ambivalences espouse this myth but quite a few, in the name of restoring agency, deliberative capacity, and crucial self-consciousness to victims, and to register the voice of native informants, end up viewing the construction of colonial cultures and ideology as the joint product of a dialogue between the colonizers and the colonized.[31] This is far from the bitter truth. In short, it is hard to deny the cultural injustice of colonialism.

Does this mean that the extremist view is correct after all? This does not follow. This perspective is useful for some societies (African), for some elites of many colonized societies, and for most elites of such societies that are in an important middle phase of colonialism. What is questionable in this view is not that colonialism took this coercive form and generated grave psycho-cultural injustice or that it threatened to bring grave cultural injustice about but that this happened everywhere, all the time. In short, the disputable feature of this view is that it makes pure coercion a necessary and grave cultural or psycho-cultural injustice a constitutive feature of colonial rule. This is not so for societies such as India. It is, of course, true that large sections of Indian elites were virtually forced or seduced into breaking away from their own identities and that they submitted to colonial modernity but this happened in one phase of colonialism. In another phase, a sustained critical examination of this self-surrender began to develop. The rebirth of self-questioning implies that even when there was a sustained assault on their indigenous culture, their collective *capacity* to reconstruct it was never damaged. On the whole, Indian elites were not victims of grave psycho-cultural injustice and Indian society did not suffer from grave cultural injustice.

The Moderately Negative View on Cultural Injustice

The perspective which denies that grave psycho-cultural justice was not a pervasive feature of colonialism, but admits that a variety of systematic cultural injustices were constitutive of it and therefore, which challenges the extremism of both the first and the second perspectives may be called the moderately negative perspective on the cultural injustice of colonialism. For this perspective, it is important that we see that

---

[31] On this, see Nicholas B. Dirks, *Castes of Mind: Colonialism and the Making of Modern India*, Delhi: Permanent Black, 2002.

colonial rule operated with different mechanisms. In particular, that some of the more effective mechanisms of colonial rule have depended on voluntary and contrived consent of culturally co-opted elites and the cultural exclusion of the masses. In short, colonial regimes achieved their domination by creating partial consent. This consent was partial, first in the sense that the threat of coercion always surrounded it and second, in that it was given only by those incorporated within the regime, not by those excluded from it. Incorporation and exclusion were two intrinsic features of colonial cultural modernity.[32]

How was incorporation of elites achieved? Initially, assimilation was sought by a deliberate attempt to intellectually destroy the culture and history of the colonized on intellectual and moral grounds. As Ranajit Guha explains, colonial historians tried to do this in India so that they could then go on to fill the void with their own civilizational ideas. The substitution of Indian by colonial culture was meant to be completed in two successive phases. In the first, the historic culture of the Hindus was to be demolished by showing that it was superseded by the culture of Muslims and then, the culture of Muslims was itself to be shown as inferior. Taken together, these two movements were to result in the virtual deletion of the entire pre-colonial past of our people, who were then to be 'compensated for that loss by the gift of a new history—a fore-shortened history with the colonial state as its subject'.[33]

Had they succeeded in wholly destroying India's past and its culture or in demolishing their ability to resist and rebuild them, the extremist perspective would have got it just right. Fortunately, this did not happen. However, colonialism did succeed, for long periods, in partially destroying the self-respect and confidence of elites in almost every colonized society. This happened in India too. This is the grain of truth in the extremist claim. This is why it is hard to accept the blanket assertion that 'there was no rupture with the past', or that 'traditional identities were not disrupted', or that 'colonialism introduced no more than one new idiom, one new strand in the complex mosaic of the societies subjected to it'. Or finally that 'the alleged schizophrenia induced by the conflict between traditional and modern identities did

[32] Incorporation is necessary because 'it is an essential feature of colonization to try to create an institutionally complete society'. This requires that 'natives adjust to the language, pattern of work and mental habits of the colonizers, if they had any hope of survival leave alone flourishing'. See Will Kymlicka, *Multicultural Citizenship*, Oxford: Clarendon Press, 1995, p. 15.

[33] Guha, *Dominance without Hegemony*, pp. 75–80.

not quite exist'.[34] As I have mentioned, sections of the Indian elite, in at least one phase of colonialism and to some degree, experienced some rupture with the past, a great deal of disruption of their own received identities, some form of schizophrenia and that the colonial modern was not merely one among several but the dominant idiom of self-understanding and the understanding of societies. Colonial society as a whole escaped this fate because a majority of its people were excluded from colonial culture and, therefore, also escaped many defects it created in the elites.

If cultural destruction did not succeed as a strategy of incorporation, by what mechanism were Indian elites incorporated into the colonial system? Incorporation was achieved by shaping the beliefs and desires of the elite and altering their identity. Fundamental to this alternative strategy was to get the colonized to believe in the worthlessness and inferiority of their own culture.[35] In the nineteenth century, many Indian things began to be denigrated. For example, the architect of early Indian liberalism, Ram Mohan Roy, felt that the government policy of support to Sanskrit and Arabic-Persian education would only serve to keep India in darkness.

The inferiorization of indigenous cultures, necessary for the exercise of colonial power, was effected by the generation of colonial discourse by western political theorists, advisors to colonial governments, colonial administrators, official historians, and teachers of English literature. Following Edward Said, several scholars have argued that colonial power functioned by producing a discourse about the Orient, crucial to European self-understanding, premised on a binary opposition between the West and the non-West and that quite fundamentally misrepresented and traduced the latter. Thus, in the writings of apologists of colonialism such as James Mill, Indian history was assimilated into the history of Great Britain and used to mark a major difference between the people of two countries. One constituted the white rulers, materially prosperous, much better civilized with a superior religion and belief system. The other were the ruled, ethnically black, vastly

[34] Jan N. Pieterse and Bhikhu Parekh (eds), *The Decolonisation of Imagination: Culture, Knowledge and Power*, New Delhi: Oxford University Press, 1997, pp. 2–3 (first published, London: Zed Books, 1995).

[35] Fanon understood this well. For him, 'the colonized people are not simply those whose labour has been appropriated but those in whose soul an inferiority complex has been created by the death and burial of its local cultural originality.'

underdeveloped at a much lower level of civilization and inferior religion and belief system.[36] The colonizers had their own explanation for this superiority. By keeping their sexual appetite under control and working hard, Europeans produced a mature, morally complex civilization. The Orient was lazy and barbaric and at best, primitive, childish, and morally simple, lacking the psychological growth of the European.[37] Similarly, the irrationality of the colonized was contrasted with rational Europeans. In the primitive mind, thought and reflection were largely absent and instinct predominated. Delayed gratification of desire was unknown to the non-European.[38] This made them hard to be rational.

Cultural colonialism, then, was largely a project of the inferiorization of colonized cultures whose members were seen by it in the image of a child, if not exactly treated as barbaric.[39] Two things followed, once this inferiorization was in place. First, since it generated a loss of self-esteem and self-respect, those among the elites who could escape their own 'inferior culture' did so and became 'more British than the British' in those spheres of societies that really mattered. They became, as Fanon puts it, 'people with black skin and white masks'. They did not entirely leave the whole of their culture but became uncomfortable with almost every one of its features. This discomfort with different aspects of their culture and tradition was indiscriminate and pervasive among Indian elites in one long phase of the colonial period. Second, those who could not or did not wish to escape their culture were condemned to be treated as inferior by their own, precisely those elites who had forsaken it. This led to new cultural divisions and to a system of graded inequality.[40]

This needs further explanation. No matter how much the colonized elites emulated their colonial masters, they were not accepted by them

[36] See, Guha, *Dominance without Hegemony*, p. 3.

[37] See Uday Singh Mehta, *Liberalism and Empire: India in British Liberal Thought*, New Delhi: Oxford University Press, 1999; Nandy, *The Intimate Enemy*; Sterba, 'Understanding Evil: American Slavery, the Holocaust, and the Conquest of the American Indians', pp. 424–48; Gauri Viswanathan, *Masks of Conquest*, New Delhi: Oxford University Press, 1998.

[38] See Mehta, *Liberalism and Empire*, pp. 27–35.

[39] As Mehta points out, childhood is a theme that runs through the writings of British liberals on India. For these liberals, 'India is a child for which the empire offers the prospect of legitimate and progressive parentage and toward which Britain, as a parent, is similarly obligated and competent.' Ibid., p. 32.

[40] This term was used by Ambedkar, the great leader of the so-called 'untouchables' of India.

as their equals (hence, the schizophrenia, the resentment, and later, the resistance).[41] Not that the colonizer discouraged the elites to mimic him, but nor did he entirely permit them to attain a European identity. In the last instance, their emulation was met with disdain. The colonized elites could not escape being culturally victimized. However, the more inferior they felt vis-à-vis the colonial masters, the more they tried to inferiorize their own people from whom, by virtue of their adoption of colonial culture, they increasingly became culturally estranged. In his writings, Ashis Nandy has made this point differently. He agrees that a colonial system perpetuates itself by forcing the colonized to accept new social norms and cognitive categories by a system of socio-economic rewards and punishments.[42] But, for him, it does this even more so with the help of a more dangerous and permanent system of inner rewards and punishments, the unconscious, secondary psychological gains and losses from suffering and submission under colonialism.[43] Over time the victim begins to identify with the aggressor and develops an inner resistance to even recognize what colonialism does to him.[44]

[41] This is what Tagore had to say, 'we had just graduated and undertaken to translate such foreign phrases as equality, liberty, fraternity, etc., into Bangla, we thought that Europe, with all its physical prowess, acknowledged the weak as its equal in terms of human right. We, the recent graduates, were absolutely overwhelmed and looked upon them as gods whom we could go on worshipping for all time and who would go on helping us for ever with their beneficence.' 'The point I want to make,' wrote Tagore, 'is that an idea is fast gaining ground in India as well as in England itself that European principles are meant for Europe alone. Indians are so very different that the principles of civilization are not fully suitable for their needs.' Thus, even the most eminent of Indian liberals—one who believed in the universality of culture more than many of his contemporaries—was finally not deceived by the universalist claim of English liberalism. Tagore, quoted in Guha, *Dominance without Hegemony*, pp. 68–71.

[42] To transform Indians into white men was a conscious colonial policy of the British after mid-19th century. Lord Macaulay famously evolved a strategy guided by the need 'To form a class of persons, Indians in blood and colour, but English in taste, in opinions, in morals, and in intellect.' Quoted in Mehta, *Liberalism and Empire*, p. 15.

[43] See Nandy, *The Intimate Enemy*.

[44] Ibid., p. xiv. Indeed, a colonial culture is one in which the ruled are constantly tempted to fight their rulers within the psychological limits set by the latter. For example, even anti-colonial protest is modelled on this new valorized image of masculinity. For Nandy, it is no surprise that the West has produced not only its servile imitators and admirers but also its circus-tamed

Colonial education played a major part in encouraging the emulation of the colonial masters. It taught Indian elites 'to appreciate colonial conquest as a triumph and achievement, when triumph meant their own defeat and achievement the loss of independence'.[45] Moreover, colonial education displaced popular Indian traditions. Once English became constitutive of thought itself, it cut the elites off from their own tradition. This was noted by the famous Bengali thinker, Bankim Chandra Chatterjee, who said that 'the term *sikshita* has now become the usual designation for those who have been educated in the Western mode,' and is antonymous to *vidya*. Those who were sikshita were naturally alienated from traditional learning, entirely unacquainted with the systems of ancient Indian thought. One major consequence of colonialism then was this: it opened a wide schism between a western-ized colonial modernity and Indian tradition and this made it impossible for the new generation of the educated to communicate with the older generation of traditional scholars.

To sum up: colonialism did not destroy every indigenous culture. Nor did it objectify and dehumanize every colonial subject or treat him as barbaric. It did not even annihilate the basic self-confidence of all colonial subjects. However, by interfering in other cultures, colonialism began to distort them. It did so by shoving into margins hitherto central strands of indigenous culture and by pushing to the centre those of its elements that were dormant or peripheral. This displacement often continued till elements centrally organizing the experience of the colonized people began to survive only as memory and were displaced by facets that were considered by them to be insignificant and worthless. This is how I understand Ashis Nandy's claim that colonial culture altered the cultural priorities of the colonized culture. Now, this movement of elements from the centre to the periphery and vice versa and change, more generally, is common to all cultures. It occurs partly because culture is a complex and unsystematized whole without a coordinating authority. So, it is not change as such that is morally objectionable. Nor is the marginalization of once dominant strands. Rather, disapproval stems from the fact that this change was partly

---

opponents and its tragic counter players performing their last gladiator-like acts of courage in front of appreciative Caesars. Nandy claims that the standard opponents of the West have been integrated within the dominant consciousness as 'ornamental dissenters'.

[45] Guha, *Dominance without Hegemony*, p. 171.

orchestrated by an authority with enormous political and economic power, which did not have the capacity to live the indigenous culture from the inside, and that forcibly changed the direction of indigenous cultures—bringing about changes in it almost wholly behind its backs. Ironically, the agents of this change were usually colonized elites and sometimes, their white masters themselves.

Of the many examples Ashis Nandy furnishes, I mention one. Colonialism, he says, produced a cultural consensus in which political and social power symbolized the dominance of men and masculinity over women and feminity. Both androgyny and psychological bi-sexuality in Indian men were obscured and marginalized and dislodged by middle-class European sexual stereotypes. These stereotypes were soon internalized by Indians who slowly resurrected the ideology of martial races latent in the traditional Indian concept of statecraft and made them central to their experience and thinking. Henceforth, kshatriyahood became the indicator of authentic Indianness. Pre-colonial Indian culture, Nandy tells us, made subtle distinctions between different forms of androgyny and subjected them to evaluation. Some forms of androgyny were good and some others damaging. Colonialism lumped all these forms together, devalued them, and opposed this crude diminished form to an undifferentiated, newly valorized form of masculinity. For example, the Bengali writer, Madhusudan Dutt, rewrote the Ramayana and reversed the value hierarchy between Rama and Ravana. From Dutt's point of view, and in keeping with the cultural elevation of masculinity, the original Ramayana began to seem like a tragedy of sorts in which Ravana, who was masculine, courageous, proud, competitive, achievement-oriented, and technologically superior, was defeated by a feminine, weak-kneed, self-abnegating, and technologically inferior god, Rama. After the colonial transvaluation of values, Madhusudan Dutt grafted this masculinity to Rama himself. Rama becomes a modern kshatriya king competing with and defeating another kshatriya king, who is alien but shares the same cultural codes. So, in keeping with colonial ideology, a recessive feature of traditional Indian culture was now made salient.

I have so far spoken of two kinds of cultural injustice: first, the inferiorization of indigenous cultures and second, the enforced marginalization of elements of indigenous culture by the colonizers. But, there is a third kind in which the basic cultural form of indigenous cultures was transformed by the intentional and unintended acts of the colonizers. Let me give three examples of this transformative process.

First, in colonial cultures, group classification became more important than individualization. Albert Memmi reminds us that very often the mark of the plural was a sign of the depersonalization of the colonized. 'The colonized is never characterized in an individual manner; he is entitled only to drown in an anonymous collectivity.'[46] This is not uncommon when a group encounters strangers. It sees them only as an undifferentiated mass, through a crude stereotype, as if they are all the same, each merely instantiating the broad features shared equally by all. Individuation and individuality is frequently denied to the unfamiliar. Colonialism institutionalized this and evolved policies based on the idea that the conception of an individual was simply absent in the colonized and only group identity mattered in their traditions.

Second, related to the first, is the invention in India of a new conception of caste and its elevation as the central symbol of Indian society. Pre-colonial India had multiple social identities and their relations and trajectories could be understood only as part of a complex and dynamic social and political context. An individual could be a member of a temple community, territorial group, family unit, occupational reference group, agricultural or trading association, faith network, and so on. He was also a member of a *jati* (also translated as caste), which was only one category among others, one way of organizing and representing identity. Not much evidence exists that the people of pre-colonial India ever used a single term to express the diverse forms of identity and community in their own life-worlds. Colonialism displaced the idea of jati with *varna*—the classification of all castes into four hierarchical orders with the brahmin on top—gave it the sanction of religious scripture, thereby making caste a matter of a person's religious identity and finally, turned it into the central, pervasive, and centralizing feature of Indian society and Hindu religion.[47]

The colonial encounter more than just gave salience to groups in general and caste in particular. It transformed how people conceived their own faiths. The great scholar of comparative religions, Wilfred Cantwell Smith, has reminded us that religion as a demarcated system of doctrines—scriptures—and beliefs is an early modern European invention and begins its existence in and through the theological

---

[46] Quoted in Loomba, *Colonialism/Postcolonialism*, p. 70.

[47] Dirks, *Castes of Mind*, p. 13–14; D.L. Sheth, 'Caste and the Secularisation Process in India', in Peter deSouza (ed.), *Contemporary India: Transitions*, New Delhi: Sage Publications, 2000, p. 237–63.

disputes of the sixteenth and seventeenth centuries.[48] Under the impact of colonialism, this category came to India and obliged Indians to think of themselves as members of one exclusive religious community, not just different from but opposed to others.[49] It is, of course, true that gods and goddesses, ethical norms and prescriptions, even rituals and practices that we now associate with Hinduism did exist in some form in the past. But that is not at issue here. Rather the point is that these were not all thought to be part of one single entity so that those who owed allegiance to any one of these set of practices did not think of themselves as belonging to a single system of belief and doctrine in competition with and opposition to all others. Elements that were later seen to be integral to Hinduism were not a reified ideological entity with the potential of being mobilized for political purposes, for instance, for the nationalist cause. It was cultural colonialism which made this possible. This alteration has played a central part in reshaping modern lives as we now live.

It might be argued that if the colonial modern culture gave the colonized a robust but oppressive sense of collective identity and an equally restrictive sense of a unified belief system; it also gave them a cultural technology to escape from them—a technology that included conceptions of individual freedom and social justice. But this argument misses the point here. It concedes that the basic cultural form of indigenous cultures has been altered, bypassing their own understanding and reasoning. And this is a loss of cultural autonomy in a very deep sense. If so, it is a major cultural injustice. Besides, once older conceptions of individuation, multiple belongings and fluid selves, as well as notions of faith are displaced or lost, there is a narrowing of reasonable options for the colonized to choose from. This, too, is loss of cultural freedom and therefore, a definite cultural injustice.

Allow me to summarize. The extreme negative perspective is useful as an interpretative and explanatory tool for several African societies. It has great value for the understanding of internal colonialism. However, it is only of partial relevance to the understanding of European colonialism in societies such as India. The 'contact zone' perspective offers some insights, but overshoots its point. It is true that new contact zones emerged between hitherto disconnected cultures and that this resulted

[48] Wilfred Cantwell Smith, *The Meaning and End of Religion*, Minneapolis: Fortress Press, 1991 (original edition, 1962).

[49] There is no word for religion in most Indian languages. The Sanskrit word, 'dharma', into which it is usually translated is not adequate for this purpose.

in synthesis and crossovers. Yet, all this happened within an overall context of asymmetries of power and knowledge. The third, relatively moderate perspective on cultural injustice goes to the heart of the matter and reflects features found in all forms of colonial rule. Always and everywhere and at the very least, colonialism displaced, distorted, and inferiorized cultures and altered the basic cultural forms of indigenous peoples. By forcefully interjecting a wholly new knowledge system, it not only violated the cultural autonomy of the colonized but generated new socio-cultural divisions among them. All this was unjust. My concern in the remaining part of this chapter is with claims of the moderate view and focuses therefore on how we must respond to the specific injustices to which it draws our attention. Since the cases of cultural injustice dealt with here involve special kinds of perpetrators, namely, those who misrepresent, calumniate, and inferiorize the common life or culture of other peoples, I shall call these perpetrators, traducers. I shall call victims of misrepresentation, calumny, and deliberate falsification, sufferers. These are terms of art designed to name perpetrators and victims of cultural injustices, used here to distinguish them from perpetrators and victims of other graver injustices, including cultural and psycho-cultural injustices to which I have referred earlier.

CULTURAL INJUSTICE AS HISTORIC INJUSTICE

So far, I have assumed that the cultural injustice of colonialism is continuous over time. But this assumption can be challenged. It might be objected by some that colonialism is a thing of the past. It did, at one time, inflict injustices, including cultural injustice on the colonized, but now, the objection goes, the era of colonialism is over. In instances of historic injustice, there is no clear or determinate way of correcting past wrongs. After several generations have passed, some wrongs are simply not worth correcting.[50] If so, we should let bygones be bygones, and forget and forgive the colonizers. No further response is required. At any rate, a situation of a dialogic encounter between cultures may not have existed under conditions of colonialism but it does exist today. If so, the claim that something needs to be done now by way of correcting those wrongs need not be addressed because historic injustice has been superseded. Any action now may result in some other cultural injustice.

[50] See Jeremy Waldron, 'Superseding Historic Injustice', *Ethics*, vol. 103, no. 1, October 1992, pp. 4–28.

I offer three points against this claim. First, Jeremy Waldron, one of the principal protagonists of the idea of the supersession of historical injustice admits that his thesis does not pertain to communally owned, non-material goods. Even material goods such as land are not covered by his thesis when the disposed subject is a tribe or community, and where the landholding of it which has been dispossessed is particularly important for its sense of identity.[51] If his thesis of supersession of historic injustice is not relevant to material goods with symbolic significance to the community, surely it cannot be valid for irreducibly social cultural goods. Finally, Waldron's thesis of supersession of reparative entitlements holds only if it is replaced by a proper theory of prospective justice. If one can show that no sustained effort is forthcoming to rectify current global cultural injustices, then there is no case for the supersession of historic injustice.

Second, this objection is premised on the view that cultural injustice ended with the cessation of colonial rule. But has it? Arguably, cultural injustice may have become more acute since the demise of formal and direct colonial rule. Several scholars point out that the colonialism of thought and categories may not only have survived the demise of empires but intensified. For example, Nandy claims that proper cultural colonialism began in India in 1947 and that the inner supports of colonial culture were resurrected just as its outer supports were being removed.[52] Others claim that the experience of colonialism is a continuing psychic experience that would have to be dealt with long after the actual colonial situation formally ends. In some form, the anxiety and schizophrenia generated by a sudden break from one's own culture and knowledge systems persists among elites even today. Generally, those who have written of cultural injustice of colonialism maintain that it is a continuing injustice. For example, the world over, those who express their protest in non-masculine ways are treated with contempt. Since recognizable forms of protest must have a masculine character, protest is not even acknowledged as such when it does not have a masculine form. The hegemonic ideal of contemporary masculinity, a product of colonialism, continues to be sustained by a wide variety of social and cultural practices. For example, inspired by colonial role models of masculinity, Hinduism continues to grow more aggressive and intolerant.

[51] Ibid.
[52] Nandy, *The Intimate Enemy.*

In northern India, those who are unable to speak English continue to feel inferior and be treated as such. Similarly, given the organization of research programmes and the structural design of modern universities, ancient Indian manuscripts gather dust as there is no incentive to properly examine them. Sanskrit, which ought to be recognized as an appropriate research tool, is artificially and farcically revived as a 'living language' in news broadcasts that few people understand or care about. It is probably better nurtured in Kyoto, Jerusalem or New York than in Indian universities. In fact, entire intellectual traditions that were once alive in Sanskrit or for that matter in Persian have been forgotten to such an extent that they are barely objects even of historical research. Courses on the history of social and political thought begin with the Greeks and end with Mill and Marx without a single reference to Indian thought. This happens predictably in all western universities but also surprisingly in Indian universities. There is an occasional urge to do a history of Indian concepts but material for such work is either unavailable or cannot be properly understood. Scholars do not have an inkling of how to dredge up concepts that began life much earlier but are still embedded in social, political, and cultural practices. A creative use of ancient traditions for contemporary purposes is virtually non-existent. In short, whole traditions of intellectual enquiry are virtually dead for modern Indian scholars today. Indeed, the gap between traditional pundits and modern scholars has probably grown after political independence. It would be fair to say that some degree of natal alienation is still present in the formerly colonized elites. Thus, it is precisely because cultural distortions and unequal relations of colonial rule are reinscribed in current practices of post-colonial societies and contemporary imbalances between First and Third World countries, that we need to think today of some response to this injustice.

Critics may still not be satisfied. They may agree that the cases mentioned earlier are instances of cultural injustice but then add that these are all newly born injustices. They may require rectification but to drag European colonialism into their discussion is normatively irrelevant. For how can we be sure that psychological injuries (inferiority complex, etc.), the displacement of basic cultural forms, and the loss of communication between western, modern, and older local systems of beliefs and knowledges are connected in a causally relevant way to past injustice? A person has a reparative obligation only if he is responsible for the injustice. He is responsible only if he has intentionally brought about the harm which constitutes injustice. How can a reparative demand be made on people who are not intentionally responsible for the injustice? Consider the case of a young unruly adolescent who drives without licence and kills an innocent bystander. Surely, he is responsible for the death of the person. But in a sense, his parents too must share responsibility. After all, the child was brought up in their care and it was their business to make him rule abiding, and to ensure that he did not drive without licence. In modern societies, such reparations must be the responsibility of the family. But, what if the parents point a finger at the company their child keeps, at the school, even at the larger social environment in which he lives that is neither morally sensitive nor rule abiding? Must the demand for reparation be directed then at all these other agents, at society at large? Or consider another possibility. What if after his death, the family of the victim is destitute and his son, angered by his condition, robs a bank and gravely injures the bank manager? Is the family of the unruly adolescent at least partly responsible for the injury to the bank manager? Must they pay damages to him? This seems counter-intuitive. It is true that the killing of an innocent bystander is an injustice. It is also true that the injury to the bank manager is a new injustice. But how are the two injustices linked to one another? If they are not, then how can reparative obligations for both injustices, the old and the new, be imposed on the family of the unruly adolescent? Similarly, the current cultural disadvantage of a people may be a result of several disconnected historical injustices and the people responsible for them may be too many, existing at different points of time in a very long period between the initial injustice and the present harmful condition.[53] How can reparative obligations be imposed on all of them for each of the disconnected injustices?

A number of assumptions implicit in these questions must be made explicit. First, that we are responsible only for our intentional acts. Second, that these intentions are properties of individuals, not collectivities. Third, that injustices which appear to be disconnected *are* indeed disconnected and further that there is only one account of the way injustices are connected or disconnected. Each of these assumptions can be challenged. To do so, allow me to begin with what Bernard Williams has suggested are 'universal banalities'. When human beings act, their actions cause things to happen, sometimes intentionally and sometimes not. What is brought about is sometimes rejoiced and sometimes

[53] See, Janna Thompson, 'Historical Injustice and Reparation: Justifying Claims of Descendants', *Ethics*, vol. 112, no.1, October 2001, pp. 114–35.

regretted or deplored, by the agent himself, or by the beneficiaries, or victims of the act, or by both. Regret or its opposite, say a feeling of satisfaction or elation are not the only responses, however. For example, if a bad result is generated by virtue of something that a person did and therefore, for which he is retrospectively responsible, then it becomes his prospective responsibility to repair the damage, to make amends. Such a demand that the retrospectively responsible person make up for the bad state of affairs produced by him may come from the agent himself, or from his victims, or from both. This is self-evident when the damage is caused by an intentional act. If my rash driving causes an accident damaging the other person's car, then the entire responsibility for repairing or replacing it falls on me. My offer to make amends and the expectation of the injured party that I do so are both appropriate. But, I may have to make amends even when the bad state of affairs ensues without my intentionally causing it. For example, if I lose a book that I borrowed from a friend, it is only proper that I offer to replace it and for my friend to expect that I do so. Both responses are equally legitimate, no matter how I lost it. I could not have *lost* it intentionally. But, this may have happened either because I am a careless person who is prone to losing things or because my life had gone so bad that particular day that the unusually preoccupied state of my mind induced me to forget it on the bus that brought me home. This shows that I am responsible and can be blamed for acts I did not even intend. As Williams puts it, 'the responsibilities we have to recognize extend in many ways beyond our normal purposes and what we intentionally do'.[54] Again, he says 'those who have been hurt need a response; simply what has happened to them may give them a right to seek it, and where can they look more appropriately than to you, the cause.'[55]

This is true not only for acts which I perform on my own but also for those I perform jointly with others.[56] A group has collective responsibility

[54] Bernard Williams, *Shame and Necessity*, London: University of California Press, 1993, p. 74. On this and related points, also see Richard Swinburne, *Responsibility and Atonement*, Oxford: Clarendon Press, 1989. Also, see the discussion of these issues by Thompson, *Taking Responsibility for the Past*, pp. 44–6.

[55] Williams, *Shame and Necessity*, p. 70.

[56] On a defence of the idea of collective responsibility, see the essays by David Cooper, 'Collective Responsibility (A Defense)', in Larry May and Stacey Hoffman (eds), *Collective Responsibility*, Maryland: Rowman & Littlefield Publishers, 1991, pp. 35–46; Joel Feinberg, 'Collective Responsibility (Another Defense)', in May and Hoffman (eds), *Collective Responsibility*, pp. 53–74; Larry

for the suffering its acts cause to others, whether or not its members intend them. Going back to the example mentioned earlier, we all must share responsibility, though in different degrees, for the death of the innocent bystander because we all have contributed to generating and sustaining a morally insensitive environment in which people break the law with impunity. Moreover, this collective responsibility may spread not just horizontally but also vertically. We may be responsible for the current harm to persons if we unintentionally contribute to practices that cause the suffering and which were initiated much before we were born. Those of us who do nothing to prevent the culture of lawlessness that we only inherited but did not create are still at least partly responsible for the action of the unruly kid who ran over his innocent victim. The entire case for reparations for injustices committed in the past is based on a notion of collective responsibility that stretches over time and is distributed among persons who live at different times. Thus, it is neither true that we are responsible only for our intended acts nor that responsibility is the property of individuals.

But, what about the argument that no connection might exist between two distinct injustices in the past or between any injustice in the past and a current injustice? I am persuaded by Janna Thompson's response to this objection. According to her, injustices that happen over a period of time can be linked to one another. Consider the policies towards Aboriginals adopted by different Australian governments over a long period of time. These policies may have changed and may have been different and just but they all had in common the assumption that Aborigines were racially and culturally inferior. Thus, the injustices of each of the policies, seen from one point of view, are disconnected from one another but they can also be seen as 'inter-dependent components of a history of disrespect'. It is this history, according to her, that is relevant to reparative claims.[57] Past injustices 'often belong to an interconnected history of wrongs that ought to be treated as a whole for purposes of reparation', a point not fully appreciated by those who claim that reparation is warranted only for the automatic effects of the initial wrong act.[58] Thus, it is clear that in the complex historical processes of

---

May, 'Metaphysical Guilt and Moral Taint', in May and Hoffman (eds), *Collective Responsibility*, pp. 239–54; and Howard Mcgary, 'Morality and Collective Liability', in May and Hoffman (eds), *Collective Responsibility*, pp. 77–88.

[57] Thompson, *Taking Responsibility for the Past*, p. 82.

[58] For this point, see ibid., p. 79.

injustices, a plausible narrative can be built of continuing injustice. It would not then be a case of the earlier injustice having been superseded and a new injustice requiring rectification but rather a matter of a continuing injustice requiring a holistic reparative policy. In any case, if the roots of a current injustice lie in the past, then it is hardly likely that it can be rectified without acknowledging the past injustice.[59]

RESPONSES TO CULTURAL INJUSTICE

Traducer Response and Sufferer Response

I have spoken earlier of two responses. The first is demanded by the victim from the perpetrator. The second is a requirement imposed by the perpetrator on himself. Because these are both responses demanded of the perpetrator, let me call them perpetrator responses and since we are concerned here with particular kinds of cultural injustice inflicted by traducers, let these be called traducer response. A reparative response may be demanded not only of the perpetrator/traducer, however. It may come from the victim as what she owes to herself. No matter who caused the damage, we all have some responsibility to repair our own broken life. The victim has some obligation to bring herself back from the dead, even if there is no response from others, including from the person who caused the harm. Let me call this victim response and in the context of cultural injustice, sufferer response. Both perpetrator/traducer response and victim/sufferer response are necessary in situations of injustice and something is amiss when one or the other is absent. A situation in which the victim demands a response from the perpetrator/traducer but the latter, not acknowledging responsibility, makes no demands on himself, goes ineluctably towards the growth of the unjustified belief that by generating a blame culture, victims are unduly perpetrating a new wrong. Nor will a situation of injustice be fully rectified if perpetrator/traducer response is not accompanied by victim response. A pure victim response will also not take us very far. If former perpetrators do not participate in their rectification, then old injustices may continue or new injustices may be created. If our objective is to eliminate injustice, then we must ensure both kinds of responses in an appropriate form.

---

[59] For discussion of this point, see Tan, 'Colonialism, Reparations and Global Justice', in Miller and Kumar (eds), *Reparations*.

Post-colonial literature has made important contribution to our understanding of cultural injustices. However, it appears to pay insufficient attention to responses. When it does attend to them, it focuses purely on sufferer response. This sufferer response is dominated by a rhetoric of resistance that excludes the traducer from any strategy of liberation and therefore, asks practically nothing from him. This suits the traducer fine because it helps him to continue living his life as if no wrong has been done. There is no expression of agent regret at the cultural injustices of colonialism. Nor does he have a sense that in the aftermath of colonialism, it might be morally required of him to contribute to repairing damaged selves and cultures and restoring the self-confidence and self-respect of the colonized. There is a widespread belief shared by everyone, by both the colonized and the colonizers, that after the transfer of political power, justice is fully restored. The colonized believe that the sole responsibility for restoring self-confidence and self-respect in themselves is their own. So do the colonizers.

There are many reasons for the belief that ordinary people of colonizing countries bear no responsibility for continuing injustices. This belief is due, first, because of a common sense morality, according to which we are answerable only for actions that we intentionally perform. If the misery of a person is caused by our unintended acts, then that suffering is his or her personal misfortune—a case of pure bad luck. Since few people intentionally cause harm to the cultures of the formerly colonized people, no one can be held responsible for their continuing distress. Even if this continuing cultural disadvantage is recognized as a form of injustice inflicted by actions of members of one's community in the distant past, how can people today be held responsible for past actions? And if they are not responsible, then why should they be asked to make amends?

Second, it may still be a moral requirement that the personal misfortune of human beings not be left entirely unattended. But the relevant agent who must do this attending, so modern sensibility tells us, is the state. The state, however, is meant to ameliorate suffering not of people generally but that of its own citizens. If so, the cultural injustice of communities must be remedied by their own state, not by the state of others. Third, most modern colonizing cultures, on the one hand, make a special thing of some ethical emotions recognized separately as guilt and, on the other hand, make relatively less of the reactions they recognize as shame.[60] This is unfortunate because though guilt directs us towards victims, it continues to restrict our attention to voluntary and intentional acts. I am believed to be guilty only if my intentional and wrong actions have caused suffering to others. And, only under these conditions may the wronged person demand reparations from me. Otherwise not. Why, if I am not guilty, should the victim direct his anger at me or demand that I make amends? Now, since guilt explores the relation between intentional acts and the wrongs they cause, it pays insufficient attention to those unintended acts which flow from the kind of people we are and the harms they cause. Generally, it is other ethical emotions such as shame that push us to examine the moral defects of our character. Ideologies that overemphasize guilt over shame are unable to guide the attention of the perpetrator to himself and his deficiencies. Guilt does not quite reach the self-related depth to which shame does and this failure successfully blocks the acknowledgement of some responsibility where it is due. This puts former colonizers in a situation where they feel neither adequate guilt nor adequate shame at continuing injustice.

But, what if the colonized publicly identified the role of the colonizers in sustaining cultural injustices? What if they tried to shame them: 'look this precisely is your role in the perpetuation of injustice. You must own up responsibility for what you have done and for being the kind of person who could do such wrong things.' The basic experience of shame, Williams tells us, is that of being seen, inappropriately by the wrong people in the wrong act or condition.[61] When this happens, the natural reaction is to hide oneself, for example, to be embarrassed because in being seen by others, one's sense of self is diminished. Are the colonizers ever embarrassed and diminished when told that the colonized have finally caught them in the wrong act in perpetuating cultural injustice? It appears not.

Shame is not just a matter of being seen by any odd observer. But rather, of being seen by an observer of a certain kind, with a particular type of view.[62] The observer in question must be someone you respect and be one who, as a result of having seen you in the wrong act or condition, has a poor view of who you are. We feel ashamed only if poorly viewed by an observer whose opinions carry weight with us, not

---

[60] Williams, *Shame and Necessity*, p. 91.
[61] Ibid., p. 78.
[62] Ibid.

by those who do not matter. The colonizer feels no shame because the colonized still does not carry enough social weight in his moral life. The poor opinion of the colonized makes no different to him.[63] Sufferers fail to induce the appropriate traducer response: no agent regret or remorse is seen or heard.

In a context where colonizers do not experience appropriate ethical emotions or acknowledge responsibility, they feel no moral need for reparation either. Over time, even sufferers give up demanding a response from traducers. Beyond a point, it is useless to look for any remedial action from the traducer. Therefore, it is no surprise that sufferer responses abound and they take the form that they do: a persistent and shrill rhetoric of isolated, monologic resistance. Underlying it are motives of revenge: to defeat the colonizer by violence, or by deceit and manipulation, or else, a tit-for-tat strategy of inferiorization. Thus, one familiar response is to lump cultural injustice together with other injustices and to have the same crude solution for all of them, that is, vengeful counter-violence. This is manifest today in what is believed to be anti-colonial, counter-hegemonic terrorism, though elements of it are also found in Fanon's radicalism.

A second response is also inspired by Fanon. Algerian women must veil themselves to frustrate the colonizer, he had announced, so that they can see without being seen.[64] The veil, he said, was historically dynamic because its use can be changed strategically, according to the circumstance. The cultural meaning of the veil must be read within the social space of those who wear them. It is about privacy, identity, rank, class, and kinship status and not necessarily about the subordination and oppression of women. The colonizer must be defeated by the cunning deployment of local cultural meanings that he can never fully understand. A third form of sufferer response is to impose on one's own society an iron-curtain, for instance, by banning 'foreign culture'—films, TV, books, and so on. This sufferer response uncritically accepts the idea of discrete cultures that interact with one another only as a zero-sum game. This fiercely parochial stance indiscriminately views all outsiders as cultural aggressors and forces them to lay off. It then tries to build a cultural and intellectual world in reaction to and

[63] On these and related issues concerning imperial indifference on the opinion others hold of the actions of superpowers, see Rajeev Bhargava, 'Ordinary Feelings, Extraordinary Events: Moral Complexity in 9/11', in Craig Calhoun et al. (eds), *Understanding September 11*, New York: The New Press, pp. 321–32.

[64] Frantz Fanon, *A Dying Colonialism*, England: Penguin Books, 1970.

isolation from the colonizing West—a pure, uncontaminated, original world, radically decolonized and dewesternized. It further branches out into two different kinds. The first tries to establish its own superiority vis-à-vis the culture of the colonizer. The second seeks neither to be exploited nor to exploit. Since cultural interaction must make one either the traducer or the sufferer, the only escape from a relation of domination is to not interact at all. Rather, it is to discover the authentic sources of one's own culture and live by them in isolated splendour. To these three typical responses, we may add one more: to deny cultural injustice and pretend that it does not exist.

Reparations for Cultural Injustice

None of these responses can, in the long run, really address the cultural injustices of colonialism. Is another response possible then between violence and forcible exclusion on the one hand and silence and denial on the other? What possibly could this response be? How should we respond to continuing cultural injustice? What should the sufferer demand from the traducer or from himself? I take it as given that prosecution is an absurd remedy for cultural injustice. If any morally adequate response is appropriate, then it must take some form of reparation. Why so? And what should be the content of such reparative claims?

Recall the attributes of cultural injustice:

1. The displacement and dislocation of indigenous cultures and of the loss of their basic cultural forms.
2. The generation of damaged selves and schizophrenia in the colonized.[65]
3. The imposition on the colonized of a position of a perpetual chaser of the colonizer. Because he is cast as an imitator, he is forever condemned to be behind the colonizer, always pursuing purposes not of his own making. Such a situation leaves no scope for alternating and reciprocal leadership.
4. The inferiorization of the culture of the colonized.
5. Given to inferiorizing the colonized for long, the colonizer develops grave indifference to the fate of the colonized. He is morally deadened to the vulnerable and the estranged—a massive moral defect.

---

[65] As Fanon puts it, 'colonialism forces the people it dominates to ask themselves the question constantly: "In reality, who am I"'. Frantz Fanon, quoted in Robert Young, *Postcolonialism: An Historical Introduction*, Oxford: Blackwell Publishers, 2001, p. 139.

In sum, at the deepest level, colonialism not only gravely damages colonized cultures and selves but also relations between the colonized and the colonizer.[66]

How are damaged cultures and broken relationships to be mended? Should the colonizers financially compensate for the damage and dislocation they caused to the cultures of the colonized? It is hard to calculate the monetary value of cultures and anyway, inappropriate to do so. Therefore, like prosecution, this too seems an absurd requirement. What then should be the content of such reparative claims? A significant cause of broken relationship between the colonized and the colonizer is the failure on the part of the colonizer to extend the principle of moral equality to the colonized. How can moral indifference be replaced by an attitude that grants equal moral standing and worth to people of formerly colonized cultures? How can the basic attitude of the colonizer be changed? How can the circulation of crude stereotypes about other cultures be stopped? This is related to other questions. How can asymmetries of cultural power be transformed into relations of cultural equality? How can monologic interactions become dialogic? Two reparative strategies are relevant here, if we have traducer response in mind. First, an apology for past wrongs. Apologies, as Minow reminds us 'acknowledge the fact of harms, accept some degree of responsibility, avow sincere regret and promise not to repeat the offence'.[67] Sincere apologies depend on experiencing shame and then making a positive use of this emotion to improve oneself, and to reconstruct the world in which one has to live, a relevant traducer response is to feel shame.

The promise not to repeat the offence is as difficult as, and presupposes, the acknowledgement of harms and the acceptance of responsibility. Because if the promise is to be fulfilled, it must be accompanied by a genuine cognitive resolve to change the ways in which the colonizers have viewed the colonized. This entails a major transformation in

[66] Janna Thompson has helpfully made a distinction between two theories of reparations which she calls 'reparation as restoration' and 'reparation as reconciliation'. I locate my own perspective on reparation within the second theory, that is, as part of a broader theory of reconciliation. On my own perspective on reconciliation, see Rajeev Bhargava, 'Restoring Decency to Barbaric Societies', in Robert I. Rotberg and Dennis Thompson (eds), *Truth v. Justice: The Morality of Truth Commissions*, Princeton, New Jersey: Princeton University Press, 2000, pp. 45–67 (republished in this collection, see Chapter 8).

[67] Martha Minow, *Between Vengeance and Forgiveness*, Boston: Beacon Press, 1998, p. 112.

the way in which western knowledge systems have been organized and regulated. It is also linked to the second reparative strategy: truth telling. Thus, stories of empire building, colonialism, and imperialism and the cultural and cognitive damage they caused must be constructed. History, social science, humanities, the arts, and the media more generally, each have a role to play in dismantling these powerful intellectual-cum-cultural colonizing systems and showing the collusion between belief-systems and colonialism. Coming to terms with the past is not only a political but a powerful cultural and intellectual act of truth telling. Such truth telling must be inspired by a persistent and engaging search for ethnocentric biases. New theoretical structures and strategies of perception are required to contest the previous dominant western ways of saying things. Once upon a time, every single story was told from the standpoint of the colonizer. The colonized was included as a mere object, never as a subject. Changing this requires a major conceptual orientation towards the needs of the non-western world.[68]

Let me give an example from my own experience. Indian universities generally tend to be lukewarm to social and political philosophy. This is partly because of a lack of interest among academics in normative issues but also because of certain features of political philosophy itself. Its content may well be universal but its form is certainly parochial, no doubt partly because there are few non-western scholars who take it up. Much of academic political philosophy takes little inspiration from non-western societies, makes hardly any references to the problems they face, and takes little notice of how cross-cultural issues acquire a distinct inflection in their cultures. Most of the examples discussed in political philosophy have no immediate relation to these societies. Besides, there are few non-western philosophers who could become a role model for Indian students. No wonder that political scientists in India take virtually no interest in political philosophy. All this makes the task of a political philosopher in India very difficult. These difficulties are compounded by the unavailability of journals, all of which are published abroad. It is hardly surprising therefore, that Indian students, though enthused by political philosophy, do not display a great deal of self-confidence or competence in doing it. Changing all this means literally turning the world upside down.

It means looking from the other side of the photograph, experiencing how differently things look when you live in Baghdad rather than in Boston and

[68] Young, *Postcolonialism*.

understanding why. It means realizing that when the West looks at the non-western world, what it sees is often more a mirror image of itself and its assumptions than what the non-west is really like and how non-western people actually feel and perceive themselves.[69]

This requires sustained intellectual commitment that is framed by a larger moral commitment to equal consideration and respect for all, including the vulnerable and the stranger, and a resolve to build common spaces where different cultures can enter into dialogue with one another on equal terms. It also requires building a larger culture that allows ordinary people in colonizing countries to morally disassociate themselves from those practices of their governments and multinational corporations that perpetuate injustice.[70]

This resolve may also carry financial implications. The rectification of intellectual blunders committed in the past may be possible only by the institutionalization of systematic learning about other cultures and civilizations. This may require more than a token gesture of setting up an area studies' programme or a research institute. It may involve setting aside huge sums of money for research and education, for educational scholarships, and for the hiring of people with knowledge and understanding about these cultures. It would most certainly require correcting imbalances in the media by instituting more scrupulous policies of selecting the right people for the job and for ensuring adequate and culturally sensitive coverage of events in formal colonies.

I have spoken earlier of traducer response. Let me turn my attention once again to sufferer response. What is an appropriate sufferer response? I believe it, too, must change its character. Monological resistance may well be justifiable as a temporary act of defiance. But in the long run, sufferer responses must cease to be restricted only to sufferers and must encompass the traducer. Surely, to rectify continuing cultural injustice, we need not monadic, isolated, and disengaged responses but those which, though separate, are mutually engaged. This mutual engagement is mandatory for another important reason. I have hitherto spoken of colonizers and the colonized and assumed that all colonizers are traducers and all colonized are sufferers. This is incorrect for two reasons. First, those descendants of colonizers who have unambiguously disassociated themselves from the acts of the colonial state and

---

[69] Ibid., p. 2.

[70] On moral disassociation, see Sterba, 'Understanding Evil: American Slavery, the Holocaust, and the Conquest of the American Indians', pp. 424–48.

colonizers should be included, if at all, with the greatest of caution. The mere fact of being a white man or a white woman does not make one a traducer. Second, those among the colonized who had begun to collaborate and had benefited from colonization, and those of their descendants who have still failed to morally disassociate themselves from the process of colonization can barely be counted among the sufferers. The mere fact of being, say, an Indian does not make one into an unambiguous victim or sufferer. I do not mean to suggest that colonizers and the colonized elite share equal responsibility for the suffering of the colonized people. However, the colonized elite has some responsibility, if not for their own initial suffering, then at least for the contribution they made towards the suffering of others in the reproduction of cultural injustices. Such people were surely morally tainted. It is no longer possible then, as it once might have been, to identify all perpetrators of injustice as western and all victims as non-western. The historical responsibility for the continuing cultural injustice of colonialism is distributed among both the colonizers and at least a part of the colonized elite. From here on, therefore, when I speak of traducers, I exclude some descendants of the colonizers and include some descendants of the colonized. Likewise, when I speak of sufferers, I do not mean to imply that every colonized person was a victim of cultural injustice to the same degree.

These points must be kept in mind when we are thinking of appropriate responses to cultural injustices. If what is mentioned is correct, then within the larger plot of working out a better understanding and reconciliation between colonial traducers and colonized sufferers, is the sub-plot of better mutual understanding and reconciliation between colonized traducers and colonized sufferers. The colonizers have an obligation to the colonized. Among the colonized, the elites too have a special obligation towards the colonized sufferers. The collaborative nature of the colonial enterprise, at least in its middle phase, implies that a proper response to it must also be worked out jointly.[71] An intellectual coming to terms with the past, a proper acknowledgement and telling of the truth about cultural colonialism must be the result of a joint effort of western and non-western intelligentsia.

---

[71] This point was important also because reparative claims presuppose that we have properly identified both the claimants who are entitled to reparation as well as those who have the obligation to provide it. On these points, see Thompson, *Taking Responsibility for the Past*, chapter 3.

However, this is easier said than done. No matter how complicitous the non-western elites were or are in the production of cultural injustice, there is no getting away from the fact that huge asymmetries of knowledge and power still remain intact. We must reckon with the fact that western people, including those who have disassociated themselves from colonialism, continue to function with little knowledge of the non-western world. This is not the case with non-western intellectuals. Indeed, it is impossible for them to function as intellectuals without a great deal of knowledge about western intellectual traditions. I do not here mean merely that there are inequities of empirical knowledge of each other. I have in mind something deeper. The very assumptions and presuppositions underlying our enquiries into our own world are shot through with categories derived from western experience. It is self-evident by now that the categories of western thought are inadequate for our experience and life world. Yet, it is these categories with which we cannot help begin. We recognize that they should be neither the starting point of our investigations nor its finished product. Yet, this is an ever present danger of our enquiries. We know, for example, that contemporary political theory is useful for our societies but we know better still that it is a product of a context that has practically no relation to our own. In short, the deep problem today for the sufferers of cultural injustice is that western categories have both an undeniable universal potential and that they are fully intermingled with the specificity of western practices and worse, possess a deep imprint of western domination and hegemony. We can neither ignore western ideas nor fully show how they can be rescued from the pernicious effects of their own imperial imprint.[72] Western thought to non-western people is both recognizably their own *and* alien.

It appears then that apart from working jointly with their western counterparts, the sufferers of cultural injustice also have to work on their own and work out their own distinctive responses. To begin with, they must know which responses to eschew. First, they should not yield to the temptation of 'post-colonial revenge'.[73] They should not retreat from anything western merely on the ground that it is western.

---

[72] Some of these issues are also raised by Dipesh Chakrabarty, *Provincial-izing Europe: Postcolonial Thought and Historical Difference*, New Delhi: Oxford University Press, 2000; and Pieterse and Parekh (eds), *The Decolonisation of Imagination*.

[73] I borrow this phrase from Leela Gandhi, *Post Colonial Theory: An Introduction*, Sydney: Allen and Unwin, 1998, p. x.

They should neither blindly reject nor accept it. Second, they should avoid the pitfalls of a naïve and dangerous nativism or an intellectually impoverished cultural nationalism. Third, as already implied earlier, the elites among the formerly colonized should not behave as if they had no hand whatsoever in their own victimization or that of their fellow citizens. Indeed, they should more openly acknowledge their active role in the neglect or inferiorization of their own tradition and culture.

What then should they do? First, sufferers of cultural injustice must turn their bi-culturalism into a strength rather than perpetually view it as a sign of their subjection. As they identify the Eurocentrism and parochialism of western categories, they should also see in this an invitation for the creative renewal of a potentially common tradition—that is one among many and yet shared. This can be done only if it is reinvigorated by non-western peoples with their own outlook and interests in mind. Western traditions were also frozen by the impact of colonialism or by the sheer intellectual lethargy of its inheritors. It needs 'outsiders' to rejuvenate it. This is already happening with concepts such as secularism and democracy.

However, the renewal of western traditions by non-western people is not possible unless they are committed to a focused, collective effort to retrieve their own forgotten and neglected traditions. This entails the examination of texts that have so far been gathering dust in unknown sites. But can these indigenous traditions ever be recovered? Can cultures of the colonized be restored to the state in which they were before colonization? Can they be relocated where they were before their displacement by colonialism? Can basic cultural forms be recovered? It is doubtful if 'original cultural forms' can ever be recovered. There is a sense in which there is no going back to pure indigenous cultures because every rediscovery is at least partly a reinvention. We know that every revival of tradition has turned out to be its reinvention. Restoration may be possible for cultural artifacts that are physically embodied but for artifacts such as conceptual frameworks that are largely disembodied, this is extremely difficult. Yet, the slow painstaking process of a part recovery of the voice and history of the colonized can begin by putting together and reinterpreting traces of evidence and meaning present in largely forgotten texts.

Retrieving intellectual traditions is not, of course, just a matter of locating texts and reading them creatively. It also means connecting with those people who escaped the deep impact of colonial modernity and who, therefore, are still steeped in traditions from which elites had cut themselves off. It is this collaborative effort between modern scholars, traditional pundits, organic intellectuals, and people on the ground that will help to rebuild forgotten cultural and intellectual traditions. This would also help articulate concepts embedded in social and cultural practices so that they are available as a resource for creative use. Only thus might the sufferers of colonialism be able to construct alternative modernities that are shaped by the experience of interacting cultures on an egalitarian basis and which respect the autonomy of all participants.

This is not as hopeless a task as might seem at first sight. In a way, it has been happening less self-consciously during much of the colonial encounter. In any encounter between cultures, some lending and borrowing is inevitable. This certainly is the grain of truth in the 'contact zone' perspective. In the making of the modern Bengali novel, modern and our traditional conventions were mixed freely. Bankim drew freely from conventions of classical Sanskrit drama and epic poetry in order to describe nature, from Vaishnav lyrics to represent sexuality and eroticism, from folk comedy to create farcical effects, from ballads to directly address the reader, and from Hindu mythology to prophesize and to represent other forms of providential intervention.[74] Anti-colonial movements reworked local resources to mobilize for decolonization.[75] Gandhi's movement for swaraj built on local resources in its methods at the same time as it borrowed from western authors such as Tolstoy and Emerson.

One version of this attempt is already present in Gandhi's response. He took it upon himself not only to liberate the non-western peoples but also the West from the history and psychology of British colonialism.[76] For example, Gandhi believed that he could use the resources of androgyny available both in the East and in the repressed, marginalized western traditions to challenge the hyper-masculine world view of colonialism. In his view, activism and courage could be liberated from aggressiveness and made compatible with the feminine principle.

Gandhi identified with the marginalized traditions of the West and made them his own. For him, 'India held in trusteeship aspects of the West lost to the West itself'.[77] Borrowing from the West was

[74] See Guha, *Dominance without Hegemony*, p. 179.

[75] On this, see Pieterse and Parekh, *The Decolonisation of Imagination*, p. 6.

[76] See Bhikhu Parekh, *Gandhi*, Oxford: Oxford University Press, 1997. For an illuminating discussion of these issues, see Nandy, *The Intimate Enemy*.

[77] Ibid., p. 74.

never for him a problem by itself. Choosing to borrow an object or an idea to suit one's own purposes is very different from being forced or manipulated into having it. Indeed, Gandhi freely acknowledged that the idea of non-violence had its roots not in the sacred texts of India but in the sermon on the mount.[78] Yet, it was important for Gandhi to make sense of the West in Indian terms. This entailed grasping that the modern West offered one possible lifestyle among many, which unfortunately for both the West and India became cancerous, so Gandhi thought, by virtue of its disproportionate spread and power. In the end, however, it was not enough for Gandhi to make sense of the West in Indian terms but also to have a genuine place for it within Indian civilization. This was the very least he also expected from the best proponents of western civilization.

The general point that emerges from Gandhi's project is this: what we have hitherto believed as universals is only one particular masquerading as such. These are false, abstract universals. If we are to arrive at genuine, concrete, trans-cultural universals, then we must first accept that we are different, unfamiliar, strange. There are no easy and neat short-cuts to communication across cultures. Once we accept the difficulty and messiness of translation across cultures as also the initial circle of prejudice that surrounds us, we may be able to find a morally acceptable place for each other in our respective cultures. Then we can also hope for a richer, greater commonness.

[78] Ibid.

8

Restoring Decency to Barbaric Societies*[1]

This essay consists of three claims, which together clarify the proper objectives of truth commissions. My first claim is that the primary function of a truth commission is to help a barbaric society become minimally decent and, in the aftermath of evil, to reinstate confidence in norms of what the philosopher, Stuart Hampshire, calls basic procedural justice, a term that connotes fair procedures of negotiation.

The distinction between symmetrically and asymmetrically barbaric societies forms the basis of my second claim: when a society moves away from symmetric barbarism, then, all things considered, some mechanism to deal with gross injustice of the past, such as a truth commission, is necessary and sufficient for achieving minimal decency. However, when a society moves towards minimal decency from asymmetric barbarism, it is more or less imperative to have a Truth and

* This paper was first presented before the Truth and Reconciliation Commission, Commissioners, and Staff at a conference held at Somerset West, Cape Province, South Africa, in May 1998. It was subsequently published as 'Restoring Decency to Barbaric Societies', in Robert I. Rotberg and Dennis Thompson (eds), *Truth v. Justice: The Morality of Truth Commissions*, Princeton, New Jersey: Princeton University Press, 2000, pp. 45–67.

[1] I am grateful to Veena Das, Robert Meister, Mahmood Mamdani, Neeladri Bhattacharya, Kumar Shahani, Shalini Advani, Sudipta Kaviraj, and especially to Tani Sandhu and Alok Rai for helpful discussions on this essay. Thanks are also due to Robert I. Rotberg and Dennis Thompson, for invaluable suggestions.

Reconciliation Commission (TRC), although it is not enough. In such contexts, we might say that the TRC is necessary but not sufficient.

In a minimally decent society, former victims are not reconciled with their former oppressors nor are groups with inherited hostilities towards one another reunited. If so—and this is my third, entirely negative claim—then it cannot be the primary objective of a truth commission to achieve reconciliation between victims and perpetrators.[2] A future cancellation of estrangement is not ruled out, however. Indeed, though not immediately apparent, a truth commission creates conditions for future reconciliation. When this happens, a truth commission may also be seen as a facilitating mechanism of forgiveness.

TRUTH COMMISSION FOR A MINIMALLY DECENT SOCIETY

Minimally Decent Society, Basic Procedural Justice

I begin by clarifying a distinction crucial to understanding the point underlying truth commissions, that is, the distinction between what I call a minimally decent and a barbaric society. A minimally decent society is governed by minimal moral rules. A complete breakdown of such rules characterizes a barbaric society.[3] In this context, what makes

---

[2] The term 'reconciliation' can be interpreted in two ways. In the first, stronger interpretation, reconciliation means a cancellation of estrangement via, say, forgiveness in order to establish substantive agreement on moral issues. In the second, weaker interpretation, it means cancellation of enmity with the help of a culture of reciprocity and mutual respect in order to have minimal disagreement on moral issues. As I understand it, this is roughly what Amy Gutmann and Dennis Thompson have in mind in their contribution to the volume in which this piece originally appeared. See Amy Gutmann and Dennis Thompson, 'The Moral Foundations of Truth Commissions', in Rotberg and Thompson (eds), *Truth v. Justice*, pp. 22–44. In my view, truth commissions may be unduly burdened if they aim at reconciliation in either of these two senses. Reconciliation presupposes a firm consensus on thick values. The objective of a minimally decent society presupposes much less; there need only be a diffused sense all around that we have had enough of evil, that we must get away from it, and the means by which we do so must not themselves be evil. The necessity of getting over estrangement or dealing with one another with mutual respect is not felt, at least not in the immediate aftermath of evil.

[3] Throughout this essay, I have used the term society instead of the bulkier term 'social formation' and by social formation, I have something specific in mind, which I must briefly explicate. Formation refers to both the manner in which something takes form (is formed) and the thing so formed. Social formation

these rules moral is their capacity to prevent excessive wrongdoing or
evil and not their ability to promote a particular conception of the good
life, including a substantive conception of justice. Such moral rules
include negative injunctions against killing, maiming, or ill-treating
others, and also a system of basic procedural justice.

Thomas Nagel has urged us to develop secular theories of evil
consistent with universal claims of positive morality and has emphasized
the need for a conception of human beings that accommodates not
only their capacity for morality but also for monstrosity.[4] I believe
Stuart Hampshire has given us such a conception, and his idea of basic
procedural justice is part, precisely, of a minimum morality to deal with
this capacity for monstrosity and evil.[5] The Second World War and in

---

then refers to the manner in which a certain type of human collectivity comes
into being as well as to that human collectivity. Such a collectivity may be a
small configuration within a community, a large community within a society,
interacting communities within a large political order such as the nation-state,
or indeed, the entire world order or a part thereof. So, as I have used the term
'society', it is possible for there to exist a minimally decent social formation
within a larger barbaric society and likewise, for there to be a barbaric social
formation within a larger minimally decent society. One of the cases I mention
later, the massacre of Sikhs in Delhi in 1984, is a barbaric social formation on
a relatively small scale. Its existence did not imply that the whole of India had
turned barbaric. Of course, the entire socio-political order such as a nation-
state may be barbaric or minimally decent. Although my use of these terms is
flexible enough to include both small communities and large societies, I realize
that it would not be entirely wrong for the reader to get the impression that I
have only nation-states in mind. Two further points must be noted. First, all
societies remain at the edge of barbarism. None is able to permanently cross
the threshold of minimal decency. Indeed, many societies sustain their own
decency by directly perpetrating evil upon other societies. Second, the terms
'minimally decent' and 'barbaric' cut across the usual typology of socialist and
capitalist social formations. Both capitalist and socialist societies have been
known to be equally barbaric or minimally decent. In my view, we need a
complex, two-tiered morality to judge social formations: first, to test if they
have crossed the threshold of minimal decency and then, begin making other
cross-societal, moral judgements.

[4] Thomas Nagel, *Other Minds*, New York and Oxford: Oxford University
Press, 1995, pp. 213–14.

[5] S. Hampshire, *Innocence and Experience*, Cambridge: Cambridge University
Press, 1989, p. 75. The association of the concept of evil with the idea of original
sin and, more generally, with theology is certainly one reason why secular
philosophers are reluctant to give it the attention it deserves. But its neglect is

particular, the horror of the Nazi regime provided the occasion for Hampshire to recognize it:

> I learnt how easy it had been to organize the vast enterprises of torture and of murder, and to enroll willing workers in this field, once all moral barriers had been removed by the authorities... Once notions of fairness and justice are eliminated from public life and from people's minds and a 'bombed and flattened moral landscape' is created, there is nothing that is forbidden or off limits, and the way is fully open to natural violence and domination.[6]

One now witnesses evil: 'a force not only contrary to all that is praiseworthy, admirable, and desirable in human lives but which is actively working against all that is praiseworthy and admirable.'[7] It is only against the background of evil that the importance of some of the most ordinary, but indispensable decencies of public and private life is illuminated. For Hampshire, such evil cannot be prevented by substantial conceptions of justice over which there may be little agreement in society. He argues that what is required in such situations is basic procedural justice. This procedural justice is part of 'a bare minimum which is entirely negative and without this bare minimum as a foundation no morality directed towards the greater goods can be applicable and can survive in practice.'[8] Justice, in this context, involves fair procedures of negotiation, a sort of machinery of arbitration that forms the basis for the recognition of untidy and temporary compromises between incompatible visions of a better way of life.[9] It is a means of enabling

---

due also to post-war euphoria—a general sense of well-being throughout the industrialized world—and to a motivated lack of interest in theorizing the great injustices of colonialism and its destructive consequences in the non-western world. By giving us the idea of basic procedural justice and with his renewed emphasis on evil, Hampshire has filled major lacuna in political philosophy. My use of the term 'evil' follows L.M. Thomas' account of an evil act. An evil act must be a wrongful act, done in an appropriate way that has the right moral gravity. The right moral gravity of an act is characterized by either its inherent or quantitative hideousness or by both. For example, the rape and massacre of a large number of women. See L.M. Thomas, *Vessels of Evil: American Slavery and the Holocaust*, Philadelphia: Temple University Press, 1992. See also James P. Sterba's review of the book in *Ethics*, vol. 106, no. 2, 1996, pp. 424–48.

⁶ Hamprshire, *Innocence and Experience*, pp. 8, 69.

⁷ Ibid., p. 67.

⁸ Ibid., p. 72.

⁹ Ibid., pp. 72–8, 109.

different conceptions of the good life to coexist and as far as possible, to survive without any substantial reconciliation between them and without a search for the common ground. This coexistence is possible by virtue of a restraint accepted by everyone on unmeasured ambition, on limitless self-assertion, and on the obsessive desire for an ever larger slice of the cake, and because people involved in even the fiercest of disputes are prepared to recognize the need to balance argument against argument, concession against concession. Basic procedural justice makes possible a minimally decent life, which has a value independent of any wider conception of the good.

Further reflection on the notions of minimal decency and basic procedural justice and on the relationship between the two enables a better grasp of the context and function of truth commissions. For a start, the phrase 'minimally decent' implies that the best available ethical standards in a society, even by its own lights, remain unrealized. A minimally decent society is not free of exploitation, injustice, or demeaning behaviour. It may not even embody political equality. Yet, it is a social order where almost every voice is heard, some visibility for everyone is ensured in the political domain, and even the most marginalized and exploited are part of negotiation, howsoever unequal the conditions under which it takes place. There remain asymmetries in such a society, but it is not asymmetrically (or symmetrically) barbaric. In short, a system of basic procedural justice keeps negotiation going and thereby prevents barbarism. On the other hand, in a barbaric society, where basic procedural justice is dismembered, the entire mechanism of negotiation and arbitration has vanished. Usually, the violation of norms of procedural justice begins with the politically motivated deployment of excessive force. In the early stages of regression into barbarism, gross violation of basic rights, that is, physical intimidation, torture, murder, even massacres occur on a fairly large scale. Active deliberation and opposition is brutally terminated. As indifference and submissiveness are routinely generated in a depoliticized environment, the initial use of massive force makes physical coercion more or less redundant. The point worth making here is that in either case, the demise of basic procedural justice is a *political* evil, which creates political victims.

A person who is robbed on the highway or systematically exploited on agricultural land or in the factory is a victim but not a political victim. A political victim is one who is threatened, coerced, or killed because of her attempt to define and shape the character of her own society, and to determine the course of what it might become in the future. When political victims suffer violence, they are not merely harmed physically, however. The act of violence transmits an unambiguous, unequivocal message—that their views on the common good, on matters of public significance do not count; that their side of the argument has no worth and will not be heard; that they will not be recognized as participants in any debate; and finally, that to negotiate, or even reach a compromise with them is worthless. In effect, it signals their disappearance from the public domain. When excluded from the political domain, such persons may be described as politically dead, as was the case with the law-abiding but politically silenced subjects of former communist states.[10] If the collapse of basic procedural justice brings about political death, then clearly its restoration marks the political rebirth of members of a society. This helps explain why, by making the restoration of basic procedural justice their primary objective, truth commissions focus primarily on the rehabilitation of political victims.

I should mention here that political victims usually, though not always, are also victims of structurally generated *social* injustice. Exclusion from political processes is frequently accompanied by severe social and economic disadvantages. Clearly, not all forms of grave injustice in the past are of a political nature.[11] But, if truth commissions focus on the rehabilitation of political victims, then it is not part of their brief to aim at the social rehabilitation of victims, to deal with gross social injustices of the past. Since, some measure of social justice to groups who have in the past suffered grave social harm is usually necessary for reconciliation, an important reason is clarified as to why truth commissions need not aim at reconciliation.

But why should they not aim higher? A better understanding of the precise context within which TRCs operate clarify why their objectives must be restricted to restoring a minimally decent order. Here, it is crucial to remember that when transiting from a barbaric to a minimally

---

[10] The idea of 'political death' is similar to the notion of 'social death' deployed by Orlando Patterson in *Slavery and Social Death*, Cambridge: Harvard University Press, 1982.

[11] Mahmood Mamdani draws a distinction between injustice within the legal framework of Apartheid and the injustice of Apartheid itself. Once this distinction is drawn, we can focus alternately on victims of Apartheid narrowly defined, that is, militants victimized as they struggled against Apartheid and those victims who suffered under the 'day-to-day web of regulations that was apartheid'. Mahmood Mamdani, 'Reconciliation without Justice', *South African Review of Books*, November–December, 1996, pp. 3–5.

decent condition, societies are beginning their ascent from hell, are taking the first faltering steps away from a situation of gross injustice on a massive scale brought about probably by people with profoundly deadened moral sensitivities. When it comes to such societies, standing precariously on the threshold of moral restoration, it is important that we look at it bottom-up rather than top-down. I mean that we must remain firmly anchored in low-level ground realities and begin our search for relevant moral principles from here. We must not first reach out for high, near perfect ethical standards only to subsequently judge ground realities with their help. And, in the ground reality of such societies, the only reasonably certain thing is a diffuse agreement that enough of evil has been wrought and that relief from it is urgently required.

It is important to fully understand the significance of this. It does not mean that enmity or estrangement has ceased between victims and perpetrators or between conflicting groups. Nor that they have begun to view each other with equal respect. Such attitudes may not even be in the distant horizon of a society resurfacing from an evil past. However, it does mean that a space has opened up for a new order on terms not entirely unfavourable to all political actors, that a temporary reprieve from civil war or tyranny exists as also the hope that this can be prevented in future. It also means that force has begun to give way to negotiation, and although relative advantage still accrues to one group, no one has a sense of complete victory or defeat. To be sure, relations of force characteristic of barbaric societies are not totally dismantled but the process has begun to loosen their tenacious grip.

Normally, such transitional moments emerge out of a settlement in which former oppressors refuse to share power unless guaranteed that they will escape the criminal justice system characteristic of a minimally decent society. Alternatively, they typically arise because former victims do not fully control the new order they have set up and lack the power to implement their own conception of justice. However, such transitional moments can also come about by other routes. It is entirely possible that former oppressors are comprehensively vanquished but current victors, victims of the previously existing barbaric society, refuse on moral grounds to avenge themselves, or fully implement the conventional criminal justice system. In short, former victims refuse on moral grounds to don the mantle of victors, something someone like Gandhi might well have done.

Clearly, at issue here are transitional situations of extreme complexity, replete with moral possibilities, including, of course, with grave moral danger. The danger is obvious: victims may forever remain victims and their society may never cease to be barbaric. But what is often missed is that seeds of moral progress are also present herein because former victims are saved the awesome responsibility of wielding absolute power and therefore, may escape the devastating consequences of being corrupted by its use. As a result, the possibility is foreclosed that past wrongs will be annulled only by fresh acts of equally excessive wrongdoings (I have in mind the former Soviet Union). Instead, we are presented with the possibility of confronting past wrongs by means other than the use of force or the wilful manipulation of the criminal justice system. So, what may begin as mere political constraint opens up (minimally) moral possibilities and it is these possibilities that lend moral weight to mechanisms like the truth commission.

The obvious lesson to be drawn from what I have said is this: a proper moral response must be formulated with the greatest possible sensitivity to evil and its aftermath. Not all conceivable moral responses are contextually appropriate. In my view, at least three possible responses exist. A morally relevant distinction is not made by the first between a stable society governed by rules of basic procedural justice (a minimally decent society) and a society moving gradually towards procedural justice or at the start of a process of consolidating it (the transition of a barbaric society to a minimally decent one). This first position argues that the same system of moral rules is applicable to both these situations. When people kill mercilessly, betray friends and family, save their own skins at the expense of loved ones, they breach the same moral norms that a serial killer violates when he strikes. If so, the moral response to this violation must be identical. The second position recognizes the difference between a minimally decent and a barbaric society. It also recognizes that reliance on a substantial morality or even on the complete set of rules of procedural justice is impracticable during a period of transition from a barbaric to a minimally decent society. However, it does not adequately see, as the third position does, that the issue is not merely one of impracticability but of sensitivity to standards of appropriateness in relevant situations. It cannot understand that the move to a minimally decent society also requires that a group or even an entire collectivity be re-educated into a system of morality. Basic procedural justice is a cultural artifact, not natural instinct and individuals can lose their moral moorings if the group with which they identify drops altogether out of the institution of morality. The third position carefully notes this significant fact and admits that is mistaken to elide the distinction between stable and transitional societies and unwise, even morally dangerous, to ask for more in transitional situations.

A further point to note is to do with the impact of the breakdown of basic procedural justice on the personal lives of victims. Hampshire rightly points out that when Hitler deliberately substituted force for negotiation, creating thereby a pliant and demoralized mass fit for domination, he destroyed morality itself in public life.[12] However, I wonder if he is correct in saying that 'morality survived in families, among friends, in professions and perhaps in commerce'.[13] Evil has a way not merely of spilling over from the public into the private domain but of pervading our intimate realms. When morality is destroyed in public life, it does not leave the rest of the social world unaffected. Friends, lovers, members of the family can all be complicitous in crime. The world is peopled with intimate enemies. No one may be presumed innocent. The very distinction between friend and enemy, between those who you love and those you intensely hate is blurred. The Indian sociologist Veena Das, reporting on victims of the massacre of Sikhs in Delhi in 1984, talks of how the traumatic violence of the crowd suddenly revealed to one of its victims the fragility of her kinship universe.[14] Shanti, the victim, disclosed that

It was my own mama (mother's brother) who had advised my husband to hide. He revealed the hiding places of the Siglikar Sikhs to the leaders of the mob. He bartered their lives for his own protection. Go and see his house. Not even a broken spoon has been looted.[15]

Tina Rosenberg gives a moving account of Vera and Knud Wollenberger, husband and wife, dissident members of the peace circle in communist East Germany who risked their jobs and their freedom and were constantly spied upon by the Stasi. After the fall of the Berlin Wall, Vera joined the East German parliament and campaigned for Stasi victims to access their personal files. When she eventually succeeded in accessing her own file, it was full of reports from a Stasi informer with code name 'Donald', containing information that could have been known to only one person. 'Donald' was her own husband.[16]

[12] Hampshire, *Innocence and Experience*, p. 75.

[13] Ibid.

[14] Veena Das, 'Our Work to Cry: Your Work to Listen', in Veena Das (ed.), *Mirrors of Violence*, New Delhi: Oxford University Press, 1990, pp. 347–8.

[15] Ibid.

[16] Tina Rosenberg, *The Haunted Land*, New York: Random House, 1996, pp. xi–xii.

The horror of this monstrous universe can hardly be overstated. The misfortune of complete friendlessness, a life without love is one of the greatest evils that can befall human beings. And, precisely this state results from the breakdown of basic procedural justice; not only are people deprived of a minimally decent public domain but also of love and affection in private life. Conversely, the restoration of basic procedural justice revives not only a healthy public arena but also intimate living. If the function of truth commissions is to reinstate basic procedural justice, then they have a crucial role to play in eventually restoring warmth among friends and family.

How do Truth Commissions Work?

How then does a truth Commission facilitate the transition from a barbaric to a minimally decent society? How does it stabilize basic procedural justice? For this to happen, for the moral threshold to be crossed, the entire society and, particularly, the victims of barbarism must begin to *believe* that conditions of civil war, tyranny, or gross injustice have receded, and that from now on decisions are likely to be made by negotiation rather than by brute force. They must begin to trust one another and have faith in the process. This is unlikely to happen if a widespread feeling among victims persists that the wrong done to them in the past is not even properly acknowledged. It is crucial, then, for developing faith in the process of negotiation that grave injustice in the past is publicly acknowledged as grave injustice, as an evil, that perpetrators of this evil own up full responsibility for their wrongful acts and victims move from passive disengagement with the world to active engagement with it. This re-engagement is effected by the fulfilment of two characteristic obligations. First, an obligation to oneself, to learn again to live one's life and rebuild relations with fellow citizens as well as with friends and family. Second, an obligation to others, particularly to the loved ones who have been killed. Victims and survivors need to tell stories of their victimization, relate their version of events, point out the aggressor, and amplify his aggression. In doing so, victims express retributive emotions of deep resentment, moral hatred, and the cry for justice. Because physical injury also leaves them mentally scarred and without any self-respect, they also need to reclaim their self-esteem. A truth commission helps achieve all this and is an instrument by which a belief in the end of an era of gross injustice is collectively generated and reinforced. In fact, by announcing that basic procedural justice is firmly installed, a truth commission helps bring to life a new (minimally) moral order, an important symbolic requirement. When a truth commission successfully performs these functions, it restores the public health of a traumatized society and helps mend the deeply fractured intimacy amongst victims of barbarism. For all these reasons, we might say, truth commissions are necessary (morally required) in transitional societies.

Against the argument that truth commissions are necessary in societies transiting from barbaric to minimally decent societies, two opposing criticisms can be levelled. For some, truth commissions inherently do more than is required in such situations. Those who hold this view inundate the victim with advice to check emotions. Rather than tell publicly and remember past injustice, victims are exhorted to forget. They are asked to contain hatred and overcome resentment; in short, to condone or immediately forgive. Revenge to which resentment may lead them, they are told, is unbecoming of civilized people, full anyway of terrible consequences for society. These critics draw a distinction between the felt needs of the victim and the real needs of the entire community and suggest that the two often run against one another. Instead of focusing on the past, the victim is told to think of the future. In brief, in this view, truth commissions are dangerous or at best, unnecessary.

The opposite view holds that a truth commission does far too little and is inadequate or merely cosmetic, at best. Its fact-finding function can be performed by narrowly conceived commissions of human rights abuses. Its cathartic functions can as easily be performed by private organizations. What the victims need, so the argument goes, is real social justice, not symbolic reparations that follow forced forgiveness. Besides, how can murderers be allowed to walk free merely by disclosing what is public knowledge anyway? Therefore, truth commissions neither provide an adequate strategy to deal with past injustice nor achieve reconciliation. The very idea of a truth commission, they say, is flawed.

Why Not Forget?

It is well known that remembrance of past harm reinforces asymmetries of power. The fear of physical suffering in the future feeds on the remembrance of past acts of repression. It encourages passivity and obedience in victims, which, in turn, serves the interests of the powerful. But such remembrances cut both ways. If memory of suffering is kept alive, reprisal may occur at future, opportune moments. Therefore, among former perpetrators, a motivated forgetfulness of their own wrongdoing, accompanied with the hope that former victims will quickly forget past suffering is not uncommon at a time when asymmetries of power are in the process of being dissolved. In this context, calls to let bygones be bygones, to wipe the slate clean or start afresh, work unabashedly in favour of perpetrators of crime. In any case, forgetting cannot be brought about intentionally. The demand on the victim to forget past injustice is, in reality, an injunction to forgive or to not publicly recall past injustice.

Most calls to forget disguise the attempt to prevent victims from publicly remembering in the fear that 'there is a dragon living on the patio and we had better not provoke it.'[17] But, it is doubtful if this is a good strategy for repairing wounds or achieving reconciliation. When a person is wronged, he is made to not only suffer physically but is mentally scarred, the most injurious of which is the damage to his sense of self-respect, if he is left with any residue of it. As Jeffrie Murphy points out, when a person is wronged he receives a message of his marginality and irrelevance.[18] The wrongdoer conveys that in his scheme of things, the victim counts for nothing. Since self-esteem hinges upon critical opinion of the other, the message sent by the wrongdoer significantly lowers the self-esteem of the wronged. In these circumstances, the insult and degradation inflicted constitutes a deeper moral injury. The demand that past injustices be forgotten does not address this loss of self-esteem. Indeed, it inflicts further damage. Asking victims to forget past evils is to treat them as if no great wrong to them has been done, as if they have nothing to feel resentful about. This can only diminish them further. Forgetting specific wrongs anyway fails to achieve its putative objective, a point to which Jeremy Waldron has drawn our attention:

When we are told to let bygones be bygones, we need to bear in mind also that the forgetfulness being urged on us is seldom the blank slate of historical oblivion. Thinking quickly fills up the vacuum with plausible tales of self-satisfaction, on the one side, and self-deprecation on the other.[19]

[17] Quoted from Tina Rosenberg, 'Reconciliation and Amnesty: Latin America', in Alex Boraine, Janet Levy, and Ronel Scheffer (eds), *Dealing with the Past*, Cape Town: IDASA, 1997, p. 66.

[18] Jeffrie G. Murphy, 'Forgiveness and Resentment', in Jeffrie Murphy and Jean Hampton (eds), *Forgiveness and Mercy*, Cambridge: Cambridge University Press, 1990, p. 25.

[19] Jeremy Waldron, 'Superseding Historic Injustice', *Ethics*, vol. 103, no. 1, October 1992, p. 6.

Beneficiaries of injustice then come to believe that gains accrue to them due to the virtue of their race or culture and victims, too, easily accept that their misfortune is caused by inherent inferiority. Waldron is on to something important here. The call to forget reinforces loss of self-esteem in the victim. Furthermore, moral injuries that are neglected putrefy demoralization in the victim. Under these conditions, perpetrators feel that they can get away with murder and grow in confidence that such injuries can be inflicted without resistance even in future. Therefore, rather than prevent, forgetting ends up facilitating wrong acts. If so, it is difficult not to conclude that proper remembrance alone restores dignity and self-respect to the victim.

A proper remembrance is critical if wounds of the victim are to be healed. It is also necessary to fulfil the collective need of a badly damaged society. This view sits uneasily with the uncomfortable fact to which Sheldon Wolin has drawn our attention that while societies remember their heroic deeds, they suppress memories of collective injustice.[20] Wolin wonders if collective memory is an accomplice of injustice and whether, by its silence on collective wrongs, it does not signify the very limits of justice. But, he also asks if a society can ever afford to remember events in which members feel tainted by a 'kind of corporate complicity in an act of injustice done in their name.' Can France publicly remember the Saint Bartholomew massacre; America, its civil war; or India, its partition? Can these horrific events be remembered by being represented in civic rituals? One philosopher, Wolin reminds us, who thought collective forgetting necessary, was Thomas Hobbes. For Hobbes, suppression of memories of past wrongs was essential because if society is treated as a building made of stones, then some stones that have an 'irregularity of figure take more room from others' and so must be discarded.[21] Hobbes' covenant was a device to incorporate social amnesia into the foundation of society, a necessary condition of which is the dehistorization of human beings.

But is dehistoricization possible? I think not. 'Muslims' invaded India in the twelveth century but for many Hindus, Muslims continue to be invaders who may kill, destroy, and convert them. The conquest of Quebec by the English happened more than two centuries ago but for Quebec nationalists, their nationalist project 'involves a reconquest

[20] Sheldon Wolin, 'Injustice and Collective Memory', *The Presence of the Past: Essays on the State and the Constitution*, Baltimore and London: Johns Hopkins University Press, 1989, pp. 32–46.

[21] Ibid., p. 37.

of the conquest'. A large part of nationalist agenda all over the world, Ignatieff rightly reminds us, is about settling old scores. In so many countries, people remarkably similar in essential respects appear to go at each other's throat simply because once upon a time one ruled over the other. A simple strategy of forgetting has simply not worked. Besides, it is to live in a fool's paradise to imagine that as grievances recede into the past and are half-forgotten, they will somehow cease to be real. As Ignatieff puts it, 'Collective Myth has no need of personal memory or experience to retain its force.'[22] Only an appropriate engagement with the past makes, then, for a liveable common future. It is true, of course, that one must guard against cosmetic remembrance. An engagement with the past must take place simultaneously at the level of gut, reason, and emotion. If not properly addressed, grievances and resentments resurface. Oddly, animosity between groups is sustained even when it goes against their current interests. This happens because emotional reactions ingrained in the human mind remain insensitive to altered circumstances and are bequeathed from generation to generation. Like property, animosities are inherited too![23]

Nonetheless, former victims and fragmented societies eventually need to get on with their lives rather than be consumed by their suffering. Perhaps victims need to forget just about as much as they need to remember.[24] People who carry deep resentment and grievance against

[22] M. Ignatieff, *Blood and Belonging*, New York: Farrar, Strauss & Giroux, 1993, p. 153.

[23] On this see David Hume, 'Of Parties in General', in Stuart D. Warner and Donald W. Livingston (eds), *Political Writings*, Indianapolis and Cambridge: Hackett Publishing Company, 1994, p. 160.

[24] Michael Lapsley, member of the African National Congress, was a victim of the letter bomb in which he lost both his hands and an eye and shattered his eardrums. He writes, 'For a very small amount of time I thought it would have been better to have died. I had never met anyone without hands so I did not know that life could be meaningful. I was faced with some important questions and one of them was: Do I allow my life to be consumed with hatred, bitterness, self-pity and desire for revenge? (Later) I realized that if I was to spend the rest of my life looking for revenge or hunting for those who had sent me that letter bomb, it would consume me. The result was that I was able to say: "I am going to live my life as fully, as joyfully, as completely as possibly and that is my victory."' See Lapsley, 'Experiences Under Repression in South Africa: Personal Accounts', in Boraine, Levy, and Scheffer (eds), *Dealing with the Past*, pp. 27–8. Veena Das notes that the behaviour of women victims of the Sikh massacre in 1984 in Delhi—their tendency to grab everything from various relief agencies—did not match middle-class expectations of dignified

one another are hardly likely to build a society together. Therefore, to ask people to forget is not entirely unreasonable. I believe timing is the essence of the issue here. Forgetting too quickly or without redressal, by failing to heal adequately, inevitably brings with it a society haunted by its past. One can't forget entirely, too soon, and without a modicum of justice. Clearly, while some forgetting at an appropriate time is necessary, a complete erasure is neither sufficient nor desirable for healing or for the consolidation of a minimally decent society. Moreover, while specific acts of wrongdoing need to be forgotten eventually, a general sense of the wrong and of the horror of evil acts must never be allowed to recede from collective memory. Such remembering is crucial to the prevention of wrongdoing in the future. I conclude that without a proper engagement with the past and the institutionalization of remembrance, societies are condemned to repeat, re-enact, and relive the horror. Forgetting is not a good strategy for societies transiting to a minimally decent condition.

Remembrance as Acknowledgement

Two kinds of remembering are needed to deal with crimes committed in the past. The first is a kind of commemoration, usually embodied in constitutional guarantees and collective rituals or social memorials, which ensures that the moral dimension of certain events never eludes the collective memory of society.[25] The point behind such generalized remembering of wrongdoing is to prevent its recurrence.[26] Truth

---

behaviour and was initially very puzzling. Later, she saw it as a healthy sign of women recovering and re-engaging in life. 'The need to corner as many relief goods as they could get gave some structure to women's activities and helped them to think of the future, to symbolize it in the new commodities that relief was bringing in their lives.' See Das, 'Our Work to Cry', in Das (ed.), Mirrors of Violence, p. 366.

[25] For an illuminating discussion of these issues in the context of the USA, and for the view that the national memory of the figure of Lincoln performs a function in US political culture similar to the one performed by truth commissions in other nations, see Robert Meister, 'Living in the Aftermath of Evil: Notes on the Political Culture of National Recovery', unpublished article, 1997.

[26] Indeed, this determination is also entailed by acknowledgement of the second kind. An acknowledgement that an act was immoral is a moral judgement and like all moral judgements has implications for action. Therefore, to acknowledge past injustice is to commit ourselves to avoiding it in the future.

commissions may indirectly facilitate this form of remembrance, but they must primarily be concerned with the public recall of specific wrongdoing. This second kind of remembrance enabled by them is contrasted with deliberate concealment. Public recall of a crime brings it out into the open, challenges its denial by its perpetrators, and contests versions that, by sanitizing events, distort their true character. The purpose behind it is to get perpetrators or complicitous beneficiaries to admit to the knowledge of, and to own up responsibility for, the crime. People need to replace a generalized, diffused sense of what has happened with a more accurate account. They simply need to know the facts: is the missing person alive? If dead, how did he die, the cause and conditions of death and on whose orders? Where is the burial site? Or, did he get a proper funeral? They need, wherever possible, to identify government officials who have direct responsibility for the crime as well as the wider set of people collectively responsible for harm. More importantly, there exists a need to know not only the nuts and bolts of the repressive machinery but, where relevant, to acknowledge a pattern of political injustice, of harm, injury, and suffering inflicted on generations of victims by structured legal and political institutions, and highlight the less visible pain and damage caused by them. This is important because behind the drama of political repression, of detention, torture, and murder, there also lies a painful story of lives mutilated by unjust political institutions, the half visible story of broken families and personal betrayals.[27]

Getting this second kind of acknowledgement is not easy. It is not always easy for victims to publicize their injuries. Without conditions that bolster confidence and reduce fear and, in extreme cases, treat traumatic emotional disorders, victims are usually reticent about entering the public domain. It is well known that only a minuscule proportion of rape victims acknowledge, leave alone file cases.

[27] Albie Sachs must have this distinction in mind when he says that: 'It is enormously frustrating to me to know there are millions of people who want to share this country, to share their humanity and open up their hearts—not just Mandela who is noted for this. But they cannot do it because the other side will not acknowledge that Apartheid was more than a mistake. It not only caused pain—it was fundamentally humiliating, inhuman and cruel. It is one thing to recognize the facts of Apartheid, it is another to acknowledge the pain, humiliation and indignities it caused.' Albie Sachs, 'Experience under Repression in South Africa: Personal Accounts', in Boraine, Levy, and Scheffer (eds), *Dealing with the Past*, pp. 23–4.

Andre du Toit tells us that in South Africa, the disproportionate number of women who came forward to tell their stories hardly ever talked about themselves but focused on husbands, sons, or other men in their lives.[28] Veena Das, in a study of survivors of the riots that followed Indira Gandhi's assassination in Delhi in 1984, notes how male survivors felt both guilty of survival and ashamed at having failed in their obligations to the dead—traumatic emotions that induce loss of face and extreme reluctance to talk.[29] Das explains the public withdrawal of these men by reference to their sense of having betrayed close kinspersons, to their shame at having escaped in the garb of women, and their humiliation and loss of self-esteem at having cut their hair and shaved their beards— both important signs of Sikh identity. Compounding all of this is a sense of impotence generated by the failure to take revenge. Innumerable cases exist of victims and survivors for who the overwhelming need to tell is matched only by a serious inability to do so. In many instances, this is due to the psychological process of numbing that protects the inner self from unbearable external assaults.[30] It is also caused by a certain framing of time by which victims typically fail to distance themselves from the past. Shanti, who lost her husband and three sons in the massacre and later committed suicide, could not bring herself even to think of the immediate future.[31] Such persons have to relearn how to live again, or be taught how to re-engage with their world before they can make their stories public. Besides, victims are frequently unable to risk re-engagement fearing that in the process they may forget what happened to their dead.[32]

A further problem has to do with how such persons frame their stories. Das tells us how it is not untypical of victims to depict a massacre as a natural disaster. 'She carries on as if she were the only one to suffer a loss. Look at the world around us. Everyone was affected. A storm came upon us and it destroyed everything in its way. Can we save anyone from such a storm?'[33] If the source of grief is purely natural, why not suffer it with dignity in silence? Why narrativize grief that must be endured? Why bring into public domain grief that is not even caused

---

[28] Henry J. Steiner (ed.), *Truth Commissions: A Comparative Assessment: World Peace Foundation Reports*, Cambridge: World Peace Foundation, 1997, pp. 25–6.

[29] Das, 'Our Work to Cry', in Das (ed.), *Mirrors of Violence*, pp. 384–8.

[30] Ibid., p. 358.

[31] Ibid., p. 359.

[32] Ibid.

[33] Ibid., p. 349.

by another human agent? A final issue concerns the nature of the public arena where stories are told. People need to be convinced that public spaces specifically chosen for this purpose are significant and that their listeners are serious, sympathetic, and unbiased. Both the arena and the persons therein must possess a stamp of authority. Initially I found it puzzling why victims require official recognition and validation of their stories. I subsequently realized that this must have to do with the authoritativeness of the modern state, and the accompanying premium attached to citizenship. Among people living in relative poverty, especially in societies such as India, this must also have to do with a certain normative attitude towards the state: viewing it as an intimate benefactor. When presented with the massive evidence of the state being continuously distant and uncaring, victims, if they are to publicly recall, need to regain confidence in it as an intimate benefactor. In other cultural contexts, people must regain trust in the impartiality of the state before they begin to tell their stores to state officials.

To get perpetrators to acknowledge responsibility for crime and beneficiaries to admit complicity or even their knowledge of it is as difficult. An entirely different psychological process is in motion here that demands almost as much attention as the one that concerns victims. Fearing excessive punishment, perpetrators may not confess. Acknowledgement anyway is awkward, deeply embarrassing and unlikely to come by voluntarily or smoothly. There is a deeper problem in that the authority of ideological rhetoric compels most people to actively censor the testimony of their own experience. Besides, why surrender if you can cope with your guilt? I have often wondered how people can live with the fact of grave harm they caused others. One unsavoury answer is that even purely negative self-assertion generates a great sense of accomplishment in people. The gain in pride and in the sense of power can be achieved as much by helping others as by hurting them. Sadly, some get an enormous kick out of kicking others. Humans, in pursuit of self-affirmation, have a vast capacity to shrug off wrong done to others. A lot of nationalist passion thrives on a rhetoric of self-affirmation propelled by people uniting around imaginary grievances against others.[34] Sometimes, lies and denials of crimes also feed into negative self-assertion. Thus, not only the fear of punishment but false pride and negative self-affirmation prevents people from acknowledging the wrong which they know or have committed, when it suits them

---

[34] See the excellent discussion in Ignatieff, *Blood and Belonging*.

to do so. The TRC in South Africa has faced this difficulty. Even De Clerck, who ritualistically offered an apology to those who suffered the indignities and humiliation of racial discrimination, continues to deny any knowledge of some of the worst abuses of human rights.[35] This is why truth commissions must be commended if they succeed in getting perpetrators to acknowledge their crime.[36]

Acknowledgement as an Operative Act

Acknowledgement is an achievement for another reason. Public remembrance of past injustice and its acknowledgement by the wrongdoer, I claim, is part of a series of acts which John Skorupski calls 'Operative'.[37] This point needs elaboration. A social fact is not a fact because it is out there in the world independent of people's beliefs about it but, as is well known, is partly constituted by beliefs. For it to remain a fact, the beliefs constituting it must remain stable. This stability is achieved not by an inner steadfastness on the part of individuals but largely by collective acts which function to mark them out *as* facts. Similarly, the significance of events or states of affairs is also constituted by collective practices. Their particular human significance has no publicly perceptible form other than that given by collective practices within a particular culture. There is no way in which this significance can be publicly known unless they are made known through these practices. In short, social facts and their significance depend for their perpetuity on stable beliefs and focused remembrance, neither of which is possible without collective practices. This role of pointing out the public significance of things is traditionally performed by rituals and ceremonies, more generally by what is called 'symbolic action'.[38] The fence that marks out a property boundary is not an optional extra but crucial to people retaining a continual sense of private property. The act of coronation confirming the new king in office is not a superfluous luxury but central to recognizing the new status of the person, which,

[35] See Timothy Garton Ash, 'True Confessions', *The New York Review of Books*, vol. XLIV, no. 12, 1997, pp. 33–8.

[36] In this respect, the South African Truth Commission may well have failed, for far fewer of the violators have come forward to acknowledge their wrongdoing than was expected.

[37] On Operative Acts and, more generally, on Symbolic Acts, see John Skorupski, *Symbol and Theory*, Cambridge: Cambridge University Press, 1976, pp. 93–103, especially.

[38] Ibid.

in turn, is a precondition for the efficacy of any future act of the royalty. Among such Symbolic Acts are those performed solely to set up new patterns of rules, that is, Operative Acts. The example of coronation just given not only establishes a social fact and underlines its significance but, in an importance sense, creates it.

Now, my claim is that the kind of public acknowledgement which truth commissions make possible constitutes such an Operative Act. A body of citizens through a complex set of institutions, including the truth commission, launches a new order bound by a new set of rules and possibly, a system of rights. One function of the truth commission is to contribute to the performance of such Operative Acts that mark the inauguration of a new moral order. The recognition that grave wrongs have in the past been committed, that people have been severely victimized, and the identification of individuals, groups, even whole communities for their crimes announces and underlines this new moral regime and gives former victims the confidence required for the re-entry into political processes of negotiation. True, this is a symbolic function but its symbolic aspect must not be treated as something one can do without; rather it is constitutive of a system of basic procedural justice. Critics who dismiss this symbolic function do not understand the complex point underlying it and more generally, fail to grasp elementary aspects of social existence. It is no doubt also true that truth commissions cannot perform this function entirely on their own. It is a mistake to believe that truth commissions can carry this burden exclusively on their shoulders. But, it is equally mistaken to fail to see their contribution in the inauguration and announcement of a new order.

Against the view that we should simply forget and bury the past and look to the future, I have claimed that forgetting either benefits past oppressors or leaves complex problems relating to the past unresolved. Against the contrary view that public acknowledgement of evil does too little for the victim, I have argued that, if properly understood and appropriately secured, such acknowledgement must in be seen as an achievement. Both arguments together constitute a defence of the idea of a truth commission as a complex strategy by which to deal with the past and help societies stabilize a system of basic procedural justice. They establish that a struggle for minimalist morality (the third response) is not a shameful compromise but an appropriate response in the aftermath of evil. The question that still remains to be answered is whether truth commissions can achieve more. Can they fix collective responsibility and also, become appropriate mechanisms of forgiveness? But before I do that, I would like to return to the difference within barbaric societies alluded to earlier—the distinction between asymmetric and symmetric barbarism.

SYMMETRICAL AND ASYMMETRICAL BARBARISM

Norms of basic procedural justice can come apart if either all relevant parties withdraw their consent to them or even when only one of them does so. When no party abides by norms of basic procedural justice, then we descend into a symmetrically barbaric society. When only one violates these norms and others are keen to enforce them, then an asymmetrically barbaric society results. The condition of Jews in Nazi Germany and of blacks under the Apartheid regime of South Africa illustrates asymmetrical barbarism. So does the massive repression by the state of its own citizens in Argentina and Chile. On the other hand, the violence that plagued Hindu–Muslim relations in the two years or so before and after the partition of India exemplifies symmetrical barbarism. To deliberately withdraw one's allegiance to norms of basic procedural justice, to abandon the moral viewpoint is to aim at evil and to guide one's action by it. In an asymmetrically barbaric society, a particular group (an ethnic/religious/race-based community or the class of political elites), by its violation of minimally moral rules, bears primary responsibility for evil. Other groups in this situation, normally the victims, bear no such responsibility and indeed, continue to hold on to a distinctively moral viewpoint. The case of symmetrically barbaric societies is different. Everyone in the society, altogether beyond the pale of morality, shares the responsibility for social and political evil. All hell has broken loose, and, to slightly alter a phrase borrowed from Hampshire, there is 'madness in *every* soul'.[39] Therefore, the very distinction between perpetrators and victims appears here to have collapsed. Given this distinction, my claim is that some mechanism like the truth commission is necessary and sufficient for restoring minimal decency in symmetrically barbaric societies. However, in asymmetrical barbaric societies, a truth commission is necessary but not sufficient.

As it stands, the claim is open to at least two objections, however. The first revolves around the distinction between symmetrical and asymmetrical barbarism, the other around the robustness that stems from talk of 'necessary and sufficient condition', the implication being

[39] Hampshire, *Innocence and Experience*, p. 189.

that such talk formulates the issue in an overly simplistic and therefore, unsustainable manner. Allow me to respond to these objections.

It is important to clarify how I wish the claim about 'necessary and sufficient conditions' to be understood, and what precisely it is about. To arrive at a minimally decent order, a society transiting from barbarism necessarily requires forward-looking and backward-looking institutions. Forward-looking institutions are so called because they are justified primarily in terms of principles that deal with current or future issues and problems, say, an electoral commission to ensure fair and free elections or a market-regulating institution to rectify current economic injustice. Institutions are backward-looking when they are justified primarily in terms of principles which compensate, say, for past harm. They are designed to deal specifically with grave injustice in the past. I take the TRC to be such a backward-looking institution, designed primarily to rehabilitate political victims. This clarified, I can now sharpen my claim: some backward-looking institution is necessary (morally required) in the transition to a minimally decent society. When societies are moving away from symmetrical barbarism, a TRC will suffice for this purpose. However, in the case of asymmetrical barbarism, a TRC is not sufficient to even deal with grave justice in the past.[40] Remembrance, acknowledgement, and admission of collective responsibility are not enough. Other strategies and institutions will be necessary to bring about a stable, minimally decent order, say, public trials of the most notorious of perpetrators or policies designed to restore political self-confidence among former victims. It should be equally plain by now that even in cases of transition from symmetrical barbarism, my claim is not that truth commissions suffice for a minimally decent order; also required, for instance, are forward-looking institutions. And, it has never been my claim that truth commissions suffice in dealing with other non-political forms of grave injustice in the past, say, structured social inequalities, forced migration, and other kinds of social victimization that frequently result from political exclusion.

The deeper difficulty, however, may be with the very distinction between symmetric and asymmetric barbarism. To deal with it, I must

---

[40] A TRC is one of the many backward-looking institutions available to deal with past injustice. In symmetrically barbaric societies, it is sufficient. In asymmetrically barbaric societies, we need a TRC and other backward-looking institutions to deal with past injustice. Strictly speaking, then, a TRC is an unnecessary but sufficient part of an insufficient but necessary background condition for the realization of a minimally decent society.

first dispel the impression that I mean all barbaric societies to fall neatly into one or the other category. I do not mean to suggest that that all barbaric societies must either be symmetrical or asymmetrical. This would be to view the distinction between symmetric and asymmetric barbarism as a dichotomy and to distort or obscure the real phenomena we are after.[41] Rather, we need to place barbaric societies in a rough sort of ranking along a reasonable continuum where moral responsibility for evil is ascribed.

But why must this be done? Quite simply because it matters just where along the continuum a real society is placed in relation to these pure and abstract ideal types. It makes a difference to the precise moral content of our judgements and eventually, to how we must act vis-à-vis it. It has to use a common political term, policy implications. The strategies and institutions designed to secure minimal decency will differ as we travel along the continuum.

It might still be difficult to argue with those who claim that this distinction fails to illuminate most real-life situations. What if most barbaric societies really crowd around the middle of the continuum, leaving all other places entirely empty? Or, quite the contrary, what if all barbaric societies eventually slide into or move closer to the slot at one extreme, say become asymmetrical. Either way, a stable distinction eludes us, and without this stability, the distinction is unlikely to have any firm policy implications. Now, there may be something to this argument. Most societies without basic procedural justice tend rapidly to slide from one kind of barbarism to another. Two warring groups may be equally brutal with one another up to time T1 (symmetrical barbarism) but a severe offensive from one at T2 may render the other utterly devastated and hopelessly incapable of retaliation (asymmetrical

[41] The philosopher Hilary Putnam—reporting his conversation with Noam Chomsky—laments the habit, common among colleagues, of 'taking perfectly reasonable continua and getting into trouble by trying to convert them into dichotomies', for most dichotomies, Putnam goes on to add, are 'distorting lenses which prevent us from seeing the real phenomena to their full extent and significance'. However, it is an implication of Putnam's statement that dichotomies may capture, not 'to their full extent and significance' but roughly speaking, what reality is like. With this broad, initial picture in hand, we may 'get out of trouble' and gain access to a more focused, fuller, deeper view of reality, by first readily acknowledging that we possess only an approximation and then, by relocating the dichotomy along a series of imprecisely demarcated distinctions along a 'reasonable continuum'. See Hilary Putnam, *The Many Faces of Realism*, Illinois: Open Court, 1987, pp. 27–8.

barbarism). More confusion sets in because a victim today can easily be a perpetrator tomorrow. Victims resisting their oppressors may deploy disproportionate violence, end up turning into perpetrators of greater evil and completely annul the moral advantage they previously possessed. A still camera shot in situations where a cinematic treatment is indispensable can, therefore, be desperately misleading. But this precisely is what this distinction appears to offer us: a frozen snapshot, and this is why, the argument goes, it may be of very dubious value.

However, this objection proves only that the structural placement of a barbaric society along points on a horizontal continuum depends upon the vertical time frame we choose for the society, that is, the period over which we wish the society in question to be considered. Indeed, if time is a factor here, then whether a society is symmetrically or asymmetrically barbaric will depend also on *who* places it there.[42] I suggest, therefore, that the question whether a barbaric society is symmetrical or asymmetrical be viewed as being asked always from the inside, by members of a society on the threshold of minimal decency, who must arrive at a judgement informed by their own lived history on what kind of barbarism they leave behind. Therefore, the relevant question is: are *we* about to extricate ourselves from a symmetrically or an asymmetrically barbaric society? And this question needs asking at least partly because the society in question must decide whether the restoration of minimal decency requires an explicit appeal to the substantial conception of justice of any one group, whether or not a set of group-specific reparations is necessary. In short, the answer must provide a general guideline to members of that society: if asymmetrical, if one of the groups within our society has caused suffering to another, then we, the members of the group of wrongdoers, must atone for it, undergo some punishment, perhaps compensate the victimized group. This is not so if we exit from a symmetrically barbaric situation where a coarse and rather primitive system of justice, based on revenge, has already been implemented.[43] I believe opportunities for reaching a minimally decent order frequently turn up in barbaric societies but are missed partly because of motivated misjudgements by its members on

[42] This is not surprising because such distinctions are not part of some natural, 'readymade world' but made partly by our evaluative interests within quite local and, in such cases, I should add, first-person perspectives.

[43] It does not follow that in symmetrically barbaric societies, victims are not entitled to aid from the state. But this may be done on an individual rather than on a group-specific basis.

the kind of barbaric societies they inhabit. And, with every misjudgement, each chance missed, a barbaric society regresses into deeper cycles of revenge and self-destruction.

It follows, in my view, that a tendency to elide or failure to maintain this distinction has disastrous practical implications. It is not enough, therefore, to have minimal decency as an objective. Necessary also is a sensitivity to the kind of barbarism left behind. If in transiting from situations of asymmetric barbarism, we behave as though we are getting away from symmetric barbarism or vice versa, then despite our best intentions, we may regress further into already existing circles of hell. Consider the period of the partition of India. The fear and radical uncertainty generated by new borders drawn on the basis of religion forced people from their homes in the hope of living securely with people of their own ilk. More than ten million people crossed borders. It is an understatement to say that this 'transfer of populations' was violent. Nearly a million were slaughtered, and almost 100,000 women were abducted and raped by marauders belonging to a religion other than their own. Responsibility for this savagery cannot be laid at the door of any single religious group, however.[44] It makes little sense in such situations to revive the distinction between victim and perpetrator or to make the 'victim's status as victim the constitutive pillar of a new political order'.[45] The restoration of the moral order and in particular, the consolidation of basic procedural justice is the primary need in such situations, and a truth commission or some equivalent mechanism is

[44] For a discussions of partition-related violence in India, see Urvashi Butalia, *The Other Side of Silence*, New Delhi: Viking, 1998; Mushirul Hasan (ed.), *India Partition: Process, Strategy and Mobilization*, New Delhi: Penguin, 1993; Ritu Menon and Kamla Bhasin, *Borders and Boundaries*, New Delhi: Regency Publications, 1998; the special issue on South Asia, 'North India: Partition and Independence', *Journal of South Asian Studies*, vol. XVIII, 1995; and especially, Swarna Aiyar, 'August Anarchy: The Partition Massacres in Punjab, 1947', *Journal of South Asian Studies*, vol. XVIII, 1995, pp. 13–36.

[45] I here react to the discussion among Kanan Makiya, Charles Maier, and Yael Tamir at the International Meeting on Truth Commissions, organized by the World Peace Foundation. I believe that the distinction I draw between situations (b) and (c) help clarify what is at stake. Clearly, there exists a situation where the new moral order must not immediately erase the status of the victim, just as it would be wrong to retain it in another. The answer to Kanan Makiya's question: should we establish commonality on the basis of rights or on the recognition of pain must be determined contextually. See Steiner (ed.), *Truth Commissions*, p. 31.

necessary and sufficient for this purpose. Consider, alternatively, South Africa today. It occupies a delicate, unstable ground and, unless fully alert, its members can easily walk into two explosive moral landmines. If former victims don the mantle of victors and seek comprehensive retributive justice in either its no-nonsense, revolutionary, or its majoritarian democratic form, then they may instantly transform former perpetrators and beneficiaries into current victims. And, if the distinction between victims and perpetrators is obliterated, South Africa may tragically degenerate into a situation faced by parts of India during its partition. This would be a disaster because South Africa has so far been characterized by asymmetrical not symmetrical barbarism.

Rwanda provides an apposite lesson here, demonstrating not only how hard these judgements are but why we need to make them at the right time.[46] For, on the face of it, one could not find a clearer instance of asymmetrical barbarism. Rwanda has recently been in the grip of a great evil; crimes of great magnitude were committed by one group against another—a million Batutsi were exterminated in three months flat. Plainly, the Bahutus are the perpetrators and Batutsi the victims of this massive wrong. Its identification as asymmetrically barbaric society has certain policy implications: the Bahutu must be punished, at least those among them who did the planning, issued the first orders; compensatory programmes designed for the Tutsis must be floated; and Bahutu may be altogether excluded from government.

Matters complicate when the grave happenings of today are placed within the larger historical context in which the Batutsi have long dominated the Bahutu.[47] Given this history, it is hard to hold on to a clear and satisfactory judgement. To an observer taking a snapshot in 1994, the evidence is plain and therefore, the judgement self-evident that Rwanda is asymmetrically barbaric with Batutsi as clear victims. But Rwandans, reaching the threshold of minimal decency, wanting to

[46] For an illuminating discussion of Rwanda, see Mahmood Mamdani, 'From Conquest to Consent as the Basis of State-Formation: Reflections on Rwanda', *New Left Review*, vol. 216, 1996, pp. 3–36.

[47] This is true not only of the pre-colonial period in which a Batutsi pastoralist aristocracy dominated a Bahutu subject peasantry, but also of the colonial era in which a Batutsi dominated state-apparatus, operating under an overall Belgian colonial authority, imposed enormous hardships on Bahutu. Belgian rule was often severe, and translated into practice so cruelly and with such impunity by Batutsi chiefs that to escape oppression hundreds of thousands of Bahutu peasants fled to neighbouring Uganda.

secure it from future erosion, and asking themselves the same question with the experience of having lived that history may view matters differently. There appears to be a general feeling in Rwanda that, in the long run, shades of symmetrical barbarism exist, that both sides have wronged one another, and that, therefore, even if some Bahutu must be punished, they must not be altogether excluded from government.

TRUTH COMMISSION FOR FUTURE RECONCILIATION?

My third, entirely negative claim is that a TRC must not aim to bring about reconciliation, but try only to accomplish a minimally decent society—a no mean feat, anyhow. By reconciliation, I mean a cancellation of enmity or estrangement via a morally grounded forgiveness, achievable only when perpetrators and beneficiaries of past injustice acknowledge collective responsibility for wrongdoing and shed their prejudice, and victims through the same process regain their self-respect. The view that truth commissions should aim at reconciliation is usually criticized for two reasons with which I disagree. The first challenges the coherence of the notion of collective responsibility and therefore, finds the very question of collective forgiveness redundant. The second argument criticizes the idea of forgiveness as morally inappropriate. I do not find the notion of collective responsibility incoherent, nor the idea of forgiveness morally unworthy. For me, a victimized group can forgive former perpetrators if they own up, collectively, responsibility for wrongdoing and repent. Allow me to elaborate this point. In my use of the term, 'responsibility' does not amount to a legal liability for an act.[48] It is linked rather to what men and women decide to do. I believe that most of our acts and decisions are irreducibly social and therefore, responsibility for them is social too.[49] Three things follow, if this is true. First, the domain of moral responsibility spills over beyond what is directly caused by an individual. Second, an entire collectivity can be held responsible for harm to others.[50] Third, guilt and blame must be

[48] For a discussion of collective responsibility, I rely entirely on Larry May, *Sharing Responsibility*, Chicago and London: University of Chicago Press, 1992, pp. 38, 106. For my purpose, I do not, unlike May, distinguish collective and shared responsibility.

[49] My own views on the irreducibly social nature of human action is to be found in Rajeev Bhargava, *Individualism in Social Science*, Oxford: Clarendon Press, 1992, pp. 199–220.

[50] Of course, this is entirely consistent with the view that members of such a collectivity are responsible in varying degrees, depending largely on the quantum of power exercised by them.

seen to lie on a continuum which also contains shame, remorse, regret, and the feeling of being tainted.[51] In short, groups may be held morally responsible for wrongs and individuals can partake that responsibility, be guilty, or feel tainted.

Allow me to move from the perpetrator to the victim. Why should the victim forgive? Forgiveness implies forswearing resentment towards the person who inflicted moral injury.[52] It is hard to take the view that the forswearing of resentment is always morally appropriate. After all, there is nothing intrinsically wrong in resenting perpetrators of evil. Indeed, since such emotions are woven into one's sense of self-respect, a person who does not resent wrong done to him invariably lacks self-respect. Under what conditions then is it morally justified to forgive? Clearly, only when the self-respect of victims is enhanced by forgiveness, or at least is not undermined by it. This, in turn, happens when former perpetrators admit their wrongdoing, distance themselves from the wrongful act, and join the victims in condemning the act as well as their own past. Only under these conditions can the self-respect of victims be restored and enhanced. Is it possible to achieve this within the functional parameters of the TRC? Truth commissions cannot aim to bring about reconciliation through this process of collective acknowledgement of grave wrongs-cum-forgiveness because reconciliation requires a profound change in the identities of people—a deep, rather long, drawn-out process. The experiential process of shedding prejudice and owning up responsibility for wrong done to others begins with the wrongdoer admitting the absence of a good reason for his act. This must turn into an acknowledgement that the bad reason for his action springs from the deepest recesses of his being, simply from the kind of person he is. Since a genuine confrontation of this fact takes place not just in the mind but at the level of gut and feeling, the acknowledgement that 'I have hitherto been the wrong kind of guy' is bound to be extremely painful. We might say of such a person that in such moments his soul is punished. This punishment of the soul must necessarily involve a profound change of identity, which must be witnessed by the victim if he is to be convinced that forgiveness is appropriate. Truth commissions which must operate within a com-

[51] May, *Sharing Responsibility*, p. 34.

[52] See the excellent discussion of this issue in J.L. Mackie, *Persons and Values*, Oxford: Oxford University Press, 1985, pp. 206–19 and Murphy and Hampton (eds), *Forgiveness and Mercy*, pp. 24, 46–7.

pressed time frame, in the immediate aftermath of evil, are simply not equipped to bear the burden of effecting or encompassing this fundamental transformation.[53] Of course, TRCs can contribute towards creating conditions for reconciliation in the future. But such reconciliation, if and when it comes about, can only be a fortunate by-product of the TRC, and not intentionally brought about by it.

It might, however, be argued that it is improper to have forgiveness even as a long-term goal. One well-known argument against forgiveness is that it is deeply tied to Christian morality and, at any rate, it takes us beyond ordinary morality into the domain of high religion. Victims in South Africa have complained bitterly that the justification of forgiveness derives from a particular moral vision with which they do not identify and therefore, it is not incumbent upon them to heed the plea to forgive. Others object that forgiveness must come from within and only the victim has the proper standing to do so. One can't forgive under compulsion, and nor can others forgive on behalf of the victim. A third criticism of forgiveness is that it has the effect of erasing wrongdoing, that it is an invitation to reconcile with, rather than conquer, evil. Finally, it is also argued that the plea for general amnesty with which it is linked can only lead to enraged victims opting for personal acts of vengeance. The demand for forgiveness, in this view, can only exacerbate settling of scores outside the rule of law.

It is true that Christianity provides an important source for the justification of forgiveness.[54] Within Christianity, it is widely recognized that since the propensity to wrongdoing is pervasive, forgiveness should be generally available too. As original sinners, we seek forgiveness from god. As sinners in our day-to-day existence, we must seek forgiveness from each other. From the availability of a virtue in one

---

[53] In my view, anxiety over the capacity of truth commissions to promote reconciliation is groundless and, at best, premature. See the report by Kate Dunn, 'Will S. Africa's Report bring Action?', *The Christian Science Monitor*, 30 November 1998, where the veteran anti-Apartheid campaigner, Helen Suzman, wonders whether the TRC succeeded in promoting reconciliation. Truth commissions are meant to encourage the controlled expression of 'difficult and troubling emotions', not suppress them. And the expression of such emotions is bound to temporarily exacerbate tension between groups, not bring about immediate reconciliation. This incidentally is why truth commissions must aim to consolidate a minimally decent society and not aim for 'higher' goals, such as reconciliation.

[54] Ibid.

religious tradition, it hardly follows that it is unavailable in others.[55] More importantly, atheistic humanism, with no connection whatsoever to religion must have place for forgiveness too. Even unbelievers can and should admit that in the course of living our lives we wrong others, particularly those about whom we care deeply. If we care about people we have wronged, we would certainly want them to forgive us. Indeed, a humanist must accept that at the heart of the human condition lies a radical fallibility that is futile to try to totally overcome. We need forgiveness from each other, alas, because without god-like features, we often commit wrong and because there may be no god to forgive us. As Murphy notes 'we do all need and desire forgiveness and would not want to live in a world where forgiveness was not regarded as a healing and restoring virtue.'[56] Furthermore, the domain where this virtue is exercised needn't only be private. We need and expect forgiveness even within the wider public domain. Therefore, I am not entirely convinced with the view that forgiveness is exclusively tied to one religious tradition or that unbelievers have no need for it.

The criticism that forgiveness bypasses the act of wrongdoing is not justified either. To forgive is not to convert a wrong into right. It is not to justify the wrong done. Nor is it identical with excusing the wrong done, as when one excuses a child for causing some harm on the ground that he can't really be held responsible for it. The process of forgiveness begins only after proper recognition of wrongdoing and is conditional upon it. Since the wrong is not simply white washed, to forgive is not to compromise with evil. Nor does forgiveness entail amnesty. Forgiveness is not to be confused with mercy.[57] This confusion may well have lain at the heart of the South African Truth Commission in its early stages.[58] Reasons for forgiveness are not automatically reasons for mercy. A victim may forgive the wrongdoer but not be entitled to

[55] For example, Gandhi believed that in Hindu scriptures, forgiveness is the highest virtue. See, *The Collected Works of Mahatma Gandhi*, Vol. CXXXVI, New Delhi: Publications Division, 1982, p. 70.

[56] See Murphy and Hampton (eds), *Forgiveness and Mercy*, pp. 30–1, 53. See Rosenberg, 'Reconciliation and Amnesty', in Boraine, Levy, and Scheffer (eds), *Dealing with the Past*, p. 67.

[57] Murphy and Hampton (eds), *Forgiveness and Mercy*, p. 34.

[58] The TRC, it may be recalled, had to decide who gets amnesty in return for a complete description of political crimes committed by the perpetrators. Many fear that this amounts to something like a general amnesty. Critics of the TRC, such as President Designate Mbeki, have repeatedly asserted that a general amnesty will never be accepted by the people of South Africa.

free him of legal accountability. Conversely, we may, out of mercy, reduce punishment for the wrongdoer but not forgive him. To act out of compassion is not to forgive, though the two may be related. Finally, forgiveness is not a virtue in all contexts and is appropriate only when it is consistent with the dignity and self-respect of the victim. One cannot forgive for the future good of the society no matter what it costs to do so. The good of the community cannot provide reasons for unconditional forgiveness. A perpetrator cannot be forgiven if he neither acknowledges nor repents for his crime. Nor is the victim ready for forgiveness if he retains the feeling that his suffering is not properly acknowledged. Without proper repentance, the person who has killed or tortured may repeat his crime. If there is no forgiveness from within, 'then the door is open to private acts of vengeance and retribution'.[59]

My overall objective in this essay has been to defend a scaled down idea of truth commissions. This, I have maintained, is not possible without a finely tuned understanding of the precise context in which they are needed or the modest but important functions they can be reasonably expected to perform. An inflated and ultimately misguided sense of their capacity not only thwarts the realization of objectives within their reach but also undermines the basis of valuable, higher ideals that supervene on them and to secure which they are more or less indispensable.

---

[59] See Rosenberg, 'Reconciliation and Amnesty', in Boraine, Levy, and Scheffer (eds), *Dealing with the Past*, p. 67.

9

Ordinary Feelings, Extraordinary Events

Moral Complexity in 9/11*

UNDERSTAND THE WHISPERS

In India, as elsewhere, every person understood that cry for help, the horror and fear writ large on terror-stricken faces, the trauma in the choked voices of people who saw it happen, the hopeless struggle to control an imminent breakdown in public, the unspeakable grief. For one moment, the pain and suffering of others became our own. In a flash, everyone recognized what is plain but easily forgotten that inscribed in our personal selves is not just our separateness from others but also sameness with them, and that despite all socially constructed differences of language, culture, religion, nationality, perhaps even race, caste, and gender, and over and above every culturally specific collective identity, we share something in common. Amidst terror, acute vulnerability, and unbearable sorrow, it was not America alone that rediscovered its lost solidarity but across the globe, almost everyone who heard, saw, or read about these cataclysmic events seem to reclaim a common humanity.

As we empathized with those who escaped or witnessed death and relived the traumatic experience of those who lost their lives, we knew of a grave, irreparable wrong done to individuals, killed, wounded, or

* Originally published as 'Ordinary Feelings, Extraordinary Events: Moral Complexity in 9/11', in Craig Calhoun, Paul Price, and Ashley Timmer (eds), *Understanding September 11*, New York: The New Press, 2002, pp. 321–31.

traumatized by the sudden loss of family and friends. These individuals were not just subjected to physical hurt or mental trauma, they were recipients and carriers of a message embodied in that heinous act: from now on they must live with a dreadful sense of their own vulnerability. This message was transmitted first to other individuals in New York and Washington, then quickly to citizens throughout the democratic world. The catastrophe on the east coast has deepened the sense of insecurity of every individual on this planet.

However, this was not the entire text of messages sent by the perpetrators. The rest is revealed when we focus on our collective identities or rather on the collective dimensions of the tragedy that unfolded on that terrible, terrible Tuesday. Unlike the first, which allows a plain and simple good to be distinguished from unambiguous evil, these messages were disturbingly ambivalent, morally fuzzy, and less likely to sift good from evil, more likely to divide rather than unite people across the world. One such message which the poor, the powerless, and the culturally marginalized would always like to have communicated to the rich, powerful, and the culturally dominant, although not in this beastly manner, is this: we have grasped that any injustice done to us is erased before it is seen or spoken about, that in the current international social order, we count for very little; our ways of life are hopelessly marginalized, our lives utterly valueless. Even middle-class Indians with cosmopolitan aspirations became painfully aware of this when a country-wise list of missing or dead persons was flashed on an international news channel: hundreds of Britons, scores of Japanese, some Germans, three Australians, two Italians, one Swede. A few buttons away, a South Asian channel listed names of several hundred missing or dead Indians, while another flashed the names of thousands with messages of their safety to relatives back home.

Hard as it was to acknowledge it in the immediate aftermath of 11 September, it must be admitted that the attacks on New York and Washington were also meant to lower the collective self-esteem of Americans, to rupture their pride. Not all intentional wrongdoing is physically injurious to the victim but every intentionally generated physical suffering is invariably accompanied by intangible wounds. The attack on 11 September did not merely demolish concrete buildings and individual people. It tried to destroy the American measure of its own self-worth, to diminish the self-esteem of Americans. Quite separate from the immorality of physical suffering caused, is not this attempt itself morally condemnable? Yes, if the act further lowered the self-worth of a people already devoid of it. But, this is hardly relevant in the case of America, where sections of the ruling elite ensure that its collective self-worth borders supreme arrogance, always over the top. Does not the Pentagon symbolize this false collective pride? Amidst this carnage, then, is the sobering thought that occurs more naturally to poor people of powerless countries that, occasionally, even the mighty can be humbled. In such societies, the genuine anguish of people at disasters faced by the rich is mixed up with an unspeakable emotion which, on such apocalyptic occasions, people experience only in private or talk about only in whispers.'

The whispering did not continue for long. Soon, left-oriented intellectuals the world over appealed vociferously to the Americans to explore the deeper reasons that underlie terrorism, pointing towards America's dubious foreign policy that has caused millions to suffer in Vietnam, Chile, Palestine, Iraq, and Sudan, to name just a few countries. Madeline Albright's infamous remark that justified the suffering and death of Iraqi children ricocheted from newspaper reports to television channels. Americans were coaxed to re-examine what their leaders do in their name. American ignorance and innocence were ridiculed: if only ordinary Americans cared to look at what was really going on alongside the American way of life and the rhetoric of freedom, they would begin to understand what happened on 11 September and why many ordinary people in the non-western world were overcome with the feeling that it was more or less what America deserved, 'damnable yet understandable pay back, reaping what the empire has sowed'.[1]

ANTI-AMERICANISM

Naturally, American intellectuals reacted with horror and disdain for such 'ideological excuses for terrorism'. They asked if a grave wrong committed today can be justified by a wrong committed in the past, in a different context and time? Could America never do anything right and Americans never allowed to be victims? Surely, there has to be a deep-rooted anti-American prejudice in most such intellectual responses from the non-western world. They could respectfully listen to reasoned political opposition to American foreign policy but not

[1] See Todd Gitlin, 'The Ordinariness of American Feelings', *Open Democracy*, September 2001. Available at www.opendemocracy.net/forum/document_details.asp?CatID=98&docID=723.

accept the pathetic ideological reflex that was characteristic of these anti-American responses.[2]

It is hard to deny the presence of prejudice, rhetoric, and the sledge-hammer of ideology in current critiques of America. And, even harder to accept is the view of the sceptic that denies the very distinction between rhetoric and argument, between ideology and reasoned political theory. It is true, of course, that both reasoned political argument and ideology seek to win over others, but they do so in dramatically opposite ways. One, steadfastly committed to transparency, provides every conceivable reason for its principles and value-based conclusions, whereas the other short-circuits moral values, reduces principles to formulae, almost always privileges the use of rhetoric over reason, and permits half-truths, even lies.

Yet, for all the validity and usefulness of the distinction between reasoned political argument and ideology, we must try not to seal them off altogether or wholly overlook what they have in common.[3] For a start, the world of the political theorist is not entirely devoid of rhetoric and emotion, nor is the universe of the ideologist completely lacking in reflexiveness, internal coherence, or rational thought. Likewise, no matter how well justified, a rationally defended belief system still contains an element of extra-rational preference and some prejudice. For all the justified complaints against ideology, should we not acknowledge, in the end, the grain of truth it might contain about us and our world? No matter how exasperating its form and how crude its technique, should we not address its content? Anyhow, any rate, ideologies are shaped by their practical function, by the inherent logic of what they are meant to deliver, that is, a broad conceptual map of the social and political world without which a political agent can not think, decide, or act. Ideologies are necessarily gestural, uncertain steps in the dark that may lead to invaluable and indispensable insights about the social and political world. Surely, it must be admitted that reasoned political argument is not always necessary for this purpose and never sufficient. Reason may fine-tune some ideologies or help defeat others but it cannot replace them. Alas, even those of us who loath the form of ideology must closely attend to its content. The ideology of anti-Americanism must not be dismissed as prejudice standing against enlightened reason.

[2] Ibid.

[3] On the distinction and the relationship between ideology and political theory, see M. Freeden, *Ideologies and Political Theory*, Oxford: Clarendon Press, 1996.

However, what appears to have invaded the public sphere well before and certainly after the air strikes is galaxies away from not only the careful, issue-based reasoned opposition to the US foreign policy but also from the ideology of anti-Americanism. Way beneath the anti-Americanism of the ideologue lies a magma of impression, emotion, and confused thought of ordinary people that just a while ago was self-directed and is now suddenly targeted at the other. It is this chaotic, sweltering, cesspool that non-western intellectuals are trying to hold in their hands and then carrying into the international public domain. It is quite wrong to call this ideology. Such mixtures of impressions and feelings, having settled slowly over the years, independent of our will, suddenly and unexpectedly reveal themselves under the impact of cataclysmic events. They are not content-less, however. Often, they are beliefs masquerading as feelings, the common man's interpretation of larger social and political situations based on directly felt experience and the itsy-bitsy information filtering through to him; the ordinary person's very own causal account of her suffering, produced in her view by a chain of oppression that resides in her home but originates and begins its devious journey from somewhere in America. The cognitive content of these feelings is this: the world is governed by two sets of international laws, one exclusive to American and its allies, and the other for the rest of the non-western world. A single American life is worth more than a thousand others. Is it such a remarkable fact that struggling, harried people, breathing a trifle freely for the first time, sometimes in an incipient egalitarian society, wish not to take any personal responsibility for their own enduring woes, and that they over react with anger, blame, and schadenfreude? Not any more than to discover that people with excessive wealth and power are generally insensitive to those without it, that they do not even notice their existence.

IS MICHAEL WALZER RIGHT ON TERRORISM?

Non-western intellectuals are trying to open a chink for people in America in order to give them a glimpse of these convoluted feelings. This is frequently done not in the language of reasoned political theory but in a somewhat defective, insensitive, shockingly brazen form that, alas, is yet another import from the West. Most American intellectuals, reacting adversely and perhaps hastily to expressions of anti-American feelings, are unable to catch what is going on here. This inability is linked, no doubt, to that peculiar narrowness of vision which accompanies power and wealth. Most Americans fail even to see the problem under discussion. Some do, but then quickly wish it away by telling themselves that it is so huge and intractable that nothing can solve it. A very, very tiny group is willing to acknowledge the problem, can even see the need to do something about it but cannot bring itself to identify the causal connection between the conduct of their government and business corporations and the abysmal condition of the poor. They cannot grasp that the global political and economic order is deeply structured in a manner that benefits the rich in the developed world and severely harms the global poor.

Of course, not all American intellectuals are myopic or insensitive. The best among them recognize that most rich countries are particularly protectionist about precisely those sectors in which developing countries provide tough competition. They can see that the technical and intellectual preconditions of a more equitable trade are non-existent in most poor countries, that few poor countries can afford to bring their cases to the World Trade Organization (WTO), or even have missions at the headquarters in Geneva, and that such factors have a gigantic impact on employment, income, tax revenues, and economic well-being in the developing world.[4] Such intellectuals also know that Central Intelligence Agency (CIA) funds were committed towards organizing the Muslims of the world into a global jihad against communism and that American assistance to the Afghan Islamists ran into billions of dollars. They are not unaware of the nefarious activities of their government in Chile, Nicaragua, Guatemala, Haiti, and a host of other countries. They support reasoned international opposition to their government's unjust policies. But, even the most celebrated of these intellectuals were puzzled, disturbed, and enraged when confronted with the morally ambivalent statements of left-liberal intellectuals that, in the same breath and the same narrative, condemn both the terrorist and his enemy, and sympathize with both those facing continuing oppression and the most recent, unexpected sufferers at the hands of the terrorist. What they want instead is outright condemnation, without pause, qualification, equivocation, and somewhat curiously, even understanding. At the very least, they wish to postpone understanding in the belief that any attempt to understand the act now is to condone it. Surely, they would say, this is time for elementary not complex morality.

---

[4] On these issues, I have benefited from discussion on trans-national justice with Thomas Pogge.

Take Michael Walzer's typically incisive piece in *American Prospect*.[5] He writes 'As Americans we have our own brutalities to answer for—as well as the brutality of other states we have armed and funded … None of this makes Terrorism morally understandable. May be psychologists have to say on behalf of understanding'. There is much in this piece which I admire and with which I agree. But I wish to draw the attention of the reader to something in it which is quietly discomforting.

Walzer correctly notes that an act of terror, though chosen collectively and strategically, is so unambiguously evil that even its perpetrators cannot morally justify it. However, for many left-liberal intellectuals, the disavowal of moral justification of terror stops well short of its condemnation. Indeed, Walzer claims, a whole politics of ideological apology has spawned in the West since 11 September. Foremost among these excuses for terror is that it is used as the very last resort. The image presented is of an oppressed and embittered people 'who must be terrorists or nothing at all' because they have 'tried every form of legitimate political action, failed everywhere, unless no alternative remains but the evil of terrorism'. For Walzer, far from attempting and exhausting every political action and then having run out of options, terrorists typically choose terror as the first option.

Walzer is right about terrorists; terror is indeed their first option. Quite simply, the description that 'they (the oppressed) have tried all political possibilities and failed' does not apply to them. But it does fit a category of agents not mentioned by Walzer. A group of moderates, oppressed but not embittered, exist out there who have tried every conceivable form of legitimate political action, exhausted all options and failed, but who refuse all along any form of violence, most of all terror. Unfortunately, the political space vacated by their persistent failure and subsequent retreat is swiftly occupied by an impatient, embittered, almost lunatic fringe predisposed to deploy terror and previously sidelined, for that very reason, by the moderates. The extremists, particularly the terrorists among them, gain squarely at the expense of the moderates.

What causes the failure of the moderates? What mechanism brings this about? First, the obdurate indifference by the state to the peaceful, legitimate demands of the moderates. The state, the enemy of the terrorist, hears the voice only of unreason—shrill polemic and

[5] The article, 'Excusing Terror: The Politics of Ideological Apology', sent by e-mail by a friend, is published in *The American Prospect*, vol. 12, no. 18, 22 October 2001.

deafening, hysterical psychobabble. Moderates who have 'learnt the art of repetition, who do the same thing over and over again' are left unheard, unattended, and eventually unsung. Shown to be ineffective by an unresponsive state, and drowned by the fervent hyperbole of the extremists, they gradually lose legitimacy in the eyes of their own supporters, the ordinary people. The matter does not end here. Despite contrary appearances, the state is always an active player in the game, ignoring moderates, often responding quickly to extremism, and almost always creating conditions conducive to unreason. In a sense, the state colludes with terrorists to defeat moderates because deep down it knows that its own interests do not match the real interests of ordinary people and that only moderates, who properly reflect these interests, pose a real threat to its existence. The plain truth is that the terrorist is a minor player in the larger struggle of the moderates (and the people represented by them) with the unjust state they confront.

Every struggle between the oppressors and the oppressed operates, at least, at two levels: the hard-nosed, forceful battle over brute power and the even more significant one, over moral legitimacy. We fight oppressive situations because they are morally reprehensible—the reason why our cause is just. But, some ways of fighting oppression not only fail to alter this inherent immorality of the situation of the oppressed but induce further moral regression. This, at least temporarily, changes the moral relations between the oppressor and the oppressed. By awarding moral advantage to the oppressors, a morally reprehensible act by the oppressed actually helps the long-term interests of the oppressor. This is how acts of terror perpetuate the injustice they allegedly fight. When people are seen to be represented by terrorists rather than by moderates, they are virtually identified with them, seen to be terrorists themselves, and from then on, their cause no longer enjoys the wider legitimacy it once possessed. Therefore, it is always in the interest of oppressor states to infect moderates with terrorism, to act in ways that increases the probability of an extremist victory over moderation.

How accurate then is Walzer's picture of the situation on the ground? In my reckoning, only partly. For Walzer, there exist two active combatants in the struggle, the terrorists and their enemy, typically the state. But, as we have seen, what is witnessed on the ground is a tripartite struggle between three deeply implicated agents: moderates, extremists, and the oppressor state/states. The success of one directly affects the chances of success of others. When moderates begin to lose and run out of options, the extremists come marching in. When extremists step in, the oppressor state appears ever more reasonable and gains moral ground. By not responding to moderate demands, the state ensures the future success of extremism. And so on. What, in that small but significant piece, Walzer does not then fully appreciate is that the oppressed is not one agent but many. There are different types of agents fighting for the same cause. Which is why it is possible to at once condemn the terrorists but support other agents against oppression. It is possible to condemn terrorism, and without giving excuses for it, to try and understand its underlying causes. It is even possible to find something morally worthwhile in a cause which terrorists undermine by their endorsement. The moral justification of our claims against oppression disappear neither when terrorists hijack them nor when terrorists are defeated. What looks like an ideological excuse for terrorism may really be a moral justification of the struggle of the marginalized moderates against unjust practices of their own states and against the support frequently extended to them by western powers.

I have been pleading with American intellectuals that they should attend to the content of feelings, not obsessively demand that they be expressed in their preferred form and to not confuse the moral articulation of the just demands of moderates with an ideological apology of terrorism. But my non-American intellectual friends should introspect too.[6] Insensitivity and ignorance is not a unique American fault. Much of the Indian elite is shockingly insensitive to the appalling conditions under which their fellow citizens live and alarmingly ignorant of the horrors in large parts of Africa. How can we then expect the even more wealthy, powerful, and privileged to be any different? Humans everywhere in the world tend to build a wall around themselves, and the more comfortable they are within these walls, the less likely they are to notice those outside such walls. Perhaps this is a time for all of us to look within and catch this ugly, decidedly uncomfortable truth about ourselves.

I had also spoken earlier of two dimensions to the message hidden in the mangled remains of the destruction of 11 September. The moral

---

[6] A word on these intellectuals: many of them remain personally committed to the best ethical ideals developed in the West and are close cultural cousins of a typical western intellectual. In all probability, they are not even liked by the people whose message they so earnestly carry. Culturally estranged, they appear shallow and hypocritical to them. In aligning themselves with the oppressed, and in trying to communicate their feelings, these intellectuals sow in themselves the seeds of a permanent schizophrenia.

horror of the individual dimension of the carnage was unambiguous and overwhelming. But, as we examined its collective dimension, a less clear, more confusing moral picture emerged. How, on balance, after putting together these two dimensions, were we to evaluate this complicated moral terrain? The answer had to be swift and unwavering. The focus then had to remain on the individual and the humanitarian. To have shifted our ethical compass in the direction of the collective would have weakened the moral claims of the suffering and the dead. And this was plainly wrong. Nor was it enough to have merely made a passing reference to the tragedy of individuals, a grudging concession before considering the weightier political crimes of a neo-imperial state. Then, as always in such situations, the moral claims of individuals are supreme. To have aggressively emphasized the collective dimension of the tragedy at an inopportune time was horribly indecent. But equally, to have screened off the collective dimension, to have ignored what ordinary people in the non-western world feel would have obstructed our understanding of how tragedies of individuals can be prevented in future; surely, this would only perpetuate another already existing moral wrong.

DIGNIFIED RESPONSE TO 9/11

Victims of 11 September reacted with quiet dignity in the face of overwhelming grief, not uncommon in people benumbed by the horror that has recently visited them. But soon there was extreme moral revulsion also and perhaps an understandable expression of the need for vengeance. Even as some people unfairly, preposterously became the victims of this newest hatred, there were calls for revenge. How are these feelings to be assessed?

Can anything at all be wrong with hating ruthless strategists who achieve their political goals' ends by the indiscriminate slaughter of innocent civilians, by random acts of violence designed to terrorize ordinary people? How can it be wrong for a woman to hate the rapist who has permanently scarred her or for victims to hate organizers of mobs that lynched them? At issue here is not the feeling of *ressentiment*, an intense desire to hurt others in order solely to gain comparative advantage for oneself. Of course, malicious hatred is morally obnoxious. But people overcome by hatred towards the perpetrators of the carnage on 11 September were not driven by malice or spite. Hating the wrongdoer is not morally inappropriate. If so, it must be morally permissible to desire to hurt the wrongdoer. There must be some room in our moral topography for what the philosopher, Jeffrie Murphy, calls retributive hatred.[7] It is extremely abnormal if self-respecting persons do not experience righteous anger, even hatred towards those who have wronged them.

Yet, it is not always wise or morally appropriate for victims to act on these feelings. It is imprudent because retaliatory action sparks off escalating cycles of revenge and reciprocal violence, certain to plunge the entire world into greater suffering, pain, vulnerability, and insecurity. Besides, the same motive of revenge is known to unleash even greater tragedies. How do we make sure that today's victims do not become tomorrow's perpetrators of much worse? Can they be prevented from committing horrific excesses? What if the original motive of revenge unravels an unappeasable thirst for violence? If lessons of history teach us anything at all, it is that the barbaric acts of one group solicits equally barbaric acts from others. No matter on whom the first blow was struck, if our aim is to terminate barbarism, then, it must be stalled now, suddenly and abruptly. In the shifting sands of the complex ethic at work here, the entire moral advantage rests with victims of the immediate crime, and if the vision that generally motivates them is to come good eventually, it is best, all things considered, to forgo the temptation to act on retributive hatred and feelings of vengeance.

To restrain vengeful motives is wise for another reason. When the mighty retaliate, they do not usually do so to grant equal status to offenders. It is rather more likely that, by a massive display of strength, the offenders are shoved further back in their less than equal place. The not so hidden text of such retaliation is to teach an abject lesson to all to never again dare the supremacy of the powerful. Therefore, it never surprises anyone when a disproportionate and symbolic show of force to maim and crush the enemy flows from the very same motive of vengeance. It is true, of course, that some acts of revenge are the wellspring of equality and refute claims of supremacy by wrongdoers. However, the spectacular show of violence on 11 September and in the days to come were always going to reveal a different logic of alternating claims to superiority in a competitive struggle for standing.

* * *

---

[7] See Jeffrie G. Murphy, 'Hatred: A Qualified Defense', in Jeffrie Murphy and Jean Hampton (eds), *Forgiveness and Mercy*, Cambridge: Cambridge University Press, 1990, pp. 89–90.

Eleventh September should have become a watershed event that began the serious questioning of this warped logic and that set new standards of international retributive justice, not revenge. This, as we all know, has not happened. American might should have been restrained, perpetrators brought to book in an international court of justice and tried for crimes against humanity, our common humanity. This would have just been a beginning. A larger process of reconciliation should then have been set in motion by, first, decoding messages of marginalized collectives hidden under the gruesome rubble of Tuesday's destruction and then, placing them for discussion by moderates from all over the world. Only by properly understanding the social, cultural, and spiritual basis of self-respect in these troubled times could we ever have begun to address the problems violently thrown at us on 11 September.

Has not the defeat of the Taliban justified the use of force? Is not the cost worth paying? This attitude reflects not an impartial but a narrow, wholly western standpoint. Recent estimates of civilian casualties in Afghanistan are around 12,000, which is at least more than twice the number tragically killed on 11 September.[8] We may not have witnessed ghost towns with terror-stricken faces and choked voices, desperately crying for more help, but we need no imagination to sense the scale of the problem there. Besides, it is still too premature to judge whether the Taliban has really been defeated. True, a Taliban-led government has fallen but its forces have simply melted away into the rural areas, not disarmed and demilitarized. The Taliban militia may have become inactive but have not lost the capacity to reassert themselves. Nor have members of the Al-Qaida been captured. They, too, have simply dispersed. As for those orphaned in this recent war, only time will tell how they would behave a few years from now. As is well known, much of the Taliban was constituted by children orphaned and brutalized by the civil war and fuelled by their hopelessness, discontent, and anger. With the Bush administration openly nurturing a desire to extend the war to other areas, and with the Afghan issue itself far from settled, who can say with confidence that the world has come out of the vicious cycle of revenge?

---

[8] On this, see Paul Rogers' insightful pieces on the war in Afghanistan in *Open Democracy*. Available at www.opendemocracy.net/forum/document_details. asp?CatID=103&docID=889.

10

Literature, Censorship, and Democracy*[1]

A week before attending a conference in Taiwan in 1995, I learned that the following couplets, written some 17 years ago by an Urdu writer, Mohammad Alavi, but printed this year in a magazine with a small readership, were causing a furor in parts of India:

Aghar Tujh ko fursat nahin to na aa,
magar ek acchha nabi bhejh de.
Bahut nek bande hain ab bhi tere,
kisi pe to ya rab, vahi bhej de.
(O Lord if you do not have the time to visit us, don't,
but do at least send us a good prophet.
There are many good souls you can call upon,
Bless O lord at least one with your divine revelation.)

They provoked a *fatwa* from the local imams, and Alavi was compelled to apologize: 'I hereby delete and cancel those two couplets and I am not going to incorporate them in the next edition of the book. I repent before Allah, the Almighty, and I hope he will forgive me.'

Earlier in the same year, a veteran Indian journalist and writer casually remarked in public that although Tagore was a great poet, his

* This paper was first presented at a conference organized by The Comparative Literature Association of the Republic of China, at Tamkang University, between 18 to 20 August 1995. It was subsequently published as 'Literature, Censorship, and Democracy', *Tamkang Literary Review*, vol. XXVI, nos 1 and 2, Autumn and Winter 1995.

[1] I thank Tani Sandhu for her comments on an earlier draft of the essay.

novels and plays fell short of exacting literary standards and therefore his status in Bengal as a novelist was greatly exaggerated. He found himself not only in the throes of a legal suit but faced from the Rajya Sabha, the upper house of the Indian parliament, the strongest possible strictures for having 'defamed a national leader'. However, the most glaring example of illegitimate restriction of speech in recent years was the ban of an exhibition by Sahmat, a cultural organization working tenaciously within the secular–democratic framework of India for Hindu–Muslim amity. The exhibition on Ayodhya, site of the Ramjan-mabhumi–Babri Masjid dispute, was first vandalized by a violent mob and then banned all over India, allegedly because it blasphemed the Hindu deities, Rama and Sita. Sahmat's 'offence' was to have exhibited different versions of the Hindu epic, Ramayana. It did so without inter-fering with the text of a Buddhist version in which Rama and Sita are siblings. It is historically documented that in order to maintain purity of descent, it was not unknown for royal brothers and sisters to marry.

My concern for free speech is fuelled by its precarious status in dem-ocratic India. It is also propelled by a deeper unease that the standard justifications for free expression, formulated either to counter blatant repression in dictatorial regimes or to meet problems generated in one phase of western, liberal societies, are inadequate for polities such as India. Three features make problematic the applicability or extension to India of standard justifications of free speech: (i) India is not a dictator-ship. It has all the requisite political institutions of a vibrant democracy;[2] (ii) its civil institutions are embedded with authoritarian traps that make political censorship easily possible or entirely redundant; and (iii) the language deployed to justify civil authoritarianism relies exclusively on home-grown cultural traditions, in sharp contrast to the justificatory language protesting violations of free speech that appears to exclude reference to such cultural traditions. My aim in this essay is to address

---

[2] My argument presupposes a democratic polity. However, the existence of democracy does not automatically solve the problem of censorship. As Rushdie, in a different context, put it, the big test will come after the end of dictatorship, after the restoration of civilian rule and free elections, wherever that is...because if leaders do not then emerge who are willing to lift censorship, to permit dissent, to believe, and to demonstrate that opposition is the bed-rock of democracy, then I'm afraid the last chance will have been lost. For the moment, however, one can hope. See George Theiner, *Casualties of Censorship: They Shoot Writers, Don't They*, London and Boston: Faber and Faber, 1984, p. 87.

the tricky question of censorship in such troubled democracies, with the hope that it will develop better forms of justification against restrictions of speech.

TWO POSITIONS: LIBERTARIAN AND AUTHORITARIAN

Liberals and democrats in India have reacted to the events cited earlier with some fear and disgust. This is indeed how it should be. The strong feeling of revulsion against censorship, the ban or strict regulation of speech by oppressive social groups or state institutions, seems wholly appropriate. On the face of it, liberal reaction that the Indian state ought to have protected the right to speak freely is justified. However, attention must also be directed at the form of this response and at the precise justification that underlies it. In conditions where the morally legitimate expression of speech is not backed effectively by the state and where no restraints are placed on the growth of intolerance, it naturally assumes a pure libertarian posture. When legitimate freedom of persons is denied and when argument and thought give way to raw emotions, at least some people are bound to demand that everything, literally everything, should be permitted in speech, that nothing should be censored or banned. The aptness in this context of a pure libertarian intuition appears unquestionable: why must we not be free to say what we believe, to communicate to others what we feel is right, to express an opinion on any matter and in any form? Nothing is sacrosanct or out of bounds. As Rushdie put it, everything is worth discussing. There are no subjects which are off limits and that includes god, includes prophets.[3]

It will not take long to convince many of us that we all possess these libertarian intuitions. However, I believe, we also nourish the contrary, authoritarian intuition, though we conceal this fact from ourselves and do not wish to acknowledge that we share it with opponents of free speech. Not infrequently, we are drawn by the temptation not only to get others to accept but to impose our own conception of the good life on them. Don't we all live in the hope that at least some of what we believe to be good will be believed by all? Would it not be wonderful if all males ceased to believe in the inferiority of women, if all believed in the possibility and desirability of a free and equal society? The stronger our commitment to a particular world view, the greater our belief in the utter worthlessness of anything opposed to it, and the more intense

[3] Quoted in Simon Lee, *The Costs of Free Speech*, London: Faber and Faber, 1990.

our desire to get others to think and behave like us. I doubt that there is anyone who has not felt, at some time or other, an irresistible urge to impose his opinion on others, especially when he believes that, all things considered, his opinions make for a much better world. Right or wrong, we are lured into paternalistic coercion, at least whenever our views are threatened by beliefs that appear to produce disastrous consequences anyway.

Both these intuitions—the libertarian hunch fostered by the fear of political power and the authoritarian one bred by an excessive partiality to one's own views—have been formalized as political positions.[4] The first, civil libertarian intuition, takes a formal view on freedom of speech—formal because it is content-neutral. Speech must be free no matter what its content. This perspective on free speech is often based on the assumption that mental harm can never be as serious as physical injury. Words never cause real damage to people. Interference, the argument goes, is necessary when there is a threat to the body but not when mental equanimity is endangered. No speech can hurt enough to require interference, especially from the state. Absolute toleration is possible because speech does not impose any real costs on anyone.

The second, authoritarian intuition, grounded in substantive values, can also be expressed as a distinct view, though it has no identifiable label. For this position, freedom of speech is conditional upon content. Speech that promotes the good life is by definition good, but speech that denigrates it is bad. Besides, bad speech causes real harm to people. Therefore, only speech with desirable content needs to be expressed freely. Bad speech must be restricted. Moreover, degrees of badness exist to which must correspond degrees of restriction. The really bad speech may be banned, the less harmful may be regulated. What is crucial is the realization that toleration of free speech has distinct limits. Such a position on free speech cuts across the divide between conventional left and right or between traditionalists and modernists. Though commonly associated with religious orthodoxy, it is not unusual to find its espousal by others. For example, feminists find it impossible to tolerate what they consider to be male chauvinist rubbish. Those who value individual autonomy may not be able to stomach feudal–paternalist diatribe. Both may wish, indeed with good reason,

[4] For a good discussion of some of these issues, see T.C. Grey, 'Civil Rights and Civil Liberties: The Case of Discriminatory Verbal Harassment', in E.F. Paul, F.D. Miller, and J. Paul (eds), *Reassessing Civil Rights*, Cambridge, MA: Blackwell, 1991, pp. 81–107.

to regulate such offensive speech. Clearly, this is a substantive rather than a formal position on free speech, one that is content-biased, not content-neutral. More importantly, once we recognize the motivation underlying it, we may begin to understand, with some discomfort, that when the fuss over speech has not arisen out of political calculation or mischief, there may be good internal reasons for people to express resentment against what they take to be defamatory remarks against Tagore, or even demand that the Sahmat exhibition be banned.

I have tried to make both these intuitions credible, but, in my view, their credibility can be sustained only up to a point. I understand but do not endorse either. Both intuitions are absolutist, even coarse and insensitive. Moreover, the debate between these opposing sides has long reached an impasse. Indeed, to take it forward, a distinct, third position, carrier of a complex intuition, has since been articulated.

THE THIRD POSITION: ABSTEMIOUS LIBERALISM

To understand this third position, let us once again ask the question of whether we have a near absolute right to free speech. Is everything under the sun really permissible? Must all speech be tolerated, or are there limits to the toleration of free speech? An elementary, technical point about speech acts may answer this. A quick examination of any speech act will show that it not only possesses a form and a content but is always performed in a context. Consider the sentence: 'We are discussing free speech'. The content of this sentence is obvious: the discussion of free speech. But it also possesses a certain form, a term of art by which I mean both its mood and its emotional resonance. For example, in its present shape the sentence has a declarative rather than an imperative (Discuss free speech) or the interrogative mood (Are we to discuss free speech?). And though this is not immediately apparent, it must have an emotional texture. For example, we may suppose that it is spoken calmly rather than angrily. Finally, it is uttered in a context: for instance, published in an academic journal, rather than spoken at a public meeting.

Notice that the meaning conveyed by the sentence is transformed not only with a change in its content but also when, despite identity of content, its form or context alters. Suppose we ask, 'Are we to discuss free speech?,' not quietly, but with an air of utter incredulity, or with impatience bordering on hysteria. Here, it is no longer an innocent question, but conveys the redundancy of any discussion on free speech. 'A discussion on free speech! Isn't the value of free speech already firmly secure? Does it really require any discussion?' Or, consider how its meaning changes when, say, instead of stated in an Oxford seminar, it is uttered publicly in Saddam's Iraq. Obviously, a sentence can be uttered in many different ways, conveying by the same content quite different meanings.

What does all this have to do with freedom of speech? The third position on free speech claims that the libertarian intuition can be rescued and simultaneously put in its place. It purports to do this by suggesting that anything may be said, no matter what its content, provided it is uttered in a certain form and in specified contexts. There does exist a near absolute right to free speech with the single proviso that it be form-sensitive and context-appropriate. The content-neutrality of speech can be protected when certain normative constraints are met. In some contexts, anything goes.

What then are the contexts within which anything can be said? At least three contexts come immediately to mind. First of all, I must be free to say anything to myself and therefore, think anything what-so-ever. This is an important freedom whose value to us can hardly ever be overestimated. After all, the most insidious censorship takes the form of people concealing thoughts and feelings from themselves. A quick look at the work of Czech writers and Hungarian filmmakers under Stalinist repression easily foregrounds the importance of this freedom. Second, content-neutrality must be respected in all contexts of intimacy. For example, no restrictions should be placed on the content of speech, on what all is said in private conversations among friends.[5] Finally, content-neutrality must be observed in public forums. For example, discussions conducted in formal, face-to-face situations, such as seminars, or in academic journals and specified sections of magazines and newspapers, must not have to consult a what-is-to-be-said-where manual. It need only maintain a requisite form, that is, possess a hypothetical intent; every opinion expressed must be an invitation for further discussion, not the declaration of a dogma. It must be a proposal, not an injunction and uttered with humility and restraint, not with recalcitrant fervour.

In all these contexts, provided speech is form-sensitive, anything can be said, and anything means everything. So, it must be totally permissible to make statements like 'the ban on a book is no solution', 'God

[5] Example: an hour after the declaration of emergency, a minister in Mrs Gandhi's cabinet spoke informally to a friend that this kind of 'danda raj' (rule by coercion) will not work for long in India. Next day, he was dropped from the cabinet.

does not exist', 'we are free to question and reject anything', 'women are equal to men in many significant respects and superior to them in some', as well as statements like 'Blacks have a low IQ', 'Muslims are inherently fanatical', 'Hindus are intrinsically hierarchical', 'women are inferior to men', 'idolatory is sinful', and 'the Holocaust never occurred'.

This point about the contextual validity and desirability of the free expression of all shades of opinions has long been noted by courts in India. Way back in 1880, some Hindus in Moradabad, India, allegedly in retaliation to offensive and obscene allusions to Hindu deities—Vishnu, Brahma, and Shiva—published pamphlets 'in favour of Hinduism and in disparagement of Islam'.[6] Defending the pamphlets, the counsel claimed that they cannot be censored or banned because of their contribution to debate among rival faiths. The judge agreed that a religious controversy in the public arena was welcome: 'No one would wish to interfere with the publication of such things as are necessary for the legitimate purpose of controversy. But for anyone to suppose that the cause of his faith could be benefited by the publication of works of such character would indicate a depravity of moral sense and mental incapacity,' the judge declared and thereafter banned them.

The abstemious liberal position outlined here hopes to retain the spirit of the civil libertarian view without falling into glaring absurdities. Recall that the libertarian believes that everything is permitted in any form and in any context. Against libertarianism, this position maintains that content-bias cannot be wholly abjured in the evaluation of free speech. At the same time, against the second, authoritarian position, it argues that content-neutrality of speech that is sensitive to form and context must at all costs be protected. The whole point of free speech is lost if it can be restricted arbitrarily by external values. Simply put, to be able to speak freely in some context is part of any plausible conception of the good life. Free speech is good in itself and not a value merely in the service of other more important values. It needs to be tolerated even when it causes some mental anguish.

I have claimed that abstemious liberalism admits contexts where everything is tolerated. It is important here to distinguish two interpretations of what toleration requires, and to point out that the abste-

---

[6] I am here referring to a famous judgement, Emperess v. Indarman (1881) ILR 3 All. 837. For a discussion of some of these issues, see Rajeev Dhawan, *Only the Good News*, Delhi: Manohar, p. 305.

mious liberal view relies exclusively on one of the two. The first, one-dimensional account, enjoins upon people with differing faiths and sensibilities a live-and-let-live policy. Suppose that you believe in X, and I believe in Y, and that X contradicts Y. Why should this fact be a reason for us to criticize or interfere in each others' lives? Your life is yours and mine is mine, and that is it. On this view, the contradiction between beliefs X and Y creates an internally riven existential situation when X and Y are held by the same person, but why should it result in social conflict when they belong to different people? This account of toleration is not favoured by the abstemious liberal view. It espouses the second view of toleration for which our worlds cannot be insulated in the manner envisaged by the first account. Mutual criticism is unavoidable because if X and Y contradict each other, then an affirmation of X implies a criticism of Y. Therefore, to refrain from criticizing the other is to abstain from a complete affirmation of oneself which can be extremely frustrating. Tolerating the other, it is argued, cannot be done at the expense of stifling oneself. And if this is so, the first view on toleration can hardly be imposed as a moral requirement on us. In any case, it has an unrealistic assessment of our own motivations, that is, it fails to see the extent to which self-affirmation in public matters to each one of us. So, on the two-dimensional account of toleration, given that mutual criticism is inevitable, toleration requires only that we restrain our manner and therefore, that our criticism be serious and respectful, not frivolous and offensive. The feelings of others must not be hurt by sarcasm or insulting language. We must not mock the deepest convictions of others.

The abstemious liberal position appears to be eminently reasonable, with potential to accommodate traditional as well as the more recent justifications for free speech. For example, admitting controversial issues into the public arena for debate is fully justified by the traditional Millean argument from truth (formulated and defended earlier by Milton).[7] Recall that for Mill, a free discussion of an issue and an uninhibited exchange of opinions is necessary if truth concerning that matter is to emerge. But suppose that there are some issues about which there is no truth of the matter. Consider, for example, a range of ethical issues that are marked by a high degree of indeterminacy. Here the

---

[7] See Jeremy Waldron, *Liberal Rights*, Cambridge: Cambridge University Press, 1993, pp. 134–42. See also, Susan Mendus, *Toleration and the Limits of Liberalism*, Basingstoke: Macmillan, 1989.

Millean argument from truth naturally fails and scepticism or pluralism may be in order. But the abstemious liberal position does not rely exclusively on the Millean argument. It may undergird the need for free expression not in truth but in, say, requirements of self-affirmation, consistent with both scepticism and pluralism. It can also be defended on grounds of autonomy and equal respect.

I believe the abstemious liberal position on free speech goes a long way towards overcoming—in the Hegelian sense of cancelling and pre-serving—the libertarian and the authoritarian positions. By making bet-ter sense of the motivations behind censorship, and by not side-stepping important issues of identity and shared values, it shows, without falling into the authoritarian trap, what's wrong with untrammelled libertari-anism. It is also better able to match the complex reality of liberal and democratic societies. These points need elaboration.

Let me first address this last issue. The liberty to express is legally prohibited in many contexts in most societies with a deep commitment to the value of free speech. There exist laws on (i) libel, (ii) copyrights, and (iii) contempt of court; laws protecting (iv) official secrets and (v) confidences; and laws (vi) prohibiting or restricting obscenity and racial or religious hatred. The impossibility of following the absolutist position on free speech condemns it to mere ideological posturing, useful only when push comes to shove over the issue.

Second, the absolutism in libertarian positions is such that it makes people jump at the very mention of a ban. 'Is it not undemocratic to ban speech?', libertarians ask. It is of course true that a ban on speech amounts to its criminalization, and much else can be done before its eventual imposition. It is also undeniable that severe restrictions are accompanied by high risk. Yet, we must distinguish, as the abstemious liberal does, between legitimate and illegitimate restrictions. Legitimate restrictions are neither entirely undesirable nor incompatible with democracy. But this shifts the burden of argument to the notion of legitimacy. What does legitimacy mean? The brief liberal answer to this would be that legitimacy requires some form of unanimous agree-ment.[8] And who or people with what kinds of motivations are to be party to unanimous agreement? Here we are asked by the abstemious liberal to imagine individuals who first abstract themselves from all

[8] For a good discussion of these issues, see E. Barendt, *Freedom of Speech*, Oxford: Clarendon, 1987. See Thomas Nagel, *Equality and Partiality*, Oxford: Oxford University Press, 1991, pp. 33–40.

cultural contexts and then arrive at a no man's land from which a dispassionate and impartial view of principles is possible. Such principles automatically enlist unanimous consent and therefore, are legitimate. So, against the libertine position, the abstemious liberal claims that forms of speech may be censored, provided this prescription is supported by justificatory principles acceptable to all.

Third, the formalism and content-neutrality of the libertarian position is a sham, and the motivations required to sustain it too artificial and humanly unattainable. A libertarian position has its own substantive values of which it is either unaware or that it deliberately ignores. The libertarian is as committed as the authoritarian to substantive, even common values. In short, the libertarian belief that the question of free speech can be detached from shared values and identity is a hopeless illusion. Consider, for example, the motivations of those who defend Rushdie. Do they support him because of their commitment to a formal principle or because of the values they share with him? Although it is analytically possible and often desirable to distinguish the general defence of free speech from the defence of speaking freely about matters of special value to us, our complex motivations in real life are sufficiently suffused with each other to make difficult a firm hold over these distinctions. It is possible, then, that the unease felt at the attack on Rushdie is caused less by the blow to a formal principle and more by our recognition that he is one of us—an artist, a secular humanist, a modernist, an intellectual in exile, an anxious non-believer in a world of rigid certainties.

We feel a special obligation to someone who appears to be one of us rather than be moved by an impartial commitment to a wholly abstract principle. To be sure, blind conformity is undesirable but, over many issues and to a much greater extent than we realize, we expect some degree of conformity from each other. We eschew persistent disagreement (disagreement may be good for us but we rarely pursue it as a good). We want our views accepted far more than we want them contradicted. It is not unlikely that the fulfilment of this expectation in Rushdie moves us to defend him and the disappointment caused by the failure of its fulfilment in his opponents prompts us to decry them. The power of solidarity should not be underestimated; it is greater than the authority of an abstract principle. But, libertarians deny that their commitment to free speech springs from common values or frames of identity—both associated usually with authoritarian intentions. This is a powerful objection to which even the abstemious liberal may be equally vulnerable, but let me first attend to some other problems that abound in this position.

CRITIQUE OF ABSTEMIOUS LIBERALISM

To begin with, in a society cleft with deeply differing faiths, it is extremely difficult to avoid offence to the sensibilities of the other. Indeed, as Waldron puts it, 'it is hard to see how free expression could do its work if it remained psychologically innocuous.' The third position sanitizes our emotions. This is one reason I have called it abstemious. Is it possible to disagree with some position but not feel hostility towards it? The abstemious liberal may here reply that in appropriate contexts, expression of hostility is acceptable, indeed even encouraged. In the pure world of make-believe, in a near, uncontaminated world of fantasy and playfulness, anything in any form is allowed. In these contexts—in the somewhat esoteric world of art and the more mundane world of everyday humour—literally anything goes in any form. How can the liberal deny that upsetting conventional forms, including the forms of utterances, is one of the constitutive objectives of performances within this context? But this is to miss the point of the criticism. For restricting hostile emotions to the domain of the arts merely begs the question about the sanitization of emotions. Can emotions be compartmentalized in this way? Besides, the claim here is that hostility may be expressed as an integral part of one's self-affirmation more generally. For example, the mere affirmation of one's faith may be deeply offensive to the other. How does one here sustain an environment free of offense and counter-offense? For some Hindus, the performance of rituals is impossible without music, but Muslims may find it against the diktat of Quran. Muslims and Jews find it offensive even to admit that Jesus is the son of god. Can the whole of Christendom be charged with blasphemy? Muslims find idolatry deeply repugnant. Shall the whole of Hinduism be outlawed? Form and content, style and substance, emotion and thought are too intertwined here to be separable in the manner desired by liberals.

Second, the abstemious liberal position is too middle class or elitist in the following sense: it antecedently over-values propositional speech to which the elites are accustomed. The language of victims, the poor, and the marginal is so thickly woven with emotions that it may have scant respect for speech with 'proper' propositional form. The persistent exclusion from public arena forces speech to be loud, shrill, and offensive, making it difficult to fit it into the traditional mould favoured by the third position. What justification exists to inhibit the expression of forms of speech to which the victims are accustomed, and to allow or encourage only those forms that are culturally unavailable to them? In the formally educated milieu of the middle class, the moderate position works well; but does it succeed in other contexts and for other people?

Finally, as it stands, the third position is still trapped in an unacknowledged, false universalism insufficiently sensitive to cultural difference. This is a point I have made already, but which needs elaboration.

CULTURAL RELATIVISM AND FREE SPEECH

For the abstemious liberal position, offensive speech is to be tolerated as long as it is restricted to one domain, say, the sphere of the arts. But, it can be argued that the exemption of literature from form-compliance is itself a culturally specific phenomenon, not possible without a separation of spheres characteristic of modern western societies. Where art has not detached itself from magic, religion, and everyday life, the special place accorded to literature may be unwarranted. Only in societies where literature has gained a certain degree of autonomy, can certain kinds of haute literature be exempt from those constraints under which less exulted literature is routinely placed in other societies. Abstemious liberals also claim that critique and discussion among rival faiths is generally permissible as long it conforms to a certain form, that is, without causing offence to anyone and with equal respect to all. The point about equal respect and the necessity to place restriction on offence is well taken, but this view fails to fully acknowledge how the assessment of what counts as offence changes with variations in public and formal contexts and in modes of address, how varied cultures are in their understanding of the dynamics of these relationships, and how cultures may ultimately differ even in the weight they accord the value of speech.

Some faiths permit jokes about god, while others require that even the name of god be uttered, under stringent conditions, only by a distinct class of persons, for example, by males not only born pure but continuously purifying themselves! Or consider the contrast often drawn between modern–western and traditional–Islamic cultures. It is said that it is easier in modern western societies for people to remark about each other on paper what they dare not say in person. In traditional–Islamic societies, on the other hand, private speech between individuals is much freer than when it is written.[9] Whether or not it is morally permissible to say something varies, therefore, with whether or not it is written.

Let me take another shot in my attempt to capture the relevant contrast. Perhaps it is the difference between formal and informal contexts, and not between written and oral speech, that is doing the relevant work here. Anything said formally, with the appropriate modes of address, may be socially, morally, and even politically acceptable, and this may include all written and some oral expressions. By contrast, in some cultures, it may be morally impermissible to make a host of statements in formal contexts, and because all written speech is thought formal, one may not be able to say in writing what one is able to say face to face. So, societies have different moral conventions and the permissibility within a culture of a certain form of speech is shaped by whether or not it is written, how formal it is, and what weight is placed in the given culture on speech as a mode of expression. It may even be argued, not very convincingly in my opinion, that the importance of free expression depends on the value attached, in the background culture, to autonomy. Given that societies have different cultural and moral values and further that the weight they place on the same values differs, it is likely that the way they resolve conflicts between free expression and other values is different, too. Indeed, theoretically at least, it is possible that in some cultures free speech has no value at all. But whether or not this is so, there is much plausiblity in the claim that the value of a statement depends on whether it is written or oral, delivered formally or informally, in public or in private, and all this affects our judgement on what place the statement occupies on the tolerance/intolerance continuum. Since cultures differ on the former, variations in the latter are to be expected, too. Any theory espousing the cross-cultural value of free speech must take cognizance of these issues, but abstemious liberalism appears not to do so.[10]

These critical remarks suggest the following dilemma. On the one hand, it seems right to allow all kinds of offensive speech in public space—the ironical, satirical tone in literature; the wit and humour of ordinary persons in their everyday life; and, in the case of the weak and the victim, even their 'hate speech'. On the other hand, cultural

[9] Waldron, *Liberal Rights*, p. 139.
[10] I refer to the work of Malise Ruthven, discussed in Simon Lee, *The Costs of Free Speech*.

relativity suggests, at least at the far extreme, that we should not expect from some cultures a degree of respect for any form of speech, and therefore, censorship of speech must appropriately be viewed from the inside. How do we get over this conundrum?

I start my response to this difficulty by employing an important point made by Jeremy Waldron.[11] Waldron has forcefully argued that the question of free speech must be protected from the more pernicious forms of cultural relativism. Curtailment of free speech cannot be justified by a facile appeal to cultural relativism. For Waldron, the urgent question is whether or not we shall have free expression in the world, not whether this culture or that, from within its own perspective, permits it. I agree. Because the issue of free speech responds to a fundamentally human and universal need, it must be rescued from the more vertiginous forms of cultural relativism. The challenge is to formulate a universal defence of free speech allowing maximum sensitivity for, not stepping over, cultural context. It is of course true that a particular formulation and defence of free speech should not masquerade as universal. But, it is equally important that the aspiration to formulate a concrete universal of free expression is not wholly abandoned. Contra the abstemious liberal position, we need, perhaps, to arrive at it not by following a single course of reasoning but by allowing different persons, reasoning from within their own distinct cultural perspectives, to converge on something common.

This brings me to another related issue. The abstemious liberal position never really abandons the view that a consensus on principles justifying restrictions on free speech hinges on the impartial motivations of agents. This is hopelessly utopian. Convergence must be sought on the basis of a more realistic appraisal of motivations that takes into account not only the particular projects and commitments valued by the agent but also the special obligations to his family, his community, his culture, or indeed, even his nation. Human beings inhabit two worlds at once: an impersonal and a personal universe, and though a balance may never be achieved—dwelling in one more than the other is the norm for most people—the influence of one never quite ceases even when the other gains dominance.[12] The challenge, therefore, is to admit at the outset that we start from different cultures but still reach a consensus

[11] In short, this liberalism is abstemious because it holds back on emotions, shies away from deep cultural difference, and is too proper to accommodate the language of the marginalized.

[12] Waldron, *Liberal Rights*, p. 139.

on some principles that endorse, in specific contexts, protection or restriction of speech. The Rawlsian idea of an overlapping consensus is not inappropriate here.[13] So, against the libertine position, and as an improvement on the abstemious liberal view, we may claim that forms of speech may be protected or censored provided there is support from justificatory principles arrived at by an overlapping consensus.

THE NEED FOR FREE EXPRESSION

But can we ever hope to arrive at an overlapping consensus in a culturally divided world? What if the taste for free speech is really specific only to some cultures? What if it is a mere preference of the modern, logocentric West? Let me begin by dismissing a particularly bad formulation of this issue. I have often heard people say that a commitment to free speech is a luxury of the modernized elite, that the poor have no need for it, or that free speech thrives only in cultures where the very idea of the sacred has been renounced, and not, say in South Asia, where faith overrides everything else and where compared with rituals, the discursive has low priority anyway. Two points make a brief riposte to this argument. First, going merely by people's tastes, preferences, and interests, free speech does not appear to matter very much even in the West. A catalogue of people' interests in the West displays a relatively low place given to free speech. By their own account, people's interests are far better served, say, by a secure job, by decent human relationships, by a safe environment, etc. Why free speech, rather than all these, is accorded special protection in the West is a widely acknowledged 'liberal puzzle'.[14]

Contrary to my own intuition, and for the sake of argument, let me assume that free speech is indeed a cultural preference. I now counter the relativist argument by using two distinctions between: (i) expression and speech; and (ii) need and preference. While free speech may indeed be culture specific—the short- or long-term preference of some individuals in specific cultures—free expression, I wish to claim, is a basic, universal need. Further, assuming the inescapability and desirability of equality, I argue that we must respect, and therefore allow, the precise form of expression chosen or endorsed by others. Let me elaborate.

---

[13] On this, see Nagel, *Equality and Partiality*, pp. 10–20.

[14] John Rawls, *Political Liberalism*, New York: Columbia University Press 1993, pp. 133–68.

First, the distinction between need and preference.[15] A need is a desire which belongs to us largely in virtue of the kind of beings we are (example, desire for food or sleep). Preference, by contrast, is a desire we have because we have adopted it (the taste for beef rather than pork). Second, the distinction between speech and expression. Speech in the narrow sense is the deployment of sentences with some propositional content. This must be distinguished from symbolic forms and what Taylor calls expression.[16] Expression has five features. First, it is embodied meaning. Second, the meaning so embodied may be a belief, desire, or feeling, or a set thereof. Third, its embodiment implies the necessary presence of a material medium. Fourth, the meaning so embodied is manifest, directly present for all to see, that is, publicly available. Fifth, it is public not merely in the sense that it is displayed after it is produced and polished, but in that it is formed in public and to be the expression that it is, constantly requires collaboration of and corroboration by participants in relevant public spheres. As the term is used here, expression includes not just speech in both the narrow and wide senses, but any symbolic activity, such as art and ritual.

Now, in this sense, expression is neither culture specific nor a mere preference but rather a common human need. People cannot help expressing themselves one way or another, in one or another form. More strongly stated, for humans it is a way of being in this world. The value of (public) expression lies in its existential significance for humans. But, as judgement on the value of particular expressions is a social achievement, the more able the relevant others are to corroborate our expressions, the more satisfactory these expressions become and correspondingly, the better our fulfilment of this need.

But forms of expression can be misrecognized, restricted, and even wholly thwarted, either because they conflict with and threaten other forms, or because of the overwhelming tendency among humans to believe that their own particular good is generalizable, or because of genuine human failure to overcome one's given conceptual universe. At any rate, the particular form of expression favoured by individuals or cultural groups can be inhibited in public for these reasons. Freedom of expression needs protection because of the persistent tendency among humans to restrict expressive activities of other persons or groups

[15] Joseph Raz, *Ethics in the Public Domain: Essays in the Morality of Law and Politics*, Oxford: Clarendon Press, 1994, p. 131.

[16] See Charles Larmore, *Patterns of Moral Complexity*, Cambridge: Cambridge University Press, 1987, p. 139.

and because it is undesirable to do so.[17] Freedom of speech is a value, derived from the general need for free expression, that may be of special importance to some cultural groups, even perhaps to some individuals within those groups, but its protection is required on grounds of the general egalitarian principle that forms of expression of a group or individual matter equally—of one as much as of the other—and therefore, when restrictions are imposed, it is mandatory to furnish consensual justification. So, free speech may need special protection, despite the general rather than the culture-specific perception that it is not as vital as other interests. Even supposing that it is a cultural preference, its protection is still required by the general egalitarian principle stemming from the need for free expression in all human beings. I know that what I have here offered is not an argument but a mere point of view, but I believe an argument along these lines has to be constructed to reach a common perspective that accommodates cultural diversity.

Now, it might be argued that the thesis established by a fully worked out argument of this kind is so general and trivial that no workable political principles concerning free speech could flow from it. But this would be to miss the point of my claim. For, in response to the fair charge of cultural parochialism, all I am seeking is a refinement of the abstemious liberal view and not its replacement. A narrow defence of free speech in societies today must be complemented by a broader argument in favour of the need for self-expression. Unless this is done, a defence of free speech will cut no ice with cultures that do not understandably and immediately see its importance.[18]

I believe the thin argument just developed can be used against censorship of some kinds of literature. However, what about 'offensive literature'? As it stands, the argument from need for expression does not apply to it. The expressive need can be met in many ways. Why, it might be argued, must it assume a form offensive to others? Now, we have already acknowledged that offensive expressions cannot be entirely eliminated from the public sphere because of the mutual implication of affirmation and offence. Given the relationship between expression, affirmation, and offence, it appears that those offended

[17] I rely here on Charles Taylor, *Philosophical Papers*, Vol. 2, Cambridge: Cambridge University Press, 1985, p. 219.

[18] The danger arises because misrecognition is almost always built into the very process of recognition. Expressions need others to be the expressions they are, but are also distorted just as they are formed. Protection is required, one might say, to tilt the balance in favour of recognition.

by such self-affirmative acts (I assume that the relationship among expression, affirmation, and offence is self-evident or can be reasonably demonstrated) must learn to live with it, and bear the costs of offence.[19] The matter need not be left at this, however. I wish to supplement this claim with another universalist argument from equality of respect and with the assumption that it is a universally acknowledged fact that some of the deepest questions concerning life and death, good and evil, have a persistent hold on all humans. Now, these issues are not only inescapable but stretch our intellect and imagination to their limit. If they are inescapable, we must deal with them. If they strain our psyche, we must forever ferret out new ways of exploring them and this must include not only 'the whole kaleidoscope of literary technique—fantasy, irony, poetry, wordplay and the speculative juggling of ideas,'[20] but also all modes of communication. Not only sacred and secular art, literature, and philosophy, but all other expressive forms must unleash on each other all the resources at their command to deepen our understanding of these issues. If we are to respond effectively to the criticism that haute literature should not be privileged, then we must throw the net wide enough to cover all forms of expression that explore these deep questions.

Of course, toleration of all such expressions has costs. Opening ourselves up to all possible cultural expressions may be volatile, particularly when we may neither be able lay down to each other the terms on which those issues shall be tackled nor 'respectfully tiptoe... around each other's cultural and psychological furniture.'[21] But it may also have benefits. We might eventually come to the realization that a deeper understanding of some of these perennially perplexing issues is inhibited, in this case, by the narrowness of our cultural forms. By implication, we may realize that we invite offence by a personal lack of catholicity. This does not mean that we endorse the other's cultural vision but, by recognizing our own limitations, we may better come to terms with a common human frailty.

[19] Similarly, a better defence of free speech must recognize the cultural specificity of offence and cultural variations in the relation between what counts as insult and modes of address, and so on. Here, I only point to the need to address the issue but am unable to fully address it myself.

[20] Perhaps the knowledge that such costs are equally shared, that those who appear to inflict them also bear such costs in other contexts, makes life more liveable.

[21] Waldron, *Liberal Rights*, p. 140.

Two problems in this fourth view still need addressing. First, in an ideal world of equal relations, offensive, indeed any speech that hurts may be tolerated. But the real world is full of structured inequalities. When speech unfailingly and repeatedly comes into conflict with the principle of treating persons as equals, when it deliberately and persistently inflicts, directly or by creating a pervasively hostile climate, a sense of inferiority on an individual or a group, lowers self-esteem and self-confidence, humiliates or stigmatizes—in short, whenever it persistently damages the sense of one's identity—then speech need not be tolerated. Recall the notorious incident in an American university where white students harassed and heckled an Afro-American woman, shouting 'we have never taken a nigger'. Even from within the abstemious liberal perspective, the inflictors of this speech forfeit the right to toleration. Their speech must be restricted.

Does this contradict the claim that offending the identity and sense of dignity of people may, in some cases, be unavoidable? It is clear from the given example that the 'sense of hurt' is much stronger when inflicted by persons belonging to a powerful group who 'talk down' from a superior platform to oppressed individuals or groups. We can't escape the fact that hurtful speech from an equal is easy to brush aside, but when it comes in conditions of asymmetricity and hierarchy, from the arrogant or the powerful, then it can't be shrugged off by those who are generally alienated, insecure, or oppressed. Moreover, individuals who are culturally ill at ease in society tend to band together and greatly value collective self-definition, and those with a strong collective identity find it even more difficult to ignore denigration aimed at their group. Words cause special damage to them and when the intention is manifestly, deliberately, and persistently to injure, then they are left with no reason to tolerate hurtful speech.

In brief, the presence of structured inequalities requires that special attention be accorded disagreeable speech, that is, speech which has an immoderate, disagreeable form, uttered in inappropriate contexts, coming primarily from the arrogant or powerful, and that persistently offends the self-respect of others. The standard view of free speech that restricts individual libel but protects group libel has no principled justification going for it in contexts where the relationship between the relevant groups is demonstrably asymmetrical. Only consequentialist reasons favour toleration of group libel by powerful groups.

Second, can disparagement of an entire way of life of a people, even in an ideal egalitarian universe, be permitted? When not merely one or the other of its aspect but indeed, the entire moral system of a group is severely maligned by speakers who show no evidence of understanding of the moral belief of the concerned group, then surely the ground from which they demand toleration is gone. This is tricky as it is formulated and needs distinguishing from an observation by Joseph Raz. Raz claims that every opinion expressed embodies a wider net of opinions and sensibilities which, taken together, constitute a form of life. The free expression of an opinion validates, therefore, a whole way of life. The censoring of this opinion, on the other hand, implies an authoritative condemnation, not just of the particular opinion censored, but the whole style of life. The problem is this: assume the holist view on expressions and then consider persons X and Y. X may, in expressing his culture, offend or even disparage, not just an aspect but almost the entire culture of Y. Since this is intolerable to Y, she may seek assistance from the state, and in attempting to help Y, the state may, by banning X's expression, end up officially condemning the entire culture of X! I confess there is no simple resolution to this problem. It is, nonetheless, sensible to distinguish between cases where offence is caused by implication and where it is intentionally brought about. The former must be tolerated, the latter need not be.

Let me conclude: I have argued against the libertarian view that disallows all bans and forms of censorship. Against the authoritarian view, I have claimed that censorship cannot always depend on content of speech. The abstemious liberal view is an improvement on both, but fails to come to grips with the cultural relativity of speech and is so sanitized that it inhibits much offensive speech that ought to be morally permissible in the public sphere. I doubt that it will be able to justify free speech in non-western, troubled democracies or work even in the full-blown, multicultural character of western democracies. Finally, I struggle to articulate a fourth position that begins to meet some of these objections. I cannot claim to have been successful in building an alternative, but I do hope to have shown both the need for reaffirming the value of free speech and the difficulty this entails. Free speech must be specially protected, but not with justifications that we have come to associate with it.

IV
MODERNITY AND IDENTITY

11

Religious and Secular Identities*

In the last decade or so, a view in the social sciences on the relationship between modernity and religion has become immensely popular. On the face of it, it is entirely explanatory. It tells us why modernization and the politics of secularism has marginalized the believer and encouraged the growth of zealotry. But sotto voce and in a what-else-do-you-expect sort of reasoning, it also justifies, if not fanaticism and religious dogmatism, at least a full-bloodied attack on modernity and secularism. Now, there is a good deal of justification in expressing discontent at the dominant form assumed in Third World societies by modernity and secularism. Some very powerful reasons exist for subscribing to this view, but I believe a few at least are not entirely honourable.

It is these reasons that I try to bring into focus in this essay. So, I am neither concerned with the explanatory part of the story nor with all the justifications it offers for the misdemeanours of modernity but only with those that I find unconvincing. But, before I dig deep into the issue, let me indicate some of the reasons for my unease with this view. For a start, it is plagued with an excessive them–us syndrome. It ridicules the dichotomies of modernity without the slightest awareness of its own fractured vision. It is obsessed with the spirituality of traditional religion but unashamedly obscures the spiritual roots of modernity. It is oversensitive to the linkages of power, wealth, and privilege with

* This paper was first presented at a conference organized by Bhikhu Parekh at the University of Hull, sometime in 1991. It was subsequently published as 'Religious and Secular Identities', in Bhikhu Parekh and Upendra Baxi (eds), *Crisis and Change in Contemporary India*, New Delhi: Sage Publications, 1995, pp. 317–49.

secular but not with religious discourse. It fluctuates between a perilous purism for which a value loses all its import even when slightly tainted with power and a vertiginous relativism for which high values are at base plain, lowly desires. In short, I detect in this reasoning a dash of motivated simple-mindedness, an oversimplification that has dangerous consequences in times of trouble.

Forgive me if I frame this issue in slightly personal terms. For some time now, those of us with a modern, secular identity find ourselves increasingly alienated not only from the neo-religious and the anti-secularist but more so from many fellow secularists. Being secular, we can hardly feel at home amidst the current deluge of 'religious' hysteria everywhere in the country. Yet, something about the dominant discourse of secularism is equally disconcerting. We find ourselves wedged between secularists in power and the religious who wish to usurp this power from them. However, it appears to me that among those who are threatened are also some believers who as a matter of plain fact can neither identify with what can be called the state–secularists nor with neo-religious ideologues and neo-traditionalist militants. Why is it that some secularists and believers are equally threatened when the accepted wisdom of our time adjudicates that all secularists and believers are fundamentally divided? The divide between the secular and the religious is something like a cultural institution in our country. Is it time, however, to challenge it? Could it be that that some varieties of secularism exist which have more in common with religion than with state–secularism? If this is really so, is a modern, secular identity always opposed to a religious identity?

I believe we cannot begin to answer these questions unless we have some understanding of what it is to have an identity at all. In the first part of the essay, therefore, I ask, with a generous dose of abstraction, what it is to have an identity. I propose first a general framework of answering this question and then claim that within it there exist at least four ways of formulating conceptions of identity. In the second part, putting this framework into effect, I ask what it is to have a religious identity and if it is different from other forms of cultural identities. Is religious identity like any other cultural identity or does it possess a unique structure? Can it be subsumed under the general notion of cultural identity or is it distinct enough from other cultural identities to require special treatment. Finally, in the third part, I explore what relationship exists between religious and modern, secular identities. My main claim in the essay, as may already have become obvious, is that some forms of secular identities have more in common with some variants of religious identities than they do with members of their own fold, and that a common culture cuts across the familiar divide between the religious and the secular.

WHAT IS IT TO HAVE AN IDENTITY?[1]

In logic, it is commonplace to claim that the concept of identity has to do with sameness: the identity of an object is its sameness with itself. Likewise, though it is trivially true to claim that anything whatsoever is the same with itself at any instant, it is also true that it becomes different at the very next instant from what it was only a moment ago. If an object has to retain its identity, remain same with itself, it must resist the myriad ways in which change threatens its very character. So, the question of identity is related to the question: what keeps an object the same despite the many changes it suffers over time?

It is related to another question as well: just as a thing is identical with itself only if it remains same over time, just so it can be identified with something else provided the features it possesses are the same as those present in others. Two discernible things can be identical if they have the same attributes. However, if they are discernible, what brings them together under the same description? What unifies an object with other objects despite its ostensible difference with them? The problem of identity is related, therefore, to the problem both of stability in the face of transformations and unity within diversity.

However, it is impossible for anything to remain same with itself in *all* respects all the time. To demand that it do so is to impose such a stringent requirement that no object can meet it. It renders any object incapable of ever retaining its identity over time. A thing can remain identical with itself in *some*, not in all respects. Equally, if sameness over time of any odd set of features of an object was sufficient for its identity, then everything would always remain identical with itself. And if nothing ever lost its identity, then the *problem* of identity cannot even arise in the first place. As a matter of fact, to say that a thing has remained the same with itself over time is almost always elliptical for the statement: a thing has remained the same with itself over time in some relevant respects. A criterion of relevance is built into a statement of identity.

[1] Readers who find this discussion too abstract may skip the entire section and go straight to the next section, 'Forms of Identity'.

This is equally true of a thing's identity with other things. At a given instant, there are any number of respects in which a thing is the same with other things and a number of other respects in which it is different. To talk of the identity of something with some other thing makes sense, therefore, only within a preselected domain; once again, identity is crucially linked to some principle of relevance. In short, a thing is the same with itself over time, or the same with other things at any given time, only with respect to some features selected according to some criterion of relevance.

To repeat, sameness of relevant features over time is integral to any notion of identity. To have an identity, a thing must have features that are both relevant (essential) and enduring (permanent).[2] If this is true of the identity of all objects, it must equally be true for the identity of that special entity, the human person or the self. To remain same with itself over time, to possess an identity, a person must be identical with some of her enduring and relevant attributes or attributes of entities that she recognizes as her own.

This conforms to the minimal sense of identity with which we are all acquainted, with a simple phenomenology of identity. To have an identity is to recognize the presence of something stable in the midst of change and diversity. It is to be located somewhere, to possess a tangible sense of being at home in the world. More importantly, this sense of being anchored is obtained by identifying with something that, on the face of it, appears different. I must be able to say: this, that appears different, is the same as me. I must be able to call it by the same name with which I call myself, or at least, call it my own. Assertions of unity assimilate, synthesize, and establish connections among diverse things that go so deep that little point remains in calling them by a different name. Conversely, to lose one's identity is to be dispossessed of one's bearings and the ability to see where one stands, to be unhinged, detached, and to feel insecure. It is to fail to choose or discover something that is one's own, to be unable to find the relevant sameness with anything.

[2] Robert Bellah says that an identity is a statement of what a person or a group is essentially and permanently. Erikson says that the term identity connotes both a persistent sameness with oneself (self-sameness) and a persistent sharing of some essential characteristics with others. See his, 'The Problem of Ego Identity', in Maurice Stern, Arthur J. Vidlich, and D. Manning White (eds), *Identity and Anxiety*, Glencoe, Illinois: Free Press, 1960, pp. 37–8.

It more or less follows from what I have just said that bodily identity cannot be a sufficient condition for the identity of a person. To be sure, some relevant bodily features of a person must endure for a person to have an identity. But no person can be exhaustively identified with her body alone. The identity of a person cannot be reduced to bodily identity; at best, it is supervenient on it. This is so because a person is a person only in so far as it has mental attributes. Strawson is surely correct in viewing a person as an entity to which both corporeal characteristics and states of consciousness can be ascribed.[3] The identity of a person must minimally but crucially depend on the identity of states of her consciousness—a condition for the possibility of the phenomenology of identity described in the previous paragraph.

But, what can the identity of states of consciousness mean? States of consciousness are of two kinds. To begin with there exist states such as sensations, by which are generally meant bodily feelings such as pain and tickling, that cannot occur without their minimal awareness by the subject. Roughly the same reasons that disqualify the body as the sole criterion of personal identity apply to sensations. However, there also exist beliefs and desires, that is, those states which are characterized by what Brentano called 'intentionality' and the ascription of which always involve the use of a that clause, as in 'The VHP believes that a temple should be built on the site of the mosque'. Beliefs and desires must possess an intentional content. Now, unlike sensations, beliefs, desires, and the acts they guide do not require that in order to have them we be conscious of them. These states do not presuppose consciousness. At the same time, no person can have all her beliefs and desires without some minimal awareness. To be a person at all, an individual must be conscious of some of her beliefs and desires. It is necessary, therefore, that to have an identity, a person must consciously be able to identify with some of her beliefs, desires, and acts.

Beliefs and desires can be conceived in two fundamentally different ways, however. Their intentionality ensures that they necessarily possess a content. But, this content may be individuated wholly independent of anything external to the individual mind or may be seen to crucially depend on natural environment and social context, in particular the linguistic practices of the community. The first atomistic and psychologistic view of intentional content I find utterly

[3] Peter Strawson, *Individuals*, London and New York: Methuen, 1964, p. 104.

unconvincing.[4] I cannot, here, go into the reasons for why I reject the atomist, psychologistic view but if indeed I am correct in doing so, on the assumption of the centrality of beliefs, desires, and acts to the whole issue of personal identity, it may be said that the identity of a person is constituted in large measure by the language she uses, by her vocabulary. A person's identity, one can legitimately say, is defined by her language.[5]

A person then has the beliefs and desires she does largely because of the words she uses. She cannot identify with her beliefs and desires without identifying with the conceptual framework embodied in the vocabulary provided by her language. Identification with beliefs and desires is impossible without language because she would not know what these beliefs and desires mean and therefore, what they are, unless she has a language. Since entry into a world of meaning is crucial for the formation of beliefs and desires, personal identity is related to a world of meanings.

Moreover, this world of meanings can be held only in common with others. To identify with beliefs and desires is to identify with something which is ineluctably social, necessarily shared with others. A human individual recognizes her identity in socially defined terms.[6] Indeed, since these desires and beliefs emerge through interaction with others, we might legitimately say that the identity of a person is largely a matter of social construction. Identities develop in the participation and accomplishment of a world with others. Briefly put, I identify myself both with my language and with members of my linguistic community. That is why one identifies oneself, as one is identified by others, by being located in a common world.[7]

This common world of meaning can be further disambiguated into a frame of reference shared with others and a common intensional grid. To share a common vocabulary is to partake, first of all, in a common world of reference, that is, the terms used by us must refer to the same

[4] For a statement of reasons why I oppose this view, the reader may see, Rajeev Bhargava, *Individualism in Social Science*, Oxford: Clarendon Press, 1992.

[5] Here I speak of language as word-dependent expressions with meanings, but I mean to extend this point to word-independent forms of expression too.

[6] P. Berger, *The Social Construction of Reality*, London: Penguin Books, 1967, p. 108. Similarly, Soddy says that identity is the anchorage of self in social matrix.

[7] Identity, with its appropriate attachments of psychological reality, is always identity within a specific, socially constructed world.

entities. We do not invent names for things in isolation, independent of each other; rather, we achieve this classification together. We get initiated into the practice of cutting up the world, slicing it in one rather than another manner. When I identify with a common world of meaning, I declare that I belong to a particular tradition of drawing distinctions. Snow, for the Inuits, must be classified in more than twenty ways. For the Karam of New Guinea, bats are birds but cassowaries are not. Most Indian languages must be able to mark boundaries within their world to create a world of *jatis*. There is a minimal sense in which I identify myself not only with this way of classifying and categorizing the world but with all those who share this classification. Furthermore, we also possess a common intensional grid equally essential for our identity.

By the possession of a common intensional grid, I mean only that a linguistic community must share the sense of terms they use. Of course, this hardly implies that every word within a language possesses one meaning for all members of the linguistic community. It does mean, however, that the sense of each word is in principle available to all, that even if they do not agree on its sense, they have minimal grasp of it. It is because of this shared grid that we understand each other or indeed ourselves. This understanding is crucial for my identity, for the sense of sameness both with myself and with others. My identity is linked to this understanding, to the stock of self-interpretations available to me. It is this understanding that provides the ground on which any explicit unity and solidarity, crucial for my identification with others, is built. All this may not be always too evident to me but the issue is thrown into sharper relief when I am flung in the midst of those who I do not understand. It is crucial for my identity that I continue to remain with those who I understand, that I retain a shared intensional grid or else, I shall lose sense of my own identity.

FORMS OF IDENTITY

Of the many enduring features ascribable to a person, I have picked out the linguistically and socially constructed beliefs and desires as the ones relevant for her identity. However, a person has many beliefs and desires, not all central to her identity. The criterion of permanence and relevance must enter our discussion of identity in order not only to pick out beliefs, desires, and acts but also to specify which of these are critically defining. Obviously, not all but only enduring beliefs and desires, which people persistently strive to hold and realize, are crucial for identity. More importantly, of the ones that endure, only the relevant ones count. A person must view them as relevant, they must matter to her, if they are to enter the definition of her identity.

Wantons and Strong Evaluators

This issue of how things matter to persons needs to be probed further, for it leads straight into a discussion of the different ways of conceptualizing human identity. One way of conceiving relevance is to view it merely as a matter of intensely felt desires. Of the wide variety of desires and beliefs, those towards which I feel intensely attracted, enter my identity. Mattering here is a simple issue of how intensely I desire something. In this view, a person's identity is constituted not by any set of beliefs and desires but only those she intensely desires. I call this the identity of wantons and the social universe inhabited by such wantons as shaped by what can be called a *culture of unfettered desire*.

What is a wanton? A wanton has desires, strongly felt desires, even perhaps the desire to have certain desires (second-order desires), but it does not bother her one bit if none of her acts are ever guided by second-order desires.[8] A wanton never cares which of her many desires will be effective, that is, which of them will move her all the way to action. A person who wants to smoke is a wanton. One who wants not to smoke may also be a wanton. What classes both as wantons is simply the fact that neither is bothered which of these two wants will eventually determine her acts. In other words, a wanton is not, what Frankfurt calls, a reflective self-evaluator[9] or in Taylor's words, she lacks the capacity of strong evaluation.[10] In short, her criterion of relevance is not constituted by strong evaluations. What is relevant is what she strongly desires, not what she might have strongly evaluated. Unlike a wanton, a person with a capacity for strong evaluation, who can be called a strong evaluator, may have conflicting wants, the desire to smoke and the one not to smoke. Her desire to smoke may even be stronger than her desire not to smoke but it matters to her that she has not given up smoking. In other words, she is moved by a value distinct from and seen by her to be superior to her strongly felt desires. To acknowledge strong evaluation is to accept that a human agent is not

[8] On the notion of wanton, see Harry Frankfurt, *The Importance of What We Care About*, Cambridge: Cambridge University Press, 1988, p. 16.

[9] Ibid.

[10] Charles Taylor, *Philosophical Papers*, Vol. 1, Cambridge: Cambridge University Press, 1985, p. 16–21.

moved by desires alone but also by a will that in some sense she has helped form. Whether or not she manages to be moved by her second-order desires, she prefers her will to be constituted by her paramount desire. She not only deliberates on how to fulfil her desire but also on *what* she must desire.

For both Taylor and Frankfurt, a fully human person is a strong evaluator. Correspondingly, the identity of a strong evaluator is informed by the language of strong evaluation, by a vocabulary of goods that she values rather than simply desires. The identity of a person is defined not by any odd set of beliefs but those she holds firmly, with good reason, and by values that cannot be reduced to mere desires, that she judges to be more important than mere desires. It follows that the vocabulary or the conceptual framework necessary for the identity of strong evaluators must be one that incorporates qualitative distinctions between things she values and those that she devalues or merely desires.[11] A person cannot have an identity in the absence of such a framework because it furnishes the criterion of relevance constitutive of identity. What is relevant for a person's identity is what she values. Only those beliefs and desires that a person values and finds worthy, are crucial to her identity. Since my identity is formed within an enduring framework, not to possess it is to fail to have an identity.[12]

A framework provides a person with a springboard from which to aspire to do or be something. This aspiration to be moved, whether or not one is successful, by some values that are regarded as better than others is central to the notion of commitment. To strive for some values, no matter how unattainable, is to be deeply engaged with them, to have entrusted oneself to them. It is to constantly judge my desires and to hope to guide my actions by standards set by these values. It is to want my life to be directed by them. Hence, the tie between commitment and identity. Indeed, my identity is defined

by the commitments and identifications which provide the frame or horizon within which I can try to determine from case to case what is good or valuable, what ought to be done, what I endorse or oppose. In other words, it is the horizon within which I am capable of taking a stand.[13]

---

[11] The best recent statement of this view is found in Charles Taylor, *Sources of the Self*, Cambridge: Cambridge University Press, 1989, chapters 1–4.

[12] Ibid., p. 19–20. To possess an identity is then to have a framework and to know how one is placed in relation to it.

[13] Ibid., p. 27.

For without a framework, a person will not be able to properly tell what the world is like and how to orient herself to it. A crisis in one's identity results precisely when that happens.

Types of Strong Evaluators

Strong evaluators can be further categorized into two types: on the one hand, there are those who see the world divided starkly and exclusively into low-placed wantons and high idealists; and on the other hand, exist those who, somewhat suspicious of high ideals, are happy to occupy a space between the world of wantons and a universe of ultimate ideals. Some strong evaluators are high idealists, while others are committed to many worlds of smaller ideals. The social universe of high idealists is shaped by what I call a *culture of high ideals*, while that of the second type is moulded by what can be called *the culture of multiple goods*.

To be sure, the identity of the high idealist is constituted by beliefs, desires, and actions but the criterion of relevance by which identity-constituting beliefs, desires, and actions are selected is shaped entirely by high ideals.[14] One's identity within this culture is non-negotiable or almost so. It is possible that I am not simply born into it. There may even be an element of choice here but when acquired, it leaves no scope manoeuvrability or escape. Getting out of it is next to impossible.

In a culture of multiple goods, one's identity is not formed by any single high ideal. From an existing repertoire of identities, a person partly selects and shapes her identity. One cannot radically alter this existing stock, nor can any individual pick up any one and mould it exactly as she pleases. The entire repertoire is not up for grabs and all identities are not immediately negotiable. But, all values are placed in this culture within specific contexts and therefore, the identities they shape are context dependent. The only general principle to be found here is that as one moves from one context to another, one must also

[14] By high ideals, I mean values that are incomparably higher than desires, even other values. They are of ultimate importance, override all other values and desires under all circumstances and all times. These command our fundamental, deepest commitment. Consider, for example, A. Wheelis' view that identity is founded on those values which are at the top of the hierarchy—the beliefs, faith, and ideals which integrate and subordinate all values. See A. Wheelis, *The Quest for Identity*, New York: Norton, 1953, p. 200. Throughout this essay, by high ideals, I usually mean incomparably high ideals and use the terms 'high ideals' and 'ultimate ideals' interchangeably. Given another chance to write this essay, I would have more carefully made a distinction between ultimate and high ideals.

be able to shift one's identity, negotiate it. There is a greater sense of fluidity here. Not only is this culture different from the world of ultimate ideals but also from the culture of unfettered desire. This is largely because it neither reduces values to desires nor elevates any single such set above all contexts. Standards of values exist and objectively, they also vary from context to context. Correspondingly, there cannot be a single, overarching set of ideals that legislate on everything irrespective of the circumstances.

Finally, there may also exist another culture that combines elements from the second and the third. Here, a single but extremely thin spiritual ideal guides and integrates smaller ideals without subordinating them. Smaller ideals are accompanied by a sense of high ideal but not determined by it. This culture can be called a *culture of plurality infused by a sense of high ideal*. Because it finds ample room for smaller ideals, this culture is different from a culture of high ideals but as it does not altogether discard a single, high ideal (albeit a thin one), it is not collapsible to a culture of multiple goods. This culture allows us to get to a higher ideal by passing through and not past smaller ideals. It can never exist independently of the culture of multiple goods nor aspire for something wholly transcendent. It has a down-to-earth spirituality.

Four Cultures, Four Forms of Identities

Let me recapitulate. I began by saying that to have an identity is to have an integral connectedness to a stable and relevant set of beliefs, desires, and acts. Since these beliefs, desires, and acts are constructed and sustained socially, to have an identity is to be integrally connected also to all those who share the conceptual framework that generates these beliefs, desires, and acts. To have an identity is not only to have a language but also a community with which to identify. It is to live in a common world, a world defined by a common vocabulary, generating a particular set of orientations that impel us to act in some rather than other ways. These, I claimed, constitute conditions for the minimal identity of a human person. Not to be able to have even this is to not be human at all.

I then distinguished four different cultures within which identities are formed and therefore, four different forms of identities. The first culture provides a minimally stable sense of one's identity and meets the weakest possible criterion of relevance; weakest because no more stability or fixity can possibly be expected from desires or pro-attitudes on which alone it is grounded. But identities are rooted in stronger criterion of relevance, shaped by values that are distinct from desires. Such identities formed within frameworks of strong evaluators can be of two types: the identity of high ideals and of multiple values. Finally, I specified yet another type of identity formed within a culture that I called a culture of plurality infused by a sense of a high ideal. This concludes the first part of the essay. The reader must now be looking for illustrations of these different cultures and for the relevance of these distinctions to the stated objective of the essay. Let me turn now to these issues.

RELIGIOUS IDENTITIES

Even the slightest acquaintance with religion is evidence enough that our dominant conception of religious identity firmly places it within the culture of high ideals.[15] To have a religious identity is to possess a framework that enables us to make qualitative distinctions between what is worthy and trivial, the strongly valuable and merely desirable, superior and inferior, sacred and profane, the highest good and the downright evil, the admirable and the contemptible, and the glorious and the despicable. In short, our ultimate ideals and their converse, including that which is merely pleasant, beneficial, or advantageous but not of enduring, overriding significance.

Consider, for example, the identity of a Sikh.[16] On the dominant interpretation of the issue, a Sikh, if he is a Sikh at all, must aim ultimately to liberate himself from the cycle of transmigration and attempt to achieve this by *nam simran*. Furthermore, he must venerate all the ten gurus, affirm the sanctity of the Guru Granth Sahib and the place where it is permanently lodged, namely, the gurudwara. The teaching of the gurus, found largely in the Granth Sahib, have far more relevance and worth, greater validity than any other moral or educational book. Their value, for him, goes so deep that in the long run, life without them will not be worth living; a Sikh will not properly be able to define his situation, orient himself, discriminate the right from the wrong, the

[15] By religion, I mean a set of beliefs and practices concerning the trans-temporal, the eternal, the other worldly, or god. By secular, I mean the view that either negates the existence of the other world (implying a commitment to whatever a suitable interpretation of the general terms agnosticism and atheism designate) or, at least, one for which human beings, living or dead, have no relevant or meaningful relation to.

[16] These examples, needless to say, are greatly oversimplified and present only one, perhaps even a caricatured, view of the issue but, I believe, for the purpose of this essay they would do.

good from the bad, which is to say he will not just be able to act humanly at all.[17] Any attack on the gurudwara, whatever the provocation, is evil and has to be denounced. The teachings of the guru are inviolable, no matter the change in circumstances. These values have to be observed whatever the cost.

The Buddhist Bhikkhu too has his set of high ideals, values that lie so deep that without them he will not be able to keep going in this world. It is of profound concern to him whether or not the *Dhammic* order exists.[18] An *adhammic* world is a world of suffering, *dukkha*, of the rule of desires that are fleeting and ephemeral, born largely out of ignorance. The ultimate ideal, therefore, is to liberate oneself from this world of impermanence, to attain true knowledge, quench one's cravings, and attain a state of nirvana. He does this not by chanting the name of god but by following the eightfold path in this world.[19]

Likewise, the world of at least some Hindu brahmins, striving to remain free of pollution (especially caste pollution) to preserve their purity represents a pursuit of high ideals. The world on this brahamani-cal interpretation is full of things and deeds that possess the capacity to incur temporary or permanent impurity. The brahmin must avoid permanent impurity and must, by ritual practice, purify himself when temporarily polluted. Impurity is related, first of all, to organic aspects of life, to organic waste and secondarily but equally importantly, to those whose work relates to it. Since the world of the untouchable is lowly and demeaning, he must refrain from straying into it, and if by accident he does, then by appropriate ritual he must immediately decontaminate himself.[20] But, even his image of ultimate hell is that of

---

[17] See, for example, W.H. Mcleod, *Who is a Sikh*, Oxford: Clarendon Press, 1989, particularly pp. 91–121.

[18] For a recent statement on the life of a Bhikkhu in Sri Lanka, see Mark Juergensmeyer, 'What the Bhikhu Said: Reflections on the Rise of Militant Religious Nationalism', *Religion*, vol. 20, 1990, pp. 53–75.

[19] This immediately makes its inclusion among religions highly suspect. Buddhism is more metaphysical and moral wisdom than religion in the full sense. But I ignore this point for present purposes.

[20] I recognize that the contrast between a culture of high ideals and a culture of unfettered desire tends to break down here. The world of the untouchable is not even a world of desire, it is a universe of degraded bodily existence. To accommodate this example, one requires a category wider than even bodily desire. From the point of view of the brahmin's ideals, the world of the untouchable does represent chaos, or valueless anarchy. It is a world from where the good has altogether vanished, though not arbitrarily.

a place where rules governing pure and impure objects/practices have ceased to be observed. What must be prevented at all costs is not just the descent into an impure world (do not forget that there is auspicious impurity as well[21]) but the collapse of the caste system, the regression into a culture of unfettered desire.

Indeed, all religions build their own picture of hell, of disorder and chaos, of dispersion, of desires run amok, and of valueless anarchy. The greatest fear of all religions is that the world will lapse not straight into a state of war of all against all, but into one marked by an erosion of high values. Loss of religious identity is a fall from a culture of high ideals to a culture of unfettered desire.

Is this the only form of religious identity available, an identity formed by high ideals in direct opposition to a weak and unstable one constituted by desires? In a brilliant little book, Geertz introduces an important distinction between the religious and the religious-minded, the latter a result of the ideologization of religion.[22] Similarly, in an extremely influential article, Nandy distinguishes religious zealotry from two other forms of religion, religion as faith and religion as ideology.[23] Presumably then, there exist three kinds of religious identities, the identity of the zealot, of the faithful, and finally, of the religious ideologue. In what follows, I shall first try to explore these three different kinds of religious identities. To these I shall then add three other types: religion as lived spirituality (religious spiritualism), spiritless religiosity, and what I call, religion as pastiche.

What is the identity of the person with faith? Faith, not surprisingly, is an elusive term. Philosophers of religion have seen faith either as a form of belief, or as trust, or as both. For some, especially the Thomists, faith is just a form of theoretical belief, a set of statements concerning the existence of god deemed to be true.[24] To have faith is to believe that god exists. Luther did not entirely dispute this meaning but from his point of view, more importantly, faith is a form of trust. A person

[21] See Veena Das, *Structure and Cognition*, New Delhi: Oxford University Press, 1982, p. 128.

[22] Clifford Geertz, *Islam Observed*, Chicago: University of Chicago Press, 1971, pp. 18, 61.

[23] Ashis Nandy, 'The Politics of Secularism and the Recovery of Religious Tolerance', in Veena Das (ed.), *Mirrors of Violence*, New Delhi: Oxford University Press, 1990, pp. 69–93.

[24] See Richard Swinburne, *Faith and Reason*, Oxford: Clarendon Press, 1981, chapter 4.

who has faith does not as much have a theory about god but trusts him. Faith, then, is less a matter of convictions and more a matter of attitude and orientation. For pragmatists such as Pascal and James, faith is entirely a matter of trust grounded in probabilistic, practical not deductive, theoretical reasoning. Clearly, a person with faith is either a devout believer or one who lives his entire life trusting god.

Conceptions of faith have also differed with the exact meaning of 'belief'. To believe, according to Wilfred Cantwell Smith, is not to state something that could be true or false, not to opine but to devote oneself to whatever one has faith in.[25] It is to set one's heart upon it, be powerfully attracted to it, to love it. Faith, then, is belief but the believer is one who loves the object of her belief, one who is wholly devoted to it, not someone who has theoretical beliefs. Recall once again the minimal conditions of identity: an identity is formed by beliefs, desires, and acts that are permanent and relevant. The identity of a person with faith is constituted by his firm, unshakeable belief in the existence of god or in the possibility of the existence of a world governed by high ideals. Furthermore, he loves and is devoted to god, to a godly order, or to his own high ideals. The two—firm belief in the ideals and love for them—reinforce each other. Love and devotion, moreover, are powerful emotions and like all similar emotions, they have a strong hold on the person who experiences them.[26] A religious person is in the grip of these overwhelming emotions that are long lasting and affect him deeply. It is these emotions that give a reason for living, a meaning and direction to the life of the man or woman of faith. Implicitly or explicitly, this world of faith, love, and devotion is different from and superior to the mundane, everyday world governed by ordinary desires. The identity of a person with faith, so characterized, is subsumed without remainder within the notion of religious identity outlined earlier.

Does this capture what Nandy has in mind? It appears not, for according to him, faith is a way of life, not exclusively a matter of beliefs and devotion. Whatever could this mean? Nandy says little on this but it is not difficult to conjecture what could possibly be implied. I said that a man or woman of faith has firm beliefs. But firmness of

---

[25] See Terence Penelhum (ed.), *Faith*, New York: Macmillan, and London: Collier, 1989, p. 11 ('Introduction').

[26] See the short but excellent section on emotions in Jon Elster, *Nuts and Bolts in the Social Sciences*, Cambridge: Cambridge University Press, 1989, pp. 61–70.

beliefs can also mean something entirely different from the emotional charge suggested in the previous paragraph. As Wittgenstein pointed out, firmness of beliefs is not a matter of the intensity of feeling with which they are held.[27] A belief is firmly held not when it is strongly felt but when it guides one's entire life. To have firm beliefs is to participate in practices that make some beliefs natural to hold. To have firm beliefs in the relevant sense is just to engage in a way of life. Kolakowski says something to the effect that the point of religion is often lost when stated in doctrinal terms, that 'religion is not a set of propositions but a way of life in which understanding, believing and commitment emerge together in a single act'.[28] To have faith, then, is to have your identity constituted in and by those practices in which understanding, believing, and commitment emerge together.

However, Nandy means something more than this. For him, religion as faith is 'definitionally non-monolithic and operationally plural'.[29] These are somewhat obfuscating phrases, but they make clear that Nandy has made faith by fiat into not just *a* way of life but as implicating several, differing ways of life. He goes on to say,

unless a religion is geographically and culturally confined to a small area, it has as a way of life, in effect, to turn into a confederation of a number of ways of life which are linked by a common faith that has some theological space for the heterogeneity that everyday life introduces.[30]

There is a grain of truth here but one should be cautious in accepting it. Cautious, because monolithic and operationally unilateral faiths do in fact exist, and even when they have been born and bred in smaller areas, they contain within themselves the propensity to spread. It all depends on context and opportunity. Geertz makes much the same point as Nandy and is aware of the ever-present contradictions of religious faith which, for him, is:

as much a particularizing force as a generalizing one ... whatever universality a given religious tradition manages to attain arises from its ability to engage a widening set of individual, even idiosyncratic, conceptions of life and yet somehow sustain and elaborate them. When it succeeds in this, the result may indeed as often be the distortion of these personal visions as their enrichment,

[27] Quoted in J.L. Mackie, *The Miracle of Theism*, Oxford: Clarendon Press, 1982, p. 218.

[28] L. Kolakowski, *Religion*, London: Fontana, 1982, p. 218.

[29] Nandy, 'The Politics of Secularism and the Recovery of Religious Tolerance', in Das (ed.), *Mirrors of Violence*, p. 70.

[30] Ibid., p. 102.

but in any case, whether deforming private faiths or perfecting them, the tradition usually prospers. When it fails, however, to come genuinely to grips with them at all, it either hardens into scholasticism, evaporates into idealism or fades into eclecticism.[31]

The coming together of many faiths is as much an enriching as a distorting process. The universalization of faith, whatever its cause, external or wholly internal, does not produce a happy plurality alone but also a dangerous monism with all the accompanying distortions of identity. Despite this caution, we simply have to concede that religion can also embody a plurality of local ways of life, and being plural, it contains seeds of tolerance. Such a religion cannot be shaped by a simplistic culture of high ideals with a single contrasting vision of its other, the culture of unfettered desire, but must resemble the cultural world of multiple values. Correspondingly, the religious identity it produces must reflect this plurality and tolerance, and must accommodate a number of seemingly incompatible values.

Religion as faith, then, is a form of love, trust, belief, or a way of life. It can be monolithic or pluralistic, universalizing or particularizing, and divisive or integrative. Often it is placed firmly within a culture of high ideals but it may also closely resemble a form of life that is found within a culture of multiple values. The identities it generates or sustains, therefore, are as varied as its own diverse and malleable cast.

How does it differ from religion as ideology? How is the identity of a religious ideologue distinct from the identity of the believer, of the man of faith? Again, Geertz provides a clue here. He says that whereas the religious person is held by his religion, the religious ideologue holds it.[32] The ideologization of religion begins when the certainty of faith begins to totter. Powerful emotions accompanying belief in a world grounded in ultimate values loosen their grip. A gulf begins to appear between processes of understanding and belief, between belief and commitment. As Geertz puts it, 'people find it harder and harder to make religious rituals and symbols work, more and more difficult to draw out of them the settled sense of moving with the deepest grain of reality that defines the religious mind.'[33] This is a phase suspended between religiousness, on the one hand, and agnosticism and atheism, on the other. Love, devotion, trust, the redoubtable taken-for-granted quality of religious

[31] Geertz, *Islam Observed*, pp. 14, 48.
[32] Ibid., p. 61.
[33] Ibid., p. 102.

symbols begins to make way for doubt, not quite the doubt that religion is a storehouse of falsehood and deception but doubt about the manner in which it has been hitherto assumed. Religion begins to be a matter of theoretical belief and like any other belief, is increasingly seen to fall within the ambit of evidence and argument. Once religion becomes a set of propositions, it may, like any other statement, turn out to be false and therefore, in the face of threat from common sense or science, it becomes increasingly doctrinal and dogmatic. It first resembles and then acquires the character of an ideology.

Strictly speaking, the religious ideologue has already lost his religious identity or else he is in the process of losing it. The appearance of religious ideologies is a symptom of a crisis in religious faith. The identity of a religious ideologue is no longer firmly anchored in high ideals. Indeed, the connection between such ideals and his practice is already snapped. His actions are guided more and more by desires, by economic or political interests. He may offer a religious reason for everything he does but that reason is not causally efficacious. It either accompanies it without any determining power or is supplied as a rationalization. Even when the two are connected, and religious beliefs and values are seen to be the primary cause of action, very often this connection is not of the right or characteristic kind. High ideals hover over human actions that are, in fact, determined by ordinary beliefs and desires. The identity of a pure religious ideologue is formed less within the framework of high ideals and more in the culture of unfettered desire. Though carrying its shadow, they are not really constituted by religious ideal. The purely religious identity of such a person is, in a sense, already crisis-ridden.

What of the religious zealot? The zealot is one who has accepted that the moment of faith, perhaps even of religious ideology, has passed. He is possibly aware that both are dead, buried, and at best, can be revived in an altogether different form. He lives in a culture of unfettered desire but makes the restoration or creation of a religious order as his primary project. Typically, he speaks of going back to the original state of perfection or to a time when his society took the crucial wrong turn. He selects the eternal fundamentals of his religion by which his life and the life of all others will be governed in future. He defines his identity purely in terms of this unaccomplished project. He is moved by an earthy desire for power and by a grievous sense of real or imagined hurt, the characteristic stance of the victim, of those who are left out, who do not belong to any existing order. The ideologue believes that high ideals inform his action. The zealot, on the other hand, has no such illusions. He is cynical, instrumentalist, and a political realist: cynical of all existing high ideals, uninhibited in his use of any means to achieve his purported goal, and well-versed in the cunning and deceit of political games. Anything is justified in the name of his larger political goal of religious revivalism. Zealotry and ideology are two distinct forms taken by religion within a culture of unfettered desire.

I promised that I shall speak of three other kinds of religious identities. The first one that can be called spiritless religion is well known. Suffice it to say that a body of religious practices from which the original, living impulse has been wrenched is religion that is spiritless. Many of us have read about the conditions under which Protestantism was born, the abysmal conditions that compelled the mild reforms of Hinduism in the nineteenth century. Recall Hegel ranting against the positivization of religion, against a religion expunged of both rationality and autonomy.

In spiritless religiosity, in both its scripturalist or ritualist varieties, the body remains but the original spirit has evaporated. From what I call religion as pastiche, both the original body and intent are gone and a very poor imitation of the original impulse inhabits an entirely new set of practices. Let me elaborate. Pastiche is a term of art with a family resemblance to the notion of parody but dissimilar in significant respects. In art, pastiche is an imitation of a peculiar form 'without parody's ulterior motive, without its satirical impulse, without laughter'. Pastiche imitates the original with a grim, dead pan exterior. Parody laughs at a style, at a form. Pastiche, on the other hand, precisely because it is serious and sombre, invites laughter not at the form it imitates but at itself. Moreover, unlike parody that has a latent understanding that something normal exists of which it is a comic imitation, and that possesses a genuine feel for the original, pastiche is irrevocably delinked from it. It simply has no idea of what it is imitating. As Jameson puts it, pastiche is blank parody.[34] Pastiche religion, likewise, is an empty replica of religiosity. It has all the marks of ersatz, of the spurious. It thrives where people have forgotten what it is to have a religious experience or even the memory of it. They have no idea any longer of what it is that they seek to imitate. Pastiche then is the imitation of an imitation of religiosity, in a heavy, laboured form, the imagined characteristic of the original. Curiously, it is part of a general nostalgia of things past, one that tries to bring back sepia-edged memory of what our grandparents did. The zealot has a teleological perspective. He wants to bring about

---

[34] F. Jameson, 'Post Modernism and Consumer Society', in H. Foster (ed.), *The Anti-Aesthetic*, Washington: Bay Press, 1983, p. 114.

something using the most efficient means available to him. Those with a penchant for pastiche religion have an expressive perspective. They are on a trip of self-expression: people in search of a religious identity compelled to make do with vacuous and laughable imitations instead.

This brings me to religion as lived spirituality. Here religion is distinct from both metaphysics and morality, from speculation and praxis. The highest point in metaphysics and morality have the same object as religion, namely, the universe and its relationship to humanity but whereas praxis is an art and speculation a science, 'religion is the sensibility and taste for the infinite'.[35] Religion's essence is 'neither thinking nor acting but intuition and feeling'.[36] It is a corruption of religion to inundate it with philosophy and coerce it into a system. Religion strays when it posits essences and determines the nature of things, loses itself in an infinity of reasons and deductions, seeks out final causes, and proclaims eternal truths.[37] It also deviates when it develops systems of duties, commands, and forbids actions with unlimited authority.[38] The reckless conversion of religion into metaphysics and morals is responsible, in this view, for spitefulness and persecution, for wrecking society, and making blood flow like water.[39]

Religion is the intuition that the infinite accompanies the finite, the powerful but immediate feeling that the human world is not disconnected from the rest of the universe. The emphasis on a sense of immediacy and on accompaniment is crucial. Immediacy separates religion from logic, from rationality and mere accompaniment disengages it from causality. This overwhelming and potentially disturbing feeling should 'accompany every human deed like holy music: we should do everything with religion, nothing because of it'.[40] By their very nature, religious feelings should inhibit the strength of our actions and invite us to calm and dedicated enjoyment.

It is the drive for power or for systematic uniformity that breeds intolerance, but a person with a living sense of the spiritual sees his religion only as a part of the whole and knows that 'regarding the same objects that affect him religiously there are views just as pious and

---

[35] Friedrich Schleiermacher, *On Religion: Speeches to Its Cultured Despisers*, translated by Richard Crouter, Cambridge: Cambridge University Press, 1998, p. 103.

[36] Ibid., p. 102.

[37] Ibid., p. 98.

[38] Ibid., p. 102.

[39] Ibid., p. 108.

[40] Ibid., p. 110.

nevertheless completely different from his own, and from which other elements of religious intuitions and feelings flow, the sense for which he may be completely lacking.'[41] Religion teaches humility and modesty and a friendly inviting tolerance. 'Modern Rome, godless but consistent hurls anathemas and excommunicates heretics; ancient Rome, truly pious and religious in a lofty style, was hospitable to every god and so it became full of gods.'[42] Schleiermacher could well be speaking of some forms of traditional and modern Hinduism.

A person with such a religious identity is contemplative and tolerant. He has a matter-of-fact relation to his high ideal and lives his life with a constant sense of its presence. With such a conception of religion, the person is shaped by the culture of plurality infused with a sense of high ideal; a minimally high ideal accompanying a world of multiple values.

MODERN, SECULAR IDENTITIES

I began this essay by expressing a sense of unease with the black and white dichotomy that keeps elements of the religious apart from every element of the secular. In the first part, I claimed that the identity of a person can be constituted in four different ways that I placed in an ascending order, implying that a more mature, fully human sense of one's identity is gained as one climbs up the scale. The identity of a person is constituted, I claimed, by a culture of: (i) unfettered desire, (ii) high ideals, (iii) multiple values, and (iv) multiple values infused by a sense of high ideals. Each of these cultures is distinct from and may oppose others. In the second part, namely, 'Religious Identities', I claimed that though our dominant sense of religious identity appears to be formed by a culture of incomparably high ideals, other religious identities exist within each of the above mentioned cultures. In other words, different forms of religious identity, in potential conflict with each other, exist within any major religion. This is equally true of non-religious, secular identities. Logically, every type of religious identity has its secular counterpart. Secular identity is internally differentiated or hierarchized as well.

Let me explore this further. The connection between a modern, secular identity and the culture of unfettered desire is known too well to require a detailed treatment. But is modernity, as some traditional critics allege, first to have launched a culture of wantons? Is modern culture and the identity formed within it reducible to the culture of unfettered

[41] Ibid., p. 108.
[42] Ibid.

desire? Traditional critics of modernity believe precisely this that an exhaustive description of modern culture is in hand as soon as it is portrayed as a culture of desire hostile to high ideals. Herein is replicated the believer's, the zealot's, and the ideologue's view of modern secular humanism. They fulminate equally against modernity for embodying their vision of hell on earth, for undermining ideals, and, for negating all values. In this picture of this world, they could not agree more with contemporary nihilists and irrational relativists. Every advocate of monolithic faith endorses the post-modern view of contemporary secular world that in an ethics without god, sex drives, power, or material interests masquerade as the good. For him, only *his* ideals, soaring well above the rest of the world, can claim immunity from this muck. However, even he cannot claim that modernity has a monopoly on this culture. All religions conceive, not on the basis of speculation alone, their own distinctive picture of valueless anarchy. The ascetic Hindu has contempt for the world of the *bhogi*, the Buddhist has his own conception of the adhammic world, the world of dukkha. The Muslim pictures in similar terms the world of the kafir. All religions worry about the catastrophic moment when humanity will plunge deep into this world but will lack the cultural resources to come out it. The fact is that human beings have always carried the cross of a world almost beyond redemption that already exists or is just round the corner. This is not surprising. Each human being keeps at least one foot in this culture forever threatening to explode. Ramayana and Mahabharata are not stories about the modern condition. The modern world is, even by religion's own reckoning, only the most contemporary version of a culture of unfettered desire. It is not and cannot be the only such culture.

So, it is not the lot of modernity alone to house the culture of unfettered desire. Even so, modern secularism may still be reducible to this culture. At any rate, it might appear so for three reasons. First, this is one of modern secularism's own self-understanding. To counter the persistent contempt for desire characteristic of high ideals, the first bolder statements of modern secularism saw pure desire in everything. Modern secularism has presented itself defiantly as a form of naturalism. It is not altogether untrue to say that, on balance, it encourages a suspicion of high ideals. This is why if the principal question is posed in such stark terms: 'Are you going to obey god or follow your own desires?', then modernity must be seen as humanity's swiftest slide yet into a worthless world of pure appetite. What modern secularism occasionally chooses to understand of itself is different from what, however, it really is. It has its own high ideals. Second, it is also placed firmly within a culture of multiple values. However, without the obvious presence of a high ideal, smaller ideals, often incommensurable and disconnected from each other, possess less intensity of attachment and even lesser effect unless seen as manifestations of desire. Frequently, therefore, they are not differentiated from desire, even by those who wish to perceive them as distinct. Third, the spiritual roots of modernity that most resemble religious spiritualism are hardly ever recognized by even its most ardent supporters. In brief, a modern secular identity is formed within each of the cultures I mentioned earlier. It is formed not only by a culture of pure desire but also by a culture of high ideals, of multiple values, and of multiple goods infused by a thin, spiritual ideal. I would like to explicate each of these a bit more.

What are the high ideals of modern secularism? There are many perspectives on secularism's high ideals. I here speak of one. The modern, secular outlook developed in opposition to the view that the entire world is an embodiment of ideas, expresses meaning, and has an overall purpose. The world, for pre-moderns, is a text to be interpreted. Second, our essential identity is defined in relation to this cosmos. Questions of identity do not make sense unless formulated within a cosmology. For our fulfilment, therefore, we must place ourselves within this meaningful universe, be in touch with this cosmos, and know where we stand in relation to other things in it. One opposition to this perspective came from modern naturalism. The other principal challenge was posed by what, for want of a better term, we can call Kantian humanism. This dualistic humanism accepts that non-human nature is intrinsically meaningless, composed of distinct entities that relate to each other contingently and mechanically. After discarding the interpretative vision of nature, it goes on to claim that whatever meaning exists in human life, in society, and history, is due entirely to the conscious or unconscious acts of human beings. Society and history possess the meaning they do because of us. Human beings cannot, therefore, find their identity in relation to this detextualized world. They have to create their own identity by producing their own 'webs of significance', their own culture.

This much, perhaps, will be constitutive of any defensible version of modern secularism but from here several paths open up, one of which leads straight to one of the ultimate ideals of modern secularism, which I call superhumanism. Superhumanism celebrates the death of god but creates a new god instead; it apotheosizes man. It replicates in finest detail the structure of theological reasoning. The attributes of the subject are the same: it can plan anything and execute it to perfection. There is nothing he cannot know, predict, control; only now, it is man, not god who does this. Man's natural powers are unlimited; it is only a question of time when they would be fully realized. History may be made within constraining circumstances not entirely of his choosing now but a day will come when it will made with radical freedom. Both natural and historical processes can be fully tamed. The high ideal of modern secularism, therefore, is perfect self-creation. All else is trivial, unworthy, low. The essential identity of human beings is that of a creative producer. Human beings are defined by their ever-developing powers of self-realization. Anything is justified in the service of this ideal: devaluation of the present, the renunciation of desire, sacrifice of peace, forfeiting ordinary human relations, abandoning individual morality. Violence, suffering, even death are justified for the sake of creative existence. The high ideal of modern secularism can be as exacting and severe as its religious counterpart.

But modern secularism has developed a great distrust of such ideals also. Consider, for example, political secularism. A firmer grasp of its principles depends upon a prior understanding of what Taylor has called the 'affirmation' of ordinary life'.[43] The need to separate the affairs of ultimate ideals from the governance of this-worldly interests and values arises precisely because ordinary, mundane existence can no longer be undervalued. Whatever else it might be, modern political secularism also reflects the grudging recognition that the independent pursuit of this-worldly values is as important as the struggle to gain other-worldly benefits. The implication for us is clear: the demotion of ultimate ideals and the elevation of plurality. T.N. Madan mentions somewhere that secularism is a 'gift of Christianity'. Even if this were true, he surprisingly fails to note its universalizable potential. I say this with all the attendant risks of being misunderstood precisely because I believe we can find cultural roots in support of such 'universal' values. By Madan's own reckoning, the life of the householder, one of the small ideals of modern secularism, is also highly valued not only among the Kashmiri pandits, whom he has studied in detail, but in the entire Hindu society.[44] Just as the modern western bourgeois

---

[43] Taylor, *Sources of the Self*, p. 13.

[44] T.N. Madan, *Non-Renunciation*, New Delhi: Oxford University Press, 1987, p. 9.

who values the life of production and family must steer clear of the dangers of both reckless indulgence and ultimate ideals, just so, the Hindu *grahastha* should resist complete surrender to the *bhogi* (pleasure-seeker, sensualist) or the *sanyasi* (renouncer, ascetic).[45] It is precisely this universalizable ideal of human fulfilment in ordinary affairs of this world, a concern for peace, security, ordinary life, and its corollary, to abjure violence and avoid suffering that undergirds the modern, secular person's distrust for ultimate ideals. He knows that ultimate ideals bring about disorder about as much as unfettered desire. He knows, too, that a conflict between ultimate ideals is as irreconcilable as a clash between desires. The culture of multiple values is born, therefore, out of the recognition that all fundamental values cannot be realized at the same time to the same highest degree.[46]

But, how does modern secularism realize this? Is it not trapped within its own high ideals? I believe it achieves it by recovering its own spiritual roots, by delving deeper into the full-blown implication of humanism, by pointed reflection on what a life without god means. The rejection of a transtemporal, other-worldly life implies that we altogether eschew the habit of imagining gods, not that we replace older deities with new ones. It means also that we recognize and respect the limitations of humans and struggle with humility for smaller ideals.

This spiritualized, humanist secularism accepts that we cannot know, predict, and control everything; that there are limits to our attempts to tame natural and even historical processes; that contingency in nature or history cannot be entirely overcome; and that, therefore, some areas of the world will always appear dark, obscure, absurd. Humanism after all is just what it is: humanism, neither a theism nor a superhumanism. Spiritualized secularism recoils from the over-bloated, over-active conception of human beings. There is much in us that is not made by but given to us. We are passive in relation to a part of nature that lies both external and internal to us.[47] We can hardly afford to forget what men and women have known for centuries, that is, those who are born will grow old and die, that disease and infirmities of old age can be controlled, not entirely eliminated and therefore, suffering cannot be wholly vanquished. Spiritual secularists know that suffering is often

---

[45] Ibid., p. 10.

[46] This is a feature as much of religion as of secular perspectives. For example, the four ashrams of Hinduism reflect this point.

[47] The best statement of this to my mind is by S. Timpanaro, *On Materialism*, London: New Left Books, 1975.

man-made but they do not forget that some suffering is not made by man.

Now, this precisely is what religious spiritualism teaches us, that in everything we do we carry the sense of our relation to the universe, to the infinite; that we know our imperfections, and therefore, that we never overreach ourselves. It is in this spirit that we learn that although many human conflicts can be settled, not all circumstances are equally propitious for resolving them by reason and therefore, there are times when it is better to live with conflicts than to seek forced resolution. It is ultimately this humility which teaches us tolerance and the love for diversity. Whatever else is contained in the discourse of rights and justice, it also reflects this great humanist insight. I am not suggesting that the language of rights and justice, so central to some versions of modern secularism, has contextual validity. My plea is only that it is not always a symptom of vacuous principles. In the vicious presence of some high ideals, they also represent courage.[48] The spiritual roots of modern secularism are not as barren as they appear to be at first sight and not all that removed from the plurality and tolerance taught by all the major world faiths.

I have tried to argue that each of the four cultures mentioned earlier equally nourish religious and secular identities. Let me straight away home in on one implication of this argument. I believe it follows from what I have said that though on one level the religious and the secular are distinct from each other, another level exists where each is structurally similar to its counterpart. A religious identity informed by high ideals has much in common with a secular identity formed within the same culture. Both in turn may be sharply differentiated from any identity formed by a culture of unfettered desire. The form of identity, therefore, is as important as its content. The content of religious and secular identity is distinct but on its own, it need not lead to opposition and conflict. It is only when they assume deeply divisive forms that conflict develops.

[48] Although I am not a great admirer of most ultimate ideals, I recognize that they will not disappear overnight. They are generated under special social conditions and unless something is done about them, ultimate ideals will continue to sprout. I do think, however, that their potency can be checked. It goes without saying that I believe that all the relevant virtues associated with high ideals, to some realistic degree, can be realized in a culture of multiple values. One of the problems with high ideals is precisely that they make absolutist demands that are humanly impossible to meet.

The question, 'can religious identity be subsumed under cultural identity or does it possess special features?', makes little sense unless we specify the form of religious identity that we have in mind and indicate the precise form of cultural identity that is to subsume it. For example, the identity of the monolithic believer can be subsumed under the more general category of the cultural identity informed by high ideals. But, so can the identity of the superhumanist. On the other hand, the identity of a religious ideologue, the zealot, or of the believer in a religion of multiple faiths cannot be subsumed under the widest possible category of an identity formed by a culture of high ideals. To sum up once again, the view that a deep incompatibility always exists between religious and secular world views is at best misleading. My claim is that the incompatibility exists between different forms of cultural identity, each of which subsumes both religious and secular identity.

This analysis also helps us to better understand the identity of Indian political actors. In the article discussed earlier, Nandy makes a highly interesting fourfold classification of political actors in the subcontinent.[49] First, there are those who are believers neither in public nor in private (example, Nehru). Second, those who are non-believers in public but believers in private (example, Indira Gandhi). Third, those who are believers in public but not in private (example, Jinnah, Advani). Finally, those who are believers both in public and in private (Gandhi). Cases 1 and 4 appear to be simple and easily explicable but 2 and 3 seem complex and are usually explained in terms of a disjunction existing in modern societies between ideologies that define people's personal identity and those that legitimize their public authority. I believe the distinctions drawn by me illuminate this issue differently. First, the case of Nehru and Gandhi is not as simple as it first appears. Though Nehru was not a believer in public or private, his secular identity was drawn completely from the cultural resources of multiple values infused by a sense of high spiritual ideal. This means that he was closer to persons with a sense of religious spiritualism and to those who formed their identity with reference to a plurality of ways of life than he was to secular ideologues and fanatics. Likewise, Gandhi, a believer in public and private, who said that those who thought religion and politics could be kept separate understand neither religion nor politics had scant sympathy for scripturalists and ritualists, for religious ideologues and zealots, or for that matter, for those who saw their faith as monolithic.

[49] Nandy, 'The Politics of Secularism and the Recovery of Religious Tolerance', in Das (ed.), *Mirrors of Violence*, pp. 75–7.

He was not averse to separating *these* forms of religion from *his* form of politics. Had he had persons with such religious identities in mind, he would quite certainly have been equally at home making the statement that 'those who want to mix religion with politics understand nothing of religion and politics'. Indeed, there is nothing inconsistent in this because the intent of the two statements is similar. Keeping some forms of religion out of some forms of politics is the only way of ensuring the mingling of other forms of religion with a different kind of politics. Those who killed him understood this well. Ironically, though not surprisingly, he was misunderstood at first by almost all secularists.

The case of L.K. Advani and to some extent Mrs Indira Gandhi is even more interesting. In different ways, both are placed firmly within a culture of unfettered desire with no integral room for high ideals. As we have seen, such a culture cannot provide the requisite depth critical for multiple values. Their identity, therefore, is thin, and like quicksilver it moves quickly from one point to another. This is why it is possible for them to have one identity in private and another in public, indeed why they can quickly change their identity even within the public or the private realm. Strictly speaking, it is not true that Indira Gandhi was a consistent non-believer in public. As is well known, in the last phase of her political career, she publicly mingled not only with *babas* and *sadhus* but even consorted with religious ideologues and zealots. This is also why Advani can be an atheist in private and a religious ideologue in public, why he too can hobnob with zealots, indeed why even in public he can be a secular ideologue at one time and a religious one at another. Perhaps I am being too harsh to both Indira Gandhi and Advani. Others might claim that Indira Gandhi's identity is also constituted by a culture of multiple values and Advani's by the culture of high ideals. Whatever the truth, it is clear that Advani's world view does not have a place for multiple values, and he and Mrs Gandhi frequently acted as if high ideals do not exist.

Once different forms of religious and secular identities are introduced into the discussion, other issues may also be seen somewhat differently. Consider, for example, the claim of some well-meaning secularists that the political acts of the Bharatiya Janata Party (BJP), including the Rath Yatra, have nothing to do with religion or the opposite claim that the BJP politicizes religion. These statements are at best nebulous and misleading, in desperate need of contextualizing. It seems to me clear that while the BJP has no allegiance to religious spiritualism or to faith as an inherently tolerant way of life, it is fundamentally interlocked with religious ideology and zealotory. The claim that the BJP has nothing to do with religion and everything to do with secularism absolves religion of all responsibility for its own perversions. Indeed, it accepts the spurious assumption of religious people of all hues that, in itself, religion is perfect and that its imperfections come from its lamentable contact with base, secular culture. Communalism has as much to do with religion as it has to with secularism because it thrives in a certain culture common to both. Likewise, while there is some truth in the claim that the BJP has politicized religion, it must immediately be asked: religion of what kind, of which culture? Once again, the statement creates the impression that a perfect entity has been deliberately perverted by its unnecessary and deplorable entanglement with secular politics. But it is not the BJP alone that has politicized religion. Transformations in religion are not spurred in a social vacuum. It is only after religion has been ideologized that its politicization is possible. Similarly, the fortunes of the BJP are no doubt bolstered by the support in urban areas from people whose identity is formed by pastiche religion but the creation of this form of religion is not the handiwork of the BJP or any other political movement.

If there is any plausibility at all in the views I have offered, then we can look afresh at some important questions that continue to grip us. Is modernity incompatible with faith, with the plurality and tolerance of traditional, religious ways of life? Has it and does it necessarily plunge all societies into valueless chaos, into a culture of unfettered desire dreaded by high idealists? It is not uncommonly believed that modernity has disrupted or marginalized the life of the believer, that it has produced the religious ideologue and its pathological form, the modern, religious zealot. Is this claim plausible? Does modernity really force upon us the morally indefensible choice between the devil and the deep blue sea, between the unprincipled, individualist, wanton and the ideologue, the zealot, the lover of pastiche?

I do not deny that modernity has unleashed processes of homogenization of unprecedented scale, power, and technological force. These forces and processes are bound to transform any settled way of life, anywhere in the world. To that extent, and in so far as modernity is tied to industrialism and capitalism, they are liable to disrupt traditional faith, its plurality as well as its privileged, self-evident authority. Traditional religion can no longer be immediately persuasive because these forces wrench away from religious symbols the determining power they once possessed. Trust, unconditional obligation, the voluntary surrender of choice, powerful emotions such as love that once turned belief into faith and conviction gradually give way to reason and doubt. In these changed circumstances, belief must be supported by evidence or argument and when neither is available, it must try to stand on its own. It is this wobbly self-reliance, however, that makes it belligerent, dogmatic, and doctrinal. Modernity often turns traditional faith into a set of doctrines. So, modern secularism is ridden with glaring deficiencies. But my purpose in this essay is to suggest that it also generates cultural resources with which to counter many of its defects. It is this which is often forgotten by many of its critics.

Let me put the issue differently. It is true that modernity and secularism, in at least some of these, have assumed a mindless, horrific form. It is equally true that some of these are inescapable. When faced with this, how do we construct our responses? One can react to it either blindly by lapsing into glib support of earlier forms of religions and traditions, defending these latter against all, not just the currently dominant, forms of modernity and secularism. All said and done, this is the character of Nandy's polemical reflexes. I admire Nandy's piece on secularism not only for its sharp-witted, focused repartee but also for its sophistication. But on reflection, I cannot help feeling that for all its insights, it does not get a suitable handle on the problem after all. Its strength is derived from its complex view of religion; Nandy is sensitive to religion's internal differentiations. But, he succumbs in the end to the Achilles heel of every robust and sharp critic and polemicist: he caricatures his opponent; the view of modernity and secularism that emerges from his essay is too simplistic. In short, he works with a routine offensive strategy: call the other an absolute evil and when he protests at the loathsome presence of similar features in your own position, say that these are only temporary, accidental afflictions rubbed off by close but forced encounter with him. This is our familiar foreign hand syndrome, a deadly new form of the intellectual's own homespun xenophobia.

An alternative response does not attempt to seal off religion from modernity, or tradition from secularism but tries to see exactly how each of these operate in different cultures, in that of unfettered desire, of multiple values, of high ideals that bypasses multiple values, and in the other mature culture that passes through these multiple values. To do so is to see the strength of both modernity and tradition, of secular and religious outlooks. It is also to refuse to make easy choices that are frequently forced upon us.

It does not bother me in the least if the reader finds in this view a whiff of compromise. He might say, however, that this compromise does not work. But do we know what does? It seems to me (obvious) that a sweeping rejection of modernity is neither possible nor desirable. Accomplishing an alternative modernity is the most reasonable option available to us. I am sure that the saner among the anti-secularists, in their less polemical moments, know this already. But it is time they said so openly.

12

Are there Alternative Modernities?*

This chapter has three objectives. First, to argue against views that confront multiple indigenous traditions with a single western modernity. Instead, I defend the idea that alternative modernities have existed within and outside the western world.[1] Second, though I do not outline these alternative modernities in detail, I hope to provide a rough idea of what it means to have a genuine alternative to mainstream western modernity. Finally, I warn against confusing alternative modernities with what I call a patchwork of high-minded western modernity and an equally rigid indigenous tradition.

UNDERSTANDING MODERNITY
I begin by drawing a distinction between two ways of understanding the rise of modernity, two different viewpoints on how a modern social

* A version of this paper was presented at an international conference on alternative modernities held in New Delhi in December 1997. It was subsequently published as 'Are there Alternative Modernities?', in N.N. Vohra (ed.), *Culture, Democracy and Development in South Asia*, New Delhi: Shipra and India International Centre, 2000, pp. 9–26.
   [1] The substantive claims of this essay are interpretative rather than normative. The essay is an exercise in analytical social theory rather than in normative political philosophy. It is not my intention to demonstrate the superiority of either the modern over the traditional world view or of alternative modernities over mainstream, western modernity. No doubt, it is a pressing need of our times to conceive and, more importantly, to realize an alternative to the dehumanizing excesses of western modernity or non-western traditions. But this task of appraising and defending a different modernity is beyond the task of this essay.

formation is distinct from its predecessors. Following the philosopher, Charles Taylor, I call the first an acultural and the second, a cultural theory of modernity.[2] On the acultural understanding, an account of transformation from a pre-non-modern to a modern society need not make any reference to cultural categories. For the cultural theory of modernity, this is impossible; a description and explanation of societal transformation must invoke culture.

I can hardly proceed further without clarifying the meaning of the elusive term 'culture'. Here by 'culture' is meant a complex but specific ideational configuration, a cluster of thoughts and pictures that transforms human biological organisms into agents who lead and experience meaningful lives. It is a web of embedded understandings and representations about the self and its relation to other selves and to the natural world, and includes conceptions of good and bad, right and wrong, virtues and vices, etc. It is our culture that decides whether or not we view nature as sacred, intrinsically meaningful, or disenchanted. It is also culture that determines the extent to which we view ourselves as distinct individuals and the value we place on our distinctive individualities. In a sense, human bodies are everywhere identical but how they present themselves, what actions they perform, and how they relate to one another is entirely culture dependent. Since culture simply is the complex web of pictures, thoughts, and concepts, it exists wherever they do. It is widely believed that ideas and representations can only exist in the minds of individuals. This is not true. Although culture is ideal, it is not only mental and does not exist only in people's heads. It is of course true that it is present in the mind but, apart from being found in bodily states and dispositions, it is also embodied in collective practices. Culture is generated and nourished by communities and much of it exists as practical, unconscious knowledge and is presupposed as the essential background of the more explicit representations formed by a section of that group.

Acultural Theories of Modernity

For acultural theories, the transition to modernity can be explained without appealing to culture in the sense outlined earlier. An example of such a theory is present in Karl Marx's 'Preface' to the *Critique of Political Economy*. In perhaps one of the most famous passages in social

[2] Charles Taylor, 'Two Theories of Modernity', *Public Culture*, vol. II, no. 1, 1999, pp. 153–74.

science literature, Marx proposed a two-stage theory of social and historical transformation, according to which a change in the legal, political, and ideological superstructure of a society is determined by a more fundamental alteration in its relations of production which, in turn, are a function of the nature of its productive forces. The two key terms, 'productive forces' and 'production relations', are meant to possess an acultural content. The defining feature of a modern society, what individuates it as 'modern', is a high level of productive forces and a type of productive organization best suited to maintain this level of productivity. A society becomes modern when consequent upon the acquisition of high technology, its productivity crosses a certain threshold. To be sure, modernity is not exhausted by high technology and a certain type of economy. But the rest of modernity follows this techno-logical change because cultural transformation, that is, a change in how the self and the world is conceived and the norms which govern the self are merely the epiphenomenon of modern technology and its attendant economic structure. Other acultural explanations are not uncommon in social science. For example, modern societies may be identified with industrialization and urbanization, or understood in terms of certain political and administrative practices, or conceived to be of a piece with enhanced instrumental rationality or scientific temper.

Common to all acultural theories, their constitutive feature, is a sharp distinction they maintain between culture on the one hand and a system of technology/economic and political institutions on the other. Let me call this aculturally defined system the technology–institutional complex or IT-complex, for short. For example, a high level of tech-nology, a capitalist economy, and the bureaucratic state together form such an IT-complex.

Interpretations of Acultural Theories

Once this distinction is firmly in place, the acultural theory yields three different interpretations. The strongest interpretation, associated with vulgar Marxism and with crude modernization theorists is this: the IT-complex constitutes modernity and has strict causal priority. Once it comes into existence, the ideational configuration follows necessarily. Within this explanatory scheme, culture has no causal efficacy. Moreover, all societies, by an inexorable logic, with little choice in the matter, must transit this process. Sooner or later, every society is bound to be swayed first by this IT-complex and when that happens, willy-nilly it must acquire a 'modern outlook'. These theories contain a radical prognosis for all human societies: all cultural and civilizational differences will be erased by modernity to produce global uniformity.

A second interpretation sheds the strong teleological bias of the first but retains the rest of the theory. On this view, every society is faced with an original, existential choice: it has to either select or reject modernity. If a society opts for it, then it will have chosen the entire package; once it steps into it, there is no turning back, no escape. Since the outlook follows the IT-complex, choosing one also means choosing the other. Quite possibly, Gandhi writing the *Hind Swaraj* in 1909, believed that Indian civilization was faced with such a choice and given his own views of modernity at that time, fearing its satanic consequences, he believed that India could and should reject it in toto.

Notice that these interpretations generate or have strong affinities with what I call the twin ideologies of modernism and traditionalism. Such ideologies emerge particularly when modernity is viewed as an assault on a group that finds it difficult to handle the IT-complex, a common occurrence in predominantly agrarian societies with their local traditions of technology, production, and household management. Despite differences, ideologies of modernism and traditionalism have much in common. The modernist ideologue defines tradition as the antithesis of the modern and, not surprisingly, finds it entirely worthless. Ideologues of tradition retaliate tit for tat and pay the modernist back in the same coin. For the modernist, traditionalists are blind worshippers of the past, paranoid of disagreement and conflict, irrationally sunk in hierarchical social practices antithetical to individual freedom. Traditionalists see modernists as valueless anarchists who move from one ephemeral desire to another, deify instrumental rationality, and are blind to the larger, deeper significance of their lived world. However, both ideologues share the same understanding of how pre-modern societies are transformed and enter modernity. They accept modernity as essentially a non-cultural phenomenon. Indeed, they endorse the same interpretation of the acultural theory of modernity.

A third interpretation of acultural theory yields what I call a *patchwork* of modernity and tradition. Like the first two interpretations, this interpretation rigidly maintains the distinction between the IT-complex and culture. However, it rejects the teleology of the first interpretation and the causal linkage between the IT-complex and culture endorsed by the second interpretation. On this view, it is possible to access the IT-complex without the cultural underpinnings normally associated with it. This possibility emerges because the IT-complex and the cultural system are seen to be distinct and causally uncoupled. This view is unmistakably attractive precisely because it offers a heady mix of tradition and modernity. Since cultural identity is defined widely in terms of home-grown traditions rather than by the IT-complex, this patchwork solution is not seen as an assault on non-western societies. Quite the contrary, it is put forward as an ideal worth pursuing. Possession of the IT-complex is anyway a source of masculine empowerment, believed to be an all important quality in the contemporary world of real power relations. Every non-western society can be at once modern and traditional, deriving power from the best of both worlds. It absorbs fresh sparks flying from contact with an alien world and is equally nourished by native roots. This self-affirming strategy not only appears to give empowerment without damaging local identity but also blunts the opposition between 'their' modernity and 'our' tradition. Examples come easily to mind. In early twentieth century, our grandfathers, typically brahmins, would appear in public dressed in a western attire, bowler hat and all, but back at home would squat on the freshly washed kitchen floor and dutifully eat 'kuccha' food cooked and served by our grandmothers draped in 'pure' silk sarees. It is reflected even today in the apparent ease with which a section of our society wishes to go more nuclear or possess high information technology even as it demands a traditional dress code for women.

The eminent sociologist, M.N. Srinivas, recalls meeting a person who saw no inconsistency in driving a bulldozer for his livelihood and indulging in traditional black magic for his pleasure.[3] These two sectors of his life were completely discrete—an experience that is not unusual. Examples of people carrying over religio-magical attitudes to the technology they work with are easy to find. Every truck plying the highway passes us marked with vermilion and festooned with flowers. On the Vishwakarma day, it is customary in India to worship tools or do machine *puja*. Moreover, compartmentalization and carryovers are not the only examples of patchwork. The use of modern technology for the propagation of non-modern viewpoints provides another instance. An unaltered traditional institution working as a functional analogue of a western institution also exemplifies a patchwork solution. For example, the traditional Indian joint family is believed by many to have supported entrepreneurial growth. Timberg's study of the role of

---

[3] M.N. Srinivas, *Social Change in India*, New Delhi: Orient Longman, 1966, pp. 54–5.

joint family system in helping Marwaris transit from trade to industrial capitalism comes immediately to mind. Other studies have shown how the joint family system helps capital formation among peasants. Here, a traditional institution is reinforced because it helps the growth of a modern institution. A traditional entity, without changing, also lends itself for a modern purpose.

This patchwork of modernity and tradition, including the 'modernization of tradition', is frequently confused with alternative modernity but is neither an alternative modernity nor an alternative to it. This is so for the unambiguous reason that, as in any patchwork, the *same* unaltered western modernity is merely stitched together with an equally untouched native tradition. I return to this point later.

Let me sum up. The acultural theory of modernity is open to three interpretations, two of which generate ideologies of modernism and traditionalism, and a third that yields a patchwork solution frequently confused with alternative modernity. In short, the acultural theory secretes a high-minded modernism, an equally high-minded, rigid traditionalism, and a patchwork solution that combines both. Each of these interpretations identifies modernization with westernization.

Cultural Theories of Modernity

Cultural theories of modernity reject the distinction between culture and the IT-complex. At the very least, they find the distinction between institutions and culture unsustainable. Why so? Institutions are rule-bound practices. All practices, including those governed by explicit rules, are partly constituted by beliefs, at least some of which refer directly or implicitly to values that give these practices a normative direction—the reason why they exist, their point. Equally crucial to social practices are specific self-understandings from their participants. In short, a particular practice will not be what it is without either its internal point or these self-understandings. Consider the practice of voting. Essential to it is that a decision be reached or a verdict be delivered. Also crucial to it is that voters see themselves as autonomous beings capable of making reasonable choices. Without this internal point and self-understanding, people mark a paper but do not vote. Surely, all this unpacks a familiar claim in hermeneutic social science that social practices are meaningful.

Now, to say this is to admit the link between institutions and particular cultural configurations. After all, culture is nothing but the web of meanings that nourishes both self-understandings and the internal point of practices. In speaking of a specific set of social practices, we also refer, therefore, to particular cultural systems. Indeed, to some extent, this is true even of technologies because they too involve certain characteristic self-understandings and purposes and are not at all as culture neutral as they appear to be. If all this is true, then modernity cannot be defined merely in terms of a culture neutral IT-complex. It is necessarily a cultural/normative system that encompasses the IT-complex. So, for the cultural theory, the IT-complex is conceptually tied to a cultural and moral outlook. This is not to say that together they must form a tightly knit system, as is the case of relations in formal logic. Nor need these relations be causal. These are looser relations, like tenuous threads of a web (which by the way is why we frequently refer to culture as a web).

Let me give examples. The entire enterprise of modern science presupposes what Weber referred to as the disenchantment of the world, its objectification. The background understanding of natural science requires that the natural world consists of discrete entities without intrinsic purpose or meaning. Accompanying this objectification is the radical subjectification of human beings. From now on, meaning resides exclusively in subjects disengaged from the outer world. This radical separation of the subject and the object implies an attitude of some degree of instrumental control and subjugation of nature. If the purpose of nature is not its own but derived entirely from human beings, then humans can give it any purpose they deem fit. If no purpose is *seen* in it, then it *has* no purpose and if this is so, then it can be manipulated at will, even destroyed. Perhaps only human beings with this kind of modern subjectivity can produce science and technology. Consider likewise, capitalism, an economic system designed to generate limitless profits. The achievement of this end depends upon continuous saving and reinvestment in production which, in turn, is possible only when conspicuous consumption and the immediate gratification of desires is curtailed. This system can be worked upon only by certain kinds of people, for instance, by those who, without renouncing the world, must live by an ethic of restraint on desire and passion. Early capitalists could neither be 'sanyasis' nor 'bhogis'. They had to follow what Weber called inner-worldly asceticism.

It appears at first sight that for cultural theories, modernity must be inescapably western. Born in the West, it must remain tied to it, its origin. If technology and economic institutions originated in the West, so must the culture to which they were linked at birth. If so, we appear to arrive at the same conclusion reached by acultural theories that there exists only one, uniquely western modernity. For non-western societies, the only route to modernization is westernization.

However, this conclusion about cultural theories of modernity is mistaken. Cultural theories need not hold the view that modernity is a unique, comprehensive, and inescapably western phenomenon. What is established so far is only this: that *originally*, modernity, a complex cultural system, was exclusively western. It has not been shown that it must *remain* western. To be sure, this point about the western origins of modernity deflates another self-affirming move on the part of non-western societies, namely, that modernity could have sprouted at different places either simultaneously or at different times. On this view, every society can be modern without being western because each gave rise to its own modernity, that every society has carried within itself the seeds of its own unique modernity.[4] Since cultural theories imply the uniquely western origins of modernity, they debunk the view that different regions of the world have developed their very own distinctive, sui generis conceptions of modernity. However, they are entirely compatible with the idea that having originated in the West, modernity has travelled to other parts of the world. Equally compatible with it is the view that in its journey to other parts of the world and through its contact with other non-western cultural traditions, western modernity has been transformed. Indeed, even within the geographical territory called the West, namely, Europe and Northern America, modernity has changed over time. Within the West and outside it, alternative modernities, that is, modernities that challenge and which are different from early western modernity, have developed over time. In the geographical West, in working out different ways of breaking away from their own past, people developed their own alternative modernities (different conceptions of the enlightenment were generated, movements countering the enlightenment such as romanticism were developed and several creative attempts were made to reconcile the romantic with the enlightenment traditions; in short, western modernity cannot be equated with any one conception of the enlightenment). In non-western societies, alternative modernities emerged as non-western peoples tried to break loose not only from their own past practices but

[4] The view that non-western societies, in general, and South Asian societies, in particular, developed their own early modernities that were stopped in their tracks, thwarted, or usurped by western, colonial modernity is found in the essay by Sanjay Subrahmanyam, 'Hearing Voices: Vignettes of Early Modernity in South Asia, 1400–1750', *Daedalus*, vol. 127, no. 3, 1998, pp. 75–104.

also from the shackles of a particular version of western modernity imposed on them.[5]

Once it is accepted that modernity originated in the West but migrated elsewhere, three different possibilities still need contending. First, modernity failed on its arrival to take root because non-modern cultural systems were deeply entrenched, resilient to change, and not easily displaceable. Indian classical music is a good example, as is the caste system, at least before the introduction of representative democracy and universal franchise. Another example is the tendency to personalize all issues. Second, western modernity quite easily found a safe niche in these societies. A number of mechanisms helped its smooth passage. For instance, a powerless people, entirely lacking in self-confidence quickly lapped up anything new that came their way. There was gradual conversion by blind emulation or sheer seduction. Institutions where this happened on a large scale included the bureaucracy, the armed forces, and urban centres of education. Westernization was also adopted for purely instrumental reasons. Something akin to this process had begun as early as in the late seventeenth century, when a section of the commercial middle class were seen to be 'clad in a more stylish garb, with a head-dress of calico-coiled turban, light best, and loose trousers. They all spoke English, offered their services for small wages, and waited on the passengers to execute their business.'[6]

A rational choice to be western was also not entirely uncommon in the early eighteenth century. Furious at the abominable excesses of their own traditions, Calcuttan youth

openly adopted an aggressive attitude to everything Hindu and openly defied the cannons of their inherited religion, ... while some of them offended public opinion by their youthful exuberance, such as drinking to excess, flinging beef-bones into the houses of the orthodox and parading the streets shouting 'we have eaten Musalman bread'.[7]

In short, hyper-westernization became a form of protest against the filth in one's own traditions, something started by Ram Mohan Roy and continued to this day by dalits (the statue of Ambedkar in a blue suit,

[5] This explains the general ambivalence of non-western intellectuals such as Gandhi and Tagore to modernity.

[6] B.B. Misra, quoted in Yogendra Singh, *Modernization of Indian Tradition*, Delhi: Rawat Publications, 1988, p. 89.

[7] Charles Heimsath, quoted in Singh, *Modernization of Indian Tradition*, pp. 91–2.

with glasses and shining shoes, constitution in hand is an apt reminder). Quite possibly, changes in society necessitated the performance of certain functions and, in the absence of functional analogues within existing cultural systems, this role could be executed only by elements within western modernity. Perhaps this explains the rather easy acceptance, in India, of modern educational and legal systems. As early as 1841, 'it was noticed that the Chamars, despised untouchables of northern India were not afraid to bring suits against their landlords'.[8]

The quick absorption of western modernity had another reason. Perhaps it contained many elements that corresponded to deep mythical structures within non-western civilizations. Surface differences to the contrary, if any feature of western modernity had a deeper universal structure, its absorption was mere formality. Something along these lines is suggested by Ashis Nandy in his explanation of why cricket, an early modern English game, gained huge popularity in the entire subcontinent.[9] Finally, a third possibility exists that when western modernity began to interact with local cultural systems, something like a hybrid or composite culture began to emerge, possibly by creative adaptation, for which an analogue can be found neither in western modernity nor in indigenous tradition. These new phenomena resemble western modern and traditional entities and can be mistaken one for the other but they escape the interpretative grid and discourse relating to both. This cluster of newly developed phenomenon, forged out of western modern and indigenous traditional cultural systems, belongs to what can be called an alternative modernity.

It is important to re-emphasize the differences between alternative modernity and a patchwork of western modernity and indigenous tradition. Consider again an example of patchwork solution. I mentioned earlier that the joint family system enabled traditional 'Marwaris' traders to become industrial entrepreneurs. Now, as long as there is no structural change within the joint family system, the Marwari entrepreneurs living under and supported by the joint family system embody a patchwork. However, as soon as the joint family system is transformed and as long as it does not mutate into the highly individualist nuclear family typical of some western societies, we move towards something akin to an alternative modernity. A change in its traditional

---

[8] O' Malley, quoted in Singh, *Modernization of Indian Tradition*, p. 100.

[9] Ashis Nandy, *The Tao of Cricket: On Games of Destiny and the Destiny of Games*, New York: Viking, 1989.

structure and an equally significant difference from western modern institutions is critical for an alternative modernity to exist.

I need to mention two more supplementary points. First, a structural change does not imply a total transformation. A practice may be modern while retaining elements of the traditional, quite like a traditional practice retaining its basic identity even though it has absorbed some elements of the modern. What matters is the basic cultural form. If that has changed, the outer shell makes little difference to its identity. Consider, for example, a change in attitude towards certain kinds of foods. A person may refuse eating beef either because it is traditionally prohibited or on grounds of health, because red meat raises cholesterol beyond permissible levels. When beef is not eaten on grounds of health, the basic cultural form of the prohibition on beef eating has changed. Second, the evidence of a change in basic cultural form is to be found by examining the habitus of a social group, their embedded understanding. Basic cultural changes occur not when people say they have become different or when their more explicit beliefs are altered but rather with a change in the understanding inscribed in their social practices.

It is also obvious that alternative modernity though radically different from indigenous traditions and mainstream western modernity is *still* a version of modernity. If so, any discussion of alternative modernity naturally begs the question: what is modernity? What is it that is common to all modernities? Hardly an easy question to answer, but let me offer my tentative view on this matter. Any modernity must be identified with the following features:

1. The acceptance of some degree of disenchantment of nature.
2. A marked tendency to avoid suffering and desire material well-being.
3. The adoption of different principles for the self-identification of individuals and the groups to which they belong and therefore, the generation of new types of collective and individual identities whose relationship entailed some form of freedom for individuals.
4. Some form of equality among individuals and groups.
5. The acceptance that differences among individuals and groups are inevitable and reasonable. In fact, we can say, (2)–(4) and perhaps (5) together constitute the modern idea of social justice.
6. The presence of some degree of reflexivity and therefore critical questioning.
7. The belief that at least to some extent social structures depend on human agency.

Together these features secrete or presuppose a certain conception of the self and how they relate to one another and to the natural world. Together, they also generate the possibility of being compatible with a limited but wide range of institutional arrangements. Mainstream western modernity provides one interpretation of this complex set of features. Other modernities must interpret and articulate them differently, assign each of them different weightages.

Other points worth mentioning to clarify my position are these: first, I believe any given non-western social formation has responded to western modernity in each of the three ways mentioned earlier. Any contemporary non-western social formation contains a layer of largely unaffected non-modern practices that have shown a remarkable resilience to change as well as a layer of thoroughly westernized modern practices. In addition to these layers—and this is my principal contention in this essay—it contains a distinct layer of alternative modernities. It is not my contention that every important feature of non-western societies must be understood in terms of a unique modernity that is entirely sui generis. Rather, my point is that the habit of viewing features of our society in terms of a straightforward dichotomy of western modern/indigenous tradition has long obscured that a significant third layer has also existed in our societies. Second, none of what I have said so far commits me to a strong value judgement on any of these three layers. It is not within the scope of this essay to dwell on the good or evil present in these layers. At any rate, neither western modernity nor indigenous traditions are wholly good or bad. Much the same is true of alternative modernities. By their very nature, traditions or modernities are not amenable to simplistic evaluations.

Perhaps I need to underline this point. It is commonplace to say of mainstream western modernity that it opened up emancipatory spaces as also seeds of new forms of imprisonment. One can here cite many instances. The modernist rejection of hierarchy is accompanied by certain unacceptable forms of levelization and new inequalities. Likewise, modernity is concerned with the avoidance of suffering and with material well-being but it has also engendered excessive attention to material comfort and fostered a neurotic fear of any pain or suffering. It has encouraged individual autonomy but also merciless self-seeking. It emphasized the need to be rational but also bolstered the most severe forms of instrumental reasoning. By opening up a private space for individuals, it saved them from continual social interference and a permanent public gaze but also made them indifferent to the public sphere.

It generated new more open-ended forms of belonging but radical exclusions and xenophobia too. This ambivalent nature is characteristic of all modernities, of early western modernity as well as its later incarnations. It is equally true of modernity when it arrived on the shores of non-western societies. As we all know, even colonial modernity was a mixed blessing, sowing seeds of liberation even as it was busy suffocating us.

This is an appropriate moment to clarify my evaluative stance towards what I have called a 'patchwork' solution. In a sense, patchwork is both inevitable and desirable. It is inevitable because human beings are complex creatures with multifarious needs and desires who worry less about consistency and coherence and more about how these needs and desires are to be fulfilled. They tend to explore all kinds of diverse sources by which to meet them. It is desirable because it is pointless not to do so. It would hardly make sense for the man in Srinivas' account to shun the pleasure derived from magic simply because, at the discursive level, it is inconsistent with the scientific world view entailed by the technology of bulldozing. So, at one level, we cannot do without patchworks. Human life thrives on them, more so because without patchworks cultural interaction and exchange is impossible. All cultural borrowing begins as patchwork. Yet, patchworks are also a product of some degree of short circuiting and therefore, thoughtlessness and an accompanying shallowness. Worse still, when things patched up are deeply conflictual, then societies and individuals are torn apart, unless, at another different level, a new phenomenon is forged sublating the subterranean tension within previously patched up entities. By their very nature, patchworks cannot reconcile deeper conflicts implicit in discrete entities more or less accidentally brought together. So, patchworks are hardly an unambiguous good. They are only good as stopgap measures. For permanent solutions that meet our deepest needs, we must look elsewhere.

Third, I have no fixed idea on the reach of alternative modernity, indeed of any modernity. An alternative modernity may be a highly localized phenomenon, firmly circumscribed, say, within a town. If there is a Parisian modernity, why not a modernity that is located exclusively in Mumbai or Kolkata? It may have a national spread. For example, if there is a Japanese modernity, surely there must be an Indian modernity as well. In fact, several Indian modernities may coexist. There can even be a sub-continental modernity to be found in India, Pakistan, Sri Lanka, Bangladesh, and Nepal. Finally, a modernity different from mainstream western modernity may well have a genuine global presence.

Let me furnish some examples of alternative modernities. Functioning democracy in village panchayats, supplemented nuclear families among urban professionals, the music of Kumar Gandharva come immediately to mind. However, I would like to dwell on two phenomena: the transformed character of castes in India and Indian secularism.

Alternative Modernity: Caste in Indian Democracy

How did the caste system react to colonial western modernity? A study of caste relations over roughly two centuries reveals that it responded to western modernity in each of the three ways mentioned earlier. To begin with, neither the trade practices of the East India Company nor the political machinery of the colonial state appear to have initially affected the core features of the caste system (the system of jatis and the practice of untouchability). The colonial state followed a policy of benign neglect, leaving intact most traditional mechanisms of social control of lower castes and the subordination of untouchables. Indeed, later incursions of the state, as when it launched a massive cognitive project to bring India under administrative control, bolstered the caste system by congealing and consolidating hierarchy, emphasizing the varna system more than jatis and further extending the growing social distance between castes. A second response came largely from newly educated sections, predominantly of the upper castes who denounced it. They flouted caste taboos on contact and dining, sometimes even on inter-caste marriages and refused altogether to define their identities in terms of castes. Such rejection frequently, though not always, came from those who unwittingly embraced western models of collective self-definitions or else self-consciously identified with them.

Finally, a third, more recent response takes us straight into the arena of alternative modernity. After the adoption of the constitution, and with the deepening of the democratic process, a whole new set of people, freshly empowered, with incipient and steady vitality began to enter local and national public spheres from which they were hitherto debarred. Over time, they brought about a profound transformation in the political and, in some respects, even in the public presence of caste. In these spheres, a hierarchical structure that constituted individuals wholly and exhaustively in terms of groups and that arranged these groups in accordance with a ranking scale of purity and pollution, has now turned into a system of more or less equal relations between relatively open, politicized, semi-autonomous politico-cultural communities. Caste is now reborn as a new collective identity with room for other identity-constituting principles and belief systems. Whereas in the nineteenth century, the caste of a person was an index of hierarchical rank, it is now a marker of social differentiation and cultural identity in the Indian politics and in some areas of the public sphere. In the jargon of sociologists, instead of being a relational category, we are now faced with the substantiation of caste. More strikingly, caste today is a potent resource for mobilization in an egalitarian political democracy and even constitutes a ground for claims towards social justice. It is abundantly clear that, at least in the political domain, we no longer have a mere patchwork of traditional castes and modern political democracy. Indeed, it is doubtful if such a patchwork of caste and democracy could have lasted long. One of the two would have had to give way to the other. The internal dynamics of their interaction has transformed traditional caste relations and produced a modern Indian democracy that is hardly a replica of western democratic conceptions or institutions.

Alternative Modernity: Indian Secularism

There is a tendency in the literature on secularism in India to first posit a highly idealized version of secularism derived partly from, say, the American or the French experience and then judge the practice of the secular state in India by standards evolved from these models. (Secularists have often done this and then lamented the failure of Indian secularism. Likewise, opponents of secularism have used the ploy to first highlight the inconsistencies of Indian secularism and then conclude that the collapse of secularism in India is imminent.) To illustrate this point let me take the example of Donald Smith's *India as a Secular State*, still the locus classicus on the subject.[10] Smith's conception of the secular state involves three distinct but interrelated relations concerning the state, religion, and the individual. The first relation concerns individuals and their religion, from which the state is excluded. Individuals are thereby free to decide the merits of the respective claims of different religions without any coercive interference by the state. They are free to revise or reject the religion they were born into or have chosen (this is the liberal ingredient within secularism). The

---

[10] D.E. Smith, *India as a Secular State*, Princeton: Princeton University Press, 1963.

second concerns the relation between individuals and the state, from which religion is excluded. Here, the state views individuals without taking into account their religious affiliation. The rights and duties of citizens are not affected by the religious beliefs held by individuals, for example, no discrimination exists in the holding of public office or taxation (this is the egalitarian component within secularism). Finally, for Smith, the integrity of both these relations is dependent on the third relation, between the state and different religions. Here he argues that secularism entails separation of powers, that is, the mutual exclusion of state and religion in order that they may operate effectively and equally in their own respective domains. Just as it is not the function of the state to promote, regulate, direct, or interfere in religion, just so is political power outside the scope of religion's legitimate objectives. So, for Smith, secularism means the strict separation of religion and the state for the sake of the religious liberty and equal citizenship of individuals.

Clearly, on this account of secularism, any intervention in Hinduism—for example, the legal ban on the prohibition of dalit entry into temples—is illegitimate interference in religious affairs and therefore, compromises secularism. Similarly, the protection of socio-religious groups (minorities) is inconsistent with an individualistically grounded secularism. For example, the right to personal laws entails a departure from secularism simply on the ground that it depends on a communally suspect classification. Together, these policies violate the ideal of neutrality or equidistance which plays a pivotal role in Smith's view of secularism. Smith believed that despite these flaws, the Indian state was secular, at least in the early 1960s. However, he also believed that these features constituted serious deviations from the model of secularism and unless quickly brought in line, the secular state in India would plunge into crisis. Was he correct?

I do not think so. Smith remained in the grip of a particular model of western secularism and therefore, was unable to get a handle on the basic features of Indian secularism. The distinctiveness of the Indian variant of secularism can be understood only when the cultural background and social context in India is properly grasped. At least four such features of this socio-cultural context call for attention. First, there exists the mind-boggling diversity of religious communities in India. Such diversity may coexist harmoniously but it invariably generates conflicts, the most intractable of which, I believe, are deep conflicts over values. Second, within Hinduism in particular and in South Asian religions more generally, a greater emphasis is placed on practice rather than belief. A person's religious identity or affiliation is defined more by what she or he does with and in relation to others, than by the content of beliefs individually held by them. Since practices are intrinsically social, any significance placed on them brings about a concomitant valorization of communities. Third, many religiously sanctioned social practices are oppressive by virtue of their illiberal and inegalitarian character, and deny a life of dignity and self-respect. Therefore, from a liberal and egalitarian standpoint, they desperately need to be reformed. Such practices frequently have a life of their own, independent of consciously held beliefs, and possess a causal efficacy that remains unaffected by the presence of conscious beliefs. Furthermore, a tendency to fortify and insulate themselves from reflective critique makes such practices resistant to easy change and reform. It follows that an institution vested with enormous social power is needed to transform their character. Fourth, in Hinduism, the absence of an organized institution such as the church has meant that the impetus for effective reform cannot come exclusively from within. Reform within Hinduism can hardly be initiated without help from powerful external institutions such as the state.

In such a context, India needed a coherent set of intellectual resources to tackle inter-religious conflict, and to struggle against oppressive communities not by disaggregating them into a collection of individuals or by derecognizing them but by somehow making them more liberal and egalitarian. A political movement for a united, liberal, and democratic India had to struggle against hierarchical and communal conceptions of community but without abandoning a reasonable communitarianism. Besides, the state had an important contribution to make in the transformation of these communities; for this reason, a perennial dilemma was imposed on it. The state in India walked a tightrope between the requirement of religious liberty that frequently entails non-interference in the affairs of religious communities and the demand for equality and justice which necessitates intervention in religiously sanctioned social customs. Secularism in India simply had to be different from the classical liberal model that does not recognize groups and dictates strict separation between religious and political institutions.

If we abandon the view, such as Donald Smith's, that political secularism entails a unique set of state policies valid under all conditions which provide the yardstick by which the secularity of any state is to be judged, then we can better understand why despite 'deviation' from the ideal, the state in India continues to embody an alternative model of secularism.[11] This can be shown even if we stick to Smith's working definition of secularism as consisting of three relations. Smith's first relation embodies the principle of religious liberty construed individualistically, that is, pertaining to the religious beliefs of individuals. However, it is possible to make a non-individualistic construal of religious liberty by speaking not of the beliefs of individual but rather of the practices of groups. Here, religious liberty would mean distancing the state from the practices of religious groups. The first principle of secularism can then be seen to grant the right to a religious community to its own practices. Smith's second relation embodies the value of equal citizenship. But this entails—and I cannot substantiate my claim—that we tolerate the attempt of radically differing groups to determine the nature and direction of society as they best see it. In this view, then, the public presence of the religious practices of groups is guaranteed and entailed by the recognition of group differentiated citizenship rights (such as the right to establish and administer educational institutions of their choice). Smith's version of secularism entails a charter of uniform rights. But, it is clear that the commitment of secularism to equal citizenship can dictate group-specific rights and therefore, differentiated citizenship. Smith's third principle pertains to non-establishment and therefore, to a strict separation of religion from state, under which religion and the state both have the freedom to develop without interfering with each other. Separation, however, need not mean strict non-interference, mutual exclusion, or equidistance, as in Smith's view. Instead, it could be a policy of principled distance, which entails a flexible approach on the question of intervention or abstention, combining both, dependent on the context, nature, or current state of relevant religions.

It is important to understand that principled distance is not mere equidistance. In the strategy of principled distance, whether or not the state intervenes or refrains from action depends on what really strengthens religious liberty and equality of citizenship for all. If this is so, the state may not relate to every religion in exactly the same way, intervene to the same degree, or in the same manner. All it must ensure is that the relation between religious and political institutions be

[11] For an interesting critique of Smith's interpretation of Indian secularism as derived from the American model with an 'extra dose of separation', see Marc Galanter, 'Secularism, East and West', in Rajeev Bhargava (ed.), *Secularism and Its Critics*, New Delhi: Oxford University Press, 1998, pp. 234–67.

guided by non-sectarian principles that remain consistent with a set of values constitutive of a life of equal dignity for all.

It was largely this group-sensitive conception of secularism of the principled distance variety that legitimized the practices of the state wherein religion was alternatingly excluded and included as an object of state policy. By its refusal to allow: (i) separate electorates, (ii) reserved constituencies for religious communities, (iii) reservations for jobs on the basis of religious classification, and (iv) the organization of states on religious basis, the Indian state excluded religion from its purview on the ground that its inclusion would inflame religious and communal conflict and produce another partition-like scenario. However, the very motive that excluded religion from state institutions also influenced its inclusion in policy matters of cultural import. For example, a uniform charter of rights was not considered absolutely essential for national integration. Separate rights were granted to minority religious communities to enable them to live with dignity. Integration was not seen as identical to complete assimilation. Similar liberal and egalitarian motives compelled the state to undertake reforms within Hinduism. By making polygamy illegal, introducing the right to divorce, abolishing child marriage, legally recognizing inter-caste marriages, regulating the activities of criminal masquerading as holy men, introducing temple entry rights for dalits, and reforming temple administration, the state intervened in religious matters to protect the ordinary but dignified life of its citizens.

To sum up: (i) modern secularism is fully compatible with, indeed even dictates a defence of differentiated citizenship and of rights of religious groups; and (ii) the secularity of the state does not necessitate strict intervention, non-interference, or equidistance but rather any or all of these, as the case may be.

So far, I have argued that Indian secularism is different from mainstream western secularism of the strict separation variety. I now need to argue that it is not reducible to traditional notions of tolerance. A 'tolerant state' is not a secular state. Recall that to tolerate is to refrain from interfering in the affairs of someone (individual or group) who one finds disagreeable, even morally repugnant, despite the fact that one has the power to do so. Given this definition of tolerance, a tolerant attitude, particularly on the part of the state, can certainly bring about peace between warring religious groups. Tolerance is also compatible with, although not the same as religious liberty. But it does not encourage respect between two groups. At any rate, it is fully compatible with inequality. There is no necessity that a tolerant state encourage an attitude of *equal* respect. And certainly, a tolerant state need have no truck with political equality and therefore, with the idea of equal citizenship. However, in the view that I have outlined earlier, a state that does not show equal respect to all religious groups and its members and more particularly, a state that does not grant equal citizenship rights is not a secular state. It follows that tolerance and secularism are two different, quite incompatible ideals. Most religious traditions in India encourage tolerance but not equal respect. They certainly do not accord equal citizenship rights. Since political equality is central to secularism but absent in most religious traditions, there is a straightforward rupture between secularism and notions of tolerance found in religious traditions.[12]

It was not my intention to offer a blanket condemnation of Indian traditions or western modernity. Rather, this essay is a plea for the recognition of alternative modernities that lie unnoticed because of the hold on our imagination of a simplistic, dichotomous framework that bifurcates our world into western modernity and indigenous traditions. The institution of caste is not a mere continuation of a uniquely Indian phenomenon. Nor is secularism entirely western. Many practices and institutions in India today cannot be properly understood as entirely western or indigenous. It will also not help to construe the democratic incarnation of caste or the Indian version of secularism as patchworks of local traditions and an imported modernity. An entrenched framework, by now a disabling habit of the mind, prevents us from seeing things as they are. This essay will have realized its aim if, in a small way, it has contributed to freeing us from that limited, obfuscating framework.

---

[12] This is not to detract from the point that tolerance, even within hierarchical framework, forms an important background condition for the development of modern secularism, and elements of this background condition can certainly be found within India.

.

V
PHILOSOPHY OF SOCIAL SCIENCE

13

Holism and Individualism in History and Social Science*

*M*ethodological individualists such as Mill, Weber, Schumpeter, Popper, Hayek, and Elster argue that all social facts must be explained wholly and exhaustively in terms of the actions, beliefs, and desires of individuals.[1] On the other hand, in their explanations, methodological holists such as Durkheim and Marx tend to bypass individual action. Within this debate, better arguments exist for the view that explanations of social phenomena without the beliefs and desires of agents are deficient. If this is so, individualists appear to have a distinct edge over their adversaries. Indeed, a consensus exists among philosophers and social scientists that holism is implausible or false and individualism, when carefully formulated, is trivially true.

Holists challenge this consensus by first arguing that caricatured formulations of holism that ignore human action must be set aside. They then ask us to re-examine the nature of human action. Action is distinguished from mere behaviour by its intentional character. This much is uncontested between individualists and holists. But, against the individualist contention that intentions exist only as psychological states in the heads of individuals, holists such as myself argue that they also lie directly embedded in irreducible social practices, and that the identification of any intention is impossible without examining the

* Originally published as 'Holism and Individualism in History and Social Science', in Edward Craig (ed.), *Encyclopedia of Philosophy*, London: Routledge and Kegan Paul, 1998, pp. 482–8.

[1] See Steven Lukes, 'Methodological Individualism Reconsidered', in A. Ryan (ed.), *The Philosophy of Social Explanation*, Oxford: Oxford University Press, 1973, pp. 119–29; and Jon Elster, *Making Sense of Marx*, Cambridge: Cambridge University Press, 1985.

social context within which agents think and act.[2] *Holists find nothing wrong with the need to unravel the motivations of individuals, but they contend that these motivations cannot be individuated without appeal to the wider beliefs and practices of the community. For instance, the acquiescence of oppressed workers may take the form not of total submission but subtle negotiation that yields them sub-optimal benefits. Insensitivity to social context may blind us to this. Besides, it is not a matter of individual beliefs and preferences that this strategy is adopted. That decisions are taken by subtle strategies of negotiation rather than by explicit bargaining, deployment of force, or use of high moral principles is a matter of social practice irreducible to the conscious action of individuals.*

Two conclusions follow if the holist claim is true. First, that a reference to a social entity is inescapable even when social facts are explained in terms of individual actions, because of the necessary presence of a social ingredient in all individual intentions and actions. Second, a reference to individual actions is not even necessary when social facts are explained or understood in terms of social practices. Thus, the individualist view that explanation in social science must rely wholly and exhaustively on individual entities is hotly contested and is not as uncontroversial or trivial as it appears.

Several commentators have noted the extraordinarily muddled character of the debate that ensued in the 1950s between individualists and holists. Why this has been so is one of the enigmas of social science. The main issue was repeatedly derailed, peripheral issues were given singular pre-eminence, different versions of the doctrine remained entangled, and deeper philosophical issues in the philosophy of science were never adequately probed. What is worse, both sides persistently knocked down the weakest, most caricatured formulation of the opponent's views. Retrospectively, the battle does give the appearance of possessing a large element of sham. No wonder then that when the dust settled, many of the issues that once provoked so much controversy were resolved: motivated prejudice against the other was acknowledged, and soon, more concessive versions, plainly indistinguishable from each other, were formulated. A careful analysis of the debate can identify points of agreement between the two and, more importantly, that something significant and contentious between the two sides persists, therefore the battle is likely to rage in the future. This shall be demonstrated by first unearthing the principal assumptions of individualism

[2] Rajeev Bhargava, *Individualism in Social Science*, Oxford: Clarendon Press, 1992.

and then showing that they can be challenged from a non-individualist viewpoint.

Any further exploration of the subject must begin with a warning: it is unwise to be tempted by the view that a worthy political cause or great moral ideal is at stake in contending methodologies. The passion that Popper and Hayek brought into the debate immobilized it rather than provide the fresh impetus it badly needed.[3] On this point, Schumpeter was right: an advocacy of methodological individualism entails no commitment to liberalism.[4] Likewise, opposing it does not imply abandoning political liberalism or denying the moral value of the individual. So, it is not just that methodological individualism should not be confused with political, moral, or religious individualism but, more importantly, it must not be seen automatically to enlist itself behind any of them.

It is equally important to remind ourselves that the term 'methodological' must be understood here in the broadest sense possible to include at least three distinct but related ingredients. The first, epistemological, concerns the understanding and explanation of social and individual entities. The second, ontological, turns on whether or not social entities are anything beyond a collection of individual entities. The third, semantic, is about the meaning of words: can a term referring to a social entity be analysed without remainder into terms that refer only to individual entities? The literature on the subject abounds with attempts to turn methodological individualism and holism into purely explanatory doctrines, but disputes over the relevant type of explanatory variable or over correct explanatory form have frequently turned into sharp controversies on ontological and semantic matters. This is hardly surprising, because an explanatory doctrine presupposes or entails ontological and semantic commitments. Therefore, individualism and holism are best viewed as comprehensive strategies with all the three components just mentioned.

ONTOLOGICAL REASONS

This much clarified, it must be noted that a particular dispute, over one form of semantic individualism, is entirely settled. There are no takers

---

[3] K.R. Popper, *The Poverty of Historicism*, London: Routledge and Kegan Paul, 1960; and F.A. Hayek, 'From Scientism and the Study of Society', in J. O'Neill (ed.), *Modes of Individualism and Collectivism*, London: Heinemann, 1973, pp. 27–67.

[4] Steven Lukes, 'Methodological Individualism Reconsidered', in Ryan (ed.), *The Philosophy of Social Explanation*, p. 123.

any more for a project inspired by logical constructionism recommending that every single term referring to social entities be analysed as a collection of individual terms. However, for individualists, this failure has no ontological or explanatory ramifications. Second, one ontological dispute must be set aside. Encouraged by careless formulations and deep misunderstanding, it was once thought that holists believed in supra-substances hovering over and above all individuals; that they were carrying forward the Cartesian legacy of substance dualism by introducing yet another substance called the social. This is unfair to the holist who must be seen instead to be advocating property pluralism and emphasizing the distinctive causal efficacy of social properties.

We may compare this point with an issue in the natural sciences. Non-reductionists in biology often argue that biological organisms display teleological properties that are best understood as irreducible to but supervenient upon physical properties. The principle of supervenience views the world as stratified, with properties at one level dependent for their existence in a non-causal way on properties lying at the more basic level. However, this relation of ontological dependence is non-reductive because the two sets of properties are never identical. Thus, teleological properties presuppose the existence of physical properties without being reducible to them.

It is in this sense that social properties are said to be supervenient on physical and biological ones. This much ought to be beyond dispute. What is not clear, however, is that this entails a supervenience of the social on the individual. For much depends on what we mean by the individual. If the term 'individual' refers to a single identifiable biological organism, then the statement is true. But surely, it is not the pure and abstract biological individual in focus here; rather what concerns us is the individual with distinctive human properties. The key question then is whether these properties emerge only when individuals come together or if they already exist, independent of any relations between them. Similarly, it is fairly incontrovertible to claim that any social process is supervenient on the physio-biological movement of individual organisms. Durkheim, as good a non-individualist as any, said so much: 'It is very true that society comprises no active force other than individuals'.[5] The holist argument contends only that

---

[5] É. Durkheim (edited by Steven Lukes, trans. by W.D. Halls), *The Rules of Sociological Method*, Basingstoke: Macmillan, 1982, p. 251.

the specific pattern of this dynamic process is not reducible to the move-ment of individual biological organisms taken aggregately.

Another vital issue to register is this: the individualist/holist controversy is not identical to the structure/agency debate in the social sciences, for a number of reasons. First, individualism does not entail a commitment to free human agency. The individualist may believe agency to be restricted too, but locate all constraints on it within the individual psyche. Individualism is compatible with internal constraints and therefore, with a full-blooded determinism. Second, it is simply false to assume that anything external to the individual agent is thereby constraining. External structures are not just constraining but also enabling. Indeed, a robust view of free and active human agents is compatible with the claim that such capacities depend on the presence of relevant external structures. More importantly, individualists can develop not only a conception of internal but also of external constraints. They too can account for the very constitution of external structures, of rules, norms, and conventions constraining human action. Likewise, holists can develop a perfectly cogent account of free human action. If this is so, the principal dividing line between the two sides cannot be drawn at the level of free agency and external constraint.

This is not the dominant understanding of those engaged in this debate. Holists accused individualists of ignoring the relations of the individual to the larger social context. Individualists, on their part, blamed holists for treating individuals as mere cogs in the social wheel. One was charged with ultra-voluntarism, the other reproached for supra-determinism. At the end of a long and unsavoury controversy, however, each side realized what should have been obvious from the very start: that neither agency nor the context within which it occurs can be ignored.

Let us identify the points where agreement is undeniable. Holists do not believe in supra-individual, social substances. They emphasize social relations and their undeniable constraining effects. Individualists cannot fault these claims. Individualists, likewise, highlight human agency and show that societies consist in or are a result of people acting. Holists can hardly object to this. Furthermore, both accept that the a supra-individual social does not think; it is individuals who do the thinking. We appear then genuinely to arrive at a consensus on a set of statements so truistic that an explanatory strategy must be deemed mistaken if it fails to incorporate or is incompatible with it.

However, a plausible holist contention is that this agreement is at the price of an even greater intellectual muddle. The seemingly uncontroversial character of these statements obscures the fact that they are open to rival interpretations, one that antecedently shifts the entire balance in favour of the individualist and another which obdurately refuses to do so. The claim that individualism is trivially true may well be a rhetorical device that conceals deeper ontological and methodological issues that divide rival camps. All the dimensions of the debate are not unravelled unless another vital issue, forced upon us less by ontological than by epistemological reasons, is addressed. Sharp differences between holists and individualists are often believed to lie precisely at this point. Close analysis reveals, however, a thicker consensus on this issue. Contentious issues lurk in the background, despite this agreement.

EPISTEMOLOGICAL REASONS

The correct move here would first be to identify the relevant explanatory form and then try and show it as ontologically neutral, usable by individualists and non-individualists alike. But, contestants in the debate have not approached the issue in this way nor found it easy to identify the correct explanatory form. One reason for this is their insensitivity to another major controversy in social science, namely, the argument between naturalists and anti-naturalists. Each side has often assumed not only the absolute validity of their preferred model of scientific explanation but their monopoly over it. The second reason is the wholly opposite error of identifying the individualist/holist debate with the naturalist/anti-naturalist controversy, as if the settlement of the first dispute rests solely on the successful resolution of the second. By assuming that holism entails scientism and that therefore their victory flows automatically from the defeat of positivist naturalism, individualists such as Hayek have been prone to this mistake.[6] Clearly, many individualists are no less dogmatic about the claim that human affairs must be studied strictly with the methods of natural science. Conversely, holists can be equally steadfast in their advocacy of a distinctive method for social science. So, it is important to see both the relevance of the naturalist/non-naturalist dispute to the individualist/holist issue and *not* to identify them.

---

[6] Hayek, 'From Scientism and the Study of Society', in O'Neill (ed.), *Modes of Individualism and Collectivism*, pp. 27–67.

The other related difficulty is that the debate is conducted without disentangling different explanatory forms. We may begin by distinguishing five versions of individualist and holist explanatory strategies. Three of these deploy the deductive-nomological model of explanation. The first attempts to explain particular social facts by deducing them from laws of individual action. The second, known as explanatory reduction, explains not particular social facts but social laws by deducing them from laws pertaining to individuals. Since this reduction is achieved with the help of bridge statements which, in turn, can take two forms, we obtain two forms of reductionist strategies. The first requiring correlatory laws may be called correlatory reduction; the second, requiring identity statements is called identity reduction. This is also referred to as micro-reduction because here a macro-entity (the social) is identified with all the micro-entities (the individuals) that compose it.

The difference between each must be maintained because arguments that work against one kind of individualist strategy do not necessarily work against the other. For example, if laws are deemed essential for explanations, and if it is shown that only laws pertaining to individual action can be formulated, then the first, non-reductionist deductive-nomological version of individualism is vindicated. Holism fails because no social laws exist to explain particular social facts. Mandelbaum believed precisely this to be the target of individualist attack and therefore tried to establish the existence of social laws.[7] But an argument establishing social laws does not invalidate individualism because by deducing them from laws pertaining to individuals, one version of individualism is still exonerated. Similarly, showing the impossibility of correlatory laws does not defeat reductionist individualism because the absence of correlatory laws may indicate not the impossibility of reduction but the prior realization of a successful identity reduction.

A large part of the debate has been traditionally obsessed with these issues. However, this intellectual effort may have been futile if laws pertaining to individuals do not exist. For all these strategies depend not just on the presence of social laws but on general laws concerning individuals. And it is doubtful if such laws of human action exist. Notice that the laws in question must capture the precise features individuating human action. The same entity when subsumed under

---

[7] See M. Mandelbaum, 'Societal Laws', in O'Neill (ed.), *Modes of Individualism and Collectivism*, pp. 235–47.

other descriptions may indeed yield laws but these would be utterly irrelevant. Reductionists are not pursuing laws of physical movement or bodily behaviour. The laws they are after must refer to actions, and therefore, to the beliefs and desires of individuals. However, as Davidson has shown, precisely, such strict laws that explain or predict mental phenomena are impossible to obtain.[8] If valid, this is a decisive argument against all deductive-nomological versions of individualism. To revive this aspect of the debate, one has either to defeat this argument or give a conception of laws different from the one normally accepted.

Two conclusions may follow from this: first, that explanations in social science are not possible; and second, more importantly, that laws are not necessary for explanation. Therefore, we may explore explanatory forms unconnected with the deductive-nomological model. Forms that do not rely on the deductive-nomological model are intentional explanation and intentional understanding. The first, without invoking general laws or theoretical syllogism, explains action by showing that the behaviour of individuals is guided by beliefs and desires (intentions). The second, intentional understanding stresses the pivotal significance of understanding the beliefs and desires of agents. These strategies can be combined to give one overarching model for social science in which the understanding of beliefs and desires goes hand-in-hand with the explanation of action. In what follows, the term 'intentional explanation' refers to this model.

INDIVIDUALIST INTENTIONAL EXPLANATION

The formal structure of intentional explanation is simple and, up to a point, relatively uncontroversial: A desires X; A believes that doing Y will get him X; A does Y. The action, Y, is explained by deducing it, via a practical syllogism, from the given beliefs and desires. A crucial feature of beliefs and desires, of all intentional states generally, is that they are directed towards a real or imaginary object and that therefore they have an intentional content. Since these states are complex and in large measure linguistically constituted, we may say that they possess a linguistic content or meaning. Their ascription always involves the use of a 'that' clause. For example, A does not just believe or desire; A believes that the world is menacing and ugly or desires that it be beautiful. Clearly, the individuation of beliefs and desires depends on the meaning of words in these clauses. This presupposes that we

[8] D. Davidson, *Essays on Actions and Events*, Oxford: Clarendon Press, 1980.

capture the oblique occurrence of these expressions, where the oblique occurrence of expression is one in which the substitution of coextensive expression affects the truth value of the whole containing sentence. For example, if 'water' occurs obliquely in 'A believes water to be the most refreshing drink in the world', then replacing it with 'H₂O' will alter the truth value of the whole sentence.

This feature of obliqueness of expressions is of great significance for intentional explanation. Actions are individuated by their appropriate description, the description under which agents subsume their behaviour. To grasp their perspective or point of view, we must get the description of their beliefs and desires right, and this depends, in turn, on getting hold of obliquely occurring expressions. Likewise, a situation on which agents hold a view plays no direct role in characterizing their mental states or actions; it contributes to the explanation of actions only as it occurs obliquely, mediated by their points of view. This much is uncontroversial. But contrary to appearance, this by itself does not lead to individualism. The individualist turn comes with the further ontological assumption that these intentional states exist internal to agents, only in their heads. The individualist interpretation appears even more invincible with the second assumption that the meaning of beliefs and desires, their content, is individuated wholly internally, without reference to the external environment of the agent. These Cartesian assumptions turn action into a wholly individualist entity, bolstering the individualist belief that if the correct explanatory form in the social science is intentional explanation, then it just has to imply a victory of the individualist over the non-individualist.

THE HOLIST CHALLENGE

The widespread acceptance of these assumptions has generated the illusion of consensus. The holist challenge shatters it. It is levelled on two fronts, one at individualist theories of meaning, the other at individualist theories of action. Arguments developed by Putnam and Burge help reinvigorate a non-individualist theory of meaning.[9] Here, one begins by the fairly standard disambiguation of meaning into (i) intension and (ii) extension. Intension designates those properties the possession of which ensures that a sign applies to an entity. For example, the intension of the sign 'red' is the quality of redness, the possession of

[9] Hilary Putnam, *Philosophical Papers: Mind, Language and Reality*, Vol. 2, Cambridge: Cambridge University Press, 1975; and T. Burge, 'Individualism and the Mental', *Midwest Studies in Philosophy*, Vol. 4, 1979, pp. 73–121.

which qualifies an entity to be called red. In this sense, to know the meaning of a term is to understand the concept of redness. By extension, the other meaning of meaning, is usually meant the class of entities to which the term applies. The extension of the term 'red tomatoes' is the class of all actual or possible red tomatoes. To grasp the extension of a term is to correctly relate it to items in the world. The next move is to show that traditional theories of meaning are characterized by two assumptions. First, that intension determines extension. This can mean many things but it means, at the very least, that it helps to fix extension. Also, that sameness of intension always entails sameness of extension. Let us call this the functional character of intension. The second is the ontological assumption, already mentioned, that intension is a psychological entity that exists in the heads of individuals. So, we possess in our heads mental entities or representations that fix extensions of terms.

Putnam's thought experiment about two different substances on earth and twin earth, identical in all respects but their chemical structure, involves a long and complicated argument, the conclusion of which, on one possible interpretation, is this: that the functional and the ontological assumptions cannot both be true.[10] Since identical mental states refer to different extensions, we must abandon either the view that meaning is a psychological entity or the claim that intension determines extension. Arguably, Putnam offers sound reasons for dropping the first and retaining the second. In other words, if the conclusion forced by Putnam's thought experiment is true, we must infer that meaning is not a psychological entity in the head of individuals. What then is it? Several answers exist but perhaps the one that challenges the individualist most is the view that it is fixed by an interlocking system of beliefs and actions necessarily involving several individuals. If so, meaning is a social not an individual entity.

A related argument developed by Burge shows first that a difference in extension also affects oblique occurrences in 'that' clauses and therefore, the contents of mental states, and second, that 'communal practice is a factor in fixing and interpreting the words and attitudes of a person'.[11] In the individuation of beliefs, we must refer not just to

[10] Putnam, *Philosophical Papers*.

[11] Burge, 'Individualism and the Mental', *Midwest Studies in Philosophy*, p. 85. For original and suggestive pieces on holist theories of meaning and action, also see Charles Taylor, *Philosophy and the Human Sciences*, Cambridge: Cambridge University Press, 1985.

the internal environment of agents but also to their external context, particularly to relevant social practices. If meanings are inescapably social, then, given that beliefs are individuated by meanings, beliefs too are social, and further, given that beliefs are analytic to action, so are actions. We began by attempting to explain a social entity wholly and exclusively in terms of individual entities, namely, actions, beliefs, and desires, but we now find that all these are inescapably social. A social fact is then explained by another social fact. Individualism is challenged quite fundamentally. Also, holists do not abandon intentional explanation; they give it a non-individualist interpretation. There is no necessary dispute between individualists and non-individualists over which explanatory form is suitable for human affairs.

So, this is the crux of the matter. For individualists, beliefs, desires, intentions, and actions are intrinsically individual. This is implausible for the holist because the intention of one person already makes reference to the intention of another; beliefs, desires, and actions are already social. But what of the individualist view wherein intentions exist as internal states in the heads of individuals? And what about the ontology of irreducible social practices? To answer this, the holist opens the second front of attack, this time on the traditional theory of action. Put simply, the individualist theory of action is the widely accepted causal view according to which action can be analysed into three components: behaviour, intentional states, and the relation of causality that binds them. Action is behaviour caused by intentions. An alternative theory refuses to reduce action to anything more basic. Intentional states separate from behaviour do not exist; rather, agents intend something by their behaviour. On this view, intentions lie directly embedded in behaviour so that we see behaviour as action. Action then is a basic ability of human beings quite independent of the ability to form representations in their heads. The holist accepts this and asks us to go further. If intention can directly inhabit the bodily behaviour of one individual, it can also occupy the bodily behaviours of several individuals.

This ontological issue has consequences for explanatory strategy as well. First, the identification of beliefs and intentions of an individual, crucial for intentional explanation, requires sensitivity to the interlocking intentions of a community of agents. The perspective of the agent, the oblique expressions in which it is embedded, is still crucial but the holist holds no presumption that it is available only or completely to the agent. Second, a grasp of social practice is necessary to situate individual beliefs, desires, and actions. This is less a function of mental operations in individual heads and more of practical know-how. Without practical understanding, as anthropologists testify and as philosophers who have worked on problems of translation and cross-cultural understanding know only too well, intellectual effort, no matter how sincere, is puerile.

14

What Makes Something Social?*

Consider the following examples of social entities: a priest; capital; the high table; the state of being unemployed; the flag symbolizing the nation; the prime minister requesting the dissolution of the assembly; fascism. What must all these objects, persons, ideas, states of affairs, actions, and events possess in order to be classified as social, as distinct from merely physical or mental phenomena? What, in general, is it for something to be or have social as distinct from material and mental properties? Can a criterion be general enough to subsume within it a variety of phenomena, demarcating the lot at the same time from other types of entities and properties?[1]

A fairly common answer to these questions is to assert that the social consists of a pattern of behaviour of two or more persons involving a set of rules, norms, rewards and punishments, rights and powers, and

---

* This paper was first delivered at a workshop organized in Kota in 1990 by V.R. Mehta and later given as a lecture at IIT, Kanpur in 1991. It was subsequently published as 'What Makes Something Social?', in Bijoy Barua and R.S. Mishra (eds), *Social Reality and Tradition*, New Delhi: Rawat Publications, 2006, pp. 37–55.

[1] By criterion, I do not mean necessary and sufficient conditions, not a definition but merely a defensible set of conditions which an entity or a property must possess before it can be called social. Second, this might be taken to be an ontology of the social as well. In other words, without specifying what this relationship between words and the world is, I assume that specifying the concept is also characterizing the entity to which the word is constitutively related. I do not, therefore, see any difference, for present purposes, between elucidating the meaning of the word 'social' and disclosing features of a social entity or property.

so on. Thus, Homans claims that 'for a behaviour to be social implies that when a person acts in a certain way he is at least rewarded or punished by the behaviour of another person.'[2] Skorupski argues that a social characteristic is one whose possession is constituted purely or partly in the existence of rules.[3] On Emmett's view, it is the presence of norms which guarantees the existence of the social.[4] For Elster, the social entails the existence of a pattern of interdependencies between persons involving choices, rewards, and preference structures.[5] Finally, Cohen argues that a description is social 'if it entails an ascription to persons, specified or unspecified—of rights and powers *vis-a-vis* other persons.'[6] I believe these views to be seriously deficient for at least two reasons. First, they work with a view of the social that is too restrictive, leaving out entities or properties that cannot be relegated to the mental or the material world. Second, they fail to pay adequate attention to the possibility of the reduction of the social to the conjunction of the physical and the mental. If the defining characteristics of the social are nothing but physical or mental properties, then we are left without a distinctive conception of the social. The requirement, therefore, that we have a conception of the social which is general enough to pick out all social entities or properties, and distinctive enough to demarcate these from all other types of entities and properties, is not met. To substantiate these points, I examine in detail the views of Cohen.

For Cohen, a person is not a priest as such and nor a piece of wood by nature a high table, they become so only when inserted in a web of social relations. And not all relations are social. For example, the interaction of two persons carrying an object together has no necessary social content. When this action is performed in pursuit of an agreement or under the authority of someone, however, it does. In itself, ploughing a field or making a shoe is not social but it is so when done in exchange

[2] George C. Homans, *Social Behaviour*, London: Routledge and Kegan Paul, 1961, p. 2.

[3] John Skorupski, *Symbol and Theory*, Cambridge: Cambridge University Press, 1983, p. 96.

[4] D. Emmett, *Rules, Roles and Relations*, London: Macmillan, 1966.

[5] Elster's views can be found in Jon Elster, 'Further Thoughts on Marxism, Functionalism and Game Theory', in J. Roemer (ed.), *Analytical Marxism*, Cambridge: Cambridge University Press, 1986, pp. 202–20; and in Jon Elster, *Explaining Technical Change*, Cambridge: Cambridge University Press, 1983, p. 77.

[6] G.A. Cohen, *Karl Marx's Theory of History*, Oxford: Clarendon Press, 1979, p. 94.

for a wage. Therefore, a distinction exists between the material and the social description of things. For example, ploughing a field is a material description of an action because it does not entail the ascription of rights and powers vis-à-vis other persons, that is, no social relations. It follows that from the material characteristics of a thing, one cannot simply deduce its social characteristics. The presence of one does not entail the existence of the other. For Cohen, this shows the irreducibility of the social to the material.

A few clarifications are in order before we proceed any further. First, Cohen (or Cohen's Marx) uses the term 'material' to cover both the physical and the mental.[7] Boring a hole in the ground is a material activity but so also is the technical know-how necessary for it. Techno-logical activity is material as is the more speculative, scientific activity. Second, by suggesting that the mere act of carrying something together (or ploughing a field) is not social, he claims that the other-regarding feature of an action is not sufficient for making it social; it must be other-regarding in a special way. It is not enough that action be inten-tionally oriented to the other. Only those other-regarding actions are social whose intentional content contains an ascription of rights and powers vis-à-vis other persons. To be social, an action must possess an intentional content that is already social. Likewise, an object, event, or state of affairs is social if it possesses or entails the presence of a social intention.

Let us apply Cohen's criterion to the following sets of examples.
1. The desire to eat/desire to eat beef rather than dog meat/the taboo on dog meat.
2. Walking/walking upright/walking upright to defy a superior.
3. Bronze/a statue in bronze/the bronze statue as a commodity for sale in the market.
4. The sensation of something external and forceful/the idea of god/ the idea of god performing a distinct ideological function.

Clearly, all items placed first in each set is a physical or a mental entity. Similarly, items placed last are social entities. This much would be agreed by almost anyone wishing to make a contrast between the social and the material. However, in Cohen's view, the second item in each set is material. The desire to eat beef, walking upright, the bronze statue, the idea of god, involve only physical and mental characteristics and therefore, are not social. They do not entail the ascription of rights

[7] Ibid., p. 47.

or powers to any other person. While it is true that rights or powers are not entailed by these descriptions, their inclusion in the material rather than the social world appears odd. For we know that the desire to eat beef is not universal and particular societies have a lot to do with why it is not. We also know that the idea of a statue or that of god is specific to societies and could not just have sprung arbitrarily from the minds of individuals. Of course, to have come into existence in some and not in other societies does not by itself show that the entity in question is social but, at the very least, it provides some basis, however weak, for the view that the society in question has something to do with its existence. It follows that if we wish to include them in our inventory of social entities, we must fish out some criterion which makes this possible. We must look for a criterion of the social which is general enough to include all these entities but which continues to show these to be different from material or mental entities.

Nothing said above constitutes, even resembles an argument against Cohen's classification. But further examples help underline the oddity of his criterion: a solitary prayer, writing a diary, going alone on a summer holiday, the use of language, fashions, norms of consumption, friendship. On Cohen's criterion, all these are material, or mental, or both but not social because they do not entail an ascription of rights and powers to persons. The first three, quite simply, involve no other person and therefore, cannot be social; the remaining do but are not social because they do not entail the ascription of rights and powers. This result is counter-intuitive, however. Something about each of these examples inhibits us from excluding them from the social world.

Here, Cohen might reply that rights and powers need not be entailed but be simply presupposed by every particular description of entity, property, or act. But, I fail to see how rights and powers are even presupposed by, say, the act of reading a newspaper or brushing one's teeth every morning. Yet, both these acts seem neither merely physical or mental and seem to presuppose some fact about the particular societies where they occur. Something is amiss in Cohen's classification.

I think an analogy can help grasp what is wrong in Cohen's way of marking the distinction. Human beings are biological organisms, clearly distinguished from the rest of the physical world by virtue of certain characteristics which they alone possess. Undoubtedly, their outstanding, even defining feature is their capacity for self-consciousness. Now, it would be a terrible mistake to take this feature as the critical one which distinguishes them from the inanimate, physical world. It would even be worse if this were believed to be the individuating feature of biological creatures more generally. This would result in relegating almost all remaining biological entities to the inanimate world. Man is a biological entity but from this it does not follow that any feature that is capable of distinguishing him would also differentiate all other biological entities from the rest of the physical world. An analogous mistake is made by Cohen and others. A very specific form assumed by the social is picked out as the mark distinguishing the social from the material, thus relegating a large class of social entities to the material world. Since the social so commonly takes the form of persons involving rights or power, it has been confused with the idea of social, generally. Although every instance involving rights and powers is social, not every thing social involves rights and powers. The criterion offered by Cohen is too narrow and restrictive to do justice to the wide variety of entities and properties which to my mind are social.

However, let us suppose that the criterion provided by Cohen does cover all relevant social phenomena. One might still persist in asking: is the social irreducible to the material? As we have seen, for Cohen this is indeed the case because from a material description one can not derive a social one. This argument is mistaken. Consider an event, say, the death of a person. From the mere description of the death of person one can not derive how the death occurred. A person can die in a number of ways but from this fact it does not follow that these different ways of dying are different in *kind* from each other or from the event of death itself. All these can equally be provided a material description. Failure of logical entailment does not by itself show irreducibility. Moreover, we know that at least on one view, logical irreducibility is compatible with nomological reducibility; indeed, is a condition of nomological reducibility. If this is so, the underivability of social from material descriptions does not show the irreducibility of one to the other. Let us suppose, however, that neither of the considerations specified is relevant. Does irreducibility follow on Cohen's own terms? I fear not. Recall that for Cohen a description is social *if* it entails the ascription of rights and powers vis-à-vis persons. But power can be given a wholly physical description. Even if power is taken to be an intentional notion, it remains material, for intentionality is a mental property and on Cohen's account, all mental properties are material. Similarly, rights are a matter of expectations and beliefs and these are standardly taken to be mental entities. So, even if it involves more than one body and mind, the social content of intentions, which gives actions a social quality, is reducible to something physical and mental. The mere presence of more than one body and mind may create a new property but not a new *type* of property. A collection of material entities is still a material entity. There is nothing in Cohen's account to suggest that the social is irreducible to the material. The mere fact that entailment does not go through, at least by itself, does not show irreducibility.

I have argued that Cohen provides a criterion not of the social in general but of a specific form assumed by the social. He has arbitrarily selected one particular kind of social entity and built out of it a general conception of the social when, in fact, the social entity in question already presupposes another, more general, perhaps even more fundamental criterion. As a result, Cohen's concept leaves out a vast area of social life, wrongly relegating it to the physical or the mental, to what he calls the material. I have also claimed that even if this conception of the social was found to be the most general one available, it would still fail to be an adequate concept of the *social* because it is reducible to the mental and the physical. Even if Cohen's criterion was found to have unrestricted application, covering all types of entities with something in common, it would fail to pick out anything distinctively social. Instead, it refers to a collection of mere mental and physical entities, or physical entities with physical and mental properties. I believe this to be true not only for Cohen's but for all other criteria mentioned earlier. Any specification of the social in terms of rules or norms is still much too restrictive. Social entities, not governed by norms or rules exist. Moreover, rules, norms, rewards, etc., may, unless demonstrated otherwise, be reducible to physical and mental entities. We conclude then that we are as yet without a general and irreducible conception of the social.

In order to arrive at this criterion, I suggest that we examine the relevant work of Durkheim. Reasons for this are fairly obvious. He was the first to seek a criterion of the social that would individuate non-material entities and properties. Second, he tried to grapple with this problem with a methodological purpose in mind, namely, to establish the autonomy of the social sciences with respect to physics, biology, and psychology. He tried to argue for autonomous social explanations on the basis of a sui generis social reality. This makes his work especially relevant to the philosophy of the social sciences.

To begin with, let me set aside some utterly misplaced criticisms of the Durkheimian position. Durkheim has often been accused of overlooking the material sub-stratum of the social, that is, several biological individuals with their innate mental properties. This is absurd. He says, 'undoubtedly, no collective entity could be produced if there is no individual consciousness,' but then goes on to add, 'this is a necessary but not a sufficient condition.'[8] Nor does he deny the dependence of social phenomena upon general human nature. He says, 'the general characteristics of human nature play their part in the work of elaboration from which social life results...these can be realized only if human nature is not opposed to them.'[9] He even concedes that 'the elementary properties from which social facts emerge are contained in the embryo within the minds of individuals.'[10] But, he insists that they emerge only after 'minds of individuals have been transformed by association.'[11] If social facts are to emerge, individual consciousness must be associated and combined in a certain way. Although human nature does not directly produce or provide a specific form to social phenomena, it certainly makes them possible. It provides the indeterminate matter which the social factor fashions and transforms. Its contribution is made up exclusively of the very general states, vague and thus malleable predispositions which of themselves could not assume the definite and complex forms which characterize social phenomena, that is, if other agents did not intervene. In sum, social phenomena depend on the mental and the physical, both of which make them possible but are distinct and emergent from and therefore, irreducible to either or both. Putting the matter more crisply, one might say that the social is supervenient on the mental and the physical both in and outside the biological individual.

The non-individualist is also accused of failing to grant human agency its central role in social affairs. Durkheim has often been flayed, even by those sympathetic to him, for having committed this colossal blunder. But evidence from his methodological writings provides a different picture. He says that 'It is very true that society comprises no active forces other than those of individuals.'[12] Social things, he says, 'are realized only by men, they are products of human activity.'[13] I believe

---

[8] É. Durkheim (edited by S. Lukes, trans. by W.D. Halls), *The Rules of Sociological Method*, Basingstoke: Macmillan, 1982, p. 129.

[9] Ibid., pp. 130–1.

[10] Ibid., p. 252.

[11] Ibid.

[12] Ibid., p. 251.

[13] Ibid., p. 62.

to be a truism, hardly ever denied by any reasonable non-individualist, that only living, automated biological organisms of a specific type can make things move in the sense relevant here or invest life into non-living matter. In human societies, it is individuals who provide the 'push and pull' characteristic of social change and reproduction. They constitute the primeval active element. The social, we have already said, is supervenient on biological individuals and therefore on their activity. The social not only consists of but is also dependent upon the active biological individual. A non-individualist contesting that the social depends on forces inherent in biological individuals does so on pain of sheer absurdity. But he also points out that the activity of *biological* individuals is insufficient for the working of specifically *human* societies. The real matter in dispute between the individualist and the non-individualist is not whether human agency is explanatorily crucial but what kind of agency it is. For the non-individualist, the specifically human activity is not reducible to the behaviour of biological individuals with their primitive or innate desires, beliefs, and intentions. So, this much is clear. Social reality does not hover over and above material reality; rather it is rooted in and dependent upon it, and in particular upon the vital movements, that is, the activity of human biological organisms. This fails to specify, however, just what the social is.

It is commonly acknowledged that, for Durkheim, two character-istics distinguish social from other phenomena: externality and con-straint. Social phenomena are external to and exercise constraint over individuals. As a criterion for picking out social entities and properties, this seems extremely dubious. Neither seem necessary or sufficient for identifying the distinctively social. For a start, any natural phenomenon is both external to and exercises constraint over individuals. What then is the distinguishing mark of the social? To this Durkheim could rightly protest that externality plus constraint is not meant to provide a definition of the social but constitute useful guidelines for pragmatic identification during methodological research. In pragmatic contexts, one is looking for a useful and approximate guide, for only a rough specification, not for an accurate, comprehensive inventory of features by which something is sure to be identified. Sadly, this plea does not save the criterion, beset as it is with a number of other problems.

The first centres around the constraining property of social phenom-ena. Clearly, some social entities are both internal to individuals and do not constrain them. The ability to construct arguments belongs to in-dividuals. Qua ability it does not exist outside them. Nor does it appear to constrain them in any obvious way. Of course, arguments cannot be produced independently of the rules on which they depend, but rather than constrain anyone, rules enable individuals to achieve things that cannot otherwise be realized. Individuals are able to do a large number of things by virtue of certain social characteristics and while the exercise of these abilities may constrain other individuals, it does not in any way constrain the agent himself. Indeed, commentators have rightly noted a deep ambiguity in Durkheim's use of this notion. For him, the term 'constraint' covers the authority of rules and norms, both those enabling the successful execution of actions and those which invoke sanctions when violated, that is to say, both constitutive and regulative rules; the causal influence as well as psychological compulsion of ecological factors and crowd situations; and the more general process of acculturation which require that individuals be trained into the ideas and values of the community.[14] On what grounds, one might ask, do we put all these under one single rubric? Is this justifiable? More importantly, as Durkheim himself recognizes, not all of these are constraining. What then justifies the use of the word 'constraint' to cover all these phenomena? Even Durkheim's plea that his criterion suggests not that every social fact necessarily constrains but only that it has the capability to do so does not validate the use of this word in the present context. One can put the point simply by saying with Giddens that social facts do not only constrain but enable.[15] Therefore, the use of the term 'constraint' is, in this context, misleading, at best. However, it does not follow that some other related word cannot be used to bring together these phenomena under one rubric.

Consider the following examples. If I follow traffic rules, I shall, unless I am in Delhi, reach my workplace safely but if I do not, I shall cause an accident, incur a fine, or at least invite abuse. If an industrialist uses modern technology and techniques of management, large profits would accrue but if obsolete technology is employed, the industrial unit is likely to be ruined. If I speak a language shared by other members of my society, I will communicate with them but not if I invent my own private idiolect. Traffic rules, modern technology, techniques of management, language, are social facts which exist outside any individual and have to be endured but they enable the individual to

[14] See Steven Lukes, *Emile Durkheim*, Middlesex, UK: Penguin Books, 1982, p. 12.

[15] A. Giddens, *The Constitution and Society*, Cambridge: Polity Press, 1984, chapter 1.

achieve objectives at least as much as, in some other respect, they constrain. Indeed, it may be truer to say that they constrain the individual only to assist him realize his aims. But something which enables us in this way can hardly be called a constraint. If I wish to become a good painter, I must, sometime during my life, follow established masters. Is this a constraint on me or something which would enable me to better realize my objective?

Clearly, we require a concept that subsumes properties of the social in virtue of which it is outside and endured by us, which refers to those properties of social facts which make them impervious to easy manipulation and control by individuals. Such a concept is indeed present in Durkheim's own discussion of these issues. He says:

> we have seen that social facts possess this property of *resistance*. Far from being a product of our will, they determine it from without. They are like moulds into which we are forced to cast our actions. The necessity is often ineluctable. But even if we succeed in triumphing, the opposition we have encountered suffices to alert us that we are faced with something independent of ourselves.[16]

Again, he says, 'Even when we struggle to free from these rules and successfully break them, it is never without being forced to fight against them.'[17] On Durkheim's view, we are not imprisoned in our social world. We can break lose from it but not entirely without struggle, largely because they offer resistance to us. The notion of resistance is weaker than that of constraint. To be constrained is to be virtually paralysed, when the will of the agent is wrested away, his freedom curtailed. On the other hand, resistance can be offered even by things which help you realize your freedom. We can, therefore, readily admit that all social facts are capable of offering resistance, while denying them the power to constrain. Resistance is a property possessed both by those facts which constrain and those which do not. The manner in which resistance is offered differs from case to case but the effect is much the same. Social facts deter the exercise of one's will either to enable one to achieve one's objective or to thwart it. Though not a defining feature, the capacity to offer resistance is an essential characteristic of social phenomena.

One might now reply that for purposes of distinguishing social phenomena, the criterion of resistance is hardly better than the one involving constraint. As is fairly obvious, natural phenomena offer

[16] É. Durkheim, in Lukes (ed.), *The Rules of Sociological Method*, p. 70.
[17] Ibid., p. 51.

resistance in quite the same sense in which social phenomena do. At this juncture, it would help to underline the point behind this criterion. For Durkheim, it is meant to provide a contrast not between physical and social but instead, between mental and social phenomena. More specifically, the intended contrast here is between individually realized mental representations and social entities. The property of resistance helps us to distinguish the social from mental representations that are internal to the individual.[18] Internally realized mental representations are within the control of the individual. On the other hand, social phenomena are outside the individual and because they offer resistance, not easily manipulable. It appears then that externality and the capability of offering resistance are jointly sufficient for distinguishing the social from the mental. Social phenomena, it appears, partake of the physical and the mental world, without being reducible to either or both. With physical phenomena they have in common properties that differentiate them from the mental world and with mental phenomena they share those which distinguish them from physical entities. One implication of this is the following: social phenomena are external to individuals and offer resistance to them but not in the same way as physical phenomena. Clearly, we need to dig deeper to find those phenomena that are external to individuals and offer them resistance but are neither merely physical nor mental, though supervenient on both. What is it that is external to individual consciousness, offers resistance to individual wills but which is constitutively different from the physical in general as well as from the biological individual with all his innate mental states?

For this question, Durkheim has two answers. According to the first, the social consists of manners of acting, thinking, and feeling, even ways of being. For the second, it consists of collective representations and actions. Though distinct, these answers are also closely related. The first answer suggests that actions and mental representations cannot exist without possessing a determinate shape, a form which is social. Things with mental or physical components acquire social characteristics when they acquire form. But, for the second answer, any collective action or representation is by definition social. Collective representations resemble their individual, mental counterparts but unlike the latter, they possess features in common with the physical world: they are external to individuals who they resist. Similarly, in some respects collective actions are like the movement of a billiard ball but unlike them, they

---

[18] Ibid., p. 71.

also possess intentionality. However, their intentional content is not wholly generated internally, by the exclusive effort of the individual. The primitive action of biological individuals may be characterized by such content but not collective action, whose intentional content is produced outside any given individual and has qualities of resistance. This is true not only of collective actions and representations but also of the form of many of our individually realized actions and thoughts. If they are to resemble anything remotely human, our biological desires, perceptions, and behaviour must be cast in a social mould. Without it, our mental world is formless, our actions unstructured. This then is a plausible characterization of the social: it consists of the form of acts and representations, both individually and collectively realized, that are external and resistant to biological individuals on whom they supervene. This is what Durkheim means when he says that social life is neither material, nor an aggregate of individual psychological states and acts but sui generis.[19]

What are forms of representations and actions? The prime candidates for collective representations, in Durkheim's view, are concepts and categories. Together, categories form the stable grid that by enclosing thought make it possible. They constitute the framework of intelligence. Following Kant, Durkheim argues that categories order individual sensations into distinct experiences, but they do so in the most general way possible. Therefore, they are applicable to all types of reality. Concepts, on the other hand, have the same function as categories, but their restricted generality enables them to lend thought and experience a specificity and distinction they lack otherwise. Both are intrinsically collective and therefore, distinct from any purely mental entity. What evidence or argument does Durkheim furnish for this claim? Against the empiricists and with Kant, he argues for the irreducibility of concepts to sensations. Concepts are not sensations because they are characterized by a generality and a necessity that corresponds to nothing else in reality. Sensations and their contents, if they can be so called at all,

always rely upon a determinate object, or upon a collection of objects of the same sort and expresses the momentary condition of a particular consciousness; they are essentially individual and subjective. We therefore have considerable liberty in dealing with the representations of this origin.[20]

[19] Ibid., p. 250.
[20] É. Durkheim, *The Elementary Forms of Religious Life*, London: Allen & Unwin, 1976, p. 14.

On the other hand, concepts and especially categories have a stability that sensations lack. Nor are we at liberty with respect to concepts; rather they impose themselves upon and exercise an authority over us. For instance, we can hardly think of an object existing outside space or time. The matter can be simply put like this: sensations are the property of individuals, are momentary, unstructured, and manipulable at will. If concepts and categories grew out of or were even built out of sensations by individuals, they would have all these characteristics. However, they possess properties which differ in kind from sensations or from any other mental entity of that sort. It follows that they are not built by individuals and could not be subjective.

From where do they come then? Here Durkheim parts company with Kant and other apriorists, for whom concepts and categories exist in the mind of individuals, and are inherent in human nature. True, for Kant, they impose themselves on us just as any other fundamental element of our nature and are therefore, objective and unmanipulable but all the same, they are mental and individual. For Durkheim, this provides no explanation of concepts, however. He says, 'It is no explanation of anything to say that it is inherent in human nature.'[21] The correct answer for Durkheim is that these are built as a result of an 'an immense cooperation' of individuals,

which stretches out not only in space but also in time; to make them, a multitude of mind have associated, united and combined their ideas and sentiments; A special intellectual activity is therefore concentrated in them which is infinitely richer and more complex than that of the individual.[22]

Concepts then do not spring from a divine source or from the heads of individuals but are a result of the cooperative effort of individuals. They exist outside individual minds. We receive them and therefore, cannot on our own beget them. They force themselves on us, resist us, and are therefore not easily manipulable. Concepts have all the features of a social entity. A similar case can also be made for collective actions.

Let me recapitulate this Durkheimian view. Sensations are private and individual. Collectively held and generated categories and concepts give these sensations a shape. It is these informed sensations that are experienced by human beings. Individualized experience, then, is already mediated by a social entity. Of course, being individualized, it has a distinct internal colouration, but it also possesses a communicable

---

[21] Ibid.
[22] Ibid., p. 16.

common meaning. Similarly, mere biological behaviour is internally caused and individual in character. But no human behaviour is entirely unstructured. It has a determinate shape, a form, it belongs to a type. This format or structure, too, is collectively generated. Individually realized action, therefore, is already, in a significant sense, social. When one further examines its content, it is seen to have an additional social content, for no action is free of conceptual content and these, as we have seen earlier, are intrinsically social. Furthermore, when a socially mediated experience is realized not in any one individual but among several individuals, we have collective experience which is very strongly social. Likewise, when socially mediated action is realized not individually but among several individuals, we have a form of collective action which has a thick social character, that is strongly social.

Let us return to some of the examples mentioned at the beginning of this essay. On Cohen's criteria, the desire to eat beef, walking upright, the bronze statue, the idea of god are material entities. On Durkheim's criteria, because they involve concepts, these are not material but social entities. Individuals on their own could never develop the idea of god, an abhorrence for beef, or even imagine sculpting. All these presuppose a system of classification, a conceptual scheme, a collectively produced culture sustained by humans. This suggests that two types of social facts exist: conceptual or perhaps cultural and institutional. Conceptual facts only obliquely involve social relations, while institutional facts implicate them more directly. The two are also distinguished by the fact that one of them does but the other does not entail the presence of some system of rights and powers. Cohen's view of the social is founded wholly on these institutional entities and fails to take into account conceptual entities. This is why it is narrow and excludes a very large number of entities, properties, states, and events from the social world. Now, institutional facts also presuppose or directly involve cultural facts. This means that an institutional entity comes into being when something is inserted into an already existing social context. In other words, an institutional fact is doubly social. This precisely is what makes it strongly or maximally social. But both types of facts are social because they are produced collectively by humans. I think one of the functions of the concept of the social is to pick out entities that are collectively produced from among those which are merely given to us (within or outside us). This particular point about the social is well captured in Durkheim's account.

I believe that this Durkheimian account is along the right lines but also that it is inadequate. This is so because the representation component in the idea of collective *representation* and the collective component in the concept of *collective* action is misleading. I think the point is better conveyed by using the concepts of shared meanings and practices. However, why I think so is the topic of another, longer essay.[23]

[23] These issues are discussed at length in Rajeev Bhargava, *Individualism in Social Science*, Oxford: Clarendon Press, 1992.

15

Teleology and Ethnocentrism
in Social Science*

In much contemporary discussions, teleological thinking in social science is thought to be pernicious, a form of intellectual lethargy to be fought and overcome. I find it difficult to wholly agree with this view. Teleology, I claim, takes different forms. While some are best discarded, others constitute the very stuff of human sciences. In the first section, therefore, my purpose, is wholly analytical, to distinguish different kinds of teleological claims and sift the good from the bad.

The second section deals with problems of ethnocentrism, many of which were first recognized only when a legitimate role was accorded to *verstehen* in the methodology of social sciences. Ethnocentrism was seen as a danger only when the internal descriptions of the participants of the observed culture were taken seriously. The argument of this section is that it is necessary to acknowledge the risk of ethnocentrism not only in the understanding but also in the explanation of other cultures. I accept that explanations of other cultures should not be wholly constituted by the internal descriptions of its members. However, from this it follows neither that explanations are inevitably ethnocentric nor that they possess some magical internal property by virtue of which they escape the pitfalls of ethnocentrism. Social scientists cannot get away with the plausible plea that while ethnocentrism has to be carefully avoided in understanding persons of other cultures, one escapes it

* This paper was presented at a conference organized by the Indo-Dutch Programme on Alternatives in Development (IDPAD) in New Delhi sometime in March 1990.

the moment a valid scientific explanation is offered. Nothing in the nature of explanations makes them necessarily free of ethnocentrism. Explanations are as much shaped by cultural contexts as descriptions.

TELEOLOGY

I shall begin by noting the distinction between description and explanation. A description of something merely purports to offer an account of what the thing is or what its relationships are to other things. For example, the statement, 'A' met 'B', describes an event. Delhi is the capital of India is also a description about both Delhi and India and the way they relate to each other. Descriptions can be more or less informative. For example, the statement, A met B at time 11 a.m., is more informative than the statement, A met B. They can also be more or less accurate. A met B somewhere in Delhi is less accurate than the statement that they met at Nehru Memorial Library. Generally, descriptions answer all kinds of what, when, where, and who-questions. On the other hand, explanations are answers to why-questions, probably also of how-questions. A met B in order to discuss prospects of alternatives to mainstream notions of development is an explanation of why they met. Explanations must be more than merely informative and accurate. They must make intelligible connections between phenomena. The relation between description and explanation is asymmetrical in the sense that while descriptions are presupposed by explanation, the reverse is not true. Descriptions need not presuppose explanations. Clearly, we may know that A and B met without knowing why but if we know why they met, it cannot be that we are ignorant that they met at all.

Following this distinction between description and explanation, we may introduce a distinction between teleological descriptions and teleological explanations. A teleological description consists of a set of statements that attribute a purpose or a function to persons, things, events, processes, or states. I intend to go to the mountains; the function of a pen is to write; it is the function of the liver to maintain blood glucose levels; religion ameliorates the suffering of the masses; world history displays the progressive realization of man's mastery over nature are all examples of teleological descriptions. Biological organisms have livers because it is their function to maintain blood glucose levels, or religion was concocted or persists in order to ameliorate the suffering of the masses, or there would be no history if man did not have the objective of mastering nature are examples of teleological explanations. Here

I shall not go into the important question of what turns teleological descriptions into explanations, and while I make use of the distinction between description and explanation in the next section, I do not further pursue the difference between teleological description and teleological explanation. I have introduced this distinction only because I want it plainly recognized that my claims are restricted only to teleological descriptions and steer clear from the vexed question concerning the validity of teleological explanations in the social sciences.

Teleological descriptions assume several forms. Some are *subjectively teleological*. These descriptions necessarily involve an actor with his subjective mental states. A description involving one or more agent with desires, purposes, choices, and goals, or projects is subjectively teleological when all these are realized in their consciousness prior to their action. I turned the other way in order to avoid meeting an acquaintance; Ceaser wished to cross the Rubicon; it was part of Gandhi's overall life plan to defeat the British at their own game; most cricket teams play to win; the capitalist class produces only in order to make profit are examples of subjectively teleological descriptions. *Objectively teleological* descriptions eschew any reference to the subjective mental states of agents either because they are irrelevant or because they deal with systems without mental states. Though not in possession of any mental states, all biological systems exhibit teleological properties.[1] Descriptions attributing such properties to biological systems are objectively teleological. For instance, the function of the heart is to pump blood into blood vessels. The heart has a purpose, a goal which is realized independently of the mental states of its possessor; indeed, it is realized even in biological organisms without any mental states. Such descriptions may be called *bio-teleological*.

These need to be distinguished, however, from another kind of descriptions about objectively teleological properties which belong only to human beings and their societies. For example, we might say that the purpose of the agent was realized directly in her action without first entering her consciousness. I change the gears of my car without always planning to do so in advance. As I enter my house, I open the door of my room but I do not first think about it and then execute this action. Such actions are goal directed but do not make reference to any

---

[1] So do mechanical systems such as thermostats. However, whereas mechanical systems have derived purposes which they would not possess unless designed by purposive creatures, biological systems display these properties intrinsically.

mental states. One might also call such goals objectively teleological. Such objective purposes may even be found as properties of social practices, institutions, and whole social systems. We might say, for example, that it is the purpose of elections to select a person or a policy out of a concatenation of individual decisions, independent of whether or not all individuals believe this, or that capitalist economic relations are geared to making profits independent of the intentions and motivations of individual capitalists. In deference to the philosopher who did most to revive interest in such descriptions, I shall call them *Hegelian teleological descriptions*. Objective teleological descriptions then are of two types: biological and Hegelian.

Other kinds of teleological descriptions also exist, those that involve progressive changes over time and therefore, attribute developmental properties to processes. Such descriptions may be called *developmental*. Here, within an overarching goal, G, a series of intermediate goals (g1...gn) are progressively realized over time, each successive goal being dependent upon the materialization of the prior one. Goal, g1, may then be seen as a moment or stage towards the realization of goal, g2, and both, g1 and g2, may in turn be seen as stages in the actualization of g3...and the whole series, g1...gn, are viewed as stages in the realization of the goal, G. Developmental descriptions involve intermediate and final goals sequentially linked in an orderly fashion to generate a pattern. Any description of an ordered sequence of stages that a system must undergo if it is to reach its final goal can be designated as a developmental description. Hegel, Marx, Comte, and lesser figures such as Rostow provide such descriptions. In genetic psychology, descriptions of the moral and cognitive development of a child provided by Piaget also exemplify developmental descriptions.

Such developmental descriptions can also be classified under two rubrics. The first possess universal application and may therefore be called *monistic*. For example, one might argue that the entire world history be seen as the progressive realization of freedom (which itself is understood universalistically). Each civilization or kind of society may then be viewed as linked to each other along a developing hierarchical chain in which each successive civilization or society more fully realizes the idea of freedom present in preceding ones. Satellite societies, which only inadequately realize the conception of freedom already embodied in principal centres, must either perish or wait before they have passed through all the stages that more perfect societies have undergone. Perhaps the view that progress in history is to be measured by the development of the productive forces also exemplifies this form of teleology. But such universalistic developmental descriptions need to be distinguished from those which apply to specific societies or civilizations alone. These descriptions attribute developing teleological properties to societies without imposing on them a uniform pattern of development. Each society is seen to possess its own history, development pattern, and perhaps, a plurality of goals, some of which fit each other, while others cause disjunction. Likewise, different historical patters coexist, some peacefully and others with unease and turbulence. Such descriptions tread a discursive space between denials of historical teleology and progress altogether and affirmations of a uniform, universally applicable historical pattern, a single vision of progress. They, therefore, allow for alternative patterns of development. These may be called *pluralistic developmental descriptions*.

To recapitulate, at least five types of teleological descriptions exist. The first is designated as (i) subjective teleological. Objective teleological descriptions are classified into two types. The first I dubbed (ii) bio-teleological and the second, (iii) Hegelian. Next, I distinguished between two kinds of diachronic teleologies which I designated as (iv) monistic developmental descriptions and (v) pluralistic developmental descriptions.

When claims are made that teleology is to be expunged from social science, are all forms to be indiscriminately discarded or only some? It is now time to assess if each of these forms of teleological descriptions is pernicious. I believe the first kind of teleological descriptions would find easy and ready takers. Reductionist strategies in social science, such as behaviourism, have long been discredited. There is hardly anyone today who prescribes a logical reduction of mental terms such as purposes and goals to behavioural and physical concepts. It follows that subjective teleological descriptions such as 'Napolean planned the invasion of Russia' could not reasonably be opposed by social scientists and historians.

What about objective teleological descriptions? Of the two, bio-teleological descriptions appear wholly dispensable for the reason that distinctively human activity is shot through with concepts. Such descriptions apply only to non-concept bearing phenomena. While biological environment with teleological properties has only an external description, human environment possesses an internal description as well. That is to say, human situations and actions mean something to the agents; people have a conceptual grasp of their situation which makes all the difference to their actions. Human behaviour does not occur in order to realize a purpose; rather a large number of human actions are performed, with varying degrees of conceptual understanding of the relevant circumstances, to realize goals that matter. However, bio-teleological and Hegelian descriptions should not be conflated. Because Hegelian descriptions also refer to conceptual phenomena, opposition to the one does not entail battling against the other. We must, therefore, enquire if independent reasons against them exist.

To assess if objective goals exist independent of the subjective consciousness of agents is part of a larger exercise of examining if concepts or meanings can be objective. This is because distinctively human goals are largely embedded in concepts. Therefore, we need to ask whether objective meanings exist or if conceptual structures can exist independent of the subjective mental states of individuals. Indeed, we need to enquire if concepts are identical with mental entities.[2] Now, if one can show that concepts or meanings are not only or wholly mental entities, that they have a non-subjective, that is, objective existence, then we would have shown that a sub-set of such concepts, namely, desires, goals, and values can also be non-subjective. This is a difficult issue, requiring several long and complicated arguments, well beyond the limits of my ability and the scope of this essay. What I would do, however, is to present the contours of the argument that makes the case for such views less implausible.

There are two facets to this issue. One aspect involves showing that goals are not merely attitudes in the mind. The second involves showing that the individuation of goals involves extra-mental, physical, and social factors. That goal-directedness can be directly displayed in individual or inter-individual action is evident from one of the examples discussed earlier. There are many actions with intrinsic goals that are not manifest in the consciousness of the agent, are directly inscribed in action. This conception of mental states and action goes against the view that action is behaviour that is caused by mental states. On this view, which takes its inspiration less from Descartes and more from Aristotle and Hegel, action is a primitive term, not further reducible to anything more basic such as mental states, bodily behaviour, and causal relations; rather, purposes inhabit actions.[3] Actions

[2] I take it that, whether or not it is immediately transparent, anything realized in the consciousness or in the mind of the agent is a mental entity.

[3] See Charles Taylor, *Philosophical Papers*, Vols 1 and 2, Cambridge: Cambridge University Press, 1985.

are intrinsically intentional, directed towards something or the other, just as much as mental states are. Intentionality, in other words, can be realized either in the mind or directly in action. Goals are not just attitudes in the minds of individuals but can be immediately displayed in the action or interactions of individuals.

The second part of the issue has to do with showing that conceptual content is not mentally but physically and socially individuated. The work of Putnam and Burge is extremely helpful on this.[4] Both show the reliance of mental and conceptual content on non-mental factors. Moreover, Wittgenstein and his followers have provided strong reasons against the view that understanding concepts is identical with the possession of an image or of any other mental ability; rather, grasping a concept is to be in possession of the ability to use signs in situationally relevant ways.[5] Indeed, concepts are not mental entities but simply signs used in appropriate contexts. Identifying goals, too, is not a matter of entering an alien mind but grasping the relevant goal-related concept in its appropriate context and use. Goals do not exist only or wholly in the heads of individuals. They exist directly in practices and are identified in relation to what people are doing vis-à-vis each other. Profit making is not always an idea carried in the head by the capitalist but exists in practices and social relations. It is an objective property of these non-subjective states and processes. The purpose of a ritual can not be identified by examining the subjective states of individuals but probably lies directly embedded in the practices and can be understood in relation to the relevant social context. If this is so, Hegelian teleological descriptions cannot be expunged from social science. Those who fight this form of teleology had better give sound intellectual reasons in favour of the view that all concepts, including goal-related purposes, can only have a mental existence or else, accept this kind of objective teleological descriptions.

What about developmental descriptions? I believe monistic descriptions stand thoroughly discredited and for good reason. The view that history displays one pattern of development into which all societies must somehow fit, that there is one criteria of progress by which all

---

[4] Hilary Putnam, *Philosophical Papers*, Vol. 2, Cambridge: Cambridge University Press, 1975; and T. Burge, 'Individualism and the Mental', *Midwest Studies in Philosophy*, Vol. 4, 1979, pp. 73–121.

[5] See, for example, C. Mcginn, *Wittgenstein on Meaning*, Oxford: Blackwell, 1984.

societies are to be judged, and that some societies lie at the apex of a linear movement of the people of the world and these are better in all respects than those which have been left behind are views that can be backed neither by evidence nor by an interpretative argument. The course of the whole world simply can not be bound together by single, universal reason. Even if we agree that there is a cumulative growth in the overall freedom of the people of some societies, it does not follow that all events of significance occurred for the sake of the realization of freedom, or that they were significant solely because, to some degree, they helped realize freedom. Similarly, it is, I imagine, difficult to find claimants for the view that capitalism is superior in *all* respects to feudalism and that every existing pre-capitalist society must follow the same pattern because it is predestined to achieve capitalism and in exactly the same way as western societies. If indeed such monistic developmental descriptions are still alive, the war against them must be waged. If remnants of such descriptions are still found in social science, a battle against them must be planned. This form of teleological reasoning must be defeated.

But, what of pluralistic developmental descriptions? Critics of the first view have frequently conflated the two and attacked history, development, and progress as such. That some specific goals of particular societies have endured over time in a modified form is not always easy to deny. It is not implausible that some teleological properties of societies will form the basis of other properties that would, in future, be realized if not thwarted by other competing goals or accidental causes. Each society, in this sense, may have its own distinct pattern of development, ridden no doubt with discontinuities and fragmentation, and discernible only with legitimate interpretative fiat. I find it hard then to discard pluralist developmental descriptions.

Let me sum up: the claim that teleology is a malaise and so must be fought could mean different things. Since teleological descriptions can take at least five different forms, the claim can be disambiguated in at least five different ways. Subjective teleological descriptions uncontroversially form a large part of human life and so, the battle against them is wholly unjustified. At any rate, hardly anyone today is waging it. The validity of Hegelian and pluralistic developmental descriptions is contested but largely due to the mentalistic assumptions of competing frameworks. I believe good reasons exist not to fight them. On the other hand, the presence of bio-teleological descriptions is a malaise indeed, a form of functionalist positivism of which social science is best rid. Much the same is true of monistic developmental descriptions. Advocacy of such descriptions is a direct outgrowth of ethnocentrism. All premature universalistic claims are ethnocentric: a pattern exhibited by one society, usually one's own, is imposed on some other. The pattern of one's culture is hailed as actually or potentially present everywhere. Contemporary goals of a particular society are projected backwards, on to its past, or else, present objectives of a society are seen exclusively in the light of its past goals. This projection and extrapolation of particular goals across space and time is part of the general problem of ethnocentrism. Monistic developmental descriptions are one particular form assumed by ethnocentrism. In attacking them, one is not really assailing teleology as much as combating ethnocentrism.

ETHNOCENTRISM
The recognition of the problem of ethnocentrism in social science is tied to the decline in the dominance of reductive forms of naturalism. Generally, naturalistic modes of scientific discourse fail to see the significance of ethnocentrism for one principal reason: they bypass the self-descriptions of people. They fail to take seriously the agent's own point of view, how she sees her situation, understands her actions; in brief, they disregard her conceptual world. But, this precisely is what leads to ethnocentrism—the error of imposing on another culture the manner of seeing and conceiving one's own. It is to assume that there exists only one way of thinking and acting, that is, one's own. If we bypass the internal description of agents, we expose ourselves to the danger of allowing our beliefs and desires, thoughts and values, govern the understanding of another culture. Ethnocentric descriptions are generated when we are unable to escape our thoughts and values in the attribution of desires and beliefs to others, when the identification of the goals of other cultures is crucially determined by our own conception of possible goals.

Non-naturalist social science strives to avoid this pitfall. It sees the perils of ethnocentrism precisely because it takes seriously the internal descriptions of agents. It accepts that descriptions are context specific and cherishes sensitivity to the context of the agent as a necessary requirement for getting them right. For the non-naturalist, to understand and accurately identify something, we must grasp the description which individuates it, which makes it what it is. But such descriptions are available from within a certain specific stock of interpretations, from a particular web of significations or meanings that provide the context and the background for that thing. This holds true not only for practices, institutions, and social relations but also for things and persons. A particular way of commemorating the dead, the parliament, the relation between lord and vassal, the national flag, the aesthete, all presuppose a cultural context for their individuation. They are constructed from a particular set of conceptual resources. The internal structure of all descriptions, we might say, is shot through with specific contexts. Descriptions are necessarily context dependent. The attempt to finesse this understanding, to leap over these descriptions by forcing upon them a skin from which all the conceptual fat has been removed is the surest way of getting them wrong. To remove this context, to provide these objects with merely an external description is to construct a different object altogether. It is not merely to misdescribe but to completely misconstrue it. In any case, external descriptions claiming freedom from all contexts are brewed in one context or another. Usually, these are ethnocentric descriptions masquerading as ones unstained by prejudice; this is why one has to strive to avoid them. If we are to get under the skin of other cultures, we must eventually, if not initially, remove our own biases and preferences, and scrupulously avoid mistaking the particular for the universal.

I believe it is being increasingly realized among social scientists that we require internal descriptions to identify objects of another culture, that our understanding has to be context specific and therefore, as free as possible from ethnocentrism. However, the story in the case of the explanation of other cultures may well be different. Here, one may reasonably argue that scientific explanations need not be couched in the language available to the object-culture, that the *explanantia* might possess a description unavailable to the agents under study. To hold the view that the description of explanantia be also internally generated is to make suspect and redundant the very practice of social science. While it may be wrong to see a stark structural difference between ordinary understanding and social science, it would be equally erroneous to make them identical. Social science must make available to ordinary agents something they would otherwise not know or else, face extinction. Indeed, it might be argued that, while the positivists were mistaken in having couched both description *and* explanation in an external language, although their attempt to replace internal descriptions was radically misplaced, they might have been correct in demanding of explanations that they be context independent, free from the values and thoughts of the observed culture.

But then, how is one to escape ethnocentrism? On one important view, this is possible only by ensuring that social science possesses a special language of its own, free from both the observed *and* the observing agents. Ethnocentricity is eschewed because science employs a special language, free of all context and therefore, of all socio-cultural specificity. In particular, scientific explanations, by their very nature, are free of all actual contexts and rely only on universal generalizations. So, we need to meet an internal requirement of scientific explanation: internal descriptions must be transcended. However, this does not land us in the thick of ethnocentrism because scientific explanations are intrinsically free of all internal prejudices and preferences. A context-dependent, ethnocentric explanation is not scientific. Thus, while the scientist needs to carefully enter an alien context to understand and obtain accurate, detailed, and informative descriptions on it, and be on guard against the possible intrusion of his own concepts and values in the process of acquiring an alien cultural framework, he need only attend to the internal requirements of science to keep free of ethnocentrism. Ethnocentrism is a threat not to explanation but only to understanding. It is time we examined this important, plausible claim.

Are scientific explanations automatically free from ethnocentrism? Is the scientificity of explanation proof against ethnocentricity? At least one important view in the philosophy of science holds that scientific explanations are free of all contexts, from all pragmatic considerations and therefore, just could not be ethnocentric. Exponents of the deductive-nomological model (D-N model) argue that important though pragmatic considerations are for the help they render in understanding the uses to which we put our explanations and the complex motivations of persons who seek them, they are irrelevant to the logic of scientific explanations. Thus, Hempel, while recognizing that explanations and its cognates in some sense are pragmatic notions, likens it to the notion of mathematic proof which is not subjective in the sense of being relative to and variable with individuals.[6] Scientific research, Hempel says, seeks to account for empirical phenomena by means of laws and theories which are objective in the sense that their empirical implication and evidential support are independent of what particular individuals happen to test or apply them. Much the same is or at least ought to be true of all scientific explanations. We do and must construct a non-pragmatic concept of explanation which is a legitimate abstraction from

[6] Hempel, *Aspects of Scientific Explanation*, New York: Free Press, 1965.

the pragmatic one. This concept need not be in actual use within any scientific community. It is severely idealized, abstracted not only from everyday but also from actual scientific use. Nonetheless, it captures well the rationale and principal intent of scientific explanations. This ideal concept of scientific explanation is free from reference to any/all personal beliefs and interests of individuals as well as from all social and cultural contexts, including that of working scientific communities. As such, it is a relation between truths or pure facts and has little to do with psycho-social (pragmatic) issues like the determination of whether or not a person on a particular occasion counts as uttering an explanation.

This view that scientific explanations are logically free from all contexts has been recently challenged by some philosophers.[7] Critics of the D-N model agree that explanations are answers to why-questions but compel us to focus more on the exact nature of the question to which the proposed explanation is an answer. They mount their critique on the D-N model by first disposing of the view that the syntactical form of the question is a reliable indicator of the specific request being sought. To dig it out, we have to view the request in its proper context as a specific speech act. Let us take an example to see their point.

Consider the question: why did Franz deliver the bottle to K? That this question has as one of its presupposition, the declarative sentence, 'Franz delivered the bottle to K', is obvious enough. What is not immediately visible is that it has a number of other presuppositions, all of which can be illuminated only when the context of the question is examined. For in asking, 'Why did Franz deliver the bottle to K?', we could really be asking a number of distinct questions: (i) why did Franz rather than, say, Max deliver the bottle?; (ii) why did Franz deliver the bottle rather than something else, say a jar?; and (iii) why did Franz deliver the bottle to K rather than to B? The phrase, 'rather than', points to the fact that each of these requests points to a definite range of alternatives, or to what may be described as their contrast class. Therefore, the correct underlying structure of a question is: why is it the case that P in contrast to other members of X, where X refers to a set of recognized alternatives or identifies its contrast class. It is because we

---

[7] These philosophers do not always take their position to the logical extreme to which I have pushed it and for good reason. However, I have deliberately taken it in one direction to explore all the implications of such a view. I would be happy to learn that the perspective outlined in the remaining essay is absurd, as long as the suggestion comes from someone who has rejected any dangerous liaison with the D-N model.

have different contrast classes in mind that, despite the identical surface meaning of the sentence, different questions are obtained. A specific contrast class, then, forms a presupposition of the question. Different contrast classes embed the phenomena to be explained differently. This explains why the meaning of each of these questions is different, even though this is not indicated by its ostensible sentential form.

More importantly, a contrast class varies from context to context depending upon our interests and background information. Consider the question: why did Franz K commit the theft? At least two questions lie hidden here. Why did K rather than someone else commit the theft? Why did he thieve rather than act in some other way? Each of these questions has a different contrast class. The class of relevant alternatives in the first question is: all persons like K. For the second question, the class of relevant alternatives is different. We are not concerned with other persons here but with the class of actions that could be performed in K's condition. In the first case, we know already or are indifferent to the standing conditions which enable persons like K to commit theft. Given our background information, we are interested in why (which occasional cause was responsible for) it was K rather than some other person who committed the theft. In the second case, we know why only people like K commit theft but wish to know further what standing conditions lead them to opt for this rather than some other act. If the proximate cause is known, we might want to comprehend the standing conditions. If standing conditions alone are known, we would wish to know which occasional cause led to the event. Thus, background information and interests determine the exact nature of our question.

Differences in objects of explanation also emerge due to a prior selection of the type of description suitable for it and these are governed by interests. Consider once again the question: why did he have a heart failure? Here, we might be interested in heart failure either as a physiological event and therefore, subsumed wholly under a physiological description or as a socio-psychological event with a non-physiological description. Qua physiological event, a heart failure is explained by reference to the blockage of arteries and other such factors. Qua socio-physiological event, the answer would be: acute anxiety in societies which are prone to anomie and alienation. The explanation we prefer would depend upon the interests which guide us. To give the second answer to the first question would be wholly irrelevant. Since relevance relations are analytic to explanations, it simply does not constitute an explanation to the object to be explained.

Differences in background conditions and interests determines what counts as explanatorily relevant. Thus, differences in background information and relevance relation produce different questions; differences in question generate different objects of explanation and these, in turn, give rise to different explanations of what appears to be the same phenomena. This relativity to contrast space and ultimately to context is what one might call, following Garfinkle, explanatory relativity.[8] Explanatory relativity underlines the fact that every explanation has presuppositions which bind it to a certain and not to other class of objects. It is these presuppositions that decide which aspect of the question requires explanation. In other words, they constitute different objects of explanation thereby determining the possible explanatory factors to be sought. The complete structure of the *explanandum* or the object of explanation includes not just the proposition, P, or what it is about but also its contrast class and the relevance relation, neither of which is given by the formal meaning of the sentence.

So far, I have argued that explanations are internally constituted by or presuppose background information and interests, that they are not free from all contexts. It remains to show, however, that these interests and information, our beliefs and values—in short, our context—is socially determined. I shall here provide only an outline of the argument, which is both lengthy and intricate, to show that our thoughts and values have an inextricable social dimension. I assume that interests and thoughts are wholly conceptual and further, that they have a propositional content. What we need to find out then is whether or not this content is individuated with reference exclusively to the mental environment of the individual or if it necessarily requires the extra-mental, social factors. Tyler Burge's thought experiment demonstrates with considerable degree of plausibility that 'communal practices is a factor...in fixing and interpreting the words and attitudes of a person'.[9] Imagine, then, a person with a set of beliefs about arthritis. She believes that she has it, that she inherited it from her mother, that it aches in certain joints more than in others, more acutely in the morning than later in the day. In addition, she believes that she has arthritis in her thigh. She goes to her doctor complaining about it only to be told that it is a disease affecting bodily joints alone and could not have affected her thigh. Rational and trusting her doctor, she changes her belief.

[8] Alan Garfinkle, *Forms of Explanation*, New Haven: Yale University Press, 1981.

[9] Burge, 'Individualism and the Mental', *Midwest Studies in Philosophy*.

Now, imagine a counter-factual situation where everything about the person, that is, her phenomenal experiences, visual images, internal verbal rehearsals and indeed, every physical and non-socially described mental state is the same but her doctor attends to her immediately, offers her treatment, mildly reprimands her for not taking adequate care, confirming by his actions that she has arthritis in her thigh. The term 'arthritis' as used in this situation is different and this alone accounts for differences in mental states of the person in the first and the second situation. Thus, differences in mental contents are solely due to practices in the community and seem to 'lie outside the individual considered as an isolated physical organism, causal mechanism or seat of consciousness'.[10] Both the sense and the reference of arthritis, the concept or meaning of the word arthritis, and all beliefs involving the word are, at least in part, determined by practices in the community.

I argued first that explanations are internally tied to beliefs and interests. Second, that these beliefs and interests are socially constituted. It follows that explanations are context-bound, tied to socio-cultural factors. If this is so, not only descriptions but also explanations can be ethnocentric. The answers we provide depend on the way we construct our questions, and if these questions are bound to our interests rather than to the interests of the object-culture, our explanations will, in a predetermined manner, fall within a specified cultural space, mainly our own, rather than the other's.

Consider then the following simple example: why did R marry T? The question can be construed easily in the following different ways: (i) Why did R qua an autonomous individual marry T qua an autonomous individual? (ii) Why *did* T qua a member of a caste marry T qua a member of a caste? The way we answer these questions would vary depending upon the conceptual world within which we subsume R and T. Suppose we construe the question in the first way and then ask: why did R marry T rather than someone else. The answer here would take into account his desires, beliefs, values, commitments, life plans, and so on. Perhaps we might say that R prefers T to all others. Now suppose we give this answer to the question construed in the second way. This would be wholly irrelevant. For *any* answer to the second question would ignore R's own preferences. This would be because for

---

[10] Ibid., p. 79.

persons who construe the question in the second manner, this question simply does not exist. Here, one will not ask why R married T rather than some other person. To insist then upon the first answer, to explain R's act as resulting from his preferences would be ethnocentric. We obtain an ethnocentric explanation because of the way we construe the question, due to the manner we constructed the object of explanation. Not that the answer is wholly wrong, that no preferences of R are ever involved but largely because an answer in terms of preferences is wholly irrelevant. Factual accuracy is not enough for correct explanations; relevance matters too.

Consider another example: why was a religious ritual performed? This question can be construed in at least three different ways: (i) Why was a (religious) ritual performed rather than something else? (ii) Why was a religious ritual performed rather than some other, say, a secular one? (iii) Why was the ritual of this religion rather than that of some other performed? Clearly, our cultural context would shape which of the three questions we shall identify as the only or perhaps the central one. A society with no experience of rituals at all (of course, no such society exists) will simply not know what is going on. Suppose, however, that this problem does not exist, that we all know what rituals are and are able to identify when one is being performed. We are now faced with the problem of identifying the real question. An atheistic society, for example, will certainly not be able to identify the second and third questions. A person from that society will simply ask: why a ritual was performed rather than something else? Likewise, a person who has no background in atheism will simply not ask why a religious ritual rather than a secular one was performed. Of course, he might ask: but why was a ritual performed at all, but he might not be able to see that secular rituals also exist. Such a person then will not be able to capture the relevant contrast class. In the absence of this, he will not provide the relevant explanation. Finally, suppose that the question was asked in a cultural context where there exists only one religion. Here, the question: why this rather than a ritual belonging to some other religion, will sound absurd. A person might understand that a difference exists between religious/secular, also between rituals/non-rituals but not between this and that religion. Such a person will simply not see the third question. If we were interested only in an answer to the third question, any answer provided by him would be utterly irrelevant. Therefore, it would not be an explanation we want.

At this point, a distinction between maximally and minimally social contexts might be invoked against the point of view just stated.[11] One might agree that explanations are determined by socially constituted interests but then go on to argue that most such interests are only minimally social. Such interests do not generate prejudice; at any rate, the resulting prejudice does not lead to ethnocentrism. Or perhaps, even if ethnocentricity results, it is not pernicious.

Now, minimally social contexts are those in which certain actions, relations, and psychological states are picked out and provided some *general* significance. For example, some relations generally count as competitive, some positions count as subaltern, some activities and attitudes together count as cognitive, some attitudes count as shame, and so on. Maximally social contexts are those in which actions, relations, and attitudes are provided a *particular* significance by virtue of their association with particular groups and institutions. For example, the US veto in the Security Council of the United Nations, the activity of combating communal attitudes, the capital–labour relation, and the belief that blacks have low IQ. Minimally social entities are universally found as a matter of empirical fact. Cooperation exists everywhere, so do subalternity, shame, and cognition. Maximally social contexts vary from place to place. Communal attitudes that need combating have a specific social context, the capital–labour relation has a socio-historical specificity, and the UN is a particular institution which does not exist everywhere. To extrapolate assumptions governed in some way by the capital–labour relation on to situations of, say, classless primitive societies would be ethnocentric but not the projection of the category of subalternity. An explanation of an action in terms of the subaltern status of the agent would not be ethnocentric. Similarly, since cooperation exists everywhere, some practices of alien cultures might be explained in terms of their functionality for social integration. There are no societies which can survive without the social production of goods. Indeed, every society plans to increase the productivity of such goods. The explanation of, say, a change in social relations by reference to the growth in social productivity would not therefore be ethnocentric. In all such cases, ethnocentrism is avoided because of the universality of minimally social entities. There simply exist universal human constants

[11] Steven Lukes, 'Methodological Individualism Reconsidered', in A. Ryan (ed.), *The Philosophy of Social Explanation*, Oxford: Oxford University Press, 1973.

which are external to every particular culture only in the sense that they exist elsewhere too. When these are used as explanantia, the resulting explanations are not ethnocentric even when their descriptions are unavailable to the agents. Perhaps these explanations are both external to the agents and free of ethnocentrism.

Let us agree for the moment that such explanations are not ethnocentric. Even so, we must realize that this is so not because of some internal property of scientific explanations but due to empirical reasons. They escape ethnocentrism not because they are scientific but because they involve explanatorily relevant items that happen to be found everywhere. Recall that on the more sophisticated naturalist view, the very logic of explanations frees them of ethnocentrism. Explanations were necessarily free of all contexts and prejudices. Now it turns out that if some are free of contexts, this is so only contingently. The universality of some explanations does not damage the contextualist position on explanation presented in this essay.

Other points about minimally social explanations need remembering. First, accepting them imposes on us the responsibility of making it dead certain that they are indeed universal. If they are not and are only assumed to be so, then we are trapped into the most vertiginous ethnocentrism. Second, we must never accept them as the only valid explanations in social sciences. Some explanations, the minimally social ones, are universal and therefore, in a sense, free of ethnocentricity. Others, the maximally social ones bring along the risks of ethnocentrism. Third, neither of these explanations need be seen as more basic than the other. Minimally social explanations are not even remotely the ultimate explanations of cultural phenomena. One type of explanation is not reducible to the other. Finally, these two types of explanations often appear to be in competition with each other. But, only one of them is the explanation of the object to be explained. Consider once again the example mentioned earlier: why was this ritual performed? The answer that it was performed to enhance social integration appears to be a plausible answer. But we need to ask afresh just *which* question is being addressed. It appears relevant to the question: why was *any* ritual performed? However, it fails to answer the questions:why was a *religious* ritual performed?; why was the ritual performed of *this* rather than of another religion?; and why was *this* ritual of a religion performed rather than any other? The answer that a ritual enhances social solidarity is irrelevant to these questions and therefore, does not constitute the explanation of the phenomena under study.

16

'Objective Significance' in Critical Social Theory*

Consider the following propositions: 'The entire sphere of inner and outer reality is to be called, in a stronger sense than that reserved for art, the world of mere illusion and bitter deception rather than the world of reality';[1] 'as soon as their mystifying character is uncovered, economic conditions appear as the complete negation of humanity';[2] and 'A commodity appears at first sight an extremely obvious, trivial thing. But its analysis brings out that it is a very strange thing abounding in metaphysical subtleties and theological niceties'.[3]

What sense are we to make of these propositions? One standard response is that they are meaningless or that they are devoid of any sense because they involve simple category mistakes. A second, more sympathetic response could be that they involve the use of metaphors indicating that a conceptual framework that makes use of them is in need of imaginative understanding and reinterpretation. A third

* This paper was presented at a workshop organized by Professor Bhikhu Parekh on behalf of the Study Group on Political Philosophy of the International Political Science Association held at the University of Baroda in March 1984. It was subsequently published as '"Objective Significance" in Critical Social Theory', in Bhikhu Parekh and Thomas Pantham (eds), *Political Discourse*, New Delhi: Sage Publications, 1987, pp. 97–119.

[1] H. Marcuse, *The Aesthetic Dimension*, London: Macmillan, 1977, p. 55, quotation from Hegel's *Philosophy of Fine Art I*.

[2] H. Marcuse, *Reason and Revolution*, London: Routledge and Kegan Paul, 1941, p. 281.

[3] K. Marx, *Capital*, Vol. 1, London: Pelican/New Left Review, 1976, p. 163.

response could be that they do indeed have a descriptive meaning, that the objective reality described by them possesses precisely those attributes which are thought to render them sensible.

In this essay, I wish to support this third claim, that it is legitimate to speak of reality in the manner just stated. I would like to suggest that the one, and perhaps the only, way to support this claim is to introduce the category of objective significance in one's analysis and understanding of social reality.[4] But the decision to introduce this category into social theory is not arbitrary, not a matter of personal preference, not even a culturally determined presupposition but is imposed on us as a matter of necessity. That is, it is grounded in the deepest recesses of our being, such that we cannot think properly about the relevant subject matter without it. So, in the first part of the essay, I discuss most generally the category of objective significance, distinguishing within it two types—one that is merely inter-subjective and the other, more weighty, that has the externality and stability of things. I then try to show how one or the other or both are necessarily constitutive of any human reality and therefore, indispensable to its understanding. I admit that philosophers of meaning may, not entirely unjustly, be quick to react adversely to my caricature-like presentations of some of the deeper issues on which, I imagine, much of their effort has been spent. Far from disregarding them, I offer the plea that for my purposes, such a general account, uncontroversial in its broad contours, is both adequate and appropriate.

In the second section, I follow my argument further to show that the category of objective significance is crucial to any critical discourse. Much of what is contained in this part is an illustration of the thesis of the first. It provides the real meat to my argument, demonstrating more fully what sense one can possibly make of the propositions stated in the foregoing. I am aware that there is an important strand within social and political theory in general and Marxist theory in particular, which sees little meaning in statements of this kind and another which observes too much sense in them without providing an adequate justification for why this is or must be so. I hope that by the end of this essay, any theory which makes such a proposition integral to its account and claims to have descriptive power precisely by virtue of such an

---

[4] The term significance can be used in two senses, either to refer to the meaning of something or to its import. In this essay, I generally use it to mean the former, that is, the meaning of something. I do not mean to suggest that everything that is significant must necessarily carry some value.

account—for example, the Marxist theory of commodity fetishism—is provided the sort of weighty justification that would make it a little more amenable to appreciation from intellectual quarters that have traditionally ignored it.

OBJECTIVE MEANING AND THE SOCIAL WORLD

It had, till very recently, been taken for granted (at least among Anglo-Saxon philosophers) that meanings are attributes of words and words alone. And these words have meanings because they stand for, denote, and refer to something which is independent of them, things which are 'out there'. It is words that have meanings and meanings are their reference. Sentences are composed of words and their meaning is a function of their elementary constituents. If a word has no reference, it is meaningless. Besides, what is to count as 'out there' is something which is determined by direct or indirect experience by publicly accepted procedures. No sense can be made of a word which refers to an entity that cannot be experienced or for which no ground exists to suggest that it can be experienced. The only real entities out there in the world which possess an ontological privilege over others, or which in fact get any ontological status at all, are those which are publicly known to be experienced or are detected by some instrument whose infallibility is beyond dispute or doubt. The meaning of a statement is then a function of the experience of a referent or, stated alternatively, it is a method of its verification. There are for this theory, no intensions; a meaning vehicle, a word, has only an extension. A thing, which by definition is an extended entity and which, by the same token, exists has a word for it and the meaning or the essence of this word is precisely these extended properties. The essence, in fact, is nothing more than the sum of all the observable properties of a thing. There is obviously no essence of that which does not exist. Three important features are easily detected in this theory: (i) words are mere symbols and no more; (ii) it is words which possess meaning and they derive their meaning by referring to something which lies outside them; and (iii) elements lying outside these words have no meanings. Properties of entities are seen to possess meaning by a subjective act for purposes of utility or economy. Objects in themselves are meaningless.

This account raises some very familiar problems.[5] Don't we understand the meaning of a term without experiencing it? Or finding an

---

[5] A. Danto, *What Philosophy Is*, London: Pelican, 1971, p. 46.

instance of it? Do we not know what a unicorn is without ever having seen one? In which case, isn't there a distinction between the intension of a word and its extension? There are words which have meaning by virtue of their intension alone, even though they have no extension. Thus, we can make sense of them without ever finding their references. To conflate their sense with their references seems to involve an obvious error. This is at least one of the claims implicit in Frege's distinction between sense and reference. Sentences may be coreferential without being synonymous. 'The man who is the present president of the largest imperial power in the world' and 'the man who shot the native Red Indians in a Hollywood film in the early part of his life' have the same references but they obviously do not mean the same thing.

But perhaps this doesn't take us very far. For all that is suggested here is that anything has more than one attribute and the meaning of a thing is the sum of all its properties, each of which can be called its sub-reference. Here, we are merely speaking of a complex entity and the meaning of the sentence that describes it can be discerned by closely examining the entire set of words which enter into such a description. But what of Frege's own example made famous by innumerable references in an almost incalculable number of articles and books? The Evening Star is the same thing as the Morning Star, and yet not quite. Both these words refer to the same thing but they have quite different connotations. Nor can these two connotations be understood as attributes of the 'star', just as in our earlier example being a president is now an attribute of a man who was formerly a film star. Perhaps, then, this meaning is conferred upon this 'star–planet' by subjects and since this star has now an inter-subjective significance—not to be confused with the private associative ideas that each one of us may have about it—we can now make a distinction between reference as something that stands for what the thing is in itself (shall we say, with all its natural properties?) and sense as the inter-subjective meaning that subjects have quite contingently to being with, but now firmly, attached to it. One can even say that one needs to make a distinction between the natural meaning of something and the different meanings that men have bestowed upon it. The move from denotation to connotation, from reference to sense, has already brought us from the natural to the cultural sphere.

Indeed, the chief motivation underlying the rise of behavioural accounts of meaning in social theory, for the reduction of sense to reference, was due to the failure to give a reasonably adequate answer to the question: what sort of entities in the world could meaning qua sense be?[6] But the point is that the very question raised earlier is indicative of an epistemological bias that prevents people from making the transition from the natural to the social sphere. Even when some attempts have been made, it has been thought that the subject—individual or collective—attaches a meaning by an act of consciousness to objects that reside external to the subject. Venus does have an objective significance apart from its natural meaning; it is not merely a planet but a star. Second, it is not just one but two stars, one that appears in the morning and another in the evening. But this objective, or inter-subjective significance, rests upon a convention, an implicit agreement by which different people act without ever bothering to examine the real cognitive status of their beliefs, that there are different phenomena in the sky. Inter-subjectivity here is pure, not founded on the hard objectivity of material objects, events, or processes. Thus, for Weber, meaning is what man extends to reality by a conscious, intentional but exclusively subjective act, and the whole of material objectivity has a bearing only as a vehicle of this subjective significance. It is seen only as a means used by men to manifest their ideas and sentiments. Even for Schutz, whose intention is quite explicitly to provide depth and complexity to Weber's conception of meaning, 'meaning is not a quality inherent in certain experiences but the result of an interpretation of a past experience looked at from the present now with reflective attitude.'[7] Meaning is, therefore, not lived but only imputed or bestowed by conscious reflective acts.

Whatever the limitations of the views expressed in the foregoing, it is clear that language does not have only a denotative function; its use is not limited to that of labelling, referring, or representing something. Language articulates, but what it articulates is not always the true nature of things, such that when it falls short of meeting the standard, one is to see in it a distortion or deflection of its purpose. To get to the truth of things, and of natural objects in particular, is only one of the

[6] Ibid., chapter 2.

[7] A. Schutz, *The Problem of Social Reality*, The Hague: Martinus Nijhoff, 1962, p. 210. Against behavioural theories of meaning, Schutz says, 'social actions involve communication and any communication is necessarily founded upon acts of working. In order to communicate with others, I have to perform overt acts in the outer world...' So far the behaviouristic interpretation is justified. It goes wrong by identifying the vehicle of communication, namely, the working act with the communicated meaning itself. Ibid., p. 218.

things that we do with language.[8] This, among other things, is the point
that was forcefully made by Wittgenstein and his followers. Language
can be put to different uses and the meaning of a statement or that of a
word can be gathered only by examining their use in different contexts,
in what Wittgenstein calls language games. It is our failure to realize
this which compels us to isolate the denotative function of language
as its only function. Learning how to denote things with words, which
is often arbitrary, is no doubt a highly developed use of language but
only one among others. Not the correct matching of words with extra-
linguistic items in the world but their use in a language game—this
became Wittgenstein's key slogan.

Meaning is still tied to words and to language but language itself
is now viewed as an activity, and in fact, one that enters into a large
number of other human activities. The meaning of a word is provided
by the rules governing its use. Now, it is part of the notion of following
a rule that one can be mistaken about it and an assessment of whether
or not one is committing an error can be made only if a public criterion
of such assessments is available. That is to say, only if rules are public
or social. It follows that the meaning of most words is to be found in
their socially governed uses or in socially governed linguistic practices.
The nature of the word in question cannot be understood unless we
answer questions about its purpose or use in our practices. Meaning
is not attached to an observation that is independent of it, but is
constitutive of what one is doing. So, meaning, among other things,
is a matter of doing something. One finds now that meanings are
multiple, constitutive of socially governed linguistic practices which
often overlap with very many other social practices. And, it needs a
very small step from here to realize that a majority of words derive
their meaning not merely from their various uses in linguistic practices
but from social practices in general.[9] In fact, very often, using words

[8] The classical function of logos, of speech, reason, and theory is to try and
understand things as they are outside the immediate perspective of our goals,
desires, and activities. See Taylor, 'Rationality', in Martin Hollis and Steven
Lukes (eds), *Rationality and Relativism*, Oxford: Basil Blackwell, 1982, pp. 89–90.
Similarly, Colletti informs us of a long tradition in western philosophy (going
back to Greece) for which the natural property of man is thought and reason,
so that in him the universe realizes consciousness of himself. See his *Marxism
and Hegel*, London: New Left Books, 1973, p. 238.

[9] See P. Winch, *The Idea of a Social Science*, London: Routledge and Kegan
Paul, 1958.

in sentences, uttering sentences is doing something, performing an action.[10] To utter a sentence is not merely to express an opinion on something, communicate something, report a matter, but is just doing something (as, for instance, promising, declaring, pronouncing a verdict, praying, or marrying). What the words in the sentence mean cannot be understood apart from the practical contexts in which they are uttered, that is, unless we see them also as constituting acts. With this, we move on to yet another dimension of meaning. Meanings are properties not merely of words but of practices, at least of those practices of which language is internally constitutive.

No one, perhaps within the tradition of analytical philosophy, with the possible exception of Winch, has shown this more than Charles Taylor, who has argued that it is legitimate to talk not merely of words having meanings but also of practices and situations having meaning for people.[11] Taylor argues that linguistic meaning is for subjects and is in a field, but it is always the meaning of signifiers (for example, words) and it is about a world of referents. Thus, it has a four-dimensional structure. The other meaning—what he calls experiential meaning—has a three-dimensional structure. This meaning is also for a subject in a field but it is directly a meaning of the world itself, not a property of signifiers. One can even say that situations, practices, and actions can signify directly without the mediation of special signifiers.

The referential theory of meaning has no conceptual space to make sense of experiential meaning. Most referential theories tend to suppress (although there is no internal necessity for them to do so) that meaning is only for subjects. Of course, much of this is due to their preoccupations with the objective, natural properties of the referent, independent of the subject's conception of it. Recall that meaning for them is tied to reference and reference is not subject dependant. It follows that meaning is free from subjectivity or at least has subject neutrality. Second, these theories fail to notice the interrelations that bind individual meanings. Again, this is due to their view that meanings are derived from and tied to individual referents that exist independently of inter-subjective connotations. Third, referents do not possess any meaning directly because they are not constituents of words and it is words alone that

[10] J.L. Austin, *How to Do Things with Words*, Oxford: Oxford University Press, 1962, and Searle, *Speech Acts*, Cambridge: Cambridge University Press, 1969.

[11] Charles Taylor, 'Hermeneutics and Politics', in P. Connerton (ed.), *Critical Sociology*, London: Penguin, 1976, pp. 153–93.

have meaning. Here one sees yet another failure on their part to realize that inter-subjectivity/sociality is constitutive of some referents in the world, especially those that belong to the social field.

This precisely is Taylor's complaint against mainstream political science, indeed against much of social science, that it is obsessed with 'brute data', and the conception of social reality with which it works is objectivist, that is, free of thought, meaning, and interpretation, all of which are thought to reside only in the minds of subjects as their psychological properties. Actions, institutions, structures, and processes are thought to be identifiable without reference to the subject and its properties. Very often, subjective properties are completely discounted not merely from the identification of objective events but also from their explanation. At most, one can have the two orders interact and observe what correlations of cause and effect can be discovered or established between them. Thus, one could say that a person, because he has a certain belief, acted upon the world in the way that he did, producing identifiable consequences both for the world and for himself but the relationship between beliefs, acts, and their consequences is causal rather than conceptual, for none of these are internally constitutive of each other. Now, this attitude does not allow for precisely those kinds of inter-subjective meanings that are constitutive of social reality and that provide the common reference frame without which the correct identification of experience, situations, actions, events, or indeed structures is just impossible. As Taylor himself puts it,

some form of language is essential for some form of social reality to be what it is, and, the meaning and the norms implicit in these practices are not just in the minds of the actors but are 'out there' in the practices themselves, practices which cannot be conceived as a set of individual actions but are essentially modes of social relations, of mutual actions.[12]

With this conception, we have already moved to a view of man for whom signifying is not an activity peripheral to his real life, required only in cognition of the external world. Rather, man is seen inescapably as a signifying agent. That is, much of what constitutes human beings will be left out of any definition of man if his signifying nature were subtracted from it or if the act of signification was reduced to its reflective function alone. Man is the sort of being from whom both action and meaning are inseparable. One could even say that he confers

[12] Ibid., p. 177.

meaning on the world not only through an act of consciousness but through all his material acts. Man builds a meaningful world through meaningful acts and lives it. We have moved close to a discussion of the notion of objective significance.

Taylor spends a great deal of intellectual energy in arguing for the validity of meaningful experiences, situations, and practices, and therefore, of a meaningful social reality which is constitutive of these elements. However, there is a notion of objective significance which has an even thicker sense than the one outlined by Taylor. This is that our objective world (the world that is made up of hard-core, tangible, sensuous objects which surround man, upon which he acts, which offer him resistance, and which he has to overcome), much of this traditionally objective and natural world, has a preconstituted significance, precisely because it is already a socio-historical world whose natural boundaries, without ever being abolished, are forever retreating. In other words, this world, at any given point of time, is for us not only a world of natural facts but also a world of signs. The world that we reflect and upon which we act has an inbuilt layer of multiple meanings.

Much of the insight into this comes from the tradition that flows from Hegel and Marx. Hegel may have misunderstood and eventually underestimated the specific modality of socio-historical objectivity. He may even have hypostatized it by subsuming it under his conception of *Geist* but there is much to be learnt from his conception of objective spirit. Besides, whatever may be the misgivings of his 'the real is the rational' thesis, the important idea to which he gave a coherent formulation (that is, the idea of objective significance—whose generative aspect he once again eventually misunderstood) can be ignored only at one's own peril. Not social relations and practices alone but the so-called material objects themselves—rivers, trees, and flowers; houses and roads; tables, pencils, and paper, goods that we live with and consume, that we use for pleasure and comfort—all these are such that meaning has been conferred upon them by labour. As such, their objectivity is not the untouched objectivity of stars and planets but a new kind of objectivity on which significance is conferred and inscribed by subjectivity. There is no social object which is not an object for man, for his use, or upon which he has not conferred some value. Most objects are functional and this functionality is not something that is merely added to them, which one attaches to them by thought but is built into their own very nature. It is their 'second nature'. Objects are reborn with a significance derived from man's actions upon them, without losing their initial objectivity which is both cancelled and preserved. It is, therefore, in this hard sense that the objective world of man is significant. One can almost concur with Merleau-Ponty that here, 'spirit becomes a thing while things become saturated with spirit'.

There has always been a tendency, at least with some Marxists, unwilling accomplices in the intellectual murder of human specificity by mainstream social science, to believe that if something is objective it could not be significant. And conversely, if it is significant, this significance is only subjectively imputed by an individual or a collection of them and that it cannot therefore be objective. Perhaps Marx himself tended, at least on some occasions, to fall into this trap. Passages can be extracted from his writing to strengthen the belief that the sphere of production is exclusively material, while that of ideas involves no material processes. But this is wholly wrong. Colletti is right, although he is not one to always spell out correctly all the implications that flow from this position, in asserting that, for Marx, 'material production is simultaneously a production of ideas and hence a production of human relations'.[13]

The real world of men has a distinct kind of objectivity. It is both subjective and objective, in the traditional meaning of the terms. It is a world of facts which are also necessarily signs. It is objectively significant. Colletti goes even further to claim that, for Marx, 'production of goods is always the production of language', which I take to mean the generation, reconstitution, and redistribution of significance. There still exists a strong tendency within Marxism to shy away in the face of significations, as if time spent on them is wasteful because it is distracting from the scientific nature of one's intellectual work. But ignoring them, one only reduces the cultural order to the natural order and this has rightly been interpreted as the denial of the very freedom of man.[14] Surely, it is wrong to project human properties on to nature (as religion, myth, and magic do), to transfigure the world of facts to a pure world of signs, to invest natural processes with attributes which belong only to man. Natural science is, therefore, right in having

[13] L. Colletti, *From Rousseau to Lenin*, London: New Left Books, 1972, pp. 18–19, 70.

[14] J.P. Sartre, *Search for a Method*, New York: Vintage, 1968, p. 152. Also, Timpanaro, *On Materialism*, London: New Left Books, 1975, p. 105. However, meaning does not imply freedom or rational deliberation. A meaningful action is not one that is always done freely. It is, however, true that a free act/situation is necessarily meaningful.

de-anthropomorphized nature. Which is why, as Cassirer has pointed out, the confrontation of science with nature was intercepted by its confrontation with myth.[15] This is also why the emergence of science has to be seen not as the acquisition of skills by which nature was seen in a new way but also as a struggle against nature saturated with mythical interpretations. However, in the social sciences, that is, when one studies man, 'what can be more exact and rigorous than to recognise human properties in him?'[16] It is for this reason that any version of Marxism that takes significations seriously, which does not make an epiphenomenon of ideality, 'limps sometimes on one side, sometimes on the other'.[17]

I have so far talked about the objectivity of meaning. A couple of clarifications before I move further. First, I do not attempt to offer an exhaustive analysis of the concept of meaning here but only to give in broad outline the sort of entities they are and what they can be attributes of. It is not my intention, in this essay, to distinguish the various ways in which different actions are meaningful, nor to distinguish how the meaning of actions are different from the meaning of experiences, situations, processes, and objects, except only perfunctorily. Second, when I refer to any of these as meaningful, I never mean to convey that they have resulted from only conscious acts. All significant structures are not the result of conscious purposeful actions. Similarly, conscious, purposeful actions do not always result in meaningful structures. I also do not wish to suggest that all objective processes are significant. There are many natural processes that we know nothing of. There are many elements that we have neither seen nor touched. All these may or may not affect us. Even if they do, we may not even feel them, leave alone be in a position to recognize what they are.

With these remarks, let me dwell a little longer on what meaning is in order to understand how it has multiple layers. Now, at least a part of what is meant by objective significance is that objects have use values. This is interesting in the light of Wittgenstein's well-known demand that meaning be looked for in the use of words. The human world of objects is meaningful because nature has to be adapted to human needs by means of a change in its form. Meaning arises once the natural

[15] E. Cassirer, *The Philosophy of Symbolic Forms*, Vol. 2, London: New Yale, 1955, chapter 1.

[16] J.P. Sartre, *Search for a Method*, p. 157.

[17] M. Merleau-Ponty, *The Adventures of the Dialectic*, London: Heinemann, 1974, p. 43.

world is transformed by labour into something that serves man's needs. This seems to be an obvious point but it is often forgotten, specially in the discussion of productive structures. Thus, Goldmann has argued that all human objects and structures derive their meaning from the fact that they are functional.[18] Man is determined by and determines structures that are significant and have use for him.

However, meanings are not simply the use values of natural referents. Objects are significant not only because they have use for men but also because, in these objects, man realizes his own purposes. As Marx put it long ago,

Man not only effects a change in form in the material nature, he also realizes his purpose, and this is a purpose he is conscious of. It determines the mode of his activity with the rigidity of a law and he must submit his will to it.

At first sight, there seems to be little difference between the purpose which an object serves and the use to which man puts a natural object. However, a closer examination shows that the structure of purposes is far more complex than the structure of use or utility that objects may also have. Two reasons should suffice to suggest why purposes are not reducible to utility or function. First, whereas an element of conscious reflection of the future is constitutive of our conception of purpose, that need not be true in the case of use and second, purposeful objects may not have any material use at all. That is, they may be valued simply because they are expressions of human purpose, as is the case with art objects. Even more importantly, one of the fundamental purposes of man is not merely to use objects but to clarify to themselves through them (that is, through objectification) what their own nature is. If one can put this a little paradoxically: the use of objects does not lie in use values alone but also that, through them, man forges a meaningful relationship with others, and clarifies the meaning of his own existence to himself. This self-interpretive nature of man, while it may be encapsulated by the term 'purposiveness', cannot have much place in an account that reduces purposes to functions and none at all in an account that is guided by the utility of objects. It is, therefore, quite legitimate to claim that the human world is meaningful not only because objects have use but because they are expressions of human purposes, ends, projects, and finality, none of which are reducible to their use, although they do not entirely exclude it.

[18] L. Goldmann, 'Subject-Object and Function', in his book *Lukacs and Heidegger*, London: Routledge and Kegal Paul, 1977, pp. 67–85.

One finds that Marxists who take the Hegelian moment in Marx's thought seriously take better cognizance of this fact than those who wish to undermine or ignore Hegel's influence on him. True, the tendency to ignore use values altogether or to ignore the material force of these use values invites dangers which cannot be underestimated. Still, these interpretations do much to enrich or to highlight important segments of Marxist analysis. Thus, Lukacs models all other social activities on labour and includes purposiveness and conscious reflection as an integral element of it.[19] More importantly, Sartre argues that man is defined as much by what he is as by his objective possibilities.[20] The future of man is present at the very heart of the human present. Ends are not entities which are quite arbitrarily attached to human behaviour, nor is human behaviour charged with some mysterious end-significance that comes into play with retrospective effect at the time of reflection, rather, in much of human action, the future finds a distinguishable, although an invisible, presence. Of course, this does not mean that an analysis of human behaviour is to ignore the present determining factors at work upon it, which condition it and in relation to which it derives a large part of its meaning. Only, that another layer of intrinsic significance of human behaviour will remain undetected unless one discovers the 'relation of the existent to the possible'. Ends, as Sartre puts it, are practically efficacious. They provide unity to the act and significance to the product into which they disappear.

Again, though Hegel was mistaken in reducing all contradictions to the contradiction between existence and essence, the unrealized but objectively possible nature of spirit, he was clearly right in identifying this as at least one of the major contradictions operative in situations of social change. The contradiction between what is and what is yet to be but thought to be possible, is an important 'causal mechanism' at work at all levels of social formation, although other contradictions between already existing structures have an equal, or perhaps even greater, effectivity. It is because men are determined not only by existing objective structures but also by ends they have projected for themselves, that no activity can be explained merely in terms of material causes. It calls for an explanation in terms of 'reversed causality'—that is, finalism—a process characterized by the anticipation or ideal presence in the mind

[19] Lukacs, *The Ontology of Social Being: Labour*, London: Merlin, 1980.
[20] J.P. Sartre, *Search for a Method*, p. 93.

of the result.[21] Thus, human activity is to be understood both in terms of causal determination and in terms of ideal determination. Indeed, the same activity can be understood in terms of both kinds of determinations. Moreover, what are ideal determinations for some subjects could be causal determinations for others.

I have so far tried to argue that it makes sense to talk about objective meanings not only because they are inter-subjectively constituted and constitutive of social relations but, in the weightier sense, that what we experience to be the natural world already has layers of signification constituted in it by centuries of human labour. I have also argued that much of the multiplicity of meaning derives from the multiplicity of uses to which objects can be put and the different purposes that are embodied in them. Hegel talks of the socio-political order as the hieroglyph of reason. Marx, on the other hand, talks of value converting every product into a social hieroglyph. Both of them intend to convey by this that our intentions, purposes, and goals are embedded in the objective world and are to be read off them, through interpretations of the grains that have been grafted upon them. Marx, like Freud and Nietzsche after him, was extremely suspicious of expressed intentions, motivations, and purposes. Not that he thought that they were always symbols of malignant manipulations, nor, indeed, that the language in which they were expressed was always fractured in such a way that they lost their innocence as soon as they took part in it. But more importantly, because he thought that consciousness has different modalities, that consciousness discloses or rather confides much more in gestures, actions, situations, and objective processes than it does in the solemn resonance of words which are naturally thought to be the home of human meanings.

I do not mean to suggest that Marx thought that human beliefs and values are physically present in material objects. That indeed is an absurd claim. Nor, that these objects possess some mysterious non-natural property which was to be discovered by an equally enigmatic intuition, as indeed, Moore thought, goodness inhered in some objects and was to be intuitively detected. The ideal that is present in the material is to be detected in the form that natural elements have assumed and in the various processes that are needed to reproduce and sustain this form. This would not be possible but for human intervention. The

---

[21] L. Colletti, *From Rousseau to Lenin*, pp. 34, 66; Lukacs, *The Ontology of Social Being*, p. 3.

multiplicity of forms implies the presence of different kinds of human intervention on the same material substrate that result in different shapes, internal colouration, uses, and significance.

The situation gets a little more complicated because meanings have the proverbial lives of a cat. New significations arise but old ones do not die. They merely get deflated, displaced, distorted, or suppressed only to emerge some other time, disfigured but breathing all the same. Meanings attract each other, and in these relationships of meaning to meaning, what Ricoeur calls the fullness of language, is revealed: 'the second meanings somehow dwell in the first'.[22] It may at times reveal the first order of meanings but very often it conceals it. All this may sound like the familiar tune of an idealist discourse. However, let me assure the reader that I do not wish to detract him from either the fact that these meanings have no independent existence (independent, that is, from objective material elements) or from the insight that the properties of natural elements do have an effect, sometimes decisive, on the kind of meanings that reside in material objects. I do, however, wish to point out that linguistic and other social practices, both intentional and unintentional, do add or superimpose upon the primary meaning another set of meanings, so that what results out of this process is a field of what Ricoeur called symbols: double or multiple meaning—expressions not necessarily linguistic, which require precisely the kind of deciphering that Marx refers to in his passage on social hieroglyphic.[23] Much of our social world requires a deep interpretation of this kind. I take an example from Sartre who discusses the simplest of situations: we observe people drinking in a room. A minute later we depart and re-enter after a few hours only to find the floor littered with overturned glasses, empty bottles, and cigarette butts. All these man-made objects in a man-made setting, ripe with

[22] Ricoeur, *Freud and Philosophy*, New Haven & London: Yale University Press, 1970, pp. 30–1.

[23] K. Marx, *Capital*, pp. 12–13, 18–19, 48–52. Ricoeur distinguishes his conception of the symbol both from the narrow definition found in symbolic logic (where symbols are artificial, empty, and aim to guarantee the univocal character of words and the non-ambiguity of arguments) and from the other wider definition found in Cassirer's writings (where the term refers to the general function of mediation by which consciousness constitutes perception and discourse). Ricoeur argues that this function is better characterized by the term 'sign'. I have, in a number of places, used the term significance, meaning, sign, symbol, and signification interchangeably and have specified wherever it is used in a special sense (as, for instance, in this example).

original significations, point to yet another significant event or to significant events invisible at that instant: the fact that the guests got drunk.[24] If we examine the overturned glasses and empty bottles further, we might get more clues on how exactly the drunk persons behaved, and so on. Thus, signification is inscribed in the very order of things.

Everything, at every instant, is always signifying and significations reveal to us ourselves and our relations with others. Thus, men produce objects that are, at the same time, signs of events, situations, processes, structures of the past, present, and future, of subjectivity of different kinds; signs that are poor as well as those which are rich; domineering and selfish, and generous and accommodating; signs that endure and those which come and go in a flash; signs that are immediately perceptible and those that require arrested reflection. Examine the childlike delight of Barthes on the seashore. 'Here I am before the sea,' he says, 'It is true that it bears no message (no man-made meaning to communicate) but on the beach, what material for semiology; flags, slogans, signals, sign-boards, clothes, suntan even, which are so many messages to me.'[25]

At the end of this section, I would like to clarify a point about the ideal dependence of social reality. Sometimes, this is taken to mean that our reality is language dependent. It is then thought that our language constitutes what we see, perceive, examine, understand, and even count as real, in such a way that no other social reality exists for us except the one given to us and constituted for us by our language.[26] Now, this is only partially true. The limits of our language may sometimes constitute the limits of our world, but it should be remembered that not only is our world available to us non-linguistically but there are ways available to transcend the limits of our language.

No doubt social reality is in some ways dependent on and constituted by the beliefs and conceptions of its participants and these are

[24] J.P. Sartre, *Search for a Method*, p. 156.

[25] R. Barthes, *Mythologies*, London: Paladin, 1972, p. 112.

[26] P. Winch, 'Understanding Primitive Society', in Wilson (ed.), *Rationality*, Oxford: Basil Blackwell, 1970, p. 82. 'Reality does not give language sense. What is real and what is unreal shows itself in the sense that language has. Further, both the distinction between the real and the unreal and the concept of agreement with reality, themselves belong to our language.' It follows that every form of life has an internal criteria of reality. Reality differs not only across space and time but there is, very much in the spirit of Schutz, a scientific conception of reality, a religious one, and so on. See also Winch, *The Idea of a Social Science*, pp. 100–1.

available predominantly in the language available to them. However, two things must be remembered to avoid the pitfalls of idealism. First, although ideas are constitutive of social reality, this does not imply that all of its participants are conscious of them or indeed, any have a clear conception about them. Second, social reality may have to be defined partly in these terms but it cannot be exhaustively so defined.[27]

Moreover, the everyday language of the participants, their spontaneous thought (which is implicated in their practices and experiences) is a repository of only immediate significance and many of the forms of such reflection expressed simple category mistakes. In the simple identification of objects, we have to take recourse to the conceptions people have of them, for it is through them alone that we will start understanding their significance. It should, however, not be forgotten that what we know thereafter will only be its immediate significance, the manifest layer of meaning. This has to be placed within larger and still larger totalities which require the weaving of richer and more complex conceptual frameworks before the full significance of the object is realized. If any form of life is defined in terms of the everyday language of the people (which alone is thought to give it a criterion of rationality and reality), then one has to make a distinction between this form of life and another, perhaps more real, life of the people which has a different rationality and significance. Alternatively, a form of life is something that may not be immediately amenable to ordinary language and to the beliefs and perceptions that are embedded in it. For example, one will very rarely find in the immediate thoughts of people a consciousness of the causal mechanism of reality.

OBJECTIVE MEANING AND SOCIAL CRITIQUE: COMMODITY FETISHISM

I have so far tried to show that objective social reality can be correctly identified and understood only if we see it as significant. In doing

---

[27] Unlike the natural sciences, in social sciences, one cannot have a distinction between thought-objects and real-objects. If we agree that the real is partly constituted by thought, then the distinction to be drawn is between thought-objects and real-thought-objects. It follows that a social scientist will participate in a double hermeneutic and will have to undergo a second-order socialization—a point that has been well made by Winch, among others. A brief but fruitful discussion of these issues is found in Ted Benton, *The Philosophical Foundations of the Three Sociologies*, London: Routledge and Kegan Paul, 1977. See also, R. Bhaskar, *The Possibility of Naturalism*, Brighton: The Harvester Press, 1979.

so, I proposed that the concept of objective significance is of central importance to any analysis of social reality. In what follows, I wish to substantiate my second claim that only if one presupposes the notion of objective significance, can one make possible a critique of social reality. That is to say, a large number of concepts (with the help of which we cite, locate, and understand the limitations of society) are validated or make sense only when they are seen to be intrinsically related to the general category of objective significance. I shall choose the most obvious candidate to illustrate my point: Marx's analysis of commodity fetishism. I shall show that one can neither make sense of what it tries to convey nor use it to criticize important segments of social reality without the notion of objective significance. I suggest not only that the theory and the many statements regarding the mystified, illusory, and metaphysical character of reality integral to it or which it makes possible, make sense but that they have both a descriptive meaning (without which one cannot speak intelligibly about some social reality) and a critical sense (without which one can say little about its limitations). It follows that without the notion of objective significance, any social theory would find the idea of commodity fetishism nonsensical. Conversely if a theory is unable to make sense of phenomena such as commodity fetishism, it will not acquire a critical edge. But objective reality is significant not because a theory makes it so, but rather the intrinsically meaningful character of social reality makes possible a theory that captures objective significance. A failure to grasp this is then a theory's irredeemable limitation. In the following discussion, I take the cue from the writings of the Italian Marxist philosopher, Lucio Colletti, whose penetrating analysis of commodity fetishism provides precisely the material that could constitute an excellent point of departure—because he comes close to but does not arrive at the notion of objective significance, he shows, more than anyone else, the need to place it at the centre of any critical discourse.

In his discussion of 'bourgeois-Christian society', one of Colletti's main arguments is that Hegel had accurately perceived and understood the relationship between Christianity and modern civil society.[28] It is Christianity which affords us the recognition that men as such are free and when abstracted from all social relations, not in the world here and now but at least in the world beyond, they are equal. Similarly, God in

---

[28] L. Colletti, *Marxism and Hegel*, chapter 12. For a different reading of Hegel, see Charles Taylor, *Hegel*, Cambridge: Cambridge University Press, 1975.

Christianity frees himself from all naturalistic attributes and appears for the first time as pure spirit.

Moreover, these conceptions of freedom as independence from society and of formal equality among men, have links with the very structures and conventions that govern the social life of a modern society. There are internal links between these conceptions and the material structures in which they are inscribed. At the same time, despite all their achievements, these ideas have their weaknesses, and correspondingly, civil society its limitations. It is this insight that leads Hegel to look for the reconciliation of these ideas with the principles of substantive ethical life of the ancient Greeks which existed hitherto as the other-worldly precepts of Christianity. These precepts must now find embodiment in this world. Christianity must, Hegel demands, be retranslated into reality.

Thus, what Hegel looks for is the realization of the Christian logos—in philosophical terms, for the embodiment of the principle of idealism. Early idealist thinking worked with the analytical method and distinguished between this and the other world, between the finite and the infinite, but it failed to relate the two. As a result, it ended up with the infinite that was limited by the finite, that is, with two finite beings. The finite, which all idealists must demonstrate to be unreal, and which they are committed to annihilate, thus remained intact and the principle of idealism never realized. Hegel, with his dialectical method, showed that the finite (that which appears to be the case) is not merely unreal but is ideal. In his philosophical vision, matter gets annihilated not by being completely cancelled but by being demonstrated as the form in which the infinite appears. Finite matter has an inadequate, partial reality and it acquires full reality only when it is shown to be the form of the infinite itself. It is now pregnant with new meaning for it is no longer a natural but primarily spiritual entity, an identity it acquires by the activity of men who are demonstrated to be both vehicles and embodiments of Geist.

Although Colletti never quite realizes it, I interpret this to mean that for Hegel, this is a transformation of objective significance. The passing of the beyond into the here and now, the material incarnation of spirit, the interpenetration of God into everything earthly, His infusion into matter, His presence in all social and political institutions and processes are all meant to convey that these this-worldly beings now have an excess of meaning in them, that they overflow with spirituality. In each of these institutions is invested not only human rationality, but an extra-human one. The meaning with which they are bestowed is not only one that derives from man's labour, expressing his purpose, but one that expresses and embodies the overall purpose of Geist. The idea then is that each project, event, relation, institution, movement, and process has a multiplicity of signification, the smaller one deriving its strength from the one that is immediately larger than it and in which it is encapsulated until it finally assumes the significance of being divine. As one places a single object or an event into larger and still larger perspectives, new meanings emerge without any necessary destruction of old ones. The largest perspective in which events are inserted and which enables us to understand their complete significance and provide us with their final explanation is the one that shows them as the material embodiment of the Absolute.

I think it needs little argument to show that much of Hegel's metaphysical conception results from an inability to explain and understand reality in terms of human action and significance. Not finding the fit between human intentions, motives, projects, rationality, and the world as he saw it, he placed them in a perspective larger than anything human. Now, there is little doubt that much in the world is without an author. There are also, as Sartre says, 'constructions without a constructor', unintended consequences of human action, many of which are completely irrational. In the face of these, the gradual cultivation of new authors with a larger conception of rationality would have been one possible way out of the dilemma but the second one, which Hegel undertook, was to give a new significance to the irrational, a new finality to what from the human point of view, was a counter-finality. Hegel may have done little to understand the natural properties or propensities of various objects but he understood very well the use to which men put them in different cultures and different stages of history. He understood their multiple significance but, unable to explain them in terms of human forces and relations, he gradually developed a conceptual framework that gave cognizance to them and went beyond them. Unable to find footprints of man in history, he imagined in it the footprints of Geist. So, on earlier meanings he superimposed new ones which had the effect of trapping their immediacy, enveloping them in a mist released by his reflection. The superimposed meanings froze the mobility of earlier significations. When objects became sacred and mythical, their secular and profane reality tended to lapse into oblivion. Holy water is not just any water; bread and wine are not only bread and wine but mysterious entities, the very flesh and blood of Christ. A stone within the precincts of a temple is not a stone on which you can walk, it has a spiritual presence and evokes in the subject a mood and attitude, feelings and reactions that natural properties of no stone can elicit.

Now, this is the principal characteristic of a religious world view. It transfigures the world of natural and social facts, investing them with a special kind of meaning. All physical and social things, instead of signifying themselves, acquire a purely derived significance indicating some transcendental presence. This significance, arising from the illusory belief that attributes belonging to man are, in fact, properties of an extra-human subject, is supported by a large network of material processes and institutions, by a set of complex practices that rest on the belief that this view of the world corresponds to what the world really is. Men act as if this imaginary element did in fact exist. Traditional myths see no distinction between the signifier and the signified, between the representative and the represented; for them the word is as real as the object it designates.[29] The shadow is as ontologically privileged as the object of which it is the shadow. A certain variety of social sciences, 'by bathing everything in sulphuric acid', as Sartre so venomously puts it, by conceiving every man as if he was a molecule, acquires the status of a myth when it succeeds in this programme of levelling. Religion is different. It makes the distinction between what is here and now and the meaning which the thing acquires from its status as a sign of something beyond. I do not think that a religious man believes that when he makes bread he is actually manufacturing the flesh of Christ—such are the visual privileges only of the insane. I find, therefore, little reason to give this illusory significance the kind of weighty objectivity that I think one can grant others. In other words, although we are closer to our conception of a mystified or illusory objective reality, we are still not at it. Our analysis of the links between Christianity and civil society provides us an example of the intersubjective beliefs finding their way as a necessary moment in situations and practices, but do not constitute examples of these beliefs acquiring a genuinely objective character, embodied not merely in actions but in objective structures involving material objects. However, what this example does is to throw light on where, in what, and how to look for objective significance, particularly of a certain variety. I move ahead by making a general comment on Colletti's interpretation of Hegel, for this has relevance for what I say a little later. Colletti tends to be

---

[29] E. Cassirer, *The Philosophy of Symbolic Forms*.

reticent in acknowledging the contribution of Hegel towards the development of the category of objective significance. He takes the presence of the super-sensate in the sensate as the immediate presence of the immaterial, unreal God Himself. This implies that for him the ideal is merely the imaginary, religious ideal. This is a mistake, stemming from his failure to grasp the inescapable polyvalence of human reality, an error that arises from his overall failure to appreciate Hegel's real contribution to the understanding of social and historical phenomena.

The next example that brings us still closer to the main theme of this section is taken from Roland Barthes' *Mythologies*. Barthes argues that myth is not distinguished according to substances. It is not an object, concept, or idea but a mode of signification, a type of speech, which is to say that it is distinguished by the way it utters its message.[30] Myth, according to him, is a second-order semiological system which is attracted to anything that has meaning, towards any sign, the meaning of which it first divests only to convert it into an empty signifier, ready to be filled with fresh meaning. Now, the original meaning is never entirely suppressed; there is an impoverishment but not an annihilation. In fact, the old sign now functions in a totally new and unexpected way. As Barthes puts it, 'the meaning does not die, it loses value but not life, for if it did, myth will have been left with nothing from which to draw its nourishment.' Myth changes the original meaning, puts it at a distance, and makes it an accomplice in a new crime. It deforms, distorts, and alienates, making it signify something else, which, now pretending to be the only significance, hides the presence of the earlier meaning. As the sign grows heavy, its appearance gets more casual, its pretence less self-conscious. To quote Barthes once more,

myth is a speech, stolen and restored. Only speech which is restored is no longer that which was stolen. When it was brought back it was not put in exactly the same place. It is this brief act of larceny...that gives myth its benumbed look.[31]

Barthes' own examples of myth have to do with anything that has a language or that acts as if it had one. It is not confined only to oral or written speeches. Ordinary language, poetry, mathematics, criticism, newspaper articles, photographs, advertisements, exhibitions, events, and simple, harmless objects (like soap, milk, wine, even toys) can

---

[30] Barthes, *Mythologies*, p. 109.
[31] Ibid., p. 125.

acquire a mythical status. In other words, although myth is a speech, it is spoken by all sorts of things, including objects.[32] Here, we are in a world of objective significance which is ripe with myths. Objects have meanings that distort other meanings. They have significance which deforms that of other objects. The rich significant contents of objects is stolen from them. Emptied of their contents, they stand for something else, represent something which it was not their original intention to designate. We have different kinds of significant objects playing hide-and-seek with each other. To be sure, the original meaning of each object is only hidden, not destroyed. It lurks in the background, acting as a necessary appendage to its new master: it even makes an attempt to represent itself rather than any other thing but this is more like a gestural attempt by someone without speech trying to make sense to people who are blind. This is a thoroughly modern world whose picture Barthes draws, if only in broad outlines. But the one thing on which he remains silent, or at least ambiguous, is how exactly this world is brought about. It seems as if this world derives its mythical significance from an inter-subjective act of consciousness but not by objective social processes. I am not for a moment denying that mythical significance is the result of an act of consciousness nor that myth itself is a type of speech. However, what I am interested in is seeing how myth, or at least myth-like phenomena, can also be actions or objective processes constituting a real social reality. It is this which brings me straight to my discussion of commodity fetishism.

Like Hegel, Marx observes the link between Christianity and capitalism, but what he notices is not merely the functionality of Christian thought for the general ethos of capitalism. Nor is this relationship to be taken as an instance of the reciprocal determination between base and superstructure: Christian ideology helping the growth of bourgeois ideological structure which helps maintain and reproduce capitalist production relations. Involved here is nothing less than the presence of the formal structure and conventions of Christianity in the socio-economic structure of capitalist society. It is the abstract man of Christianity who produces, through abstract labour, values different and abstracted from use value. In other words, the real world of production acquires the form of Christianity, begets its mystery, its metaphysical subtleties, and theological niceties. Social reality is illusion; it has these strange illusory qualities.

---

[32] Ibid., p. 111.

Concrete labour, by which Marx means conscious, purposeful activity of men bound by common meaningful relations which they understand (by which natural processes are directed and natural material transformed to serve human needs, which confers significance upon the world and through which self-interpretation becomes possible) is now reduced to abstract labour. This private labour of individuals, which has no immediate purpose or use for them and which is qualitatively indifferent, produces value or exchangeable objects which have a non-sensuous, non-material, ghost-like objectivity. On the other hand, use values, the natural properties of things for human use, appear as mere by-products. The intended products of labour are not this or that determinate, sensate things but expressions of this identical ideality of expended human labour power. As Marx puts it,

the objectivity of value of commodity contrasts with the sensate objectivity of the same commodity, in that not an atom of matter enters into the objectivity of value. We may twist and turn a commodity this way and that—as a thing of value, it still remains unappreciable by our bodily senses.[33]

Thus, commodities only possess the objectivity of value insofar as they are expressions of one and the same social unit, namely, human labour. The objectivity of their value is purely social. So, as Colletti says, 'a commodity is a super-sensate thing in a sensate matter and natural body which harbours within itself the non-material objectivity.'[34]

Now, this 'non-material objectivity', this supra-sensate element in the thing is, for Colletti, the unity of the finite and the infinite, being and non-being together, the other-worldly soul present in the this-worldly body, which is why a commodity, possessing both use value and non-use value, is a contradictory thing, a mysterious object. This is also why its world stands upside down. It is interesting to note that just as in his analysis of Hegel's social philosophy, Colletti tends to suppress or ignore the important fact that invested in social and political institutions are not super-human, godly, and spiritual significance alone but also human significance, just so he tends to see—and perhaps Marx encourages him to do so—in non-material, super-sensate objectivity (that is, ideal objectivity) only religious mystery and metaphysical wonder. What, then, is a general feature of the specific human objectivity in which the subject and the object are

---

[33] Marx, *Capital*, p. 138.
[34] Colletti, *Marxism and Hegel*, p. 278.

always inextricably related appears to him to be a special feature of the capitalist world.[35]

Thus, Colletti fails to note that it is a feature of any human world, even a non-alienated one, that in it non-material objectivity coexists with material objectivity. Therefore, this by itself could not be the mark of alienation or perversion. Alienation in capitalist society is due, among other things, to a peculiarly distorted non-material objectivity. It is important to remind ourselves that the human world is sensate but the 'super-sensate' is always inextricably present in it. The traditional suspicion of the senses cannot simply give way to the more modern suspicion of reason. We cannot see things in the world with our senses alone. We must rely on our understanding as well and this is because we cannot even identify the elements 'out there' unless we also see them as significant.[36]

Most social objects are such that one cannot identify them without knowing their objective sense. The latter constitutes the former. This may appear to create a problem in that the same material object assumes different forms. But then, this is the only correct way of grasping the ontological status of social phenomena. A human entity without objective sense is an abstraction, a pure reference from which its sense has been subtracted. True, our problem is complicated by the

[35] Ibid. Colletti is brilliant in his analysis of the concept of social relations of production where he brings out these points well. See also, Colletti, *From Rousseau to Lenin*, chapters 1 and 2.

[36] That the identification of something is not possible without knowing its significance is clear from many examples. X warns Y and prevents him from falling over the precipice. The warning is identified—because of X, Y is being saved. But what is it that really saved him? It is obvious that unless Y understood the meanings of the words uttered in the warning he would have died (the example is Quentin Skinner's). Or, take the following examples from A. Danto. There are six tableaux on the north wall of a chapel in Padua, in which Giotto narrates six episodes from the life of Christ. In each of them, the Christ figure is shown with a raised arm. Materially, there is no difference, but a different kind of action is performed by means of it from scene to scene and the identity of the action is to be read from the context of its execution. Disputing with the elders, the raised arm is admonitory; at the wedding feast, it is the raised arm of the presti-digitator who has caused water to become wine; at the baptism, it is raised in a sign of acceptance; then it commands; it blesses; and finally, expels. It is clear that many of the intentions and purposes have to be read off the context which penetrate them and the identity of each action is a function of these meanings.

presence of innumerable associative ideas that surround each object but this is a difficulty one just has to contend with in dealing with human objects. The open-endedness and the multiplicity of significations does also tend to create the impression of arbitrariness and asystematicity but objective significations are structured and there are limits to their variations.

Some other passages from Marx that Colletti cites equates the social with the purely imaginary.[37] Now, social objectivity considered in abstraction is only ideal, relational objectivity and has no corporeal reality. However, it is certainly not imaginary, at least not in the sense that it exists only in the imagination or that it is pure fancy. It is imaginary only in the sense that the social cannot be grasped by pure sense. But this is an extremely flexible use of the term 'imaginary' and I am not sure if it is this and not the more restricted sense in which Colletti is using it. Indeed, this seems to be the reason why Colletti exclaims that the commodity has an imaginary, but nevertheless social existence. This is also the reason why he says that a representation too—which has an imaginary existence—is social and real only because everything functions objectively as if X did represent Y. Note that it is not that X actually does represent Y but it is as *if it* represents Y, and all social and objective processes are carried out on this assumption. The social is identified all too immediately with the imaginary which includes the as–if element, that is, merely an assumption that something is the case, perhaps even an illusion. Here, the non-sensuous becomes too much like the supra-sensate god. Now, there are certainly many objective processes that go on as if god exists and many more social processes that involve the illusory belief that something or the other exists—and representation could be an instance of one such process—but it is important to remember that it is the general nature of the social processes to involve beliefs of various kinds, often regardless of their truth or falsity. These beliefs, which constitute the significance of these processes, always escape the senses. If so, the social always transcends the sensate but this does not imply that it always involves an as-if process and is, therefore, illusory. It follows also that if we are able to see immediately the significance of things, perhaps not just one but many, then it is not our pure senses but our humanized senses, senses nurtured by thoughtful labour that experience this world

[37] K. Marx, *Theories of Surplus Value*, Vol. 1, Moscow: Progress Publishers, 1963, p. 171; and *Capitol*, Vol. 1, Oxford: Oxford University Press, 1975, p. 17.

without ever being self-conscious of this fact.[38] Also, that it is a certain kind of ideality, meaning, or significance and not ideality or significance as such that lends social reality its illusory or mysterious character. In drawing the contrast between pure material objectivity and an ideal objectivity, Colletti falls into an indefensible dualism that he inherits from Descartes and Kant. The real contrast to which he could but does not draw attention lies between different types of material–ideal objectivities. Colletti allows us to think that an ideal objectivity, in our language, a significant objectivity, is ipso facto mysterious or illusory. This is plainly false.

Thus, there is absolutely no difference in material objectivity between an object that is to be used personally, given away, or exchanged. Nor, between these and one that has been produced in order to maximize the exchange value or to valorize capital. There is no difference between an object for use and capital. What distinguishes them is their objective significance. This objective significance, as I have already pointed out, is neither purely subjective nor inter-subjective but is grounded in and is internally constitutive of the actual production of objects. It is very much 'out there'. There are material changes that are involved in and which sustain the production and reproduction of capital. In fact, new material processes come into being in order that capital accumulates and these differ from the ones that would be set in motion if the same material objectivity lacked the significance of being capital.[39] Objective ends, then, are the properties of the very system of production. They are as real as any material process that realizes them. There may have been no difference in the material production of goods for personal use, for exchange, solely for exchange, produced for maximum exchange value, or for capital accumulation. However, we find enormous differences in the general character of production of these significantly different objects. In capitalism, there exists not sensuous labour of human beings

[38] Similarly, both Winch and Weber argue that the capacity to recognize acts, objects, and relations this way, in terms of the symbolic universe to which they belong, is a condition for living any sort of social life. See Winch, *The Idea of a Social Science*, pp. 113–16.

[39] However, this does not mean that all these material processes are indispensable for production as such. Even if some of them were, it does not follow from the statement that they can be operationalized only under capitalist social relations. True, they came into being with the help of these relations, but they are not naturally bound to them, which is why they can function after capitalism as well.

producing use values but rather capital reproducing itself. Marx himself is aware that ends are central to objective social reality. In *Capital*, Vol. 3, he says,

> Capitalist production is distinguished from outset by two characteristic features. One, it produces its products as commodities...being a commodity is the dominant and determining characteristic of its products. Its second distinguishing feature is that the production of surplus value is the direct aim and determining motive of production.[40]

I do not think I need to add here that these aims and motives are not subjective but structured and constitute the objective features of the very processes of production.

It is now clear that the real question one needs to ask is: if commodities have objective meanings, then what are they? More importantly, from where does commodity acquire its mysterious character? If it is significant (like any other thing) and if this significance is not religious, then why is it still mysterious? Why is the world of commodity production illusory? Commodities are mysterious not because they have a non-material objectivity but because they tend to pass off as objects which have no meaning at all. Commodities tend to have the kind of benumbed look that Barthes' myths have. They tend to suppress the meaning that a certain kind of human labour has conferred on them. In myth, everything is equally real. In religion, two different orders of reality are recognized but the transcendental significance of objects is given more reality than its nature-groundedness. In art, the significance of an object is recognized precisely in that its value is derived from creative human work. Only in commodities does significance become natural. The whole system of production is geared to produce commodities, material processes are directly implicated and are set in motion, not as if they were commodities, not on the assumption that commodities exist (when in fact they do not) but in order to produce them precisely as commodities. Bread is produced, neither as Christ's flesh nor as bread but as a commodity, which is why illusions acquire the weighty objectivity that other objects of a similar kind perhaps lack.

To be sure, the fact that commodities are also use values can never be entirely suppressed. Paradoxically, this fact is revealed clearly in the

[40] K. Marx, *Capital: A Critique of Political Economy*, Moscow: Progress Publishers, 1959, pp. 879–80.

sphere of consumption. In fact, Marx says that commodities are both use values and exchange values. The original meaning of things does not disappear altogether. It is displaced by another, more predominant one, while for most producers, not merely its presence but even the memory of it gets blurred under the weight of ideal objectivity. Recall Barthes who shows how signs, which are pregnant with first-order meanings, are divested of their richness and transformed into empty signifiers that must seek and call out for the 'concept', look for something new to signify in relation to which and because of which they get staggered, disfigured, and impoverished. Now, what for Barthes is a mental, inter-subjective process has already been for Marx an objective social process. Private, abstract labour produces commodities which are divested of their own original meanings—use values—of all their qualitative richness. A new intentionality, a new end tames them and uses them as its vehicles. True, exchange values cannot do without use values, just as our Hegelian masters cannot do without their slaves. But use values can now survive only under the aegis of exchange value, only as a bearer of value. A shoe is not produced because it is a shoe or because it has a certain use for someone, but because it will yield maximum exchange value, profit, and capital!

What produces value, as we have seen, is labour which is indifferent to its qualitative dimension, whose own objective significance has been reduced completely to purposelessness. Labour is not merely abstract but also alienated.[41] We thus have a system of labour whose significance lies in producing values—objective significances of a type that has no relation whatsoever to the use value of the objects, no relationship to their original significance. We have an objective process whose original significance has been robbed, producing objects which too have been emptied of their significance. A meaningless process generating meaningless objects; a non-ideal, material, objective process causing material objects to happen and grow. This reads more and

---

[41] Alienation is objective. It refers both to a process of abstraction which materially separates individuals from each other and dissects social labour, as well as to a certain loss of significance. It may also be mentioned here that the notion of objective significance finds its way into even those enclaves of Marxism where one least expects it. The Althusserian notion of the materiality of ideology comes very close to it. See Althusser, 'Marxism and Humanism', in his *For Marx*, London: Penguin, 1969, pp. 219–48. Also, see Althusser, 'Ideology and Ideological State Apparatus', in his *Lenin and Philosophy and Other Essays*, London: New Left Books, 1971, pp. 121–73.

more like a pure natural process. History has indeed been reduced to nature. However, since new significances are nevertheless present, they appear as natural meanings of these strange objects. They are their natural properties. There is no objective significance, no inter-subjective sense, only a world of referents surrounded by associative ideas that are psychological properties of individuals. Social properties appear as natural properties, relations between social objects or persons who are nothing but objective personifications of the natural properties of things, appear to be relations between things. We are at the very heart of a reified world.

For Barthes, myth is a type of speech that typically distorts meanings in such a way that 'things lose the memory that they once were made'. For Marx, there are mythical actions (or rather, mythical processes) which divest meanings in a similar way such that objects lose their historical character. Objects reproduce themselves like other elements do in nature. But where is the illusory quality of this reality? It lies precisely in that it conceals almost everything from itself, hides that it is human, subject dependent, significant, that it is social as well as historical. It is not subjective consciousness that errs, that is mistaken about its own nature or of the world that lies outside, it is not subjects alone who mistake the historical for the natural world. It is this world itself which in all its immediacy, visibility, and manifest appearance, this world, which human subjects have endowed with significance, which takes the form of a natural world of meaningless objects produced by purposeless labour abstracted from that of others. It is, therefore, these phenomenal forms themselves, the form of money taken by commodities, the form of commodity taken by use values, the form of wage labour taken by labour, the form of capital taken by congealed labour, the form of associative sociality taken by the community, the form of abstracted state taken by public power, genuine freedom and equality themselves becoming abstract. It is all these which hide real relations, real causal powers, and the real capacity of agents to transform the world. Production relations, exploitative mechanisms that are built into these, the contradictory nature of these relationships, the real nature of unpaid labour that generates surplus, all these remain concealed. There is no uniform way in which this concealment takes place. Objects take the place of other objects, and physically hide them. One kind of objective significance deflects another within the same object. Real processes are set into motion (for example, that of abstraction and alienation which hide relations by replacing the field of object by an 'empty screen' in front of which only the immediacy of a single object is visible).

But all these do not concern us here. What is important is that if one remains trapped in these phenomenal forms, in those ideological structures which have a material existence, and then is seduced by them, one is not really able to act on the world that matters, or at least which also matters in a significant way. Not only that, we are unable even to see it, this more real side of our social reality.

Index

O'Sullivan, Noel 56n1
Ottoman empire 75, 110

Pakistan, demand for 117
  non-Muslim minorities in 87
Pandian, M.S.S. 118
Pantham, Thomas 66, 360
Parekh, Bhikhu 36, 56n1, 66n7,
  156n4, 170n34, 192n72, 194n76
Pascal, 275
pastiche religion 279
paternalistic coercion 242
Patterson, Orlando 201n10
Paul, E.F. 242n4
Paul, J. 242n4
perfection, notion of 73, 141
  socialist idea of 133, 137
Penelhum, Terence 275n25
Perry, Michael J. 83n9
Pettit, Philip 64n6, 160n11
Piaget Jean 345
Pieterse, Jan N. 170n34, 192n72,
  194n75
Pogge, Thomas 232n4
'political', meaning of 4, 24, 29
political death 201
political domain 120–2, 128, 200,
  306
  exclusion from 201
political philosophy 27, 35, 39, 40,
  44, 49, 51, 58, 189
political science, meaning of 22
political theory, decline of 38–41
  distinctive features of 6
  functions of 35–6, 40
  meaning of 4–5
  and modern societies 51–3
  need for 27
  relevance of 65
  types of 41–8
    contemplative 46–8
    explanatory 41–2
    normative 42–6

political thought, and political theory
  53–5
political victims 200–1
polygamy 127, 310
Popper, K.R. 315, 317
Positivism 39
Pratt, Mary 162n19
prejudice 63, 93, 195, 222, 223, 230,
  316, 352, 358, 359
principled distance, Indian
  secularism and 96–9, 309
procedural justice, basic 200, 215,
  216, 220
  decent society and 196, 197–205
  societies without 218
'production relations' 294, 382, 387,
  389
Protestant ethics 42, 93
Protestant churches, state and 86
Protestantism 83, 279
  in USA 114
Punjabi refugees, in India 123
'purposiveness' 371, 372
Putnam, Hilary 218n41, 323–4, 348

Qanoon-e-Shahadat, in Pakistan 94
Quinton, A. 40n5
Quranic injunctions 72
Quebec, English conquest of 125, 208

racial/religious hatred, restrictions
  on 247
Rai, Alok 116–17
Ramaswamy, V. 71n15, 71n18
Ramayana 174, 240, 282
Ramayya, Ekantada 70n14
Rawls, John 10, 44–5, 90n18, 253
Raz, Joseph 157n5, 254n16, 258
reciprocal detachment, politics of 122
reflections 8–9, 19
  subjective 8
  word-dependent 9–11
religion, concept of 281